P9-DXO-180

James Madison
and the
Making of America

ALSO BY KEVIN R. C. GUTZMAN

The Politically Incorrect Guide to the Constitution

Who Killed the Constitution?
The Federal Government versus American Liberty from World War I
to Barack Obama
(coauthored with Thomas E. Woods Jr.)

Virginia's American Revolution:
From Dominion to Republic, 1776–1840

James Madison
and the
Making of America

Kevin R. C. Gutzman

ST. MARTIN'S PRESS
NEW YORK

JAMES MADISON AND THE MAKING OF AMERICA. Copyright © 2012 by Kevin R. C. Gutzman. All rights reserved. Printed in the United States of America. For information, address St. Martin's Press, 175 Fifth Avenue, New York, N.Y. 10010.

Design by Kathryn Parise

ISBN 978-0-312-62500-9 (hardcover)

Book Club Edition

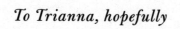
To Trianna, hopefully

Contents

Acknowledgments

I had the help of several people in writing this book. First, my agent, Andrew Stuart, saw the project's potential from the beginning and encouraged me all along. Next, the staff of the Haas Library at Western Connecticut State University, especially Meredith Halliburton, proved ever-reliable in assisting me. The library staffs at the other Connecticut State University campuses were helpful as well. At St. Martin's Press, my editor, Michael Flamini, and his associate, Vicki Lame, could not have been more professional. The book's copy editor, Martha Cameron, also did exemplary work with my draft. Peter S. Onuf, Michael F. Holt, Edward L. Ayers, Elizabeth Fox-Genovese, and Forrest McDonald guided me in various ways at very preliminary stages of the project, when my attention was mainly on other things. Tom Woods and Lee Cheek provided encouragement along the way. My parents gave me innumerable types of support. So did my kids. And Lorie. Always Lorie.

James Madison
and the
Making of America

Chapter 1

From Subject to Citizen, 1751–76

James Madison Jr. entered the world at midnight of the night of April 16–17, 1751.[1] By chance, he was an American prince.

James Madison Sr., the master of Montpelier in Piedmont Virginia's semifrontier Orange County, was the wealthiest man in the county. His lands were extensive, his slaveholdings were notable, and his family connections were impressive. In a society that privileged the wealthy to a notable degree, James Jr.'s world was his oyster.

Piedmont Virginia lay west of the Tidewater region that had been dominated by Virginia planters for well over a century. Life was cruder there, and tradition less powerful. Social status figured very strongly in a young man's life, but not to the degree that it did in the coastal counties. If ever a common Virginian doffed his hat as young Madison passed, Madison was not quite so snobbish as a Byrd, Carter, or Harrison. Still, like them, Madison knew his place.

As the scion of a prominent planter family, Madison—unlike most Virginia boys—received an enviable education. First, he attended a small school for sons of the elite in King and Queen County run by Donald Robertson. Next, from 1767 to 1769, his father hired an Episcopal priest tutor to live at Montpelier as Madison's, and possibly his siblings', teacher.[2] Finally, at age eighteen, Madison went on to the College of New Jersey (now Princeton University). Along the way, Madison read widely in Greek and Latin. He imbibed strong republican sentiments as well as a skeptical attitude toward office-holders.

Opting for Princeton was uncommon among Virginia bluebloods. Madison went there to avoid reputedly unhealthy Williamsburg.[3] More commonly, boys of his class went to England's Inns of Court or Scotland's University of Edinborough for advanced professional training in law or medicine, or, like Thomas Jefferson, they spent a few years at the colonial college, William and Mary. At William and Mary, nominally Episcopalian, the students were not notably studious and the curriculum was far from rigorous.

Princeton, on the other hand, had a president unlike any in Virginia. The Reverend John Witherspoon was a Presbyterian, a recent immigrant from Scotland.[4] As a matter of course, his attitudes about the relationship between church and state, government and religion, the conscience and society were different from those to which Madison would have been exposed at William and Mary. Witherspoon contributed substantially to the course of American philosophy through his devotion to the Scottish Enlightenment, then in full flower, and transmission of Scottish commonsense philosophy to America.

Witherspoon joined leading figures in Scotland's philosophical establishment in promoting this philosophy. It downplayed the utility of "metaphysical" thought, preferring hardheaded realism, and held that everyone carried the ability to achieve insight into the true and the good by applying his mental faculties to the world around him. Not books, but experience was the best guide.[5] In other words, Witherspoon was Aristotelian, not Platonic—with a vengeance, and he believed that the common man could participate in government along with the aristocrat.

Witherspoon taught, as a Presbyterian minister could be expected to do, that man was self-centered and not to be trusted. Among other sources for this teaching was the Scottish philosopher David Hume, with whom Witherspoon was not uniformly in tune. Famously, Madison would turn Hume's teaching to good account in Federalist No. 10—and, indeed, throughout his career. We can find many points of similarity between Witherspoon's beliefs and Madison's, but Madison clearly was not an undiscriminating student. For example, Witherspoon held state support of Christianity to be essential to the health of society and of Christianity, while Madison ultimately rejected that idea, with world-historic significance, as we shall see.[6]

Although he would later win acclaim for his learnedness, Madison was never a cold, calculating scholar. Rather, he always demonstrated an active sense of humor. Proof of this from his college days is provided by some poetry Madison contributed to an intramural dispute.

Princeton students, it seems, had organized competing literary social clubs, the Whigs and the Cliosophians. Madison took the lead among Whigs in a doggerel war in 1771–1772, contributing several poems to the ongoing conflict.[7] The editors of Madison's papers infer that the Whigs were the socially elite group, while their rivals' backgrounds often formed the grist for Whig mockery.[8] Among the choicest bits was this:

> *Keep up you[r] minds to humourous themes*
> *And verdant meads & flowing streams*
> *Untill this tribe of dunces find*
> *The baseness of their grovelling mind*
> *And skulk within their dens together*
> *Where each ones stench will kill his brother.*

In light of which, you can only imagine how Homeric the quality of the rest must have been. But I will spare you.

While at Princeton, Madison decided to study law on the side. He bought the books he thought he needed for that purpose and, in the fashion of those days, began to read them.[9] Very few American legal scholars took classes in law at the time. Instead, they commonly read leading texts and apprenticed to individual members of the bar. Madison's course, then, was nothing unusual. Nor, I wager, was his experience. Madison's first flush of tepid enthusiasm (in December 1773) soon gave way before the reality of legal study, which he described (in January 1774) as "coarse and dry." Fortunately for him and for us, Madison seems to have abandoned his hobby almost instantly.

In 1772, Madison entered upon a very interesting correspondence with one of his Princeton classmates, Philadelphia's William Bradford. Bradford, who one day would serve briefly as George Washington's attorney general, broached subjects philosophical and religious with Madison, and the Virginian responded in kind.[10]

At this point, Madison was still prone, in the fashion of his Princeton instructors, to religious speculations and philosophical diversions. For example, Madison wrote Bradford at one point that, although of course young men would be ambitious, "Nevertheless a watchful eye must be kept on ourselves lest while we are building ideal monuments of Renown and Bliss here we neglect to have our names enrolled in the Annals of Heaven."[11] Warming to the subject, Madison went on to say that, "As to myself I am too dull and infirm now to look out for any extraordinary things in this world for I think my sensations for many months past have intimated to me not to expect a long or healthy life, yet it may be better with me after some time tho I hardly dare expect it and therefore have little spirit and alacrity to set about any thing that is difficult in acquiring and useless in possessing after one has exchanged Time for Eternity." Madison, aged twenty-one, went on to advise his pal not to be swayed by the allure of "those impertinent fops that abound in every City to divert you," but to stick to his resolution to study "History and the Science of Morals." Fortunately, Madison said, his secluded perch in ultrarural Orange County insulated him from such temptations, which "breed in Towns and populous places, as naturally as flies do in the Shambles."

Bradford replied with an expression of concern for Madison's health.[12] Little could he know that Madison would be fatigued and often on the verge of death for another sixty-four years. In their exchanges, Madison made clear that he respected the ministry and wished his friend would enter upon that profession; the editors of his papers infer that perhaps he would have liked to become a minister, if it were not for his health.[13] The twenty-two-year-old Madison also noted that, "I do not meddle with Politicks." Events would soon bring a change in that sentiment.

In his letter of December 1, 1773, Madison struck out on a new path.[14] Since Bradford's Pennsylvania was, along with New Jersey and Rhode Island, one of three colonies without established churches, Madison asked him to describe the Pennsylvania "fundamental principles of legislation" and "particularly the extent of your religious Toleration." Bradford had finally decided to become an attorney, and Madison did not want to rush him.

Rather, he asked him please to provide this information once he had "obtained sufficient insight."

Displaying a systematic approach to political and philosophical topics that would soon be commented upon by his colleagues as characteristic of his statesmanship, Madison gave Bradford two specific questions to answer for him: (1) "Is an Ecclesiastical Establishment absolutely necessary to support civil society in a supream Government?" and (2) "How far is it hurtful to a dependant State?" Presumptuously, Madison suggested Bradford might attend to these issues "in the course of your reading and consulting experienced Lawyers & Politicians upon." He awaited a report on "the Result of your reserches."

Bradford's next missive included an enclosure describing the Boston Tea Party of December 16, 1773.[15] Madison responded by saying that, "I verily believe the frequent Assaults that have been made on America[,] Boston especially[,] will in the end prove of real advantage."[16]

This led Madison directly back to the issue of state churches that he had raised with his friend before: "If the Church of England had been the established and general Religion in all the Northern Colonies as it has been among us here," he erupted, "and uninterrupted tranquility had prevailed throughout the Continent, It is clear to me that slavery and Subjection might and would have been gradually insinuated among us." Next came the young Madison's historic insight, the one that would soon reshape his world: "Union of Religious Sentiments begets a surprising confidence and Ecclesiastical Establishments tend to great ignorance and Corruption[,] all of which facilitate the Execution of mischievous Projects."

Madison told Bradford that he wished to visit Pennsylvania "to breathe your free Air. I expect it will mend my Constitution & confirm my principles." His unhappiness with his own colony had arisen from the fact that, "The diabolical Hell conceived principle of persecution rages among some," including the Episcopal clergy. "This," he moaned, "vexes me the most of any thing whatever."

Madison provided Bradford the sad details: "There are at this [time?] in the adjacent County not less than 5 or 6 well meaning men in close Goal [jail] for publishing their religious Sentiments which in the main are very orthodox." Apparently Madison had raised this issue ("squabbled and scolded abused and ridiculed") among his Virginia compatriots without any positive effect. He closed by asking Bradford to "pray for Liberty of Conscience [to revive among us]." This, as history would prove, was a radically more liberal position on church-state relations than the "religious Toleration" invoked by Madison in his December 1 letter to Bradford.[17]

Madison returned to this theme again when next he wrote Bradford.[18] The May 1774 session of the Virginia General Assembly, he heard, was going to take up the matter of religious dissent. Baptist petitions and Presbyterian influence might well produce greater religious liberty. Madison doubted that any good would come of it, however, as discussion in the last session had thrown the enthusiasts (whom we would now call "Evangelicals") in a bad light. Coming to the establishment's defenders, he virtually spat upon the page, saying, "The Sentiments of our people of Fortune & fashion on this subject are vastly different from what you have been used to. That liberal catholic and equitable way of thinking as to the rights of Conscience, which is one of the Characteristics of a free people and so strongly marks the people of your province is but little known among the Zealous adherents to our [Episcopal] Hierarchy." There were some legislators who were good men on this score, "but number not merit you know is necessary to carry points there." Madison thought that the clergy, powerful thanks to its ties to English bishops and the king, would strenuously resist any relaxation of the established religion's enforcement.

As he had before, Madison next contrasted Virginia's establishment to the Pennsylvanian regime under which his friend lived. He envied Bradford, and that envy evoked from Madison an impassioned, youthful statement of his faith in religious freedom:

You are happy living in a land where those inestimable privileges are fully enjoyed and public has long felt the good effects of their religious as well as Civil Liberty. Foreigners have been encouraged to settle amg. you. Industry and Virtue have been promoted by mutual emulation and mutual Inspection, Commerce and the Arts have flourished and I can not help attributing those continual exertions of Gen[i]us which appear among you to the inspiration of Liberty and that love of Fame and Knowledge which always accompany it. Religious bondage shackles and debilitates the mind and unfits it for every noble enterprize every expanded prospect. How far this is the Case with Virginia will more clearly appear when the ensuing Trial is made.[19]

Beyond the question of the Virginia religious establishment and the treatment of dissenters, Madison in his correspondence with Bradford increasingly considered the growing imperial crisis.[20] In addition, he described news of Lord Dunmore's War, a Virginian conflict with the Indians to the Old Dominion's west. Finally, Madison told Bradford that he favored Virginia's more confrontational approach in mid-1774 to the conciliatory measures advocated by Pennsylvania. In light of his criticism of Virginia's religion policy, one cannot ascribe this preference to budding Virginia patriotism. Instead, it reflected young Madison's personal feeling: the colonies must stand up, and Congress was the mechanism. Since Bradford lived in Philadelphia, he was able to keep Madison abreast of the latest news from that body.[21]

When the Congress closed, Madison wrote that Virginians "universally approved" of its actions because "A spirit of Liberty & Patriotism animates all degrees and denominations of men."[22] Another way of putting this is that all ranks in society and all religious affiliations stood for American rights. Further, Madison hazarded that "Many publickly declare themselves ready to join the Bostonians as soon as violence is offered them or resistance thought expedient." Virginians in some parts were organizing themselves into military units, and Madison wanted the entire colony on a war footing.

Madison wrote to Bradford excitedly the following May 9 with a description of the recent colonial response to Lord Dunmore's seizure of the colonial gunpowder.[23] In the days before bullets, firearms required gunpowder, which was in short supply in the colonies, and so the Virginia governor's action amounted to an attempt to disarm the colonial militia at a stroke. Madison was thrilled by the confrontation between the militia and the governor, and particularly by Patrick Henry's forcing Dunmore to compensate Virginia for the powder. He also criticized the Tidewater planters who had urged moderation; as he lived in the Piedmont, Madison did not face the same military risks as did tobacco barons closer to the coast. They, not he, were close to the sea (hence the Royal Navy) and the governor.

When the leading men of Orange County decided to endorse Henry's actions, they selected Madison to be their penman.[24] In four resolutions and a summary, Madison, his father, and their most prominent neighbors strongly criticized the governor and heaped praise upon Henry. Dunmore's seizure, they said, had been "fraudulent, unnecessary, and extremely provoking to the people of this colony," while the Hanover County volunteers' "resentment" and "reprisal . . . highly merit[ed] the approbation of the public." In case the governor attempted to recoup the money, the Orange County resolutions called on their delegates to see that the money was "laid out in gunpowder."

The fourth resolution, finally, addressed a message to Henry and his followers (and through them, to the world). The governor's insistence that he intended to return the powder had been untruthful, they said, and so they thanked the Hanover men for "your zeal for the honour and interest of your country." By "your country," note, Madison meant Virginia. The Orange County men added that Parliament's recent Coercive Acts, while directed at Massachusetts, were really "a hostile attack on this and every other colony, and *a sufficient warrant to use violence and reprisal, in all cases where it may be expedient for our security and welfare*" (emphasis added). If Parliament could close the port of Boston and reorganize Massachusetts's democratic government into a military dictatorship, it could do the same to any other colony—including Virginia. Madison, his father, and their neighbors endorsed the use of whatever means came to hand to resist this outcome.

Fighting between British and colonial forces began at Lexington and Concord on April 19, 1775. Through the rest of the year, Madison received several additional missives from Bradford passing along rumors about the war and events in Congress. In October 1775, Madison was selected by the Committee of Safety—Virginia's executive branch in the days after Lord Dunmore fled the colony—as colonel of his county's militia.[25] That made him second in command to his father, the county lieutenant. However, as Madison recalled in his old age, he was both generally infirm and prone to "sudden attacks, somewhat resembling Epilepsy, and suspending the intellectual functions." His constitution did not hold up under the rigors of military training, so, he never served in the American Revolution.[26]

The first office young Madison *did* perform was that of delegate to the Virginia Convention, the legislative branch of revolutionary Virginia down to the implementation of its 1776 constitution. He won election for a one-year term on April 25, 1776.[27] Soon thereafter, on May 15, the Convention adopted resolutions saying that a declaration of rights, a republican constitution, federation with other colonies, and alliances must be adopted. That night, Williamsburg celebrated Virginia's independence "with a military display 'of great exactness,'" as a continental Union flag replaced the Union Jack over the Virginia capitol.[28] "The city was brilliantly illuminated," and the citizens provided the soldiers a fabulous feast.[29]

It was the Convention's decision to adopt a permanent republican constitution that made Virginia independent. Madison considered Virginia independent from May 15, 1776, as well.[30]

It seems that Madison prepared for the task before him, writing the constitution, by assembling materials on the other colonies' constitutional systems.[31] In time, his diligent application would win him a reputation as consistently the best prepared and most knowledgeable (if not always the most perspicuous) man in American politics. Princeton had prepared him well.

The Virginia Convention of 1776 is largely forgotten now. Yet it was, as John Adams might have said, an epochal event: it adopted the Virginia Declaration of Rights, the first American declaration of rights, and the Virginia Constitution of 1776, the first written constitution adopted by the people's representatives in the history of the world. In Virginia's legislative bodies, inexperienced members were expected to hang back and allow senior members to do the important work. Yet Madison, though a very junior member of this august assemblage, played a highly significant role. Arguably, his accomplishment in that body was the most significant of his entire storied career.

The Virginia Declaration of Rights served as the foundation of the Virginia Constitution. It laid out the principles on which Virginia's elite agreed that republican government ought to be based. Madison served on the committee that drafted the Declaration and the Constitution, whose leading member was the widely respected senior statesman George Mason.

Mason, master of Gunston Hall on the Potomac River, was among the most learned men in a Virginia ruling class spangled with highly educated people. His political principles owed much to the English Whig tradition, which based claims to individual and communal rights on a particular reading of English legal and political history. Unsurprisingly, with men of that turn of mind at its head, the Convention established the Old Dominion's new republican government on a firmly English foundation.

In the Glorious Revolution of 1688–1689, England first expelled its king, then adopted a bill of rights as the foundation of its government. Only when they had agreed to abide by the bill of rights were William III and Mary recognized as England's new joint monarchs.

Mason, who called himself a man of 1688, had Virginia do the same thing. As Dunmore (and through him, King George III) had fled the colony, and as the king had declared that the colonies were in rebellion and beyond his protection, the first step—removal of the king—had been taken for them. Next came the task of drafting a declaration of rights.[32] According to Madison, Mason drafted the committee version.[33]

The preamble began: "A DECLARATION OF RIGHTS made by the representatives of the good people of VIRGINIA, assembled in full and free Convention; which rights do pertain to us, and our posterity, as the basis and foundation of government."[34] With that Lockean foundation, the first section of the committee draft stated: "That all men are by nature equally free and independent, and have certain inherent rights, of which they cannot, by any compact, deprive or divest their posterity; namely, the enjoyment of life and liberty, with the means of acquiring and possessing property, and pursuing and obtaining happiness and safety." Robert Nicholas, the colonial treasurer, objected.

If Virginia went on record saying this, Nicholas declared, Virginians would instantly face a terrible choice: either they could ignore their most basic principles, or they could in the midst of a great war with the world's foremost military power throw their society into convulsion. What he meant, of course, was that a claim that all men are equally free was inconsistent with slavery. Virginians could either ignore this inconsistency and keep slavery, which would make a mockery of their stated principles, or they could adopt this language and abolish slavery, which would throw Virginia into widespread upheaval.

In Madison's day, quite a substantial share of Virginians believed that slavery needed to be at least reined in. Some wanted to see it ultimately eliminated. There had been repeated efforts in the General Assembly either to adopt a policy of gradual emancipation or at least to ban further imports of slaves. But those efforts had run aground, because elite Virginians wanted to keep slavery and because the king would not allow an import ban. A lot of Virginians feared that freeing the slaves would lead to economic doom and perhaps even race war, and so it seemed to men like Nicholas that May 1776 was a very bad time to take up the matter.

Nicholas proposed a slight change to Mason's committee draft: insert the phrase "when they enter into a state of society." So it would read: "That all men are by nature equally free and independent, and have certain inherent rights, of which, when they enter into a state of society, they cannot, by any compact, deprive or divest their posterity. . . ." Then it would not apply to slaves—who were not parties to this new social compact.

Nicholas's proposal was accepted. At the birth of its republican government Virginia effectively stated that slaves were not part of Virginia political society.

Madison did not object.

Succeeding sections said that the people were sovereign (Section 2), that a majority could replace the government whenever it wanted (Section 3), that the separation of powers principle should be observed (Section 5), that the right to vote should be widely available (Section 6), and that the military should be subordinate to the civilians (Section 13). Besides making these general claims concerning political philosophy, the Declaration of Rights also enumerated several of the most important rights of individual Englishmen-cum-Virginians: the right to trial by jury in criminal (Section 8) and civil (Section 11) cases, the right to militia service (Section 13), the freedom of the press (Section 12), and the right to proportionate and humane punishment (Section 12), among others.

When the final section of the draft came up, Madison intervened. Here, Mason—following the English precedent—had penned language guaranteeing Virginians "the fullest toleration in the exercise of religion."[35] In a day when persecution was the lot of Protestants in Spain and France, Orthodox Christians in the Turkish Empire, and Catholics in many Protestant lands, toleration served as the benchmark of liberal attitudes toward dissenting minorities. Mason rightly considered this a forward-thinking formula.

But for James Madison, aged twenty-five, that was not enough. What, after all, was the implication of a government promise to "tolerate" someone's opinion? Surely it was that government knew better, but it would put up with the individual's divergent understanding for now. Madison's proposed substitute said, "That religion, or the duty which we owe to our CREATOR, and the manner of discharging it, can be directed only by reason and conviction, not by force or violence; and therefore, that all men are equally entitled to enjoy the free exercise of religion, according to the dictates of conscience."[36] With the excision of the second "that" and the word "enjoy," this was the final language of Section 16. The convention agreed to it unanimously.

Here, then, was the fruition of Madison's anguished complaints to his Pennsylvanian friend from Princeton days about the tyrannical effects of Virginia's religious establishment. Not only did Madison wish Virginia's regime more closely to resemble Pennsylvania's, but he did something about it. He led the way in enshrining full-throated religious libertarianism in the first American declaration of rights—where it still takes pride of place today.

While the Declaration of Rights closely followed the example of the Glorious Revolution, Virginia's 1776 constitution represented the victory of the American Revolution. Although the convention's leading members rejected Thomas Jefferson's repeated pleas to be relieved of his seat in Congress, and thus freed to head to Williamsburg and join in writing the Constitution, the preamble to the Constitution was Jefferson's handiwork.[37] As his more famous Declaration of Independence would, Jefferson's preamble founded constitutional government in Virginia on an argument concerning George III's constructive abdication of his position.

Since George III's appointed governors had stood between the indigenous elite and its policy preferences, the republican governorship would be extremely weak. The governor would be elected by the General Assembly, have no veto power, serve only a one-year term, and have to win majority support of his Council of State for any major initiative. In other words, he could not do much of anything without the support of the Council.

Besides the Council of State, republican Virginians would have a bicameral legislature: the House of Delegates, which was simply the colonial House of Burgesses under a new name; and the Senate, a less numerous body named for the Roman Senate. Accustomed as we are to having the upper houses of American legislatures called "senates," we likely do not hear the Latin echo in that name as loudly as did the classically educated Virginians who first used it. The idea that it conveyed was of a select group of elite men calmly deciding important policy issues in insulation from the hoi polloi who dominated the House of Delegates. While the delegates served annual terms, the senators were to be insulated from popular pressure by four-year terms, and from then on, they were to be elected independently rather than appointed. They also had limited power regarding spending bills.

The suffrage requirements Virginians had long known, which required men to own substantial landed estates before they could vote, remained in effect. Judges of statewide courts would be elected by the legislature. County courts would continue, as in colonial days, to be selected by county elites from among their fellow members and to serve more or less for life.

Essentially, the Old Dominion's new republican Constitution put on paper what Virginians had been contending for in the crisis with Britain over the previous decade: that the House of Burgesses/Delegates had virtually all the power to legislate for Virginians. The extreme subordination of the executive and judicial branches of the new government called to mind the relationship of the House of Commons to the House of Lords and the Crown in Britain. In fact, the Constitution went even further. Perhaps it reflected overreaction by Virginians to the problems they had recently encountered. Madison, who seems not to have objected at the time, would come to think so—or at least to say so.

The convention voted to adopt the Constitution on Saturday, June 29, 1776. Patrick Henry was sworn in as the state's first republican governor on the same day. There was no looking back.

Chapter 2

Winning the Revolution, 1776–87

The following decade, 1776–1787, saw Madison carve out a name for himself as one of the foremost figures in American politics. He helped to remake monarchical Virginia into a republican society, win the American Revolution, and build the continental coalition that sent delegates from twelve states to Philadelphia for the Federal Convention in summer 1787.

Yet, after young Madison's sterling service on his county Committee of Safety and his momentous participation in the final Virginia Convention, his career in everyday electoral politics got off to a very ignominious start. The first time he ran for a seat in the newly renamed House of Delegates, in April 1777, he went down to defeat.[1]

As Madison recalled, he went into the election of 1777 intending to stand or fall on his merits. Here we see a young man devoted to principle—or, it may be, a blueblood certain that he would be given the people's gift simply because of who he was.

Traditionally in Virginia, local leading men such as the Orange County Madisons sat in the Burgesses, dominated the Church of England vestries, and monopolized the militia offices. In exchange for common men's votes, these paragons of civic virtue "treated" their neighbors into a drunken stupor; that is, they gave them more whiskey than you or I could drink.[2]

James Jr. decided in April 1777 that he should be elected without treating. It was unrepublican to offer the assembled inhabitants of Orange County anything other than his services in return for their votes, he thought. Vote for me, and I will take the office, was his message.

And so they did not vote for him, "his abstinence," as he put it, "being represented as the effect of pride or parsimony." Some Madison supporters petitioned the House of Delegates to overturn the result on the basis that one of the victorious candidates "did . . . make use of bribery and corruption during the said election," but this effort came to naught. For the first and only time in his long career, Madison had lost.

Not to worry. Soon thereafter, on November 15, 1777, Madison was chosen by the House of Delegates to serve on the eight-man Council of State— the governor's partner in administering the executive branch of Virginia's government.[3] He first attended on January 14, 1778, and he seems to have been a regular participant until his selection by the General Assembly for a seat in Congress cut short his term in December 1779.[4]

The council's business covered a broad range of military and naval matters, as well as whatever other domestic concerns the legislature chose to entrust to the executive. Ongoing difficulty with Indians to the west and the press of revolutionary business—usually involving raising troops and locating and purchasing provisions, the kind of workaday tasks that are what government is ultimately about—kept the governor and the council more than busy.[5] More significant for history than Madison's individual performance as a councilor, which cannot be established on the basis of any surviving evidence,[6] was the close familiarity he gained with the two governors with whom he served, Patrick Henry (to July 1, 1779) and Thomas Jefferson (thereafter). Henry would become a long-standing political antagonist, while with Jefferson, Madison established the most enduring and consequential political alliance in American history.

Madison appeared in Congress for the first time on March 20, 1780, at age twenty-eight.[7] He would serve there for three years, the maximum term of service allowed by the Articles of Confederation (which were ratified in 1781).[8] In that period, Madison staked out a position of leadership in the effort adequately to fund General Washington's forces, the efforts to vindicate Virginia's western land claims and secure ratification of the Articles of

Confederation, and the campaign to augment Congress's powers by amending the Articles. Ultimately, his frustrating service in Congress moved Madison to push for replacement of the Articles of Confederation.

The impression that the Continental Army might starve to death if Congress were not strengthened struck Madison from his very first week as a congressman.[9] As he described things to Governor Jefferson, "Our army [is] threatened with an immediate alternative of disbanding or living on free quarter [that is, every man foraging for whatever he could find]; the public treasury empty; public credit exhausted, nay the private credit of purchasing Agents employed, I am told, as far as it will bear, Congress complaining of the extortion of the people; the people of the improvidence of Congress, and the army of both." Desperation was not common in Madison, but he saw the situation as desperate.

One might have expected Madison to devise a plan to address the problem, then to begin to lobby other legislators to support it. That would be to overlook what Madison took to be the generally low quality of the people in Congress when he arrived in 1780. "Congress from a defect of adequate Statesmen," he wrote, was "more likely to fall into wrong measures and of less weight to enforce right ones." As a result, the states habitually weighed Congress's policy for themselves before deciding whether to cooperate. They often did not in the end cooperate, and the word from General Washington was that the army was near starvation.[10]

To Madison's alarm, Congress in 1780 could "neither enlist pay nor feed a single soldier, nor execute any other pu[r]pose but as the means are first put into their hands." This situation flowed from the resolution, adopted two days before he took his congressional seat, disallowing Congress to print money. Since the power of "emitting money on the faith of their Constituents" (that is, of printing IOUs payable after the war) had been "the only power [Congress] ever had of supporting the war," Congress on Madison's arrival was virtually powerless to do anything other than beg the state governments for support and cooperation.[11]

As Madison understood it, the danger posed by congressional weakness flowed from two directions: first, it might weaken the army so drastically as to lead to loss of the war; second, it might provoke soldiers to mutiny, as even the most patriotic veteran could not be expected to starve to death for the cause.[12] In the name of the war effort, Madison even endorsed a Pennsylvania law giving that state's government broad power to seize private property for military use. Madison feared for the war's outcome greatly in the middle of 1780.[13]

Meanwhile, Madison joined his fellow Virginia congressman Joseph Jones in taking the lead in the matter of the western lands. At the beginning of the revolution, settlement's legal western boundary had been the Proclamation Line of 1763—a line running along the peaks of the Appalachian Mountains drawn by King George III at the close of the French and Indian War. George III, desirous of avoiding the expense likely to be associated with further Indian conflict, had prohibited his subjects in North America from making further inroads into Indian territory.

Without realizing what he was doing, King George had stepped into a hornet's nest.[14] In those days before the existence of the stock market, wealthy men with money to invest frequently bought land, and western lands were a hot commodity. From John Hancock in Massachusetts through Benjamin Franklin in Pennsylvania, from George Washington and George Mason in Virginia to the Low Country nabobs of South Carolina, western land speculators dotted the colonial elites. The Proclamation Line seemed to render their land claims worthless.

Independence brought the resuscitation of western speculations. The matter was complicated by the fact that not only Virginia but other states—even Connecticut!—claimed lands in what we now call the Midwest, which in those days was the Northwest. Virginia congressmen insisted from the Continental Congress's earliest days that Congress had no power to adjudicate such disputes, that the Old Dominion had delegated it no power to resolve conflicting claims. The land, the largest and most populous state insisted, was Virginia's.

This matter had to be resolved. The Articles of Confederation, sent to the states for their ratification by the Continental Congress in November 1777, remained unratified. Little Maryland, Virginia's neighbor to the north and one of the minority of states with no western land claims, had held out those several years. As long as Virginia included that gigantic empire, Marylanders thundered, they would never agree to a stable confederation. After all, an Old Dominion that included not only today's Virginia but also West Virginia,

Kentucky, Ohio, Michigan, Indiana, Illinois, Wisconsin, and part of Minnesota would ultimately dwarf Maryland in population, wealth, and every other attribute of political power. To agree to such a union, then, would mean the negation of Maryland's existence. If the other states wanted Maryland's ratification, Virginia must cede the lands beyond the Ohio River. It must confine itself to the territory that is today's Virginia, West Virginia, and Kentucky.

George Mason proposed that now that Pennsylvania and Virginia had resolved a long-running border dispute, Virginia could cede the northern panhandle of what is now West Virginia, as well as its trans–Ohio River claims, to Congress.[15] In exchange, Congress should guarantee that the ceded territory would eventually be organized into at least two states, confirm Virginia's (rather than other states') grants of land in that region to private parties, compensate Virginia for its expenditures in defense of those lands during the revolution, and provide the land bounties Virginia had promised its veterans, among other things. Mason thought that if Congress proposed this deal to Virginia, he could steer it through the General Assembly in the upcoming session. To spur Madison and his colleagues to act, Mason added that he expected the upcoming legislative session to be his last.

The issue came to a head in Congress in the midst of dire military developments.[16] The South stood occupied, with Charleston, South Carolina, a British military encampment, and American forces had suffered significant defeats in pitched battles with Lord Charles Cornwallis. In addition to these problems, British naval forces repeatedly raided Virginia from Chesapeake Bay in 1780, demonstrating that the extensive river network that had facilitated Virginia's development as a staple producer also made Madison's home state militarily vulnerable. The Chevalier de la Luzerne, France's minister (we would say "ambassador" nowadays) to the United States, pointedly informed Congress that his king would support America's cause more energetically if the Articles were ratified. Madison, for one, believed Luzerne.[17]

Americans wanted to ratify. As we have seen, people like Mason and Madison had taken the lead in securing written constitutions for all but two of the American states. They did not want to continue with the informal arrangement that was the Continental Congress, but strongly preferred to have a written federal constitution. The Articles were it.

On June 26, 1780, Congress referred the question to a committee of five, including a North Carolinian, a New Yorker, a Marylander, a Connecticut congressman, and Madison's Virginia colleague Joseph Jones. On September 6, 1780, Congress adopted the committee's report, which called upon Maryland to ratify, called upon the states with western land claims to have their congressmen help "effectually remove the only obstacle to a final ratification of the articles," and noted how "indispensably necessary" speedy ratification was to the "public credit," "support of our army," "and "our very existence as a free, sovereign and independent people."

Immediately thereafter, Jones made a related motion, which Madison seconded. They said that in case Virginia, North Carolina, and Georgia agreed to cede western lands, those lands should ultimately be laid out into states, and the rest of the ceding states' lands should be guaranteed by Congress; that Congress should reimburse those states for the expense of securing that territory from the British; and that all purchases by individuals from Indians of land within that territory should be considered void. After making this motion, Jones retired from Congress. This left it up to Madison to take the Virginian seat on the committee to which the motion was referred, and thus to carry Virginian water in this matter for many months to come.

Congress discussed the Jones-Madison resolutions twelve days after their submission, on September 18.[18] It adopted the provisions regarding eventual statehood for the ceded lands and congressional reimbursement of the military expenses borne by the ceding states, but it rejected the provision regarding Indian purchases.[19] Madison intimated to Jones that the ceding states could affix whatever conditions they chose to their cessions, and could even annul private purchases before making their cessions; thus, congressional action in this regard was unnecessary.

Madison in this first term in Congress, and indeed whenever in Philadelphia down to his marriage in 1794, stayed in the home of Mrs. Mary House at the intersection of Fifth and Market streets.[20] Mrs. House and her daughter, Eliza, along with Eliza's husband Nicholas Trist, boarded many congressmen, including a number of Virginians. Boarding houses were commonly used by members of Congress in those days, as the shortness of congressional sessions and the difficulty of transportation made taking one's family along prohibitively expensive.

For young bachelors such as Madison, boarding in such establishments provided opportunity to fraternize with fellow politicians and live in relative comfort among members of one's own class. Often, relationships established in such contexts endured. Madison, for example, would go to his grave more than a half-century later a friend of Nicholas Trist. In addition, marriages sometimes resulted—but Madison is not known to have struck up a romance in Philadelphia.

In fact, Madison's single-minded devotion to business left some with highly negative impressions. One fellow Virginia congressman's wife described Madison in March 1781 as "a gloomy, stiff creature, they say he is clever in Congress, but out of it, he has nothing engaging or even bearable in his Manners—the most unsociable creature in Existance" [*sic*].[21] As we shall see, Madison recognized this weakness, and ultimately took a substantial step to offset it.

In the summer of 1780, Philadelphia was wracked with a contagion.[22] It was what in those days was called "the flux"—apparently some variety of dysentery. Madison recorded that "the mortality in this place exceeds any thing ever remembered." It seems that he escaped the ravages of the deadly disease, although Continental Congress president Joseph Reed's wife Esther was not so lucky: she died on September 18, barely past age fifty. Similar scourges frequently struck early modern cities, and country boys such as Madison were ill prepared to resist them.

On October 17, 1780, a three-man committee reported instructions drafted by Madison for Minister John Jay.[23] The flap that ultimately issued from this affair would affect federal politics for many years to come. Jay was charged with negotiating a Spanish alliance, and the committee wanted to flesh out his formal instructions. The United States insisted on the right to use the Mississippi River (then Spanish property), and the point was to equip Jay with an argument that allowing Americans to use the great American river was just and equitable.

The committee argued that King George III's "rights and claims in quality of their sovereign . . . devolved on [the people of America] in consequence of their resumption of the Sovereignty to themselves." Echoing an old Virginian argument,[24] the committee asserted that the king's former rights in North America had all flowed from the efforts of the Americans and their ancestors. Yes, Britons overseas had fought to vindicate American claims in more recent days, but a disproportionate share of the burden of those conflicts had been borne by the American colonists. Therefore, for Spain to recognize America's claim was only right.

The balance of the rather long letter provided various debating points that Jay might use in support of the same argument, or of the additional claim that Spain ought to grant the United States "navigation of the waters running out of Georgia through West Florida" (which is essentially to say, the coastal regions of today's Alabama and Mississippi). Whether the court at Madrid would find these assertions persuasive must always have been dubious. In the end, Jay's embassy was almost completely fruitless, not to mention personally and nationally humiliating.[25] Not for the last time, Madison's debating points proved unavailing when it came to European diplomacy. Pipsqueak, republican, Protestant Amèrica had nothing to offer and no means to threaten, and so could extract nothing; powerful, monarchical, Catholic Spain felt no sympathy, indeed wished to retard America's expansion westward, and so gave nothing.

After a half year in Congress, Madison had become convinced that radical steps had to be taken to provide the Continental Congress with money. He suggested a possibility to a Virginia legislator.[26] Taxation would not do, he said. Loans were unavailable. Specific taxes could not be counted on. "Purchases with state money or certificates" promised more inflation, which was already a besetting problem. Only one other alternative remained: the necessary "supplies" should be "*impress[ed]* with vigor and impartiality." The burden of these seizures should be somehow apportioned by wealth, and the involuntary contributors ought to be compensated with "certificates not transferrible & be redeemable at some period subsequent to the war at specie value and bearing an intermediate interest."

Madison expressed marked enthusiasm for this idea. Since the individuals thus forced to contribute to the war effort were to be compensated, "much less nicety would be requisite in apportioning" the burden than if they were not. Since the certificates were to be nontransferable, Madison reasoned, inflation seemed a less likely result of this scheme than of further issuance of state promissory notes. Virginia never adopted such an expedient, although its laws did provide for seizure of military supplies.[27]

Madison believed that a reform of the revenue system could vindicate not only America's claim to independence, but also its republican governments.[28] "The wan[t] of this article [money] is the source of all our public difficulties and misfortunes," he averred. If only Congress had "one or two million guineas properly applied," not only could America "expel the enemy from every part of the United States," but "it would reconcile the army & every body else to our republican forms of governments." People's objections to the republican form, he said, flowed from lack of money. If the government had adequate money, its military efforts would be as successful as those of any other government.

Rather than this, the House of Delegates considered another expedient: offering a slave as bounty to any man who enlisted in the Virginia forces.[29] Slaves were to be acquired by the state for this purpose through a forced expropriation of every twentieth slave owned by any man who had twenty or more. The masters from whom slaves were taken would be compensated, the legislation had it, by being given IOUs payable in eight years, with interest on this forced loan to be paid beginning after five years. Madison's source for this information told him that the concept had been developed in a "private Committee" of the House of Delegates, that it likely would pass the House, and that it stood a far worse chance of adoption in the Senate. The reason for the discrepancy between the houses of the General Assembly seemed to be that the Senate's membership came from a far wealthier segment of Virginia's population, and thus was more likely to be personally affected by the plan.[30]

Madison disapproved of the plan for enlisting soldiers with slave bounties very staunchly.[31] As he put it, "would it not be as well to liberate and make soldiers at once of the blacks themselves as to make them instruments for enlisting white soldiers?" Unlike the bounty idea, Madison held, freeing slaves who enlisted was consistent with Revolutionary philosophy: "It wd. certainly be more consonant to the principles of liberty which ought never to be lost sight of in a contest for liberty."

One reason that slave owners did not enroll slaves was the fear that armed blacks would turn on their former masters and encourage remaining slaves to do the same. Not to worry, Madison said, for "with white officers & a majority of white soldrs. no imaginable danger could be feared from themselves, as there certainly could be none from the effect of the example on those who should remain in bondage: experience having shown that a freedman immediately loses all attachment & sympathy with his former fellow slaves."

Here we have Madison's earliest known expression of opinion concerning slavery.[32] Perhaps unsurprisingly, the advocate of the rights of religious dissenters and embattled Bostonians had little to say for paying white soldiers with Africans. He preferred freeing the Africans. Madison must have been gratified to learn that the General Assembly rejected the idea of a "Negro bounty," so that Virginia did not ever join the states resorting to that expedient.[33] Whether the young congressman's views affected the outcome, we do not know. One leading member of the House of Delegates told Madison that it had been considered "unjust" to slave owners, besides "inhuman and cruel" to the slaves.[34]

Madison frequently found himself in a position to insist on Virginia's sovereignty in the face of attempts to have Congress intervene in Virginia's affairs. Thus, for example, when claimants to midwestern lands asserted rights supposedly given to them by other states' governments, Madison called Congress "a foreign tribunal" and stoutly denied that it could hear a matter between Virginia and "private individuals."[35] For it to do so, he said, would offend "the sovereignty & honor of the State."

At the end of 1780, as it seemed the war might be coming to a climax, Madison lamented a change in Congress's attitude on the question of the Mississippi navigation.[36] Only a few weeks before, Madison had been happy that Jay was instructed not to surrender that right. Now, however, he said that Georgia and South Carolina congressmen had reopened the question. As Madison explained, those southernmost states feared that the war might be concluded on a *uti possidetis* basis, which is to say with each side retaining the territory in its possession. Therefore, Georgia and South Carolina—the latter of which had been long under British occupation—pressed for Jay to secure Spain's guarantee of American independence and a substantial Spanish subsidy, and if the price was the Mississippi, so be it.

Madison feared the likely diplomatic consequences of this change of heart. Even if Congress rejected the Deep South initiative, word of the discussion would get out, and that would weaken American diplomats' hand in negotiating an end to the war. Madison judged that most states would insist that no state's rights to the Mississippi could be surrendered without its concurrence, and so he predicted that the gambit would fail. Madison encouraged the General Assembly not to alter its instructions to Virginia congressmen, but to maintain the policy that the Mississippi navigation must not be bartered away. Jay, he noted, had told Congress that Spain seemed likely to agree to share the river, if only America stood firm.[37] In any event, "Both my principles & my instructions will determine me to oppose it."[38]

As Madison and Theodorick Bland, Virginia's other congressman, disagreed concerning the desirability of trading the Mississippi navigation for Spanish aid, they wrote Governor Jefferson on December 13, 1780, requesting clarification of the state's position.[39] The General Assembly responded on January 2, 1781, that the Virginia congressmen ought to insist on navigation of the Mississippi coextensive with America's boundaries.[40] They should also try to obtain "a free port or ports" on the lower Mississippi for Americans' use.

Congress's fiscal situation continued to affect public affairs in drastic ways. Thus, Madison had to inform Governor Jefferson of the army mutiny at Morris Town, Pennsylvania, on New Year's Day, 1781.[41] The mutineers, he relayed, had begun to march on Philadelphia "in regular order . . . with a determination not to lay down their arms nor return to their obedience till their grievances should be redressed." The causes of the mutiny were "a detention of many in service beyond the term of enlistment & the sufferings of all from a deficient supply of Cloathing & subsistence & long arrearage of pay." When it became clear that the mutiny would be put down, Madison noted with an air of relief that similar complaints could easily lead to similar behavior by other units unless provisions and money were provided.[42] This, as we have seen, had long been among his pet causes.

So, too, as we have seen, was ratification of the Articles of Confederation. News that Virginia had agreed to cede its trans–Ohio River territory arrived in January. In response, Maryland ratified the Articles on February 1, 1781.[43] The Articles, the United States' first federal constitution, went into effect.

Madison's, and indeed other congressmen's, frustration over the inability of Congress to man and fund the army and diplomatic corps, as well as to finance the U.S. debt, continued unabated. Madison was appointed to a three-man committee on March 6, 1781, with the task of preparing "a plan to invest the United States in Congress assembled with full and explicit powers for effectually carrying into execution" Congress's policies.[44] On March 12, the committee reported a proposed amendment to the Articles empowering Congress to coerce states militarily.[45]

The committee's proposal, laid before Congress on March 16, was preceded by a preamble laying claim to "a general and implied power . . . to enforce and carry into effect all the Articles" against noncompliant states. On this basis, the committee proposed to give Congress the power "to employ the force of the United States as well by sea as by land to compel such State or States to fulfill their federal engagements, whether by blockade or by seizure of property." Ironically, even as the committee contemplated forcing states into compliance with Confederation policies, it purported to provide that ratification required the consent only of the states "not actually in the Possession of the Enemy." The amendment was never adopted, but it reflected widespread sentiment.

Thomas Jefferson's term as governor was to expire on June 2, 1781, and Jefferson happily wrote Madison on March 23 about his coming retirement from politics.[46] His tenure as Virginia's chief executive had coincided with the British decision to shift the theater of war to the Chesapeake. At one point, a British force commanded by former American general Benedict Arnold invaded the Commonwealth and chased the governor from his hilltop house outside Piedmont Charlottesville, near Madison's Montpelier. Jefferson came under fire on several scores, ranging from administrative failure to naked cowardice. Some of the criticism was merited, some not, but he had had enough.[47]

Madison told his older friend that particularly in the midst of the war, Jefferson's services could not be spared.[48] He told Jefferson he would lament his decision "in silence," with the consolation that Jefferson had promised to write him more often. In the meantime, Madison asked Governor Jefferson for his private opinion concerning the amendment to the Articles pending in Congress.[49]

It seems that Madison half hoped, half expected that Jefferson would lick his wounds and rush once more into the breach. A year later, with Jefferson still in retirement, Madison told a mutual friend, "Great as my partiality is to Mr. Jefferson, the mode in which he seems determined to revenge the wrong received from his Country [Virginia], does not appear to me to be dictated either by philosophy or patriotism. It argues indeed a keen sensibility and a strong consciousness of rectitude. But this sensibility ought to be as great towards the relentings as the misdoings of the Legislature, not to mention the injustice of visiting the faults of this body on their innocent constituents."[50] The General Assembly had seen the error of its ways, so Jefferson should let bygones be bygones. Common Virginians should not have to suffer the permanent loss of Jefferson's labors because of what Madison thought a momentary lapse in judgment by their legislators.

Madison returned to the issue of Jefferson's retirement in late 1782. The ex-governor's wife had died, and within a few days, Madison told a mutual friend that he hoped good might come of it. "Perhaps this domestic catastrophe may prove in its operation beneficial to his country by weaning him from those attachments which deprived it of his services," Madison wrote.[51] He hoped Jefferson would accept an appointment as one of the commissioners to negotiate the peace "as soon as his sensibility will bear a subject of such a nature."[52] Madison, it seems, was far less sentimental than Jefferson, who cultivated sentimentality intensively.[53]

Madison's communication with Jefferson made clear that for him, Confederation coercion of a state was more than an abstract notion. As he explained, "a small detachment" of the army would likely gain state acquiescence. If not, "the situation of most of the States is such, that two or three vessels of force employed against their trade will make it their interest to yield proper obedience." Immediately after launching this bombshell, Madison added that if his plan were adopted, the Confederation would maintain a substantial navy even in time of peace. Southerners ought to consider this particularly desirable, Madison concluded, for "without it what is to protect the Southern States for many years to come against the insults & aggressions of their N. Brethren." Arming Congress with a navy to use against the states would save the South from the North!

As the war ground toward its unanticipated climax of late 1781, Madison devoted his attention chiefly to the question of obtaining resources for the army. On May 18, for example, he and his colleague Joseph Jones returned to Madison's old idea when they moved that Gen. Anthony Wayne be empowered to seize supplies.[54] Unsurprisingly, congressmen from Pennsylvania (where Wayne's forces were at the time) opposed the motion, but nine other states were unanimous in their support.[55]

Madison here helped establish a landmark in favor of an implied powers reading of the Articles of Confederation. War's imperatives, it seems, overrode constitutional scruples—not for the last time in Madison's career. When he thought better of it, even while still in the Confederation Congress, Madison would say, "As Congs. it would seem they are incompetent to every act not warranted by that instrument [meaning the Articles] or some other flowing from the same source."[56] Yet, at other times, Congressman Madison argued for exclusive congressional authority over the American capital and for congressional authority to maintain a military establishment in peacetime.[57] Where necessary to its core functions, then, Madison argued for broad congressional power, even as he generally favored a strict adherence to the Articles' allocation of power to the Confederation government.

On October 1, 1781, a committee chaired by Madison reported a blistering manifesto on the issue of British depredations against American civilians.[58] With the recent burning of New London and Groton, Connecticut, by forces under Benedict Arnold's command as backdrop,[59] the committee excoriated the British for "various scenes of barbarity by which the present war has from its beginning been characterized on the part of the British arms." Americans, the committee roared, had suffered the rules of war "to be outrageously violated with impunity," but now they commanded Washington to "cause exemplary retaliation to be executed on the Enemy for all acts of cruelty committed by them against the Citizens & inhabitants of these states." In particular, the committee report proclaimed that further instances of burning down American towns in violation of the laws of war would be met with instant execution of an appropriate number of British officers then held as POWs.

Congress did not adopt this policy.[60] Instead, it referred the idea to a committee to confer with General Washington. Still, the committee's report and Congress's openness to it captured the outrage provoked among America's leading politicians by British behavior, particularly in 1781. Conveying that outrage seems to have been Madison's goal.

* * *

Meanwhile, also at the beginning of October, Lord Cornwallis found himself in his fateful fortifications at Yorktown, Virginia. Governor Thomas Nelson wrote to Madison and his Virginian colleagues with news of the initial encirclement and the British troops' first falling back from their outer fortifications on October 5.[61] Report of further progress was sent to Madison by his friend Edmund Pendleton on October 8.[62]

As the war reached its end, Congress resumed discussion of the question of the western lands.[63] Jones, Madison, and their junior colleague Edmund Randolph submitted a formal protest written by Madison. Their chief contention was this: "If the present discussion has been opened upon an opinion that Congress can assume for the use of the United States any portion of territory claimed by an individual State and supposed by them not to fall within its limits, we are now to learn the page of the Confederation in which this power is delegated." The Virginians were staking out a strict constructionist reading of the Articles. This approach to constitutionalism would later come to be associated (largely, though by no means solely, through Madison's efforts) with Virginia. They did not stop at that, however, but advised Governor Nelson to develop the argument in support of Virginia's claims in detail so that it could one day be submitted to the appropriate body, if necessary.[64]

Madison thought it likely that the Congress eventually would to some extent reject Virginia's land claims. He thought Virginia ought in that case to revoke its cession. In any event, he said, Virginians "ought in all their provisions for their future security, importance & interest to presume that the present Union will but little survive the present war." Still, the Union was necessary so long as the war continued.[65]

On October 16, Madison happily relayed to Pendleton his understanding that the British did not think that Cornwallis's besieged force at Yorktown could be relieved.[66] Four days later, Governor Nelson sent the smashing news: Yorktown had fallen, and Cornwallis had surrendered his entire army on October 19. Nelson judged the event likely to be fatal to the British cause. In fact, there would be no further significant engagements. The American Revolution was virtually over; only the negotiating remained.

The negotiating and the financing. Money continued to be the chief issue before the Congress. On January 8, 1782, Madison joined his colleagues Jones and Randolph in sending Governor Benjamin Harrison word of recent congressional legislation purporting to establish a Confederation-chartered bank.[67] "Objections were suggested against such an engagement," they said, but Congress had adopted the legislation anyway.

Those "objections" had issued chiefly from Madison, who unsurprisingly had noted that the Articles of Confederation gave Congress no power to incorporate a bank.[68] Madison was one of only four congressmen (of twenty-four voting) who voted against the resolution concerning incorporation. As he later recalled, "he considered the institution as a violation of the Confederation." It is unknown whether Madison later, having opposed this first resolution to create a bank, acquiesced in its creation at the debate's conclusion. By then, his fellow Virginian, Edmund Randolph, had succeeded in having Congress resolve "that it be recommended to the legislature of each State, to pass such laws as they may judge necessary, for giving the foregoing ordinance its full operation," which one might see as a safeguard of state sovereignty. Yet, even if the creation of the bank is seen as accompanied by that check, Congress's undertaking to legislate in an area not delegated to it certainly violated Madison's stance—often reiterated in connection with the states' western land cessions—that Congress could only do the few things the Articles specified.

Madison recognized this difficulty. Yet, he said, Congress's request that each state do what was necessary to empower the bank to operate within its territory might serve as "an antidote against the poisonous tendency of precedents of usurpation."[69] He was not hopeful in this regard, but as one member of Congress, there was little more that he (or Randolph) could do. Implicitly in his own defense, he pleaded "the dilemma in which . . . circumstances placed the members who felt on one side the *importance* of the institution, and on the other a want of power and an aversion to assume it." In general, he sympathized with Superintendent of Finance Robert Morris's desire to strengthen the institutional basis on which the Confederation's finances rested, even as the revolution had reached its denouement.[70]

Seemingly, however, the congressmen did not know that it had. Thus, Madison, Randolph, and Joseph Jones wrote Governor Harrison on February 15, 1782, that "the Enemy intend to prosecute the ensuing Campaign with all the vigor in their Power."[71] Therefore, they encouraged Virginia to provide all the men and provisions it could to the southern army.

So it went through the balance of 1782. Not realizing that Yorktown marked the war's turning point toward American victory, Madison and his fellow politicians continued their efforts to man and supply the army, continued to circulate rumors of the enemy's and the allies' comings and goings, and remained uncertain whether and when independence would be won.

All was made clear on March 4, 1782. Then, the House of Commons voted a resolution naming as "enemies to His Majesty and this country" anyone advocating or pursuing "the farther prosecution of offensive war on the continent of North America, for the purpose of reducing the revolted colonies to obedience by force."[72] Lord North, prime minister through the war—for its last several months only because King George would not accept the resignation that would have meant acquiescence in independence—had been displaced.

The result was, as Madison and his colleagues explained to Governor Harrison, the dispatch of a British general charged with "treating of peace with America."[73] In the interim, the general informed Washington, he hoped to make the war "as little destructive as possible." Yet, the new ministry disliked the idea of independence; apparently they hoped to find some middle way between subordination and capitulation.

Despite British unwillingness to face facts, the revolution was effectively won, at last. In addition to the crushing American victory at Yorktown, diplomatic developments in Europe would soon make Britain's need to disengage from North America imperative.[74] The fighting at sea might continue, and the British had not yet abandoned several important posts, but changing sentiment and international developments meant that independence was virtually assured.

Between the victory at Yorktown and the conclusion of the peace, Congress faced pressures from two sides. On one side were people who advocated effective abandonment of the French alliance at the negotiating table if such a step would yield America a better treaty than would adherence to the promise not to make a separate peace.[75] Proponents of this course seem to have thought that the former colonies' natural link was to Britain, and that it should be restored as expeditiously as possible. On the other side were those who wanted to stay in the French orbit. Madison argued for dealing with the French in good faith and considered Louis XVI an estimable friend to

America, even as he deplored French efforts to hem American territorial claims in at the Appalachian boundary.[76] Congress repeatedly considered instructions to guide the American negotiators, and Madison played a leading role in the process. Among other initiatives, Madison notably moved, on September 10, 1782, that if the British wanted restitution to Loyalists for property confiscated by the Americans, the American negotiators should insist on compensation for "slaves & other property" taken by British forces from the Americans.[77] Ultimately, John Jay saw his chance and took it at the peace talks in Paris, and so America—to the surprise of its Gallic patrons, as well as the discomfiture of its Spanish quasi-ally—ended up with the Mississippi as its western boundary.[78]

In the meantime, Madison remained concerned with the fiscal situation facing Congress. When Superintendent of Finance Morris reported that Congress had received only $5,500 from the states between January 1 and May 17, 1782, Madison moved in Congress that Morris be instructed instantly to inform the governors what the consequences would be if they did not immediately provide more money.[79] In response, Congress appointed Madison to chair a committee charged with conferring with Morris on the matter. The committee two days later reported a recommendation—not in Madison's hand—that members be sent to the individual states with the assignment of making Congress's situation clear to them.[80] Still, to Madison's and other congressmen's distress, every state—not least Virginia—remained in arrears.[81] Madison favored empowering Congress to levy an impost, among other expedients; he said that the tariff power would serve "to prevent separate appropriations by the States, to do equal justice to the public creditors, to maintain our national character & credit abroad, to obtain the loans essential for supplying the deficiencies of revenue, and to prevent the encouragement which a failure of the scheme would give the Enemy to persevere in the war."[82] The General Assembly first passed a law saying that once the other twelve states had agreed to the impost power, Virginia would join; later, hearing of recalcitrance on the part of Rhode Island, Virginia repealed its law.[83] Madison and his Virginia colleague in Congress protested that Virginia ought to support granting Congress the impost power, particularly as its example might induce other states to withdraw their assents, but to no avail: no amendment to the Articles granting Congress a tariff power was ever adopted.[84] Without independent financial resources, Congress often lacked the ability to perform even its most basic functions. The states, such as Madison's own Virginia, could not clothe the few soldiers they managed to recruit either.[85] Madison feared that in case Congress could not pay the army, further army mutinies were inevitable.[86] In that, he proved prescient: only Washington's great stature and steadfast republicanism staved off a general mutiny—or worse.[87]

Interestingly, a significant difference of impression developed between Madison, on the one hand, and state-level politicians, on the other, during these months. Madison believed that if empowered to do so, Congress could extract revenue from the people. Virginia's state politicians' appraisal of the situation was that Virginia simply could not pay more—that the people had reached their limit.[88] This distinction would later have a significant effect on Madison's place within the Virginia elite, as well as on debates within the Old Dominion on the shape of desirable federal reform.

One development in those final months of Madison's congressional tenure does demand our attention, for it was in November 1782 that Madison first undertook to keep notes of debates in Congress.[89] The first proceeding that he recorded was the selection of Elias Boudinot as president of Congress, and he would continue to take notes through the session of June 21, 1783.[90] He could not have known it then, but we now know that this new discipline would have the happy result of providing us with our most detailed record of the Philadelphia Convention of 1787, in which Madison would be both a leading participant and the note taker par excellence.

As he took up this discipline, Congress learned on February 13, 1783, that King George had proclaimed his readiness to recognize the thirteen "free and independent states" on November 30, 1782.[91] According to Madison, there followed "great joy in general" at what Madison called "the dawn of peace."[92] King George III finally declared a "cessation of arms" on Valentine's Day, 1783.[93] Congress, convinced that peace had actually come by communications it received on April 10, issued a similar declaration on April 11.[94] It then unanimously ratified the preliminary peace treaty on April 15.[95]

This did not resolve all of the problems the Congress had been facing, of course. The most important of the remaining questions was how the Union, which Madison considered essential, could be maintained in peacetime. If Congress had had a difficult time meeting its expenses even during the war,

how might it now finance its debt—meaning make the interest payments—
and handle its ongoing operating expenses?

Alexander Hamilton, Robert Morris, and others favored permanent indebt-
edness as an instrument of policy. As far as they were concerned, if the U.S.
government did not extinguish its debt, there would always be public creditors.
Those creditors, who would come from among the wealthiest Americans,
would support the U.S. government. The Union would thus be cemented.

Madison cooperated closely with Hamilton and Morris on several financial issues in the early months of 1783. Hamilton in particular pushed for
greater power to be lodged in Congress, and Madison—long distraught over
the inability of that body to meet its obligations—found him a welcome ally.
As Madison put it on the floor of Congress, "the idea of erecting our national
independence on the ruins of public faith and national honor must be horrid
to every mind which retained either honesty or pride."[96] His plea was that
Congress must be granted a revenue source independent of the state governments. The subject under consideration was the army's petition to be paid
arrears, and Madison judged that absolutely essential.

In the course of many days' tedious discussions of potential revenue
sources, methods of assessing real estate values before apportioning taxes
among the states, etc., Madison had an opportunity to hold forth on the nature of the Articles of Confederation.[97] In reply to those who insisted that
the Confederation Congress was an executive body, and thus that it would
be inappropriate to give it an independent revenue source, Madison held the
contrary. The Articles, he said, were "the federal constitution," and they gave
Congress the power "to fix the quantum of revenue necessary for the public
exigencies, & to require the same from the states. In proportion to the value
of their land." Whatever determinations Congress made on this score, Madison continued, "were a law to the States."

As Madison understood it, once Congress made fiscal policy in exercise
of these powers, that policy was binding because "the federal constitution
was as sacred & obligatory as the internal constitutions of the several States;
and . . . nothing could justify the States in disobeying acts warranted by it,
but some previous abuse or infraction on the part of Congs." Besides that, he
added, Congress had the power "to borrow money indefinitely," and in doing

so it left the states "constitutionally bound" to repay. Clearly, these powers were not executive, Madison insisted. He triumphantly concluded that to give Congress a source of money independent of the state governments would not be inconsistent with the spirit of the Articles.

On April 10, 1783, the Virginia congressmen informed the governor of Virginia that New York had offered Congress a plot of land to serve as the American capital.[98] In response, they continued, Virginia's delegates had joined Maryland's in offering Congress "a Small tract of Territory . . . in the Neighbourhood of George Town on Potowmack" as a superior alternative. That superiority, they reasoned, arose out of its "more Central Situation" and the "more ample and Enlarged Jurisdiction" they could give Congress over it. In June 1783, the General Assembly developed Madison's idea further, unanimously adopting a resolution offering Congress a choice between Williamsburg and a Potomac site.[99] Nothing came of this project in the short term, but it would germinate in Madison's mind for years—until finally he had the opportunity, under the U.S. Constitution, to give it effect.

Madison also struck up a dalliance at this time with Catherine "Kitty" Floyd, the daughter of a New York congressman who was a fellow resident of the boarding house in which Madison habitually lodged when in Philadelphia.[100] The instigator was none other than Madison's friend Thomas Jefferson, who stayed there for eleven weeks in early 1783. Jefferson told Madison that matrimony "will render you happier than you can possibly be in a singl[e] state." In Madison's absence, Jefferson said, "I often made it the subject of conversation[,] more[,] exhortation with her and was able to convince my[self] that she possessed every sentiment in your favor which you could wish."

Madison replied that yes, the lady reciprocated Madison's interest. In other words, the two had become engaged. Madison would not make final arrangements until the close of the congressional session, he said. Finally, the thirty-two-year-old congressman had found a bride in the sixteen-year-old northerner. Further, "the interest which your friendship takes on this occasion in my happiness is a pleasing proof that the disposetions which I feel are reciprocal[.]" Jefferson "rejoice[d]" at the news.[101]

Alas, by early August, Kitty had changed her mind.[102] Madison, perhaps out of embarrassment, perhaps in deference to social convention, tried to expunge the entire matter from the relevant correspondence. He destroyed much of his personal (as opposed to political, philosophical, or economic) correspondence, but twentieth-century scholars managed in this case to read through the heavy lines he drew across the Kitty-related passages. Only through their efforts do we know that Dolley Madison was not James's first love. It took no such sleuthing to tell that Jefferson sincerely regretted having facilitated the entire matter. Not to worry, he counseled his crest-fallen friend from afar, "the world still presents the same & many other resources of happiness."[103]

Madison's tenure as a member of the Confederation Congress closed out with a flight to Princeton. Congress's relocation from America's largest city to the little college town in New Jersey came at the decision of President Elias Boudinot, who thought it necessary to get Congress out of reach of mutinous Continental Army troops. At the root of the mutiny lay Congress's inability to satisfy the soldiers' just expectations regarding the pay they had been promised—a matter with which Madison had long been concerned.[104]

As Madison recorded the events, June 21 saw first Congress, then the mutineers assemble at the State House.[105] Congress asked the president of Pennsylvania, John Dickinson, to deploy his militia, but Dickinson explained that unless the soldiers resorted to violence, the militia could not be counted on to take Congress's side. Congress therefore remained inside until around its usual 3:00 p.m. hour of adjournment, when the members left. Some suffered harassment, though not violence, at the hands of the soldiers.

Members returned to their meeting place that evening. They authorized Boudinot to reconvene them at Princeton or Trenton, New Jersey, in case the situation in Philadelphia did not improve adequately. Yet Dickinson remained unsure that the militia could be relied on to intervene on Congress's behalf. Boudinot exercised his discretion on June 23, a Tuesday, by calling members to assemble in Princeton that Thursday. In the wake of Congress's removal, the participants, with the exception of the two chief instigators, submitted. Apparently having heard that Washington was speeding 1,500 troops to Congress's assistance, it seems that the mutineers decided discretion was the better part of valor.[106] By the end of June 26, the mutiny was effectively over.

Life in Princeton was a drudgery for Madison. As he explained, "Mr. Jones [his fellow Virgina congressman Joseph Jones] & my self are in one room scarcely ten feet square & in one bed."[107] "We are crowded too much either to be comfortable ourselves," he advised, "or to be able to carry on the business with advantage."[108] Members of Congress had every incentive to find a new capital expeditiously. Still, they decided not to return to Philadelphia "by a large majority."[109]

At his departure from Philadelphia, Madison had one other bit of business to transact. As he explained to his father, "Billey," his body servant, had become too accustomed to life in Philadelphia "to be a fit companion for fellow slaves in Virga."[110] Therefore, the congressman said, he would not force Billey to return to the Old Dominion with him, "even if it could be done." Besides, Madison could not "think of punishing him by transportation merely for coveting that liberty for which we have paid the price of so much blood, and have proclaimed so often to be the right, & worthy pursuit, of every human being." Exactly what Madison did remains unclear. He noted, however, that Pennsylvania law would not permit Billey to be sold for more than seven years, and he added that, "I do not expect to get near the worth of him." Seven years was a classic length for an indenture. It seems, then, that Madison signed an indenture agreement for Billey, who would have become free after.

As he pondered his departure from bucolic Princeton, Madison's friends already had begun to offer their two cents' worth concerning his future. Edmund Pendleton, who like Jefferson and Randolph had been Madison's regular correspondent while the young man served in Congress, wrote him in October 1783 that he ought to seek a seat in the Virginia General Assembly's lower house, the House of Delegates.[111] When Madison's congressional term ended on November 2, he must have had that idea in mind.

Madison arrived back at his parents' home in Orange County in the midst of very bad weather. As he explained, "We have had a severer season & particularly a greater quantity of snow than is remembered to have distinguished any preceding winter. Confined to the house, Madison put his time to good use in reading law, a subject he had long intended to pursue. As he explained, Madison wished "to depend as little as possible on the labour of slaves," while at the same time he wanted "a decent & independent subsistence."[112] "The difficulties which [he foresaw] in" law dissuaded him from pursuing that profession. Yet, he continued his reading of it. It was while thus occupied that Madison read and became an advocate of the work of the General Assembly's revisors of the laws.

That committee of delegates, spearheaded by Jefferson, Pendleton, and George Wythe—prominent lawyer-politicians all—had been given the task of combing over Virginia's common and statutory law with the goal of identifying provisions and precedents inconsistent with republican government. Among its proposals were Jefferson's pet project of abolition of feudal land tenures (done), reform of criminal punishments to make them more proportionate and less bloody (begun), institution of public schooling, and enshrinement of the principle of religious freedom. Madison suggested to Jefferson in early 1784 that the entire set of proposals be published so that the public might become familiar with the whole. Like other admirers of the revisors' product, Madison hoped that eventually the entire set of reforms would be adopted en masse; although that never happened, Madison in time would be responsible for pushing the most important of the bills through the General Assembly.[113]

Patrick Henry, too, implored Madison to make his retirement from public life brief, and to hurry to the aid of "our Country" (by which, characteristically, the great orator of the revolution meant Virginia, not the United States generally).[114] The federal system needed reform, he wrote, and many other things urgently demanded attention. Madison should help provide it, beginning in May when the General Assembly, of which Henry was acknowledged master, convened.

Madison assumed his seat in the House of Delegates, which since 1780 met in May, in the revolutionary capital of Richmond.[115] As he did so, other members already considered him "as a general, of whom much has been preconceived to his advantage."[116] As in Congress, the chief concern would be finance. Not only was Virginia unable to meet its obligations to the Confederation, but it could barely service its own debt.

The Treaty of Paris had ended the revolution on a high note. Shockingly, Britain had recognized the Mississippi rather than the Appalachians as the United States' western boundary. Yet, the treaty also required that the United States enable British creditors to collect their debts in American courts. Virginia had by the time Madison entered the General Assembly done nothing to implement this requirement. Instead, Patrick Henry insisted that American action on this question must be preceded by withdrawal of British forces from American territory in the old Northwest. The British, predictably, saw things the other way, and they likely would continue to do so as long as the fur trade with Indians in that region remained profitable.

In light of the press of financial matters and his reputation as an able politician, we should not be surprised that Madison was named chairman of the Committee on Commerce.[117] He moved by the end of May to have the House adopt a resolution to take up the revisors' work and decide on each of the approximately 130 bills they had written "as early as possible."[118] Early the next month, he joined in resolutions negating all Virginia laws inconsistent with the peace treaty—including any impeding Britons' collection of debts in Virginia courts, even as other prominent delegates favored renunciation of those debts.[119]

Among the several committees to which Madison was named and bills that he drafted in his first session back in the General Assembly, another named him to participate in what came to be known as the Mount Vernon Conference.[120] Contemporary evidence indicates that Madison authored the resolution.[121] The General Assembly intended for the Conference to resolve various issues concerning the two states' sharing the Potomac River that were then pending between Maryland and Virginia, but to his consternation, the conference ultimately met at Washington's Potomac River estate *sans* Madison. He learned of the appointed date only after the fact.[122]

The question of the old colonial laws making the Church of England the church of Virginia came before the House in an unanticipated form. The Episcopal (formerly Anglican) Church technically remained Virginia's established church. Its clergy petitioned for incorporation, which is to say legislation legally recognizing its position in its denomination.[123] That legislation legally also invested the Episcopal clergy with the old establishment's property—glebes (that is, parsonages), churches, and all. It also insulated Episcopal priests from removal from office other than by the entire convocation (that is, the assembly of the state's Episcopal priests and laymen) and empowered them to adopt canon law. As Madison explained, the proposal won Henry's endorsement (he was an Episcopalian), and Madison voted for it to stave off Henry's proposed tax to support Protestantism generally (a general assessment). Madison hoped that the people would demand repeal and that the bill would teach them "the danger of referring religious matters to the legislature."[124]

Henry's idea of a general assessment had begun to percolate. "Several Petitions came forward" for the idea, Madison explained, and the concept won the approval of the Committee on Religion. Madison found this idea authentically dangerous. A general assessment was continuation of Protestant establishment without preference. Where formerly the king's church, the Church of England, had been Virginia's state church, that arrangement had only a minority of defenders. Still, Henry, Edmund Pendleton, and other prominent Tidewater (that is, coastal Virginia) Episcopalians believed that the slackening of religious authority during the American Revolution had resulted in a general breakdown of morals in society.[125]

Their solution—Madison thought it was mainly Henry's solution—was to revive taxes to support religion.[126] Those taxes had not been collected since 1776 but might be again. What made the general assessment concept different from simple restoration of the establishment was that under the new plan, each taxpayer would select the recipient of his contributions. Thus, rather than everyone paying to support the Episcopalians, a Baptist could designate the local Baptist to receive his taxes, a Presbyterian could designate the local Presbyterian, and so on. Everyone would pay, but at least where he had a different preference, a taxpayer would not have to support the former royal church.

This was not as conservative a proposal as it seems from our perspective. Maybe Virginia had not enforced taxation in support of the favored church since the dawn of the revolution, but laws providing for such taxation remained on the books, and the Episcopalian ministers still occupied the parsonages established for them in colonial days. From that point of view, then, a general assessment could seem liberal; it certainly would have been more liberal than the contemporary system in nearly any European country or New England state.

Amazingly for its time, Madison's summary of the general assessment proposal included a criticism that "in its present form it excludes all but Christian Sects."[127] On this ground, he lamented, the "Presbyterian Clergy" had come to favor it. Unhappily for Madison, Henry's rival for dominance of the state government, Richard Henry Lee, confided that he favored it as well.[128] As Lee, the chieftain of the powerful Lee family and former president of the Continental Congress, put it, "Refiners may weave as fine a web of reason as they please, but the experience of all times shows Religion to be the guardian of morals—and he must be a very inattentive observer in our Country, who does not see that avarice is accomplishing the destruction of religion, for want of a legal obligation to contribute something to its support." Turning to a common objection to the proposal, Lee added, "The declaration of Rights, it seems to me, rather contends against forcing modes of faith and forms of worship, than against compelling contribution for the support of religion in general." So far as Lee was concerned, Islam and Hinduism fell under "true freedom" as well as Christianity did. Henry's bill, however, would favor Christianity alone.

By Christmas Eve, 1784, the bill was up for a third reading in the House of Delegates. Under the Virginia constitution, each bill had to pass three readings in order to become law. Madison and like-minded colleagues narrowly averted passage by moving to postpone the matter.

Already by then, Madison had developed extensive arguments against the idea of government support of religion. His prerevolutionary revulsion over establishment persecution of Baptists had developed into a coherent opposition to government support for religion. There are in his papers two sets of notes for speeches opposing Henry's proposal, and each of them makes a powerful case against it.[129]

Thus, in his first outline, Madison thought it impossible for courts of law neutrally to decide what "Christianity" was. He asked which version of the Old Testament—the Hebrew, the Septuagint Greek, or the Vulgate Latin—was to be preferred. And which translation? Once that question had been decided, which canon of Scripture—which set of writings—ought to be adopted: the Protestants', the Catholics', or the Lutherans'? How was the Bible to be received: as divinely inspired in every word, as divinely inspired in its essentials, as divinely inspired in general, or how? How was the godhead to be understood: in the Trinitarian way, in the Arian way, or in some other way? Must one accept the classic Protestant slogans *sola scriptura* and *sola fide*? How, in short, could a judge decide who was a Christian and who was not?

His second outline considered even more powerful arguments against Henry's proposal. It opened with a claim that religion was "not within [the] purview of Civil Authority." This whole project, he noted, tended in the direction of establishing Christianity. Having done that, he wrote, it would tend toward requiring uniformity (which had been required in England since Tudor times) and adopting penal laws in furtherance of this project.

The second heading of Madison's second set of notes against Henry's bill began by asking whether religion was necessary. It then asked whether religious establishments were necessary to religion. His answer: no. People naturally tended to be religious, he said, and history showed that establishment corrupted religion. Here, of course, Madison's opinions reflected the hard-line Protestant version of church history ambient in Virginia in his day. History, Madison noted, gave no example of a general assessment. It did, however, give examples of states devoted to religious freedom—not only Pennsylvania, but also New Jersey. Rhode Island and Delaware, he said, further supported his argument, as did the experience (if not the law) of New York.

Under his third heading, Madison mentioned the Virginia Declaration of Rights. Although his notes include only that cryptic reference, one can infer that Madison, who was Section 16's chief author, held a general assessment inconsistent with, indeed directly violative of, the guarantee that Virginians would enjoy the free exercise of religion, as well as the claim that neither violence nor force should be used to guide men into particular religious observance. Fourthly, Madison held that this semi-establishment would drive emigration from Virginia. Any such development was greatly to be lamented as far inferior to the expected immigration into the "asylum" provided by the Declaration of Rights and its liberal church-state principle.

This brought Madison to consider that matters in Virginia were not as bad as the general assessment's proponents said. If disease was rampant, well, war and bad laws had contributed to making it so. The termination of the war and the correction of the laws would yield improvement of Virginia's social situation without religious assessment. Besides that, Madison concluded, the bill would dishonor Christianity. He closed by holding up the principle of Section 16 of the Declaration of Rights as worthy of defense.

Although it had won earlier in the session by 47–32 on its first reading, the bill passed on its second reading on December 23 by only 44–42.[130] Henry was selected by the legislature to assume the office of governor, and in his absence, the prospects for his reform changed markedly. The next day, December 24, the House decided, 45–38, to put off a third reading until the following November. In the meantime, it also decided, the bill would be printed (twelve copies given to each member) for the people's consideration.

In the interim between that session of the General Assembly and the one to convene in November 1785, Virginia experienced its first truly popular, statewide political campaign. Petitions for and against the general assessment in support of teachers of the Christian religion circulated virtually everywhere. As Madison described the contest, it "ma[de] a noise thro' the Country."[131] His evaluation of the breakdown of contending sides was this: "The Episcopal people are generally for it, tho' I think the zeal of some of them has cooled. The laity of the other Sects are equally unanimous on the other side. So are all the Clergy except the Presbyterian who seem as ready to set up the establishmt. which is to take them in as they were to pull down that which shut them out." Referring to the contrast between their petition against the proposal to incorporate the Episcopal clergy the previous year and their support for the general assessment in 1785, Madison concluded, "I do not know a more shameful contrast than might be formed between their Memorials on the latter & former occasion."

The petition campaign seemed necessary to the bill's proponents because of a quirk in Virginia's political system. Recall that in 1776, George Mason had taken the lead in devising Virginia's first republican constitution. Madison had played a role in the drafting as a member of the committee charged with writing both that and the Declaration of Rights. Owing in part to Mason's conservatism, the constitution essentially retained Virginia's colonial scheme of legislative apportionment, under which each county sent two members to the House of Delegates. This made it possible for popular disapproval of a particular measure to fail to register majority support in the House, where Episcopalian Tidewater counties were drastically overrepresented. Madison's ally, George Nicholas, a delegate from Jefferson's Albemarle County, noted, "A majority of the counties are in favor of the measure but I believe a great majority of the people against it; but if this majority should not appear by petition the fact will be denied."[132] With adequate petitions, then, opponents of the general assessment would be able to demonstrate that Virginians at large opposed the plan. Nicholas, a master political strategist, suggested to Madison that he commit something to paper that might be circulated throughout the Commonwealth so that opponents' petitions could all be framed in basically the same language. Madison would soon follow this advice.

By May of 1785, Madison had received a number of positive electoral reports. "I have heard," he observed, "of several Counties where the late representatives have been laid aside for voting for the Bill, and not of a single one where the reverse has happened."[133] Yet there was more he could do. As Madison anticipated that the vote in the coming General Assembly would be "precarious," the debate "warm," he decided to put pen to paper.[134]

The result, *Memorial and Remonstrance Against Religious Assessments,* was completed in mid-June. It is his first great state paper. Madison kept his authorship a secret, and although Nicholas, George Mason, and perhaps a few others knew it, the author's identity did not become public until Madison disclosed it in 1826—forty-one years later.[135] By then, of course, he had long since retired from active public life and the establishment was long dead.

That Madison kept his authorship of the *Memorial and Remonstrance* secret should not surprise us. After all, to anger, offend, or even alienate general assessment proponents such as Patrick Henry, Richard Henry Lee, and Edmund Pendleton could not have done him any good. Besides, there was a general expectation in the 1780s that public papers would be published anonymously so that the reader would be able to exercise his own judgment rather than being swayed by a famous name.

Madison's argument in the *Memorial and Remonstrance* is relatively brief. It comes to six pages in his collected papers.[136] Yet, in that short span, he lays out the whole American Enlightenment case for religious freedom.

First, he says that the general assessment would be "a dangerous abuse of power." Next, he quotes the Virginia Declaration of Rights to the effect that "religion or the duty which we owe to our Creator and the manner of discharging it, can be directed only by reason and conviction, not by force or violence." The right is a natural right, he says, older than society. The duty is one owed by man to his creator and thus cannot be justly infringed by government. "Before any man can be considered as a member of Civil Society," Madison insists, "he must be considered as a subject of the Governour of the Universe." His duty to the creator is both antecedent and superior to his duty to his society, Madison concludes the opening section of his argument. "Religion is only exempt from [Civil Society's] cognizance."

Next, Madison argues that if civil society in general cannot regulate man's performance of his duty to the creator, still less can the legislature. Legislators, after all, "are but the creatures and viceregents" of society at large. "Their jurisdiction is both derivative and limited." For legislators to overstep the bounds of their authority would make them "Tyrants"; among the ways that they could become tyrants would be by regulating religion.

Madison's next major point is that transgressions upon liberty must be met at the threshold, because otherwise they grow worse. So, in this case, "Who does not see that the same authority which can establish Christianity, in exclusion of all other Religions, may establish with the same ease any particular sect of Christians, in exclusion of all other Sects?" If government can enforce an establishment to a limited degree, it can enforce another "in all cases whatsoever." (Here Madison echoed the British Parliament's Declaratory Act of 1766, in which the British sovereign body had claimed unlimited authority to legislate for the colonists. In 1785, this phrase still rang in Americans' ears as a pithy claim to unlimited authority—one against which they had fought the revolution that had finally ended only two years before.)

According to Madison, the bill assumed that government officials could properly use religion in support of civil policy. Madison characterized this as "an unhallowed perversion of the means of salvation." What he seems to have meant here is that the bill's supporters, including Henry, said that their aim was to revivify traditional morality. Similar claims appeared in other early republican religious establishments, such as the religion sections of John Adams's Massachusetts Constitution of 1780. For his part, Madison thought it inappropriate to consider religious observance as anything other than a good in itself.

Madison added that religious establishment was not necessary to the flourishing of religion. In fact, he posited, in its earliest days, Christianity had succeeded not only without government support but despite energetic repression. To say otherwise was "to weaken in those who profess this Religion a pious confidence in its innate excellence and the patronage of its Author; and to foster in those who still reject it, a suspicion that its friends are too conscious of its fallacies to trust it to its own merits." In fact, he said, for nearly fifteen centuries establishment of Christianity had generally had more a corrupting than a supporting effect.

Madison next repeated the point concerning immigration that he had made in the House of Delegates debate: adoption of the pending bill would have a negative effect on Virginia's population trends. People who looked to Virginia as an asylum would no longer see it that way; those who already lived in the Old Dominion might well find the general assessment a reason to leave the state.

Finally, Madison noted that the freedom of religion had been enshrined in the Declaration of Rights. If the General Assembly legislated on that question anyway, it might find in that precedent justification for future incursions upon other rights, such as the freedom of the press, trial by jury, separation of powers, and even the right to vote. Therefore, the petitioners were "in duty bound" to resist the general assessment.

As the campaign progressed, a happy development came to Madison's attention: the Presbyterian clergy at last opposed the general assessment.[137] Madison credited "a fear of their laity or a jealousy of the Episcopalians." The latter sentiment had been stoked by the act incorporating the Episcopalians.

When the next session of the Assembly opened, the "Bill establishing a provision for the teachers of the Christian religion" remained lying on the table. It never even came up for another vote. The people had spoken through their numerous petitions and pamphlets, and Madison could claim a great deal of the credit, both as author of the *Memorial and Remonstrance* and as organizer of the anti-assessment campaign.

The new session of the General Assembly opened in October. Back in the House of Delegates, Madison dusted off the revisors' report and tried to secure the adoption of all of their proposals. On October 31, 1785, Madison proposed 118 bills of the original 126.[138] Since he was chairman of the Committee for Courts of Justice, Madison had been able to guide the committee in reporting them, and now he could lead the full House in debating them. His course of legal reading clearly had enabled him to impress his colleagues with his legal knowledge.

In the debate, Madison encountered significant opposition from Speaker of the House Benjamin Harrison. When Jefferson's proposal to reform Virginia's criminal punishments—to make them less "sanguinary," in line with the latest Enlightenment ideals—came before the House, matters ground to a halt.

Frustrated at that, Madison ended up abandoning the project of securing the entire suite's adoption and pushing the bill for religious freedom to the top of his priority list. He could not have known it at the time, but this decision meant that the rest of the revision of the laws would never be adopted.

The Bill for Establishing Religious Freedom has three sections: a philosophical preamble, an operative section, and a concluding section.[139] The first section, more than two-thirds the length of the whole, laid out Jefferson's—and Madison's—views concerning religious liberty. "Almighty God hath created the mind free," it asserted, and "attempts to influence it" by punishments could only produce "habits of hypocrisy and meanness." "Even the forcing [a man] to support this or that teacher of his own religious persuasion" violated his right, it went on, to support whom he chose or to support no one. It also undercut the incentive freedom would give to pastors to behave in a way that laymen would reward.

Civil rights, Jefferson had written, "have no dependence on our religious opinions, any more than our opinions in physics or geometry." Government should act when people infringe on the "peace and good order." Otherwise, "truth is great and will prevail if left to herself." In the operative second section, then, the bill said, "That no man shall be compelled to frequent or support any religious worship, place, or ministry whatsoever . . . nor shall . . . suffer on account of his religious opinions . . . but all men shall be free to profess . . . their opinion in matters of religion, and that the same shall in no wise diminish, enlarge, or affect their civil capacities."

The third section breathes the spirit of the Enlightenment in a completely different way. The General Assembly knew that it could not bind future legislatures, it said, so it could not ensure that the act would never be repealed. Yet, to repeal or narrow this act would be "an infringement of natural right."

In the House of Delegates debate, Madison helped defeat an amendment that would have substituted Madison's Section 16 of the Declaration of Rights for Jefferson's preamble. He did accept a substantial paring back of Jefferson's original preamble, but succeeded in defeating attempts to confine religious freedom to Christians alone.[140] With that, the Virginia Statute for Religious

Freedom—Madison's greatest accomplishment—was passed into law. Madison crowed, "I flatter myself [the enacting clauses] have in this Country extinguished for ever the ambitious hope of making laws for the human mind."[141]

While this matter occupied the House, delegates also considered petitions both in favor of emancipating the slaves and in favor of repealing the law allowing manumission of individual slaves.[142] No one supported the emancipation petition, and Madison voted against the repeal idea both times it came up. Virginians would have the power to emancipate their slaves for a few years more.

In pondering the state of the federal Union, Madison arrived in these days at the conclusion that granting Congress a tariff power would achieve more than simply giving it the ability to fund its operations.[143] As he reasoned, individual states could not regulate the United States' trade, so it had to be regulated by Congress. More than that, giving Congress that power would allow the United States to respond to foreign restrictions on American trade with countervailing measures calculated to induce foreign powers to eliminate their restrictions. As far as Madison was concerned, "A perfect freedom is the System which would be my choice." Congress could only secure that with "retaliating regulations of trade." From this conclusion to his advocacy of a federal power to regulate commerce with foreign countries was no long step. For James Madison, freedom of religion, freedom to emancipate one's slaves, and free trade formed components of an overarching view of government and society.

Chapter 3

The Philadelphia Convention, 1787

Georgia's William Pierce attended the Philadelphia Convention only briefly.[1] He spoke four times, and the positions he took were enough to mark him as neither a personal opponent nor a devoted follower of Madison, but his own man. We can put some stock, then, in the brief sketch of Madison that Pierce composed in the convention's wake.[2]

"Mr. Maddison," Pierce recalled, "is a character who has long been in public life; and what is very remarkable every Person seems to acknowledge his greatness." How had Madison earned that reputation? Partly through assiduous application. "He blends together," according to Pierce, "the profound politician, with the Scholar. In the management of every great question he evidently took the lead in the Convention, and tho' he cannot be called an Orator, he is a most agreeable, eloquent, and convincing Speaker. From a spirit of industry and application which he possesses in a most eminent degree, he always comes forward the best informed Man of any point in debate." Madison was not only a careful student of American politics, however: his experience also gave him abundant resources for statesmanship. Again according to Pierce, "The affairs of the United States, he perhaps, has the most correct knowledge of, of any Man in the Union. He has been twice a member of Congress, and was always thought one of the ablest Members that

ever sat in that Council." The gentleman from Virginia had a winning personality too: "Mr. Maddison is about 37 years of age, a Gentleman of great
modesty,—with a remarkable sweet temper. He is easy and unreserved among
his acquaintance, and has a most agreeable style of conversation."

Madison never more clearly earned his Georgia colleague's description
of him as a scholarly master of public affairs than in preparing for the Philadelphia Convention. In 1786–1787, Madison devoted himself to what one
scholar of his role in that august assemblage called his "research project."[3]
Combing ancient, medieval, and modern writings on history and political
science, he mastered the history of both bygone and contemporary confederations.[4] In the main, his conclusion was that confederations tended to fail
for lack of power in the central government. Distilling this book learning
and his own experience, Madison also came to certain conceptions about
the ways that the American system needed to be improved. Those lessons
took the form of a memorandum entitled "Vices of the Political System of
the United States."[5] In "Vices," Madison identified twelve shortcomings of
the federal system under the Articles of Confederation. Madison's performance in the Philadelphia Convention cannot be properly appraised without
bearing in mind that his goal in the Convention was to address and remedy
each of these twelve flaws in the American political system by making radical
structural reforms, mainly with the aim of using a new federal constitution
simultaneously to empower the federal government and to circumscribe the
states' powers.

The twelve "vices" can be classified into two groups: shortcomings of the
federal system and shortcomings of the state governments. Among the shortcomings of the state governments were four general tendencies of those
governments. Madison had long pondered these, and his revolutionary correspondence is full of ruminations on and complaints concerning them.
First, he said, the states consistently failed to comply with Congress's requisitions. Congress did not have the power to tax; it could only requisition (that
is, request) money from the states. They often refused or failed to provide it.
In fact, every state at one time or another failed to comply fully with a congressional requisition. Madison's research taught him that this persistent
problem was virtually guaranteed to plague any government structured in
the way the Confederation was.

Madison's second vice was that the state governments since independence had frequently encroached on federal authority. He listed "the wars and Treaties of Georgia with the Indians," when Indian relations and wars were supposed to be a federal responsibility, "the unlicensed compacts between Virginia and Maryland, and between Pena. & N. Jersey," and "the troops raised and to be kept up by Massts." Madison judged some of these state infringements on federal authority necessary. Their necessity was the fault of the weakness of the Continental Congress and its successor Confederation, he believed. If the general government were adequate, the states would not have to undertake interstate compacts and Indian treaties for themselves.

Madison's third vice was "Violations of the law of nations and of treaties," which he thought the state legislatures had committed routinely. Here Madison touches on one of the central themes of his reform effort that is most jarring to our ear. Part of the problem comes, he says, from "the sphere of life from which most of [the state legislatures'] members are taken." In plain English, he means that most state legislators are too common, not elite enough, to see the problem as a problem. For James Madison Jr., son of James Sr. and Princeton product, much that is wrong in American politics in mid-1787 could be corrected if only a way were found to take power from the average Joes in the state assemblies and give it to select Princetonians at a greater distance from their constituents. While foreign governments have not yet punished the United States for violating, say, the Treaty of Paris, the French alliance, or the Dutch treaty, it is only a matter of time until one or more of them does so.

Perhaps more alarming even than the states' failure to comply with America's foreign obligations was the matter to which Madison devotes his fourth vice: the states' infractions on each other's rights. So, for example, the Articles do not prohibit it, but Madison thinks that when several states have treated trade with other states as trade with foreign countries, they have violated the Articles' spirit. Similarly, he sees debtor states' laws regarding debt as violating creditor states' rights. So, too, when Maryland, Virginia, and New York have favored their own vessels over those of foreign countries or of other states, they have violated other states' rights. Madison here seems to assume that the United States of America should be one large free-trade zone, and he considers state laws moving away from that goal as contrary to the affected states' just expectations.

Vices numbers 5 and 6 concern the absence of interstate cooperation where it is needed and, more specifically, the absence of a federal guarantee against state-level antirepublican revolution. Besides helping sister states suppress insurrection, fit objects of interstate cooperation that come to Madison's mind include establishment of universities, granting of corporate charters to canal companies, immigration policy, and copyrights.

Turning to the Confederation's structure, Madison's vice number 7 is "want of sanction to the laws, and of coercion in the Government of the Confederacy." Without "coercion," the Articles are not really a constitution, he says, but "a treaty of amity of commerce and of alliance, between so many independent and Sovereign States." Rather than experience, the Articles' framers in omitting to provide some force to the Confederation Congress relied upon "the justice, the good faith, the honor, [and] the sound policy of the state governments." Characteristically, Madison here scores a dig against the naïve but well-meaning revolutionaries whose "enthusiastic virtue" had led them to believe that government could rely on popular virtue to secure compliance with its policies. This is his understated verdict: "It is no longer doubted that a unanimous and punctual obedience of 13 independent bodies, to the acts of the federal Government, ought not to be calculated on."

Madison joined other Federalists in denigrating the states' wartime cooperation in federal policies. "Even during the war," he wrote, "when external danger supplied in some degree the defect of legal & coercive sanctions, how imperfectly did the States fulfil their obligations to the Union?"[6] Since the peace, matters had only deteriorated. This was to be expected, Madison concluded, because all measures bear unequally on different states and so those on whom a particular measure bore harder should be expected to comply more grudgingly, if at all. In fact, political figures in each state could win acclaim by opposing federal measures for their unfairness even when they were not unfair. Over time, then, the problem of state noncompliance would only grow.

The people would likely side with their states in any conflict with the Confederation, vice number 8 said, because of the "want of ratification by the people of the articles of Confederation." In some states, he noted, the

Articles had been elevated to the position of parts of the state constitutions, while in others they had simply been recognized by the local legislatures. So long as the people haven't ratified a federal constitution and thereby given it constitutional status within each state, federal policy may occasionally be made to yield to state policy—particularly since state courts will tend to enforce their policy instead of conflicting federal policy. Under the law of nations, any such act absolves the other members of their duty to abide by the Articles of Confederation.

Madison concludes his "Vices of the Political System of the United States" with four items on the laws of the states. Numbers 9 and 10 concern the sheer number and flux (what Madison calls "mutability") of the state laws. These factors combine to make it virtually impossible even for residents, let alone for citizens of other states, to maintain the requisite familiarity with state laws. Injustice and impairment of the economy result.

Vice 11 is the "injustice of the laws of States." Here Madison wrote an entire essay. First, he noted that responsibility for unjust laws might lie either in the legislatures or in the peoples of particular states. In case it lay in the legislature, one reason might be that bad men had been elected. Madison thought that the explanation for election of bad men to legislative office might lie in the pool of candidates from among whom they had been chosen. A pool of candidates might be undesirable because of their motives for seeking election, and Madison identified three possible motives: "ambition," "personal interest," and "public good." "Unhappily," he concluded, "the two first are proved by experience to be most prevalent." What tends to happen, he thinks, is that men actuated by the first two motives outnumber purer followers of the third impulse, win election, enact harmful measures, and use the electioneering talents that got them elected in the first place to maintain and even extend their harmful policies. Besides that, Madison thinks the "honest but unenligh[t]ened are apt to be duped by eloquent leaders animated by selfish views, who tend to cloak their arguments in "professions of public good." (He did not name anyone specific, to be sure, but the General Assembly's readiness to follow Patrick Henry must have been on his mind.)

The other cause of unjust laws lies in the people themselves. That the people should act unjustly is even more harmful to the republican faith than legislators' misbehavior. "All civilized societies are divided into different interests and factions, as they happen to be creditors or debtors—Rich or poor—husbandmen, merchants or manufacturers—members of different religious sects—followers of different political leaders—inhabitants of different districts—owners of different kinds of property &c &c." Since a majority will rule in a republic, what is to keep them from oppressing the minority? Madison lists people's self-interest in having society ruled according to the common good ("too often unheeded," as nations like individuals forget that "honesty is the best policy"); concern for the polity's reputation ("character"), which he judges even less efficacious than desire that the common good be sought; and religion, which is insufficient even to restrain individuals, let alone an entire society. In fact, "individuals join without remorse in acts, against which their consciences would revolt if proposed to them under the like sanction, separately in their closets." A religious majority may as easily be oppressive as restrained by its faith.

Madison thinks that a reform to empower the central government will provide a safeguard for minority rights. As he puts it, "an enlargement of the sphere is found to lessen the insecurity of private rights, . . . not because the impulse of a common interest or passion is less predominant in this case with the majority; but because a common interest or passion is less apt to be felt and the requisite combinations less easy to be formed by a great than by a small number." It may be that the prevailing opinion is wrong and that republics' problems with selfish majorities are more severe in small than in large states, he hopefully concludes. Soon enough, Madison would make this very argument in Philadelphia and, more famously, in Federalist No. 10.

Also foretelling Madison's famous tenth *Federalist* essay was his final "Vices" paragraph. There, he noted the desirability of the electoral process that would most reliably elevate "the purest and noblest characters" to public office. These men should be those who felt impelled to public service and who were "most capable to devise the proper means of attaining it." As he would explain in more detail in Federalist No. 10, Madison thought that extension of the sphere offered the best hope in that connection too.

Through this time, Madison's correspondence with William Grayson, James Monroe, Thomas Jefferson, and others disclosed two significant developments reinforcing Madison's hope for federal reform. First was the widespread adoption by state legislatures of the expedient of paper money. As far as Madison and his like-minded correspondents understood it, paper money was nothing more than a ruse for debt forgiveness; after all, where a lender had loaned out gold or silver, for a legislature to say that he must accept depreciated and constantly depreciating paper in return came to a plain transfer of property from him to his debtor.

Second, 1786 saw Massachusetts struck by Shays' Rebellion. Madison and other Federalists understood Shays and his coadjutors to be nothing more then ne'er-do-well debtors bent on upsetting established law in the Bay State. They believed that Congress should be able to intervene to prevent the overthrow of republican government

The common denominator of these developments, to Madison's mind, was that they could be resolved via intelligent constitutional reform. A new federal constitution could ban states from printing paper money, and it could empower the central government to suppress insurrections in any of the states. Here, as in many other areas, Madison saw his everyday experience reinforce the conclusions to which his political experience and his study had already led him.

A first run at constitutional revision took place at Annapolis, Maryland, in September 1786. This convention manifested a notable change in Madison's attitude. Alexander Hamilton had called for a federal convention in Congress as early as 1783, but Madison opposed that call on the ground that it might rouse "pernicious jealousies" and likely would have no positive effect.[7] Intervening experience had prompted a strong shift. By 1786, Madison had helped in calling the Annapolis Convention into being, and he took the fruits of his research into the history of federations with him.

Madison would have supported the creation of a radically stronger central government at the time of the Annapolis Convention, but he doubted even reinvigoration of the Confederation Congress was possible. To his disappointment, he arrived on September 6, 1786, to find virtually no one else in attendance.[8] In the end, only five states sent delegates to Annapolis. Even host Maryland did not. Proponents of reform, led by Madison and New York's Hamilton, decided that while they could not proceed with their reform efforts in Annapolis, some positive result might still be salvaged from the abortive gathering. They therefore joined in recommending that another convention be called for the following summer, with the idea "of extending the plan to other defects in the Confederation."[9]

The unanimous report, seemingly drafted by Hamilton, said that although they had met in Annapolis for the purpose of proposing changes to the Confederation in relation to trade, they believed that more extensive alteration of the federal system was necessary. There should be a new convention, it continued, to address all of "the embarrassments which characterise the present State of our national affairs, foreign and domestic." In closing, then, they asked for a convention to meet in May 1787 in Philadelphia "to devise such further provisions as shall appear to them necessary to render the constitution of the Foederal [*sic*] Government adequate to the exigencies of the Union."[10]

As Madison was hard at work trying to cobble together a continental coalition for constitutional reform, events in Congress threatened to scuttle his project permanently. Incoming correspondence from numerous men, particularly Madison's fellow Virginian James Monroe, made clear how significant dissension in Congress was.[11]

The minister for foreign affairs, New York's John Jay, had been instructed by Congress to negotiate a new trade treaty with Spain.[12] Though not the power it had been, Spain remained the possessor of very extensive colonial territories in the New World. Jay's initiative might prove very lucrative.

In assigning Jay his task, Congress granted him very wide negotiating latitude. It made only one stipulation: Jay must not surrender America's claim to the right to use the Mississippi River. Just as the seaboard rivers served as central arteries of transportation in Pennsylvania, South Carolina, Virginia, and other states, so the Mississippi promised to be an essential trade route for the inland territories. The southern states, in particular, held out hope that eventually ships loaded with agricultural goods would stream down the Ohio and the Mississippi to New Orleans and, from there, to America's accustomed Caribbean and European markets.

When Spain proved unaccommodating, Jay returned to Congress to note that Madrid might cut a favorable deal if the United States agreed to cede complete control over the Mississippi for a quarter century. Congress split along regional lines, with the South against Jay's request and the rest of the country in favor of it. Southerners worked themselves up into a lather by conceiving of the Mississippi navigation (as it was called) as a "natural right."[13] If Congress's northern majority was willing to barter away Southerners' natural rights in this instance, all in the name of filthy lucre, where would the tendency stop? Could a northern congressional majority be entrusted with additional powers?

James Monroe sent Madison numerous heated missives on this issue.[14] In the first of them, Monroe, assuming that the South would never surrender the right of access to the Mississippi, thought he saw unpatriotic motives at work. Jay and his northern sympathizers intended by this strategy to break the western territories off from the United States by prompting settlers there to go their own way or to prompt the breakup of the United States generally in favor of "a separate confederacy." The level-headed Madison likely recognized his longtime friend's excitability in this appraisal, but Monroe's account of the extended congressional debate over the matter cannot but have concerned him; Madison thought the Jay initiative worrisome, and at root unjust.[15]

For Madison, the congressional majority's willingness to adopt this untoward initiative provided still another illustration of the problem with American constitutions. He observed:

> There is no maxim in my opinion which is more liable to be misapplied, and which therefore more needs elucidation than the current one that the interest of the majority is the political standard of right and wrong. Taking the word "interest" as synonymous with "ultimate happiness," in which sense it is qualified with every necessary moral ingredient, the proposition is no doubt true. But taking it in the popular sense, as referring to immediate augmentation of property and wealth, nothing can be more false. In the latter sense it would be the interest of the majority in every community to despoil & enslave the minority of individuals; and in a federal community to make a similar sacrifice of the minority of the component States. In fact it is only reestablishing under another name and a more spe[c]ious form, force as the measure of right; and in this light the Western settlements will infallibly view it.

As Madison was given to understand, Monroe, Monroe's correspondent Patrick Henry, and George Mason all objected strenuously to the Jay proposal. The three of them would reach different conclusions from Madison's concerning its significance for federal reform. Madison feared that this imbroglio would prompt skepticism about federal power, and he was right.[16] Only time would tell how right.

Madison returned to Virginia in late 1786 for the new session of the House of Delegates. While in the state legislature, Madison cultivated the alliance with Washington that ultimately proved instrumental in establishing the new federal Constitution.[17] He also maintained close relations with the new governor, Edmund Randolph, the longtime attorney general, son of the last colonial attorney general, and scion of the most important political dynasty in the Old Dominion. Patrick Henry's retirement from the governorship and replacement by Randolph paved the way for the two to cooperate in federal reform.

Besides that, Madison in the General Assembly had three overwhelming concerns: shepherding the revision of the laws to final adoption (at which he failed), the economic dislocation resulting from the revolution, and the ongoing conflict with the Indians to the west. Madison worriedly reported to Washington on November 1 that "the affair of the Mississippi is but imperfectly known. I find that its influence on the federal spirit will not be less than was apprehended."[18] Madison confided that he was trying to persuade his colleagues not to link the Mississippi issue and the movement for federal reform, but things did not look good.

Washington's reply was all that Madison could have hoped.[19] "No morn ever dawned more favourable than ours did—and no day was ever more clouded than the present!" "I hope, to take the lead in promoting this great & arduous work. Without some alteration in our political creed, the superstructure we have been seven years raising at the expence of much blood and treasure, must fall. We are fast verging to anarchy & confusion!" Washington then relayed the impression made on his mind by Henry Knox's account of Shays' Rebellion, the Massachusetts tax revolt of 1786. Knox had told Washington (falsely, as it turns out) that the western Massachusetts rebels' program extended to redistribution of property. The general was shocked to hear that sympathizers ran to several thousand and that they hailed not only from Massachusetts but from all four New England states.

Washington's solution was a reinvigorated federal government. "Will not the wise & good strive hard to avert this evil? Or will their supineness suffer ignorance and the arts of self interested designing disaffected & desperate characters, to involve this rising empire in wretchedness & contempt?" Good men, it seemed, were standing by to watch as the American experiment in republicanism dissolved into anarchy. Washington observed angrily that European observers had predicted precisely this outcome to the New World enterprise. "What stronger evidence can be given of the want of energy in our governments than these disorders? If there exists not a power to check them, what security has a man of life, liberty, or property?" There must be more unity in the center: "Thirteen sovereignties pulling against each other, and all tugging at the fœderal head will soon bring ruin on the whole; whereas a liberal, and energetic Constitution . . . might restore us to that degree of respectability & consequence, to which we had a fair claim, & the brightest prospect of attaining." Washington's concern for the domestic consequences of inadequate federal government only barely edged out worry concerning the effect of Shays' Rebellion on America's reputation abroad.

Madison shared Washington's concern. More significantly, Madison was just the political operator that the Federalist cause needed if it was to exploit Washington's support of strengthening the central government to the full. Even as Washington wrote his November 5 missive, Madison in Richmond had a hand in the General Assembly's deliberations about sending delegates to the Philadelphia Convention slated for summer 1787.

On November 3, the House of Delegates in Committee of the Whole adopted a resolution supporting the idea of a Virginia delegation to a Philadelphia convention empowered to propose amendments to the Articles of Confederation.[20] Madison secured appointment to the committee to bring in the bill. The bill, described by the editors of his papers as "in Madison's hand," sounded much like Washington. The issue, the General Assembly declared, was whether "the good people of America . . . [would] by wise and magnanimous efforts reap the just fruits of that Independence which they have so gloriously acquired, and of that Union which they have cemented with so much of their common blood; or whether by giving way to unmanly jealousies and prejudices, or to partial and transitory interests they will renounce the auspicious blessings prepared for them by the Revolution, and furnish to its enemies an eventual triumph over those by whose virtue & valour it has been accomplished." The bill went on to say that Virginia's delegates should be charged to meet other states' in Philadelphia "and to join with them in devising and discussing all such alterations and further provisions as may be necessary to render the federal Constitution [that is, the Articles of Confederation] adequate to the exigencies of the Union, and in reporting such an act for that purpose to the U. S. in Congress, as when agreed to by them, and duly confirmed by the several States, will effectually provide for the same."

Virginia's delegates, then, were to see to amendment of the Articles of Confederation. The General Assembly, by adopting the language above, told them to ensure that before the necessary changes to the Articles of Confederation could become law, they must be approved first by the Confederation Congress and then by the states. The House of Delegates passed this bill on November 9, the Senate passed it on November 23, and the speaker of the House signed the enrolled bill on December 1.

By that time, Madison had received an account of the unrest in Massachusetts from Henry "Light-Horse Harry" Lee. Lee's version was even grimmer than the account from Henry Knox that had so exercised George Washington. Madison informed the general of this in the same letter in which he told the master of Mount Vernon of the general's impending appointment to head Virginia's Philadelphia delegation.[21] Washington replied that he could not accept the appointment, because he had already told the Society of the Cincinnati that for various reasons he could not journey to Philadelphia the same month as the Convention was due to commence. It would be insulting to his brother officers if, having begged out of that event, Washington showed up in Philadelphia a few days later to participate in the Philadelphia Convention. The General Assembly's request would otherwise have prompted him to abandon his retirement, he explained.[22]

Madison meanwhile maneuvered in the House of Delegates to allay the fears of delegates from Kentucky, which was still part of Virginia, concerning the Mississippi navigation. The House of Delegates on December 29 adopted resolutions penned by Madison spelling out the Commonwealth's rejection of the idea of bartering away the Mississippi.[23]

In the first resolution, the General Assembly went on record in support of Madison's idea that access to the Mississippi River for the purposes of "navigating" it and "communicating with other Nations through" it was a natural right, one "secured to [the United States] by the event of the late Revolution."[24] Madison's claim echoed Jefferson's assertion in *A Summary View of the Rights of British America* that Britain had wronged the colonists by depriving them of free trade with all the world. The second resolution asserted that "the Confederacy" had been established "on the broad basis of equal rights in every part thereof," and that trading off one part's rights for other parts' advantage would be "a flagrant violation of Justice" and "direct contravention of the end for which the fœderal Government was instituted."

Having thus laid the rhetorical groundwork, Madison concluded with a hammer blow: to trade away access to the Mississippi would be "dishonorable," would provoke westerners' "just resentments and reproaches," and would destroy "that just confidence in the Wisdom, Justice and liberality of the fœderal Councils which is so necessary at this Crisis, to a proper enlargement of their authority." Virginia remained supportive of a proper negotiation with Spain, the resolutions concluded, even as it opposed Jay's gambit. Madison's resolutions, which he called "pretty pointed,"[25] but which were not so strong as some wished,[26] passed unanimously through the House. They later gained the assent of the Senate as well, though not unanimously.[27]

By condemning the Jay-Gardoquì negotiation in strong language, Madison no doubt intended, to calm Kentucky fears. If the chief Virginia proponent of federal reform said that discussing trading away the Mississippi navigation rightly endangered the movement in that direction, then he could be trusted not to do so. His calculation paid off, as the very day after the adoption of the Jay resolutions, the House of Delegates voted to hold elections a week later for a Virginia delegation to the Philadelphia Convention.[28]

The delegates were elected on December 4, 1786. Madison was the author of the motion and among those named.[29] The day after the governor sent Madison his commission, Madison wrote to inform Washington that the general had been placed at the head of the delegation. Yes, Madison said, the Continental Army's former officers deserved respect, but this matter was so important that he joined the General Assembly majority in thinking Washington had to be appointed in spite of his reservations. Seeing Washington's name at the top of the list would make clear to all of the other leading men in the United States how seriously Virginia took the matter and would invite them to attend too. Madison hoped that Washington, upon considering it in this light, would concur.

Madison received support in the cause of federal reform from Judge Edmund Pendleton and the American minister to France, Thomas Jefferson.[30] Yet each had his trepidations. Pendleton worried lest granting Congress the power to regulate trade leave the tobacco states at the mercy of the other states' interests. Jefferson, for his part, said, "To make us one nation as to foreign concerns, & keep us distinct in Domestic ones, gives the outline of the proper division of powers between the general & particular governments." He thought there should be three branches of the federal government, as there were in the state ones. Congress might have appointed an executive committee to perform those functions, Jefferson noted, and he had himself proposed that it do so. However, it likely never would "have self-denial enough to go through with this distribution," and so "The distribution should be imposed" via constitutional reform.

Jefferson thought that the Jay imbroglio threatened the future of the Union itself. If the east continued on that path, he said, the west would eventually leave the United States of America to form its own country. "It might have been made the interests of the Western states to remain united with us," Jefferson held, "by managing their interests honestly & for their own good. But the moment we sacrifice their interests to our own, they will see it better to govern themselves." Interestingly, Jefferson thought it self-evident that in case they chose to do so, the western states could of course leave the Union: "The moment they resolve to do this, the point is settled. A forced connection is neither our interest nor within our power."

Jefferson next turned to boasting about European opinion concerning his and Madison's joint achievement, the Virginia Statute for Religious Freedom: "The Virginia act for religious freedom has been received with infinite approbation in Europe," he reported, "& propagated with enthusiasm. I do not mean by the governments, but by the individuals which compose them. It has been translated into French & Italian, has been sent to most of the courts of Europe, & has been the best evidence of the falsehood of those reports which stated us to be in anarchy. It is inserted in the new Encyclopedie, & is appearing in most of the publications respecting America."

Not only did elite European opinion hold the Virginia statute in high esteem, but so did its egotistical author. Jefferson allowed as how, "in fact it is comfortable to see the standard [that is, the flag] of reason at length erected, after so many ages during which the human mind has been held in vassalage by kings, priests & nobles." Having patted himself on the back, he complimented Madison by adding, "and it is honorable for us to have produced the first legislature who has had the courage to declare that the reason of man may be trusted with the formation of his own opinions."

When Washington answered Madison's news that the General Assembly had selected Washington to head Virginia's Philadelphia Convention delegation, he made clear precisely how delicate a situation he found himself in.[31] The Society of the Cincinnati, meeting in Philadelphia at the same time as the Convention, was an organization whose membership and activities were close to Washington's heart. He thought he owed his fellow Continental Army officers a moral debt. Yet, several leading figures, including the Adamses, John Jay, Elbridge Gerry, and Thomas Jefferson, among others, saw the society as an incipient aristocracy.[32] What with its hereditary, military service-based membership, they had a good point.

For that reason, Washington had supported a change in the society's national bylaws ending hereditary succession. Yet, several states refused to adopt that change. For that reason, Washington had declined to serve as president of the society and begged out of the summer 1787 meeting. Among the reasons he gave in declining the presidency were his ill health (severe rheumatism) and public retirement at the time of his 1783 resignation of his general's commission. Yet here Virginia was, insisting that Washington go to Philadelphia. Washington told Madison that something might arise between this December 1786 communication and the Philadelphia Convention's scheduled commencement the following May, but that at present he "should feel myself in an awkward situation to be in Philadelphia on another public occasion, during the sitting of the Society." As things stood, then, he did not see how he could attend.

Madison's response was that he saw the gravity of Washington's difficulties, but that in light of the state of public affairs, no one would hold participation in the Philadelphia Convention against the general.[33] He suggested that Washington should at least leave the door open to his attendance in case things grew sufficiently worse by the summer of 1787. Governor Edmund Randolph, in transmitting the official notification of Washington's election, painted matters in extreme terms: he should accept his appointment, "For the gloomy prospect still admits one ray of hope, that those, who began, carried on & consummated the revolution, can yet rescue America from the impending ruin."[34]

Meanwhile, Jefferson wrote to Madison from France sloughing off Shays' Rebellion as evidence of Americans' desirably ambivalent and suspicious attitude toward government.[35] Without realizing the degree of Madison's concern,[36] Jefferson opined, "I hold it that a little rebellion now and then is a good thing, & as necessary in the political world as storms in the physical. Unsuccessful rebellions indeed generally establish the encroachments on the rights of the people which have produced them. An observation of this truth should render honest republican governors so mild in their punishment of rebellions, as not to discourage them too much. It is a medicine necessary for the sound health of government." Yet, in contrast to his equanimity when informed of the Massachusetts uprising, Jefferson expressed great unease about the Jay-Gardoquì negotiation. If the western people declared their independence, he thought, "we are incapable of a single effort to retain them," because neither the militia nor the army could be induced to attack them. Likely a war involving France and Spain would result. The initiative must be nipped in the bud.

Madison returned to Congress in New York on February 12, 1787.[37] Once again, a quorum was hard to come by. Madison devoted most of his energy to preparing for the Philadelphia Convention. It was at this point that he drafted his "Vices," along with a draft plan for the Convention to consider. Chief among the topics occupying the Confederation Congress's attention were the Jay-Gardoquì negotiation, American violations of the Treaty of Paris, the movement for federal reform, and the effort of the Confederation to aid in suppressing Shays' Rebellion.[38]

Madison and his colleague William Grayson wrote to Governor Randolph at the beginning of Madison's tenure saying that Shays' Rebellion seemed to be exhausted.[39] Yet, within a week the congressmen had changed their minds and written the governor that they urgently hoped to see the Shays troubles abate, as it seemed likely that otherwise the distemper would spread not only to New York but beyond.[40]

Madison's notes of congressional debates show that he advocated a forceful federal response to Shays' Rebellion that he himself called unconstitutional and contrary to the spirit of republican government.[41] He hoped that the Congress would interfere in Massachusetts's internal affairs on the side of the government, he said, despite the fact that it was "rather difficult to reconcile . . . with the tenor of the Confederation, which does not authorize it expressly, and leaves to the States all powers not expressly delegated; or with the spirit of Republican Govts which as they rest on the sense of the majority, necessarily suppose power and right always to be on the same side." His excuse for advocating such measures was that the Confederation bore responsibility for defending the states against foreign intervention, and that it seemed not unlikely that Great Britain stood ready to exploit untoward developments in the United States to its own advantage.

Madison also exploited the congressional debate concerning the Shays matter to the advantage of the cause of federal reform. Congressmen from other states should bear in mind, he said, what effect a popular uprising in another state might have on the Union at large, and even upon their own states. It was this consideration, he explained, that had led Virginia's general assembly—usually slow to tax tobacco—to adopt a temporary tax on that product. Such a tax, Madison lectured, "wd. not have been granted for scarce any other purpose whatever."

Soon thereafter, on February 21, Congress took up the question whether to endorse the Annapolis Convention's call for the states to send delegates to Philadelphia for another go at federal reform in the summer of 1787.[42] A congressional committee charged with the task composed a report agreeing with the Annapolis Convention that the Confederation needed to be strengthened and that amendment of the Articles was the best route to take. In the debate that day, Madison's notes show that one congressman held that the Confederation needed to be divided into regional confederacies of more manageable size. (Madison also noted that for the first time, one newspaper in Boston had just proposed the same thing: a separate New England nation.) Still, a congressional majority did endorse holding a Philadelphia Convention.[43]

Madison was not very enthusiastic about the prospect.[44] The Confederation had few defenders, true, and the states' growing noncompliance with Congress's fiscal requisitions meant that it would not endure for long, but he found that "men of reflection" were "much less sanguine as to a new than despondent as to the present System." If the Philadelphia Convention failed, Madison thought it likely that "some very different arrangement will ensue." In Massachusetts and Rhode Island, in particular, "some leading minds" were turning toward the idea of a monarchy as a result of Shays' Rebellion and the democratic excesses of the smallest state. This idea would not be popular with average people, who seemed more apt to prefer "a partition of the Union into three more practicable and energetic governments." Alas, Madison noted, this idea had moved from the realm of private speculation into that of the public prints. He hoped that "the republican character" could be salvaged at Philadelphia, that the threat of disunion would "rouse all the real friends to the Revolution to exert themselves in favor of such an organization of the Confederacy, as will perpetuate the Union, and redeem the honor of the Republican name."

In mid-March came two very significant developments: first, Washington finally agreed to join the Virginia delegation to Philadelphia if his health allowed.[45] Second, ominously, Patrick Henry declined to go.[46] Madison read this as a highly negative development. As he told Washington, "there is danger I fear that this step has proceeded from a wish to leave his conduct unfettered on another theatre where the result of the Convention will receive its destiny from his omnipotence"—that is, Henry intended to leave himself free to oppose the Convention's handiwork when it came up for ratification in Virginia.

It was also during March that Rhode Island refused to send delegates to the Philadelphia Convention.[47] Although Madison, Washington, Randolph, and their collaborators in other states had hoped for deputies from all thirteen states, they surely must have seen this development coming. In 1786, Rhode Island's legislature had followed up its April currency depreciation (which reduced the value of its paper notes by 50 percent between summer

1786 and spring 1787). Soon, Rhode Island passed a legal tender law and began trying to foist off its paper money upon Congress in response to requisitions. Combined with Rhode Island's refusal to extradite Shaysites who sought refuge in that state, these events put it outside the pale. As Madison put it, "Nothing can exceed the wickedness and folly which continue to reign there."[48]

With the matter of Washington's attendance resolved, Madison's plans for the Convention now focused on Governor Randolph. Madison, recall, was slight of build and weak of voice. The governor, on the other hand, stood as tall as the typical Virginia blueblood, in the same mold as Jefferson and James Monroe, both of whom were six-feet-two in height or more. Besides that, Randolph was a polished speaker, the incumbent governor, and a scion of Virginia's leading political dynasty. He was the obvious candidate for the role of spokesman for Madison's proposed constitutional reforms. First, however, Madison had to bring Randolph around to agreeing with him on exactly what those reforms ought to be.

While Randolph wanted to amend the Articles of Confederation, Madison preferred to start with a new draft constitution and accommodate the good features of the old Articles to it. Madison also thought that individual reforms ought not to be presented for the states' approval separately, because that might let the states adopt some and not others or, worse yet, some states to accept some proposed reforms while others agreed to others.[49] In the end, that outcome would thwart the whole effort. No positive change would be adopted by all.

Next, Madison got to the nub of the matter: the type of change he envisioned. He thought that "an individual independence of the States" was "utterly irreconcileable with the idea of an aggregate sovereignty. I think at the same time that the consolidation of the States into one simple republic is not less unattainable than it would be inexpedient. Let it be tried then," Madison concluded, "whether any middle ground can be taken which will at once support a due supremacy of the national authority" and maintain the states "so far as they can be subordinately useful." On what would be the chief question before the Philadelphia Convention, Madison would endeavor to reduce the states to mere subdivisions of the centralized structure. This was far from the situation produced by the revolution, in which the states had come first, and the center possessed only so much power as they had seen fit to give it.

Among the institutional innovations Madison had in mind for this new "national" government were creation of an executive branch, establishment of a national veto over state laws "as the K. of G.B. heretofore had" (perhaps to be lodged in the upper, indirectly elected house of the legislature), population apportionment of Congress, popular election of the lower house of Congress, and popular ratification of the Constitution. Madison conceded that Randolph might adjudge his project "extravagant" or "unattainable." Madison thought it simply "essential." The change in the apportionment rules might seem at first blush unlikely to be adopted, he reasoned, but "the Northern States will be reconciled to it by the *actual* superiority of their populousness: the Southern by their *expected* superiority in this point." Once this point had been gained, Madison thought, the larger states would become willing to yield power to a new central government, and the small states would follow. Madison told the approval-seeking Randolph that many people had come to agree that absent thorough reorganization, the Union would fracture into numerous parts.

Madison left his congressional post in New York on May 2, bound for Philadelphia.[50] He thought that the Mississippi problem had been headed off, just in time to eliminate that objection to augmenting the central government's power.

The convention was to begin on Monday, May 14. Due to the terrible weather, virtually none of the delegates arrived in Philadelphia in time.[51] This gave Madison an opportunity to settle into his comfortable lodgings at the "elegant" Indian Queen, conveniently located on Third Street between Market and Chestnut, where he found Mason of Virginia and several delegates from other states among his fellow boarders.[52] As others arrived over a period of several days, Madison had time to appraise the assemblage's chances of success. He must have sympathized with James Monroe's assessment: that agreement among the states was unlikely, but if they agreed, their product would probably be too feeble to endure long.[53]

Before an adequate representation of all the states had materialized, Madison had to deal with a difficult problem. Gouverneur Morris and Robert Morris, both representing Pennsylvania, proposed that the large-state delegations hang together in insisting that voting in the Convention be apportioned among the states by population. Virginia's delegates rejected this proposal in hopes that their good faith would be requited by the small-state delegations when the question of how to apportion Congress came up.[54]

Meanwhile, the Old Dominion's delegation took advantage of other delegates' laggardness. By May 20, the Virginians had all arrived, and they had established a regular practice of meeting "two or three hours every day" to work out their common position.[55] Soon, their superior preparation would enable them to take the lead in the Convention.

The Philadelphia Convention met in Carpenter's Hall, now commonly called Independence Hall. That beautiful building had been the site of the Second Continental Congress, and thus was the place where the Declaration of Independence had been agreed among the thirteen states' delegates. In 1787, it was Pennsylvania's State House, where the legislature sat in session even as the Philadelphia Convention met.

From the day that the convention opened, Madison played the role of its chief note taker.[56] As he explained, "I chose a seat in front of the presiding member, with the other members, on my right and left hand. In this favorable position for hearing all that passed I noted in terms legible and in abbreviations and marks intelligible to myself what was read from the Chair or spoken by the members; and losing not a moment unnecessarily between the adjournment and reassembling of the Convention I was enabled to write out my daily notes during the session or within a few finishing days after its close." Along with the far less extensive notes kept by a few other delegates, Madison's record of the convention provides us with a pretty full account of what happened there.[57] Madison's work in recording the proceedings was a prodigious feat in light of his participation as a leading thinker and orator in the convention, in which the editors of his papers calculate that "he spoke more than two hundred different times."[58]

The first day that saw delegations from seven states present was Friday, May 25, 1787. Like Virginia's, the other states' legislatures seem to have taken the convention very seriously, for as Madison noted to more than one correspondent, they had sent their most eminent men.[59] The convention unanimously chose Washington to preside, and the general, product of Virginia political culture to the bone, offered the customary Virginian speech.

He was sensible of his inadequacy to the post, he said, and so he hoped that the other delegates would indulge him as he did his best.[60]

When the convention next met, on Monday, May 28, a rule allowing any member to call for yeas and nays to be recorded on any vote was debated. George Mason objected that the knowledge that their votes were being recorded would tend to impede people from changing their minds as the convention wore on, and would aid opponents of the convention's product after the convention adjourned. The rule was rejected without opposition.

The groundwork thus having been laid, the real work of the convention began on Tuesday, June 29. That was when, as the *Journal* (the formal record of the convention) put it, South Carolina's Charles Pinckney presented "the draft of a fœderal government to be agreed upon between the free and independent States of America" and, more significantly, Governor Randolph proposed the Virginia Plan.

By all accounts, the weather in Philadelphia was clear and comfortable the day that Madison's plans all came to fruition.[61] There was Washington in the front of the room, here were delegations from nearly all the states, and there stood Madison's young friend the governor, waiting to present a detailed proposal designed to correct all of the difficulties that Madison had long lamented in the federal system. Not only did Randolph present a Madisonian plan, but he did so in Madisonian terms. One can almost imagine him stopping to glance at a copy of Madison's "Vices" as he delivered his profound address, and thus set the convention's agenda for the entire summer.

Randolph began his lengthy and momentous speech, the highlight of his very distinguished career, with the traditional Virginian self-deprecation: he regretted, as Madison recorded it, "that it should fall to him, rather than those, who were of longer standing in life and political experience, to open the great subject of their mission. But, as the convention had originated from Virginia, and his colleagues supposed, that some proposition was expected from them, they had imposed this task on him."

After remarking on the difficult situation facing the United States, and the widespread expectation that the American republican experiment was about to fail, Randolph set out four lines of inquiry for the convention to follow. It ought to ask what "properties, such a government ought to possess," what "the defects of the confederation" were, what dangers the United States currently faced, and what measure might remedy the situation. He then outlined preliminary answers to these questions.

A new American government, Randolph held, should protect "against foreign invasion" and "against dissensions between members of the Union, or seditions in particular states." It should "procure to the several states various blessings, of which an isolated situation was incapable." It should "be able to defend itself against encroachment" and "be paramount to the state constitutions."

In Madison's account, Randolph next noted that defects in the Articles of Confederation could be explained by "the then infancy of the science, of constitutions, & of confederacies,—when the inefficiency of requisitions was unknown—no commercial discord had arisen among any states—no rebellion had appeared as in Massts.—foreign debts had not become urgent—the havoc of paper money had not been foreseen—treaties had not been violated—and perhaps nothing better could be obtained from the jealousy of the states with regard to their sovereignty."

"He then," Madison wrote, "proceeded to enumerate the defects." The first of Randolph's defects of the Articles of Confederation was that it "produced no security against foreign invasion." Congress had no power to punish violations of treaties or of the law of nations (which in the eighteenth century served the function of today's international law), could not prevent individual states from provoking wars, and could not fund enlistment of soldiers (which was necessary because neither militiamen nor conscripts made fit soldiers, Randolph observed).

Second on Randolph's list was that the Confederation (which Madison, typically of his contemporaries, called "the fœderal government") could neither suppress armed conflict between states nor put down rebellion within a state, since it had neither authority nor means to do so. Third, Randolph said, the United States of America could obtain many advantages not presently available to it due to its inadequate government. Among these were "a productive impost," "counteraction of the commercial regulations of other nations," laws to prevent states from printing paper money, and "establishment of great national works," as well as "the improvement of inland navigation." Fourth, "the fœderal government could not defend itself against the incroachments from the states, because it had to draw military resources necessary to that task from the state governments themselves.

Besides, fifth, "it was not even paramount to the state constitutions." After all, those constitutions, unlike the Articles, had almost all been adopted by people "elected for that purpose," while the Articles had been ratified by state legislatures.

Madison in his notes made short work of Randolph's account of the dangers America currently faced. Among other things, Randolph pointed to "the prospect of anarchy from the laxity of government every where." James McHenry of Maryland, however, provided a fuller account of Randolph's criticism of the status quo. "Our chief danger," Madison's friend and spokesman said, "arises from the democratic parts of our constitutions. It is a maxim which I hold incontrovertible, that the powers of government exercised by the people swallow up the other branches. None of the constitutions have provided sufficient checks against the democracy." By this, Randolph meant that the state legislatures were not adequately checked under the revolutionary state constitutions, and so the people's whims were too readily incorporated into law.

With that preamble, Randolph finally laid out the fifteen-resolution Virginia Plan. Yates's account of Randolph's speech says that Randolph "candidly confessed that they were not intended for a federal government—he meant a strong *consolidated* union, in which the idea of states would be nearly annihilated." Here, one hears a powerful echo of Madison's correspondence, in which Madison had said that the states should be retained insofar as they might be "subordinately useful."

Randolph proposed that where to this point each state had had an equal vote in Congress, from now on each state's weight in the "National Legislature" should be "proportioned to the Quotas of contribution, or to the number of free inhabitants." (According to New Jersey's William Paterson, Randolph observed that only on the basis of one of these schemes of apportionment could the "larger States assent to any Reform.") The national legislature should be bicameral, its lower house should be popularly elected, and its upper house should be elected by the lower from among nominees submitted to the lower house by the state legislatures. In answer to the observation that revolutionary legislatures and Congress had been too responsive to the popular will, the terms of members of the upper house should be long enough "to ensure their independency."

The new national legislature's power ought to extend, Randolph said, to "all cases to which the separate States are incompetent, or in which the harmony of the United States may be interrupted by the exercise of individual Legislation." Besides that, the national legislature ought to have a veto power over state laws and the right to employ the Union's military might against "any member of the Union failing to fulfill its duty" under the Constitution.

Randolph next proposed creation of "a National Executive." That executive ought to have "a general authority to execute the National laws" and "to enjoy the Executive rights vested in Congress by the Confederation." The executive should be a member of a committee with members of the national judiciary whose function would be to veto the laws passed by the national legislature and the national legislature's vetoes of laws passed by state legislatures. The national legislature would be able to override vetoes of its laws by supermajority vote, and the national legislature would be able to reimpose its vetoes of state laws by supermajority vote.

The "National Judiciary" that Randolph proposed would have jurisdiction over admiralty and piracy matters, interstate cases, cases involving foreigners or "the national revenue," impeachments, "and questions which may involve the national peace and harmony." The judges, he said, should serve "during good behaviour."

Among the other points in Randolph's Virginia Plan were that the new Constitution should be amendable without the consent of the national legislature, that the states' officials ought to be bound by oath to uphold the Constitution, and that ratification by each of the states ought to be by a specially elected ratification convention.

When Randolph finished his work, Pinckney presented his plan, and the convention adjourned for the day.

The convention's nationalists, emboldened by Randolph's performance, took up the next day where they had left off. Randolph withdrew his motion that the Articles of Confederation ought to be "corrected and enlarged" and offered three others in its place: a motion that "a union of the states, merely federal, will not accomplish the objects proposed by the articles of the confederation, namely, common defense, security of liberty, and general welfare"; a second motion, "no treaty or treaties among the states as sovereign," would achieve those ends; and a third motion that "a national government ought to be established consisting of a supreme legislative, judiciary and executive."[62]

South Carolinian Charles Pinckney noted of Randolph's new first resolution that if the convention agreed to it, if it voted that "a union of the states, merely federal," was inadequate, the convention was at an end. The delegates' powers extended only to recommendation of improvements to the federal union, not to its replacement with a national government, he said. When the convention agreed with him, debate concerning Randolph's first two ideas ceased, and the convention took up his third.

At this point, Charles Pinckney wondered what Randolph meant in calling the proposed new government "national." To say that it was national, rather than federal, might imply that all authority originated in the center, and so he asked whether Governor Randolph hoped to abolish the states.

Two other delegates, South Carolina's Charles Cotesworth Pinckney (not to be confused with his kinsman Charles Pinckney) and Massachusetts's Elbridge Gerry, shared Charles Pinckney's concern. They said they doubted that Congress's act recommending a federal convention or the states' commissions of the delegates could be squared with "a discussion of a System founded on different principles from the federal Constitution [that is, the Articles of Confederation]." The Pinckneys' fellow Carolinian, Pierce Butler, asked "Mr. Randolph to shew that the existence of the States cannot be preserved by any other mode than a national government."

An alternative resolution calling for the establishment of three branches, but omitting the insistence that the new government be "national," was rejected, and then Randolph's "national" resolution passed—6 ayes, 1 no, 1 state delegation divided. Another motion by Randolph, seconded by Madison, calling for scrapping the states' equal votes in the legislature in favor of some other scheme of apportionment then passed—7 ayes, 0 noes. Unable to agree on what other mode, the convention adjourned for the day.

One of the great fault lines in the convention had been exposed. While Madison and Randolph hoped for a national government—one that, in their Pennsylvanian supporter Gouverneur Morris's words, had "a compleat and compulsive operation"—other delegates would cleave to the decentralized, federal system vindicated by the revolution, in which most power remained at the state level.

The first nationalist matter that Randolph and Madison wanted the convention to decide, apportionment of representation, caused bitter division. Their proposal to drop the old system, which had given Connecticut, Rhode Island, Georgia, and Delaware the same weight in Congress as Massachusetts, Virginia, New York, and Pennsylvania, won quick assent. On the other hand, when Alexander Hamilton suggested that representation be apportioned simply according to "the number of free inhabitants," his proposal went nowhere.

Delaware's George Read then stepped in. Delaware's delegation had instructions not to agree to give up their state's equality in congressional voting, he noted. If the convention agreed to such a change, the Delawareans would perhaps have to quit the convention altogether. (Read knew whereof he spoke: foreseeing exactly this line of discussion, he had taken the lead in instructing the Delaware delegation thus. In fact, he had written the instructions.)[63]

Morris and Madison immediately rose to insist that this change was essential. Madison said that equal voices for large and small states "must cease when a national Govt. should be put into the place." In the old system, the state governments had been integral to enforcement of the Confederation's policy, but now they would not be. Therefore, state equality could be dispensed with.

Read was unpersuaded, as indeed were the other small-state delegates. Maryland's James McHenry, for example, noted that the Virginians' apportionment proposal "gave the large States the most absolute controul over the lesser ones," which clearly was unacceptable to him. His notes also show that he held the Randolph-Madison approach to be inconsistent with the Confederation Congress's call for the Philadelphia Convention. Congress, McHenry noted, had resolved "that on the 2d Monday of May next a convention of delegates who shall have been appointed by the several States to be held at Philada. for the sole and express purpose of *revising the articles of confederation*, and reporting to Congress and the several legislatures, such alterations and provisions therein as shall . . . render the *fœderal constitution*, adequate to the exigencies of government and the preservation of the union" (emphasis McHenry's).

The Virginians' proposal that the people elect the lower house of the proposed new legislature also provoked extensive discussion. The records of the debate reveal that Madison was not alone: many of the framers believed that the state governments were too democratic. In fact, rather than finding himself defending indirect elections to the Senate, Madison found himself forced to defend direct elections to the House. Roger Sherman of Connecticut insisted that the state legislatures ought to continue to select members of Congress, because "the people . . . want information and are constantly liable to be misled." Elbridge Gerry of Massachusetts, obviously affected by the recent doings of Daniel Shays and his followers in the Bay State, chimed in that he too believed that "the evils we experience flow from the excess of democracy."

Madison strenuously objected to the idea that the people should not select the members of the lower house of the legislature. "He was an advocate for the policy of refining the popular appointments by successive filtrations, but thought it might be pushed too far. He wished the expedient to be resorted to only in the appointment of the second branch of the Legislature, and in the Executive & judiciary branches of the Government." His reasoning was that basing at least that house on popular suffrage would render the new government "more stable and durable." The idea was adopted, 6 ayes, 2 noes, 2 states divided.

Next, the debate turned to the composition of the upper house, which Randolph called a senate. North Carolina's Richard Dobbs Spaight answered the motion that it be elected by the lower house by asserting that its members should instead be chosen by the state legislators. Randolph thought it should be much smaller than the lower house, because that way it would be "exempt from the passionate proceedings to which numerous assemblies are liable." A well-constructed senate, Randolph said, could serve as a check on "the turbulence and follies of democracy," which were among America's besetting "evils." The mode of selecting senators was put off for later consideration.

Then the convention turned to the question of Congress's powers. As before, Randolph and Madison either both read from the same script— essentially, Madison's "Vices"—or were so much in harmony that Randolph's every utterance sounded like Madison. Two Carolinian delegates said that the meaning of the word "incompetent" in the Virginians' motion that Congress should have power to legislate "in all cases to which the State Legislatures were individually incompetent" was vague, and that they wanted (as Madison wrote) "an exact enumeration of the powers comprehended by this definition." For the nationalist Madison's general grant, in other words, they wanted to substitute a federal enumeration.

In response to the Carolinians' complaint, Randolph instantly proclaimed his firm opposition to "such an inroad on the State jurisdictions," adding that "he did not think any considerations whatever could ever change his determination." Madison, surely sensing that matters were at a critical pass, instantly rose.

Madison said that he "had brought with him into the Convention a strong bias in favor of an enumeration and definition of the powers necessary to be exercised by the national Legislature; but had also brought doubts concerning its practicability. His wishes remained unaltered," he concluded, "but his doubts had become stronger." (The Georgian Pierce's notes show Madison saying that "he was convinced it could not be done.")

"What his opinion might ultimately be" concerning the possibility of enumerating the federal government's powers, Madison continued, "he could not yet tell. But he should shrink from nothing which should be found essential to such a form of Govt. as would provide for the safety, liberty and happiness of the Community. This being the end of all our deliberations, all the necessary means for attaining it must, however reluctantly, be submitted to." With that, Madison recorded, the question was put on giving the new national legislature power to legislate in all cases to which the states were incompetent, with a result of nine ayes, 0 noes, 1 state divided. At that point, to what must have been Madison's great satisfaction, the convention also voted to adopt the proposed veto over state laws without dissent. The day's work ended with Madison's announcement that he now opposed the Virginia Plan's provision that the new government be empowered to use the military against recalcitrant states. His proposal to postpone consideration of that concept was accepted without dissent, as well. At some point in this discussion, according to his notes, Alexander Hamilton broached an idea that Madison would soon explore in his immortal tenth *Federalist* essay: "The way to prevent a majority from having an interest to oppress the minority is to enlarge the sphere." For his part, James Wilson this day stated: "A confederated republic joins the happiest kind of Government with the most certain security to liberty."

On June 1, the convention's first Friday, it took up the Virginia Plan's executive branch proposal. Almost instantly, the delegates began to debate the number of people in whom the executive authority ought to be vested, and that led Madison to observe that they should first define the executive authority. He offered that the national executive ought to have "power to carry into effect. the national laws. to appoint to offices in cases not otherwise provided for, and to execute such other powers 'not legislative nor judiciary in their nature' as may from time to time be delegated by the national Legislature." As Rufus King noted, Madison accepted Wilson's earlier definition of the executive authority as extending to carrying out the legislature's laws and appointing high officers. Madison also came down in favor of a one-man executive and a one-term limit, and he explicitly rejected the idea that the executive authority extended to "Rights of war and peace," as the British king's did. The convention then briefly debated the length of the chief executive's term and the means of his selection before the day's work drew to an end. The delegates having decided to meet on Saturdays, the convention resumed its business on June 2. First, it rejected Wilson's proposal for an electoral college, 2 ayes, 7 noes, 1 state divided. It then agreed to have the national legislature elect the "Executive," 8 ayes, 2 noes.

Delaware's John Dickinson thought the executive should be removable by the national legislature on application of a majority of state legislatures. In presenting this idea, he spoke at length on the advantage Americans drew from the division of their country into numerous states. Some men seemed to want to abolish the states altogether, he noted. For his part, he thought that the apportionment of the national legislature ultimately would "end in mutual concession." His solution was that "each State would retain an equal voice at least in one branch of the National Legislature," with the other perhaps apportioned by the taxes each state paid. Madison noted that he certainly opposed insulating executive officials from anyone's approval. Only Delaware voted for Dickinson's removal proposal, but his position on legislative apportionment had been made clear to all. Alas for Madison, who at this point carefully side-stepped the issue, the Delawarean was not alone.

On the following business day, a Monday, the convention once again spent its time on the Virginia Plan. So, the structure of the executive was discussed, and the convention agreed to the Virginia Plan's proposal for a national judiciary. It added that there should be a supreme court and one or more inferior courts without objection.

Madison's most interesting contribution to this discussion came in answer to the proposal that, like the British king, the chief executive ought to have an absolute veto, not one that could be overridden. Madison averred that this was a bad idea because such a veto would almost never be used. Displaying his characteristic keen understanding of political reality, Madison realized that an executive veto susceptible of override paradoxically would be a more useful power. As to casting a veto that could not be overridden, Rufus King recorded that Madison said he doubted even "the Kng of Eng. wd. have firmness sufficient to do it."

According to King, Madison said that "a Check is necessary experience proves it," and so it must be structured in such a way as to make the idea that it might be used credible. If the judiciary were united with the executive in the veto power, it would "render their Check or negative more respectable." The idea that republics would end up riven into different interest groups, once seen as the calumny of republics' opponents, had now been borne out by experience. "There is diversity of Interest in every Country"—rich and poor, debtors and creditors, "the followers of different Demagogues," adherents of different religious sects. Therefore, "we must introduce the Checks, which will destroy the measures of an interested majority." The executive must be given a veto, then, for two reasons: to enable it to defend itself against the legislative and "for the safety of a minority in Danger of oppression from an unjust and interested majority."

Pierce called this "a very able and ingenious Speech." In his account, Madison set his call for a veto in the context of an analysis of the constitutional problems that befell the ancient republics. Madison then concluded that the way to avoid such difficulties was to marshal all of the wisdom of the various parts of the government, as by having the judges and the executive join in exercising the veto power.

When the question of judicial appointment came up, Madison objected to having judges be selected by the national legislature. No doubt thinking of Virginia's experience with Mason's 1776 constitution, under which the General Assembly appointed the statewide courts' judges, Madison based his objection on the fact that, "besides, the danger of intrigue and partiality, many of the members were not judges of the requisite qualifications. The Legislative talents which were very different from those of a Judge, commonly recommended men to the favor of Legislative Assemblies." Yet, he said, he was uncomfortable with the idea of giving the executive the power to appoint judges, and so tended to favor reposing it in the Senate. In conclusion, he would be happy merely striking out the Virginia Plan's language on this question and holding the matter over until later in the convention.

The convention did precisely that. The first time the convention considered the Randolph-Madison proposal that the new judges have "good behaviour" tenure and fixed salaries, it passed without demurral.[64]

Next, the convention soon came to the proposal for ratification through popular conventions. When Connecticut's Roger Sherman reflected that this idea was unnecessary, as the Articles had provided for amendment and ratification by Congress and the state legislatures, Madison was instantly on his feet.

As his notes put it, he "thought this provision essential." Where ratification was by a state legislature and the same legislature subsequently adopted legislation contrary to the Constitution, state judges could reasonably be expected to decide in favor of the state legislation. After all, the general rule was that subsequent enactments by the same body superceded previous ones.

Madison added that if the Constitution were merely a species of treaty, any party's breach would absolve the others of responsibility for adhering to it. This consideration, too, argued in favor of ratification "by the supreme authority of the people themselves." Pierce Butler of South Carolina held that since the Articles required amendments to be ratified by the state legislatures, the Philadelphia Convention's product would have to be submitted to them.

On June 6, a Wednesday, the convention considered Charles Pinckney's proposal that the state legislatures select the members of the House. He explained that there were two reasons this was a good idea: the legislators were better informed than the people, and the states would be more likely to ratify the Constitution if they were to have this power. James Wilson, who would stand consistently for a national democracy throughout the proceedings, replied that the people should have control over the legislature, and that bad selections were to be expected when districts were small. Connecticut's Roger Sherman thought that if the state governments were still to exist, they should select the members of the national legislature; that was the only way to maintain harmony between the two levels of government.

Madison's fellow Old Dominion delegate, George Mason, based his defense of popular elections upon the shift in the government's operation contemplated by the Virginia Plan. Under the Confederation, he said, the states had been represented in Congress. That made sense, because the Congress had acted upon the states, not upon the individual people directly. In light of the fact that the new government would act upon the people directly, "they ought therefore to choose the Representatives." Mason conceded that republican elections were imperfect. Yet, he said, "no Govt. was free from imperfections & evils." Republican government was to be favored anyway, given "the advantage of this Form in favor of the rights of the people, in favor of human nature." Besides, there was a potential remedy to many of the electoral problems of the preceding decades: having the states carve out larger districts. Madison's argument had won another convert.

Madison hastened to endorse Mason's effort. While the majority of speeches in the Convention to this point appear as perfunctory efforts in the published record, Madison's June 6 address on the issue of elections takes two full pages.[65] Here, Madison deployed his enormous learning in the history of ancient and modern confederacies, foreshadowing his famous argument in *Federalist No. 10.*

He began by accepting Sherman's list of "objects of the Union"—"defence against foreign danger," prevention of interstate armed conflict, treaties with other countries, and regulation and taxation of foreign commerce—but he hastened to add other "principal ones." For Madison, it was extremely important that the Union could help secure private rights and ensure "the steady dispensation of Justice." Concerns in those two areas, he continued, "had more perhaps than any thing else, produced this convention."

Connecticut's Sherman had conceded that interference with private rights and with the regular dispensation of justice had been more common in small states than in large, but Madison noted that these two types of problems had appeared in large states as well. His solution was "to enlarge the sphere as far as the nature of the Govt. would admit." Far from optional, "this was the only defense agst. the inconveniences of democracy consistent with the democratic form of Govt."

"All civilized Societies," Madison lectured his fellow delegates, "would be divided into different Sects, Factions, & interests," and he listed "rich & poor, debtors & creditors, the landed the manufacturing, the commercial interests, the inhabitants of this district, or that district, the followers of this political leader or that political leader, the disciples of this religious sect or that religious sect." This natural development posed a serious problem, because "in all cases where a majority are united by a common interest or passion, the rights of the minority are in danger."

Maxims of morality, pangs of conscience, and concern for reputation were ineffective checks, Madison said. "Religion itself may become a motive to persecution & oppression." He noted that the history of Greece and the story of Rome bore out what he had said. Americans had made the revolution because, seeing that Britain's interests were not the same as the colonists', they realized that they as colonists likely eventually would be subjected to oppression by Parliament.

Even the most foolish distinctions could cause factions to coalesce: "We have seen the mere distinction of colour made in the most enlightened period of time, a ground of the most oppressive dominion ever exercised by man over man." In the era of America's independence, "the real or supposed interest of the major number" had caused whites to oppress each other where they could, too: "Debtors have defrauded their creditors. The landed interest has borne hard on the mercantile interest. The Holders of one species of property have thrown a disproportion of taxes on the holders of another species."

To Madison, all of this proved that, "where a majority are united by a common sentiment and have an opportunity, the rights of the minor party become insecure." Worse: "In a Republican Govt. the Majority if united have always an opportunity."

Now, finally, after all the labor of research and politicking that had gone into his preparation and into bringing the Philadelphia Convention into being, Madison revealed his grand insight. "The only remedy," he warned, "is to enlarge the sphere, & thereby divide the community into so great a number of interests & parties, that in the 1st. place a majority will not be likely at the same moment to have a common interest separate from that of the whole or of the minority; and in the 2d. place, that in case they shd. have such an interest, they may not be apt to unite in the pursuit of it." The convention, then, must compose a new structure "on such a scale & in such a form as will controul all the evils wch. have been experienced."

At least, that is how Madison's notes described his speech. Robert Yates, on the other hand, said, "Mr. Madison is of opinion, that when we agreed to the first resolve of having a national government, consisting of a supreme executive, judicial and legislative power, it was then intended to operate to the exclusion of a federal government, and the more extensive we made the basis, the greater probability of duration, happiness, and good order." Alexander Hamilton objected to Madison's speech by noting that some of the greatest demagogues were patricians (he likely had the Gracchi in mind) and that while the legislators might be drawn from half the globe, they would "meet in one room"—and thus have all the tendencies to which republican assemblies were prey.

Madison also made clear on that day, June 6, why he favored having the judiciary join the executive in exercising the veto power. In a republic, he said, there would seldom be an executive so meritorious that the people would acquiesce in his serving in that office; instead, he "would be envied & assailed by disappointed competitors." Even a British monarch might not dare to veto the act of both houses of Parliament, he said;[66] having the judges join him in it would make the veto power more efficacious because more likely to be used. Unlike a monarch, a republican executive also would lack the great wealth and permanence that would put him beyond corruption. Having the judiciary join him in vetoing thus would be a necessary security against him. Besides, giving the judges a role in vetoing would allow them, in common with the executive, to use the veto in self-defense against the legislature.

After making this apt point of political science, Madison next offered up a very poor prognostication. Some people, according to Madison, opposed having judges empowered to join in exercise of the veto power (as they were in New York under that state's 1777 constitution) because they later would be called upon to construe statutes the veto power had given them a role in enacting. Not to worry, Madison held: a judge would very seldom encounter a statute "so ambiguous as to leave room for his prepossessions." Clearly, Madison anticipated a far more restrained judicial ethic than the judiciary has come to display.

Most of the other delegates who spoke on the matter said that the branches ought to remain separate to maintain executive responsibility. Madison's proposal to have the judges and executive veto jointly was defeated, 3 ayes to 8 noes.

In the wake of the day's debates, Madison sat down to report on the convention's first days to his absent friend, Thomas Jefferson.[67] Doubtless certain that Jefferson was dying to know what the delegates were up to, Madison had to disappoint him. He told him who was in each state's delegation, then explained that all had vowed to keep the proceedings private. Madison felt free only to say that the first volume of what would be John Adams's three-volume *A Defence of the Constitutions of Government of the United States of America* had appeared in the United States, and that its influence could not be good. "It will probably be much read," Madison guessed, "particularly in the Eastern States [by which he meant New England], and contribute with other circumstances to revive the predilections of this Country for the British Constitution. Men of learning find nothing new in it. Men of taste many things to criticize. And men without either not a few things, which they will not understand. It will nevertheless be read, and praised, and become a powerful engine in forming the public opinion." Adams's fame, the power of his intellect, and the poor performance of America's governments together made it likely that "the remarks in it, which are unfriendly to republicanism, [would] receive fresh weight."[68]

Besides that, Madison said that he had heard Patrick Henry was to push a new paper money law through the General Assembly. Henry also seemed apt to defeat court reform in the Old Dominion yet again. Finally, Madison wrote mostly in code, he had heard rumors from Virginia that Henry was "hostile to the object of the convention" and wished "either a partition or total dissolution of the confederacy." What Jefferson must have thought of that last idea, we can only guess. Madison would continue to make such assertions through the ratification process, without any direct evidence to support them.

In another foreshadowing of events to come, Madison confided in a different correspondent that same day that he took great pleasure in learning of

Lafayette's prominent role in the French reform movement then aborning.[69] "I sincerely wish his influence may be as great as it deserves to be," he noted.

On June 7, the convention took up a motion by Delaware's John Dickinson to have the senators be elected by the state legislatures. As Dickinson explained it, his proposal would mean that members of the two houses of the proposed legislature would draw their powers from different sources, and that would make them—like the British House of Lords and House of Commons—checks upon each other. If the senators were made numerous, they could check the lower house, because they would then tend to draw the wealthy and well-born into their ranks, which would (as Rufus King reported Dickinson saying) "check the Democracy."[70]

Madison opposed this idea vociferously. First, he said, it would mean either giving up proportional representation or having a very large number of members in that house. To give up proportional representation, Madison said, was "inadmissible, being evidently unjust." To have a large number of senators, on the other hand, would mean to surrender the qualities the Senate was meant to embody: "coolness," "system," and "wisdom," all of which the Senate should possess to balance the lower house. "Enlarge their number," Madison said, "and you communicate to them the vices which they are meant to correct." Dickinson had hazarded that a more numerous Senate would be weightier, and had called for 160 members, but Madison argued that "their weight would be in inverse ratio to their number." He argued that the history of the Roman republic proved his point, because the tribunes' power had diminished as, waxing in number, the tribunes saw their ability to act as a body wane.

Once again, it was for Dickinson to respond. He took a position diametrically opposed to Madison's—indeed, to many of Madison's fondest hopes. "The preservation of the States in a certain degree of agency," he thundered, "is indispensible." As Madison recounted Dickinson's speech, "He compared the proposed National System to the Solar System, in which the States were the planets, and ought to be left to move freely in their proper orbits." In addition, Dickinson disputed Madison's account of Roman history, among other ways by noting that the tribunes had not lost their influence as a result of the increase of their numbers, and that Madison's reasoning seemed to lead to the conclusion that the Senate ought to have fewer than ten members—the greatest number of tribunes in the Roman republic.

Madison answered that the chief problem in the federal system had been that the state legislatures tended to pass paper money laws and other pestiferous measures whenever the people wanted them. He was hard-pressed to understand how maintaining the legislatures' role in selecting members of Congress could remedy the problem. Unfortunately for him, however, his Virginian colleague, George Mason, closed the day's discussion by noting that the convention had been concerned to give the institutions of the proposed federal system the means of self-defense, and that the state legislatures should be no exception. He conceded that the state legislatures had occasionally misbehaved, but he added that the only reason one could not make similar observations about the planned government was that it did not yet exist. Surely the states needed to be able to protect themselves against the likelihood that the federal legislature would swallow them up. The vote in favor of Dickinson's proposal at this early point, June 7, was unanimous.

On the following day, June 8, the convention took up another of Madison's pet proposals. He and South Carolina's Charles Pinckney moved that the plank of the Virginia Plan saying that the new legislature should be empowered to veto state laws that violated the new constitution or treaties entered into by the Union be struck out. They further proposed that Congress instead be empowered "to negative all laws which to them shall appear improper." This would be an even greater power over state governments. Madison explained that the state governments had tended "to encroach on the federal authority" and "to violate national Treaties," which would be covered by the narrower power, but also "to infringe the rights & interests of each other" and "to oppress the weaker party within their respective jurisdictions." The broader power was necessary to let Congress prevent states from doing these things. The only alternative to a veto over all state laws, Madison said, was the use of force.

That, however, was a theory that could never be effectively put into practice. For Madison, "this prerogative of the General Govt. is the great pervading principle that must controul the centrifugal tendency of the States; which, without it, will continually fly out of their proper orbits and destroy the order & harmony of the political system." A Delaware delegate thought that the large states, insistent as they were on proportional representation, could use this veto power to dominate even the internal police of the small states; a North Carolinian, perhaps mindful of the future of slavery, objected to any measure that did not leave it to the states to control their own "internal policy" (as King's notes put it).

According to his own notes, Madison insisted that the central government must have a check over the parts. He asked rhetorically what danger there was that the new government would oppress the states. Although Dickinson, surprisingly, sided with Madison, on the ground that it was impossible to draw a line between cases over which the central government should have a veto and those over which it should not, the proposal to change the Virginia Plan's language concerning a central government veto over state laws failed. The delegations' vote was 3 ayes, 7 noes, and 1 state divided.

The next day, Saturday, June 9, was a pivotal day in the convention. On that day, New Jersey's David Brearly introduced the question of the rule of apportionment. He averred that if population were the measure, Virginia would have sixteen representatives to Georgia's one, and that Massachusetts, Pennsylvania, and the Old Dominion together would dominate the legislature. Population apportionment, he said, "carried fairness on the face of it," but "deeper examination" showed it to be "unfair and unjust."

William Paterson, Brearly's Jersey colleague, next took the floor. He drew attention back to the question that had agitated the convention at the first: what type of changes it was authorized to make. Paterson reminded his fellows that Congress had authorized the convention, and that Congress's charge to the delegates had been repeated in many states' commissions. Those commissions, he said, all charged their holders to seek "amendment of the confederacy."

Madison had Paterson reminding the convention that "the Commissions under which we acted were not only the measure of our power, they denoted also the sentiments of the States on the subject of our deliberation. The idea of a national Govt. as contradistinguished from a federal one, never entered into the mind of any of them, and to the public mind we must accommodate ourselves." The states, he concluded, must be treated as equals.

Some people objected, Paterson continued, that if the government was to operate directly on the people, the legislators must be selected by the people directly. He saw no reason why that was so. Furthermore, he said, New Jersey would never agree to a plan that provided for population apportionment, because under such a plan, "she [New Jersey] would be swallowed up." He would work against it in Philadelphia, and failing there, he would work against its ratification by New Jersey.

Two delegates responded to the proposal for population apportionment by saying this idea would only be appropriate if the states were redrawn to make them of equal size. One made this argument positively, and the other made it in opposition to the idea of population apportionment. It went nowhere.

On the following Monday, June 11, Connecticut's Roger Sherman for the first time put forward the so-called Connecticut Compromise. His solution to the problem of the large states' demanding the Virginia Plan's population apportionment of Congress while Dickinson of Delaware, Paterson of New Jersey, and other small-state delegates insisted on state equality was simple: each group should have its way in regard to one of the new legislature's two houses. Sherman said that the lower house ought to be apportioned by population and the states should have equal votes in the upper. He justified this proposal by saying that the states had to have some means of self-defense; otherwise, the three large states (Virginia, Pennsylvania, and Massachusetts) would lord it over the rest.

The convention agreed to have the lower house be apportioned in some way other than state equality: 7 ayes, 3 noes, 1, state Divided. The convention then rejected Sherman's motion to allow each state one vote in the Senate: 5 ayes, 6 noes. By the same margin of 6 to 5, the convention then adopted a large-state motion (sponsored by Pennsylvania's Wilson and New York's Hamilton) to apportion the upper house the same way as the lower. When the conversation turned toward the question what that rule should be, some delegates argued for taxation as the standard of representation. In light of later developments, it may be surprising that James Wilson of Pennsylvania, not a southern delegate, proposed that each state's representation ought to be based on its free inhabitants plus three-fifths of its other inhabitants.

Gerry of Massachusetts objected that slaves were property. If property was to be represented, he asked, why should slave property be favored over horses and cattle? At that point, Madison, perhaps seeing that this question could distract and divide the convention for a long time, interjected that the particulars should be left to a subcommittee.

The same day, the convention also agreed unanimously (on Madison's motion) to the Virginia Plan's proposals that the central government guarantee a republican form of government to each state, that the new Constitution be amendable, and that state officials be required to swear to uphold the new Constitution. (Of particular note are George Mason's arguments that the Constitution must be amendable, because it would doubtless prove flawed, and that there must be a way to amend without Congress's having a role, since congressional abuse of power might be the problem in need of remedy.)

On the following day, June 12, 1787, when the convention took up the issue of the length of congressmen's terms, Madison seconded a proposal that it be three years. He reasoned that such lengthy terms would counteract the "instability" that had been "one of the great vices of our republics," as well as providing congressmen adequate time to gain the knowledge of other states' affairs that would be essential to performance of their duties. (Yates's notes show that Madison also said three-year terms would attract the best men to seek election to Congress, while two-year ones likely would not.) Gerry held that New Englanders would never give up annual elections, but Madison denied that anyone in the convention could really know what the people thought at the moment, what they would think if they knew what the delegates knew, or what they would think six or twelve months later.

Therefore, Madison said, the convention could "consider what was right & necessary in itself for the attainment of a proper Governmt." Both the delegates' prestige and the support of the states' other leading citizens would help win popular acceptance. If the convention did not do what it ought to do, men of station would oppose the convention's product, while "little support in opposition to them can be gained to it from the unreflecting multitude."

Here, as elsewhere in his candid statements in the convention, Madison expressed his skeptical attitude toward the common citizenry. He believed that they must be in ultimate control of the government, but he also thought them wise to defer to their betters—which he was confident they would do. In his conception of politics, Madison reflected the Virginia political culture.

So, similarly, Madison on June 12 favored a proposal to give senators seven-year terms. Connecticut's Roger Sherman spoke first to the question, objecting that the people needed "an earlier opportunity . . . for getting rid of them" in case "they acted amiss." Madison's ally, Edmund Randolph, replied that "the object of this 2d. branch is to controul the democratic branch of the Natl. Legislature," and that the Senate needed firmness to avoid being overwhelmed by the more popular lower house.

Madison then added, "His fear was that the popular branch would still be too great an overmatch for it." In his account, state senates with four-year terms had in no case been able to resist the other branches. The convention had to create "a stable & *firm* Govt." [italics Madison's] or the people were apt soon to abandon the republican experiment "in universal disgust" in favor of some other type of government more conducive to their welfare.

On June 13, Governor Randolph, clearly with the experience of the Confederation government in endeavoring to comply with the Treaty of Paris in mind, noted that the prime reasons for creating a new judiciary would be "to establish . . . the security of foreigners where treaties are in their favor, and to preserve the harmony of states and that of the citizens thereof." Madison and Randolph proposed that the jurisdiction of the "national Judiciary" ought to extend to all "questions which involve the national peace and harmony." Madison conceived of members of the "supreme tribunal" as "expositor[s] of the laws," and he proposed that the Senate, rather than the legislature generally, select them. That way, he said, true qualifications for the post would be favored over mere electioneering. As he soon commented in another connection, Madison thought that the senators would be generally more capable than members of the lower house, and so he envisioned entrusting them with the most serious responsibilities under the new government.

With that, the convention had completed its work of considering each provision of the Virginia Plan and either altering or accepting it. The following day, June 14, the delegates heard Paterson say that (in Madison's words) "several deputations, particularly that of N. Jersey," hoped to offer an alternative, federal plan for the convention's consideration. With that, the convention adjourned for the day.

Friday, June 15, saw Paterson present his famed New Jersey Plan, the small-state delegates' alternative to the Virginia Plan, as amended. The New

Jersey Plan represented the work of the delegations of Connecticut, New York, New Jersey, and Delaware, perhaps with the aid of Maryland's Luther Martin.[71] Their concerns were of two varieties: (1) Connecticut and New York wanted to give Congress a few new powers, not replace it with an entirely new government; and (2) New Jersey and Delaware opposed elimination of state equality in Congress.

Madison noted that Delaware's John Dickinson, with whom he had repeatedly crossed swords on related issues, at this point explained the position of the New Jersey Plan proponents to him this way:

> You see the consequence of pushing things too far. Some of the members from the small States wish for two branches in the General Legislature, and are friends to a good National Government; but we would sooner submit to a foreign power, than submit to be deprived of an equality of suffrage, in both branches of the legislature, and thereby be thrown under the domination of the large States.

Whatever may have been the roles of other delegates, then, Dickinson saw Madison as the mastermind of the big-state campaign to secure population apportionment of both houses of Congress. To his mind, Madison's persistence in it despite repeated warnings over several weeks that the smaller states would not acquiesce was imprudent and dangerous. It threatened to wreck the convention, and ultimately the Revolution itself.

Dickinson wanted Madison prudently to compromise for the common good. Madison had said repeatedly that political principle ruled out any arrangement of Congress other than population apportionment. From Delaware, New Jersey, or Connecticut, however, that seemed to be pure posturing: Madison's own home state would have the very largest delegation in each house of Congress if he got his way.

The New Jersey Plan had several elements, each in radical contrast to the Virginia Plan. First, it said that the Articles of Confederation should be perfected. Second, it said Congress ought to be empowered to levy a tariff, a stamp tax, and revenue through the postal service, as well as to regulate interstate and foreign trade. Third, it said that the United States ought to have appellate courts to hear federal suits originating in state courts. Fourth, it said tax requisitions ought to be apportioned among the states according to the whole free population plus three-fifths of slaves, and that Congress should be empowered to enforce requisitions on states that did not pay their quotas voluntarily.

The executive section of the New Jersey Plan was mainly in line with what the convention had done with the Virginia Plan to this point, with these exceptions: it envisioned a plural executive; it would have empowered Congress, on appeal by a majority of governors, to remove the executive; and it would have banned the executive from personally leading the American army.

The New Jersey Plan also called for a supremacy clause, for a power in the federal government to enforce laws and treaties of the United States against the states, and for a federal power to admit new states. Its real meaning lay in Dickinson's upbraiding of Madison. There the Delawarean, actively and prominently engaged in the 1760s disputation with Great Britain even as Madison entered his teenaged years, made clear precisely what the small states insisted upon: a federal form of government, one in which the new legislature had limited legislative power. Most importantly, that power must be wielded by a legislature in which the states' equality was preserved. The small states, in other words, must be reassured that they would not be swallowed up by the large ones.

According to Yates's notes, his New York colleague John Lansing summarized the differences between the two plans by saying that the New Jersey Plan called for a federal government, while the Virginia Plan called for a national government. Thereupon, the convention adjourned so that the delegates could peruse and consider the New Jersey Plan.

The next day's debates began with Lansing again holding the floor. "Was it probable," he asked, "that the States would adopt & ratify a scheme, which they had never authorized us to propose? and which so far exceeded what they regarded as sufficient?" The convention, he insisted, had no power to discuss such proposals as the Virginia Plan. The power the states had given them was only to consider amendments to the confederacy. "He was sure," Madison recorded him as saying, "that this was the case with his state. N. York would never have concurred in sending deputies to the convention, if she had supposed the deliberations were to turn on a consolidation of the

States, and a National Government." Besides that, Lansing continued, "the States will never feel a sufficient confidence in a general Government to give it a negative on their laws."

Madison's Pennsylvanian ally Wilson then summarized the choice facing the delegates. In the Virginia Plan, he said, were three branches of legislature (because the executive's veto power gave that branch a role), while the New Jersey Plan looked only to one. The Virginia Plan, Wilson said, looked to representation of the people, while the New Jersey Plan rested on the state legislatures. The Virginia Plan would have apportioned the legislature by population, while the New Jersey Plan featured state equality. The Virginia Plan would have a single chief executive, while the New Jersey Plan's would be plural. The Virginia Plan envisioned a government controlled by a majority, while the New Jersey Plan's might be dominated by a minority of the people. The Virginia Plan would give a national legislature power over "all cases to which the separate States are incompetent," while the New Jersey Plan would give Congress certain additional powers. The Virginia Plan would give the national government a veto over state laws, while the New Jersey Plan relied on coercion. The Virginia Plan would empower the legislature to impeach and remove the chief executive, while the New Jersey Plan would let the governors initiate the process. The Virginia Plan provided a veto power, while the New Jersey Plan did not. The Virginia Plan called for "inferior national tribunals," while the New Jersey Plan did not. The Virginia Plan would grant national tribunals some original jurisdiction, while under the New Jersey Plan it would be only appellate. The Virginia Plan would give the national courts jurisdiction over "all cases affecting the Natl. peace & harmony," while the New Jersey Plan looked to a few types of cases only. Finally, the Virginia Plan looked to popular ratification, while the New Jersey Plan retained the Articles' model of ratification by state legislatures.

Wilson said that when it came to what the convention had been empowered to do, he thought that it could "propose any thing" but "conclude nothing." In other words, it could merely recommend, and its recommendations would not be binding.

South Carolina's ever-incisive Charles Pinckney made two points that would help shape the convention's outcome. First, he said that Carolina would support the Virginia Plan if it could retain equal representation at the same time. Second, he said that he thought the Confederation should be retained if it proved possible to do so while making provision for the necessary changes, but that the convention should propose an altogether new government if that proved necessary.

Governor Randolph added, "When the salvation of the Republic was at stake, it would be treason to our trust, not to propose what we found necessary." For his part, then, "He wd. <not> as far as depended on him leave any thing that seemed necessary, undone. The present moment is favorable," he concluded, "and probably the last that will offer." The real issue, according to Randolph, was whether a federal or a national government was needed. Experience showed him that the federal model would not do. That had been proven by "the trial already made." Thus, the convention must decide whether "real legislation" was the best way to adopt national policy, or coercion was.

The New Jersey Plan would have put the sword in the hand of Congress and threatened the states with violence in case they did not meet their federal obligations. This was, Randolph insisted, "impracticable, expensive, cruel to individuals." It was also unwise, because of its tendency "to habituate the instruments of it to shed the blood & riot in the spoils of their fellow Citizens." This kind of habituation "trained them up for the service of Ambition." That way lay despotism and civil war.

The Virginia Plan provided the solution, Madison's magnetic young friend continued. It was "a national *Legislation over individuals,* for which Congs. are unfit." After all, Congress was a diplomatic body, a meeting place of ambassadors, as John Adams described it, and to give it these powers would be to unite the legislative and the executive functions in the same hands. Besides that, his experience showed him that popular confidence in the Confederation Congress was generally low (which was a view directly opposite the one Hamilton's notes showed Paterson expressing in his speech that day).[72] Therefore, according to Randolph, what was needed was a properly constituted new government. The delegates must seize this opportunity to create one, because it was "the last opportunity for establishing one. After this select experiment, the people will yield to despair." With that, the convention adjourned for the day.

Monday, June 18, 1787, turned out to be one of the most significant days of the convention. Oddly, its significance had less to do with the outcome of the convention's work than with its effect on the course of American political history. While Madison was chiefly a witness to the day's events, the impression they made on him had huge repercussions.

Alexander Hamilton, who with Madison and George Washington had been instrumental in convening twelve states' delegates in Philadelphia that summer, had made slight mark on the conclave's proceedings in their first month. One might have expected far more, and surely thoughtful delegates familiar with the New Yorker must have wondered why he had not taken a leading role. All was about to be made clear.

Commanding the floor for nearly the entire day, Hamilton unburdened himself of suicidally candid ruminations on political science. First, he said that he considered both the Virginia Plan and the New Jersey alternative inadequate. The latter displeased him more, because retention of state sovereignty would mean adoption of an inadequate central government.

Previous speakers had erred, Hamilton said, in distinguishing as they had between national and federal government. There were federal governments that operated on individuals as well as on the constituent states, as for example the German Diet did, and as the Confederation did when it came to piracy. The New Jersey Plan, too, would operate on individuals.

Then he made a statement that would prove to be characteristic of Hamiltonian constitutionalism ever after.[73] Even if federal governments could not operate on individuals, he said, he agreed with Edmund Randolph that the convention must propose what it thought necessary. To fail to do so because of so slight a matter as the insufficiency of the delegates' powers "would be to sacrifice the means to the end."[74]

An adequate government must attend to "the great & essential principles necessary for the support of Government." Those were "an active & constant interest in supporting it," "the love of power," "an habitual attachment of the People," "coercion," and "influence." (By this last, he said, he meant "honors & emoluments.") All of these principles now weighed on the side of the states in any conflict with the central government. Therefore, any federal government would be precarious.

The only way to avoid having the states resist central authority, then, was to give the center enough power to reverse the relationship between states and center in regard to all of his "essential principles." The New Jersey Plan would not do that, but would allow the old equation to continue. As an example, Hamilton offered that requisitions from the new legislature would only be met by the states when and to the extent that they considered the legislature's policy correct, and that the refusal of one state to pay would induce others to refuse too. In short, the current problem would endure.

According to Yates's account, Hamilton here even said that it was a bad idea to enumerate rulers' powers. Enumerated powers, Hamilton said, would always prove inadequate.[75] Besides that, he said, "gentlemen of fortune and abilities" would never deign to participate in Congress, because its sessions would be long and their pay as members would be slight. "I despair," he cried, "that a republican form of government can remove the difficulties."

Hamilton also held that political science was against vesting the necessary powers in a body like Congress. "Two Sovereignties," he said, "can not co-exist within the same limits." The New Jersey Plan was therefore inadequate. Ideally, one might simply eliminate the state governments and save the associated expense. Only popular resistance argued against it. (He would make clear the next day that the state governments should be retained for the central government's administrative convenience.[76])

Warming to his subject, and never one to tire of hearing his own voice, Hamilton hazarded that, "in his private opinion, he had no scruple in declaring, supported as he was by so many of the wise & good, that the British Govt. was the best in the world: and that he doubted much whether any thing short of it would do in America." He hoped his colleagues would recollect that formerly educated opinion had held the Congress to be adequate. Now, "the members most tenacious of republicanism . . . were as loud as any in declaiming agst. the vices of democracy." This trend in elite sentiment, Hamilton hopefully declaimed, "led him to anticipate the time, when others as well as himself would join in the praise bestowed by Mr. Neckar on the British Constitution, namely, that it is the only Govt. in the world 'which unites public strength with individual security.'"

Every society will have its many and its few. Each group must have constitutional means of protecting itself as a group. The absence of such a balance accounted for America's stay laws, paper money laws, and other such problems. The British, on the other hand, had resolved the difficulty: "Their house of Lords is a most noble institution." The lords' wealth and station gave them incentive to oppose "every pernicious innovation" by Crown or Commons. "No temporary Senate will have firmness en'o' to answer the purpose." No good executive could be created consistently with republican principles, either, "it seemed to be admitted."

Besides, Yates had Hamilton add, the old adage that "the voice of the people [is] the voice of God" was mistaken. So far as Hamilton was concerned, "the people are turbulent and changing. They seldom judge or determine right. Give therefore to the first class a distinct, permanent share in the government. They will check the unsteadiness of the second, and as they cannot receive any advantage by a change, they therefore will ever maintain good government." They ought to have life terms, too, so that they could counteract the democratic element of the legislature.[77]

Yet a good government must have a good executive. "The English model was the only good one." England's hereditary king could not be bribed by foreigners or persuaded to descend to domestic partisanship.

With that as peroration, Hamilton reached his breathtaking conclusion: "Let one branch of the Legislature hold their places for life or at least during good-behaviour. Let the Executive also be for life." So long as the people chose the senators, either directly or indirectly, the system would be republican. If the chief executive served only a seven-year term, he would have every reason to keep the country embroiled in foreign wars, because crises would be conducive to his reelection; that is why his term must be for life.

Hamilton conceded that his sketch of government "went beyond the ideas of most members," but he doubted that the people would adopt the Virginia Plan either. As he understood things, Hamilton said, the Union was "dissolving or already dissolved." People were beginning to cast off their "prejudices," and in time they would realize that even the Virginia Plan did not take matters far enough. Then, according to Madison's notes, Hamilton expected that they would "be ready to go at least as far as he proposes."

Hamilton said he intended merely to describe the ends for which he would work through the balance of the convention, not to propose his plan for discussion in itself. "I confess," he said, "that this plan and that from

Virginia are very remote from the idea of the people. Perhaps the Jersey plan is nearest their expectation. But the people are gradually ripening in their opinions of government—they begin to be tired of an excess of democracy—and what even is the Virginia plan, but *pork still, with a little change of the sauce.*"[78] According to Gouverneur Morris, Hamilton's six-hour performance was "the most able and impressive he had ever heard."[79] (Then again, himself from an aristocratic family, Morris was predisposed to accept Hamilton's argument.)

Hamilton at this point sank back into the quiet observer's role he had played up to that momentous June day. In fact, he left the convention for several weeks soon after spelling out the details of the elective monarchy he preferred. The convention, for its part, rejected a motion from John Dickinson to stick to the program of proposing amendments to the Articles of Confederation (4 ayes, 6 noes, 1 state divided), rejected the first of Paterson's New Jersey Plan proposals (9 ayes, 2 noes), and returned to discussion of Randolph's (that is, Virginia's) resolutions.

Madison would not forget what Hamilton had said.

The next day, June 19, Madison kicked off the day's proceedings. According to Rufus King's account of Madison's speech, Madison began by denying that a confederation that had been unanimously adopted could only be broken up by the consent of all the parties.[80] Rather, Madison went on, "A contract entered into by men or societies may be dissolved by the breach of a single Article." This was the rule in regard to treaties, Madison lectured, and he added that "sometimes however provision is made that the Breach of a single Article shall not dissolve the Constitution or Treaty." The implication here obviously was that a party could withdraw from a "Constitution or Treaty" upon the breach of one article, if it desired to do so, unless "provision [were] made."

In the main, Madison held forth on the shortcomings of the New Jersey Plan. He insisted that it would not meet any of the goals he had laid out for constitutional reform. In addition, he said, the small states stood to suffer greatly if Paterson's plan were adopted. After all, Paterson envisioned having Congress coerce the states into complying with requisitions, and only the small states could actually be compelled. "The larger States will be impregnable, the smaller only can feel the vengeance of it."

Ignoring John Dickinson's private admonition that he cease insisting on pure population apportionment, Madison warned the small states that their firm devotion to state equality in Congress ("pertinacious adherence to an inadmissible plan") might prevent the convention from agreeing to any plan. That could lead to a breakup of the Union. If the Union dissolved, he said, either the states would be independent or there would be regional confederacies. In either case, he guessed, the small states could not expect their large neighbors to treat them as well as the Virginia Plan would.

Apportionment, Madison continued, was the main issue. Yet he still did not see any chance of compromise. Despite Dickinson's private warning that Madison risked driving the convention apart, the Virginian persisted in his blustery threats. Madison noted that some small-state delegates admitted that it would be unjust to leave Virginia with the same number of votes in Congress as states that were substantially smaller. One obvious solution, to redraw state boundaries so that they would be equally large, was impossible due to the dissimilarities among the states' "rules of property, as well as in the manners, habits and prejudices of the different States." Besides, he wondered, why would not a voluntary federation be just as easy to enter into as redrawing state boundaries?

The New Jersey Plan struck Madison as objectionable on still another practical ground as well. Soon the western territories would be divided into numerous lightly populated states. If population were the basis of apportionment, this would present no great difficulty; if each state had an equal vote, on the other hand, Congress would perhaps be controlled by a very small minority.

As Yates told it, Dickinson here intervened. The Delaware delegate thought that good elements of both plans might be adopted. Despite him, at this point, the convention voted to put aside the New Jersey Plan: 7 ayes, 3 noes, 1 state divided. As before, New York—insistent upon federal, not national, reform—went with the small-state minority.

When Madison finished, his more temperate nationalist colleagues hastened to repair any damage his repeated threats to the smaller states might have caused. For his part, Luther Martin of little Maryland insisted that the states had been in a state of nature in relation to each other at the time of independence, and that any alteration of that situation flowed from the Confederation. In both the Confederation and the convention, he held, the small and the large states had been on an equal footing. He would never agree to alter that situation so that the other states lay at the mercy of Virginia, Massachusetts, and Pennsylvania.

James Wilson, for his part, thought that the United States had only become independent as united states. Hamilton hurried to agree with Wilson. Hamilton added that a coalition among the three giant states was unlikely because they were not contiguous and their interests were markedly different. Whether Madison and his friends were playing good cop, bad cop or their personalities led them to address the small-state delegates in different ways, Martin and his fellow small-state representatives did not budge.

That same day, in New York, North Carolina's congressman, William Blount, wrote home to John Blount.[81] William was a delegate to the Philadelphia Convention in New York on congressional business, and his evaluation of the proceedings in the City of Brotherly Love thus far was that "Virginia . . . seemed to take the lead Madison at their Head tho Randolph and Mason are also great." Despite the delegates' best efforts, Blount believed that "we shall ultimately not many Years just be separate and distinct Governments perfectly independent of each other." Madison must occasionally have had the same fear.

On June 20, the convention decided to strike the word "national" from the Virginia Plan's first resolution, so that it said "that the Government of the United States ought to consist of a supreme legislative, Executive and Judiciary." No one objected. Next, it agreed to drop the same word from the Virginia Plan's second resolution, so that what remained was a resolution "that the Legislature ought to consist of two branches."

At that point, John Lansing of New York weighed in.[82] Delegated by the Empire State's skeptical antinationalist majority, along with Yates, to overbalance Hamilton within the delegation, Lansing had watched the convention's progress with growing discomfiture. Now, he gave vent to all of it. "I am not authorized," he reminded his colleagues, "to accede to a system which will annihilate the state governments, and the Virginia plan is declarative of such extinction." He said that the real issue was whether the convention would retain "the foundation of the present Confederacy," and he offered as an alternative to Virginian bicameralism a resolution that "the powers of Legislation be vested in the U. States in Congress."

Bicameralism was barred by two considerations, Lansing opined: the limits on the delegates' powers, and "the state of the public mind." James Wilson of Pennsylvania, Lansing noted, had said that since the convention was merely to propose, it might propose whatever its members wished. Lansing begged to disagree. The convention, he said, was composed of very eminent members, and so its recommendation would have great weight. In case it were rejected, that rejection would cause "great dissensions" (Madison recorded Lansing saying), even "dissolve the union" (in Lansing's own version). The failure of attempts to empower the Confederation Congress to levy an impost, he reasoned, made clear that no such reform as was presently under discussion could win the public's approval.

Besides that, Lansing said, some aspects of the proposed plan were simply undesirable. For example, the federal veto on state laws could not readily be exercised, for Congress would not have time to review all of the laws the state legislatures adopted. He also thought it absurd that Georgians should be called upon to weigh the expediency of laws adopted by the legislature of New Hampshire. In addition, he admonished, the proposal was simply too complex. Due to its novelty and complexity, no one could really say how it would work, either in regard to the central government or in regard to the state governments. One level of government, he was certain, "must absorb the whole."

George Mason answered Lansing crushingly. Americans, the senior Virginian delegate deduced, would never surrender adequate governmental power to a body such as the Confederation Congress, whose delegates were not directly elected. They had been unwilling to grant it additional powers in the past, and they would remain so. "Will they trust such a body, with the regulation of their trade, with the regulation of their taxes; with all the other great powers, which are in contemplation?" Congress was the only unicameral legislature not elected by the people in America, which Mason said explained the people's suspicion of it. Further, use of the military against the states for the purpose of tax collection would never work, but would only breed rebellion.

Despite his desire for a stronger central government, Mason closed by saying that he wanted the states to endure. "He was aware of the difficulty of drawing the line between [state and national authority]," Madison recorded Mason saying, "but hoped it was not insurmountable. The Convention, tho' comprising so many distinguished characters, could not be expected to make a faultless Govt. And he would prefer trusting to posterity the amendment of its defects, rather than push the experiment too far."

In conclusion of the day's discussion, Connecticut's Roger Sherman and Pennsylvania's James Wilson laid out the basic premises of the small and the large states once again. Sherman, for the smaller, said that the Confederation had been adequate to see the states through the revolution to a successful outcome. Yes, the government now needed power to service the war debt, but all that required was to give Congress more power.

Pennsylvania's Wilson denied that it was so. "Confederations," he said, "are usually of a short date." He gave a familiar example from ancient Greek history, averred that the Swiss and Dutch counterexamples were owing to the proximity of hostile powers, and attributed (confederated) Germany's strength in 1787 to the superintending role of mighty Austria. In America's case, he concluded, the larger states had sacrificed their just claims to more of a say in federal councils because of the urgency of the situation. Now that crisis had passed, and "the time is come, when justice will be done to their claims."

The next day, June 21, Madison addressed the general subject of the role of the states under the contemplated system. He said that the states were far more likely to encroach upon the central government's powers than vice versa. "All the examples of other confederacies," Madison lectured, "prove the greater tendency in such systems to anarchy than to tyranny; to a disobedience of the members than to usurpations of the federal head. Our own experience had fully illustrated this tendency." In general, he said, the state governments' power would not be taken from them by the central government insofar as it was useful to the people.

On the other hand, "guards were more necessary agst. encroachments of the State Govts.—on the Genl. Govt. than of the latter on the former." If the general government could exercise all of the states' power, "the people would not be less free as members of one great Republic than as members of thirteen small ones. A citizen of Delaware [the least populous state] was not more free than a citizen of Virginia [the most]: nor would either be more free than a citizen of America. Supposing therefore a tendency in the Genl. Government to absorb the State Govts. no fatal consequence could result." This line of reasoning did not apply to the opposite case, in which the state governments exhibited movement "towards an independence on the General Govt." In that situation, "the gloomy consequences need not be pointed out." It was with those consequences of the potential breakdown of the Union in mind that the states had called the Philadelphia Convention. According to Yates's notes, Madison at this point again held up the national veto of state laws, at least "in certain instances," as the type of check on state overreaching that was needed.[83] Yates also had Madison once again saying that drawing a line between state and national power was impossible, "and therefore I am inclined for a general government."[84]

Later that day, when the question of the length of representatives' terms came up, Madison opposed the idea of annual elections. While extremely common in the era of the revolution—Randolph noted that "all of the Constitutions of the States except that of S. Carolina, had established" them—annual elections to Congress struck Madison as likely to be terribly inconvenient. The country was very large, he reasoned, and the people would expect their representatives to appear among them at election time. This expectation would require incumbents to travel from their home states to the capital and back repeatedly, and travel in the late eighteenth century was extremely slow and difficult.

Madison's other ground of opposition to annual elections savored of the career politician in him. New members of Congress, he noted, would need substantial time to acquaint themselves with the matters under their cognizance. Until they did so, "their trust could not be usefully discharged," and new members "would always form a large proportion" of the whole. Therefore, they needed to be given longer terms than annual, and he was unpersuaded that even biannual elections would be infrequent enough. Although Hamilton chimed in with a reference to the British House of Commons' septennial elections, the proposal for three-year terms was defeated by a vote of 7 ayes, 3 noes, 1 state divided, and then a provision for two-year terms was substituted without objection.

On June 25, the subject of debate was the Senate—the mode of members' election and the length of their terms. Debating a motion to empower state legislatures to elect senators, Pennsylvania nationalist James Wilson predictably held that the people ought to elect the senators, just as they would the representatives. "The Genl. Govt.," Madison recorded him saying, "is not an assemblage of States, but of individuals for certain political purposes." Wilson concluded that "the *individuals* therefore not the *States,* ought to be represented in it." (Yates, interestingly, has Wilson saying that, "I must lay aside my state connections and act for the general good of the whole. We must forget our local habits and attachments." According to Rufus King's notes, Wilson in this speech also objected to the term "United States," because it was plural.) He would have liked apportionment in this house to be by population, and for the people to select electors who would elect senators. This last proposal was not seconded by any other member.

Connecticut's Oliver Ellsworth weighed in to the effect that "the state legislatures are more competent to make a judicious choice, than the people at large."[85] Election by the people would give the lower house the attribute of instability, he counseled, but the upper could be endowed with "wisdom and firmness" if the task were given to the state legislatures.

Madison's Virginia colleague George Mason countered Wilson by saying that since all agreed that each branch of the new central government must have "the faculty of self-defence," he found it strange that some denied that the state governments must have the same faculty. He insisted that the selection of senators by the state legislatures alone could meet that need. The motion to grant state governments this power passed by 9 ayes, 2 noes.

According to Yates, Madison at this point intervened to object: "We are proceeding in the same manner that was done when the confederation was first formed—Its original draft was excellent, but in its progress and completion it became so insufficient as to give rise to the present convention." No wonder Madison left this speech out of his notes!

The following day, the convention continued to consider various questions of congressional organization. Most significant was the length of senators' terms. In the midst of that discussion, Madison delivered a brief speech in which he explored both the function of the Senate and the situation he thought America faced.[86] First, bicameralism would serve as a barrier against self-interestedness in one house. Second, a small, select body with long terms could protect the people from the impulses that struck the larger, more responsive house from time to time, he held. Another reason to endow one house with long terms was that it would enable members of that house to develop expertise in difficult policy areas.

Finally, Madison said, all societies had their poor and their rich. America did not yet have the extremes of condition one found in European countries, but it might eventually. If that day came, a small, select body in the legislature might serve as a check on the impetuosity with which the "leveling spirit" already sometimes in evidence in America (he must have meant Shays' Rebellion) endangered property rights.

Madison wanted a long term for senators. Nine years sounded good. He also favored a high minimum age requirement, because with such a requirement the one-term limit he had in mind would be neither a public nor a private problem. Lest anyone thought this a hard pill to swallow, Madison closed by saying that, "as it was more than probable we were now digesting a plan which in its operation wd. decide forever the fate of Republican Govt we ought not only to provide every guard to liberty that its preservation cd. require, but be equally careful to supply the defects which our own experience had particularly pointed out."

At this point, Madison's ally, Hamilton, intervened, perhaps to Madison's discomfiture. "He acknowledged himself not to think favorably of Republican Government," Madison noted, "but addressed his remarks to those who did think favorably of it, in order to prevail on them to tone their Government as high as possible." ("High tone," in 1787, was another of saying "aristocratic or monarchical tendency.") For Hamilton, long Senate terms represented "high tone," and were desirable on that basis.

Two days later, on Thursday, June 28, the convention again considered the question of the lower house's apportionment. The day before, Luther Martin of Maryland had led small-state delegates in defense of an equal vote for each state.[87] Now, New York's Lansing moved that the word "not" be dropped from the pending motion "that the representation of the first branch be according to the articles of the confederation." Madison opposed Lansing's motion at length and with vigor.

The small states argued that equality of the states respected the states' equal sovereignty. Madison insisted on this point's irrelevance. The document under consideration was not a treaty, "in which were specified certain duties to which the parties were to be bound," but "a compact by which an authority was created paramount to the parties, & making laws for the government of them." Here, Madison said that the proper analogy was to representation of "Counties of the same States" in the state legislatures. In addition, he added, the congress proposed was to have a veto over state laws. In that sense, it would be part of each state's legislature, and so ought to be "established on like principles with the other branches of those Legislatures." (Here, Madison overlooked the fact that the Virginia General Assembly was apportioned geographically, with each county given an equal voice in the House of Delegates regardless of population.)

Martin had forecast a coalition of Virginia, Pennsylvania, and Massachusetts to dominate a new congress apportioned by population. After all, he noted, those three states together had virtually half of the United States' population. Madison countered that the three largest states shared no common interest setting them off from the other states. In fact, he said, three states could hardly have been selected that were more geographically, economically, and religiously dissimilar. He was right: Massachusetts had been founded by Puritans and still had an established church, Pennsylvania had been founded by Quakers and had never had an established church, and formerly Episcopalian Virginia had only the previous year adopted its Statute for Religious Freedom; Massachusetts was in New England, Pennsylvania in the middle of the country and centered on a major port (America's most populous city), and upper-south Virginia had nary a major city to speak of; Massachusetts had abolished slavery during the revolution, Pennsylvania slavery was on the way out, and Virginia remained deeply committed to the institution.

This trio posed paltry threat of an antiliberty coalition at the time, and in fact has seldom been found in cooperation in federal politics in the Constitution's two-plus centuries. Ever attentive to historical lessons, Madison noted an additional reason to doubt that the big three would form a league against the rest: eminent individuals and eminent nations tended to rivalry, he said, not to coalition. Rome and Carthage had warred repeatedly, France and Austria had long been rivals, and the American Revolution likely would have failed if France and Britain had not continued the pattern.[88] In fact, he noted, where large and small entities had confederated, as in ancient Greece, early modern Germany, and the Netherlands of his day, small states did better where the parts were melded into one whole. He concluded that the small states' interest lay in as close a union as they could obtain.

The next day, the convention adopted the unamended resolution to apportion the new legislature along "some more equitable ratio of representation" than the one used in the Confederation Congress. Madison insisted that the equal state votes idea was "unjust," and he foretold the small states' conquest by the larger in case their continued insistence on equal votes led to disunion.[89] According to Madison, the assumption that the states were sovereign upon which this proposal rested was false; Yates's notes show that Madison insisted that the states were "only political societies." He also shows Madison, the impractical politician and expert rhetorician, insisting vociferously on not allowing "inconsistent principles" into the new Constitution while trying to divert attention from the threat of a large-state coalition by highlighting "the great danger to our general government" from the fact of *"the great southern and northern interests of the continent, being opposed to each other."*[90] Having rejected the idea in connection with the lower house, the delegates began to consider a proposal from Connecticut's Oliver Ellsworth to give the states equal weight in the upper house.

Warming to his subject, on the following day (June 30) Madison ripped into Ellsworth with gusto. The chief divide in federal politics, he reiterated, did not depend on the states' sizes, but to some extent on differences of climate and to a greater degree on "their having or not having slaves." Any defensive power ought to be given to those two interests, the Virginian slaveholder insisted, and not to the small states as small. Madison thought the best expedient for doing this was to abandon the three-fifths ratio for counting slaves in apportioning the legislature, and instead count them 100 percent for apportioning one house, not at all for apportioning the other.[91] He continued to oppose the idea of equal state votes, but, he avowed, "I mean . . . to preserve the state rights with the same care, as I would trials by jury."[92]

Ellsworth interjected: "The Natl. Govt. could not descend to the local objects on which [domestic happiness] depended. It could only embrace objects of a general nature." His rights' preservation he entrusted to the state governments that had always borne this responsibility.

Finally, on July 2, South Carolina's Charles Cotesworth Pinckney moved for appointment of a committee to resolve the issue of congressional apportionment. Madison, seemingly realizing that matters were getting away from him, opposed this gambit. Committees were no more apt to resolve such matters than was the entire house, he averred.

The convention ignored Madison and appointed a committee. Virginia's member was George Mason, who had argued that the states must be given equal weight in the upper house so that they could defend themselves. Also on the committee were equal-apportionment advocates such as Maryland's Martin, Connecticut's Ellsworth (ultimately replaced by Sherman due to indisposition), and New York's Yates. Unsurprisingly, the committee reached a compromise the next day, July 3: the lower house, it said, should be apportioned by population and have the sole power to originate money bills, and in the upper house, "each state shall have an equal vote."

When the convention took up the report on July 5, Madison objected to it strenuously. The money bills provision, he said, was worthless. In the states that had such constitutional provisions, senates had easily circumvented them by refusing to accept any bill the lower house refused to amend. It therefore seemed to Madison that the large states were being offered nothing of substance in exchange for yielding his grand principle of population apportionment of both houses.

In the course of unburdening himself of this observation, Madison yet again warned the small states that their refusal to yield to his argument would mean disunion, and that disunion would have very grave consequences for them. Among the ones he mentioned were the need to seek foreign alliances and the continued imposition of "exactions levied on them by the commerce of the neighbouring States."

Gouverneur Morris of Pennsylvania followed Madison with an appeal to consider the effect of the committee's proposal upon the entire world. He lamented that some delegates seemed to think of themselves as representing only their particular states, when really all humanity had a stake in the convention's outcome. Like Madison's, Morris's disinterested principles led him to a conclusion that favored his large state's interests.

Madison's Virginia colleague, Mason, characteristically presented a more statesmanlike argument. Implicitly criticizing Morris and Madison, Mason said that accommodation had been the convention's goal in appointing a committee, and that accommodation had been the committee's goal in making its apportionment proposal. Accommodation on this question was necessary, he said, to a successful outcome to the convention. Noting that no other delegate's private interests can have been suffering more in his absence from home than his own, Mason said that he would happily die in Philadelphia rather than leave the city before agreement had been hammered out.

Although the committee report marked a significant development along the lines on which they had insisted, it was during the initial debate on the report July 5 that New York's two senior delegates, Robert Yates and John Lansing, left the convention. They never returned. The convention allowed their colleague, Alexander Hamilton, to cast New York's vote until July 10. At that point, since the Empire State's delegation lacked a quorum, it ceased to have a vote.[93]

One might have thought that this development augured well for Madison's overall project. After all, Yates and Lansing objected to the convention's proceedings for the general reason they had laid out at the beginning: that it was doing more than the states had deputed it to do. Subtract their (that is, New York's) nay vote, and you'd think that Madison's nationalist agenda had a better chance. Yet, on July 7, the convention voted by 6 ayes, 3 noes, 2 states divided to leave the proposal for equal state votes in the upper house in the committee's report.

On July 9, the convention considered a proposal for allocation of representatives in the first House of Representatives. Hearing New Jersey's Paterson argue that a representation was "an expedient by which an assembly of certain individls. chosen by the people is substituted in place of the inconvenient meeting of the people themselves," Madison said that yes, that was what a representation was. Since it was, he added, the pending proposal concerning apportionment in the upper house ought to be rejected in favor of some other. Madison's idea was that one house could be apportioned according to the number of free inhabitants, the other according to the number of free inhabitants plus slaves.

Surely the small-state representatives must have smiled at this idea. Madison, insistent that Virginia outweigh all other states in both houses, as it would have done if both houses were apportioned according to free population, now proposed a different mode of apportionment whose effect would have been . . . to give Virginia more votes in each house than any other state. Virginia, after all, had not only more free residents than any other state, but the most slaves, as well.

Rufus King of Massachusetts followed Madison immediately. Since eleven of the thirteen states had already decided that slaves should count in apportioning taxation, King averred, they ought to count in apportioning representation as well. Madison's initiative on this score would bear significant fruit in the days ahead.

On July 10, Madison moved, with Mason in agreement, that the size of the first House of Representatives be doubled from the contemplated sixty-five. The convention rejected their proposal, chiefly on the ground of expense, 9 noes to 2 ayes. The next day, Virginia voted to establish the three-fifths ratio as slaves' weight in apportionment. The convention accepted this idea, although Madison, uncharacteristically, said nothing. The day after that, the convention unanimously decided that "direct Taxation ought to be proportioned according to representation." This locution was dubbed more fitting by James Wilson than an explicit reference to slaves. Pierce Butler of South Carolina noted on July 13, "The security the Southn. States want is that their negroes may not be taken from them which some gentlemen within or without doors, have a very good mind to do." Butler need not have feared: the South had won its way, and then some.

On July 14, the convention again considered the question of the upper house's apportionment.[94] Charles Pinckney of South Carolina moved that although smaller, the upper house be apportioned by population in the manner of the lower. Madison concurred, calling Pinckney's idea "a reasonable compromise." A New Jersey delegate, on the other hand, warned, "The smaller States can never give up their equality." Gerry, more reasonably, said that he "should like the motion," but noted that it would never be accepted and that some kind of "accommodation must take place."

Once again, Madison held forth in the longest speech of the day on the small states' "improper principles." Some said that the government was to be partly federal and partly national, he noted, and on that basis they held that one house should be federal and one national. Yet he could think of no sense in which the government would actually be what he called "federal"—that is, in which it would act on the states rather than on the people directly.

Therefore, by the small states' own argument, both houses ought to be apportioned by population. Madison also reminded the small-state delegates of Paterson's statement about proper representation.

Madison at this point unveiled a new argument in favor of population apportionment: that it would aid in the defense of slavery. At the moment, he reasoned, eight states lay north and only five lay south of the line between slave and free states. Over time, however, population was migrating southward and westward, which would tend toward an equilibrium. If each state had the same voice, however, the equilibrium would be slower to come, if it ever did.

The bottom line, however, remained the impermissibility of "bad first principles."

On July 16, the convention turned to the Virginia Plan's provisions concerning the powers of Congress: "That the Natl. Legislature ought to possess the Legislative Rights vested in Congs. by the Confederation" (which was adopted without objection), "and moreover to legislate in all cases to which the separate States are incompetent; or in which the harmony of the U. S. may be interrupted by the exercise of individual legislation." Pierce Butler responded to the clerk's reading of the latter resolution by asking for a definition of the word "incompetent," and by lamenting that the whole was so vague.

Nathaniel Gorham of Massachusetts replied that vagueness in the general statement laid the groundwork for a clear elaboration, and Butler's fellow South Carolinian, John Rutledge, moved that a committee be appointed to clarify the resolution. The convention rejected this motion.

As if that were not enough, the next day found the convention once again considering, and rejecting, Madison's other pet proposal: the congressional power to veto state laws. Madison said that he "considered the negative on the laws of the States as essential to the efficacy & security of the Genl. Govt. The necessity of a general Govt. proceeds from the propensity of the States to pursue their particular interests in opposition to the general interest. This propensity will continue to disturb the system, unless effectually controuled. Nothing short of a negative on their laws will controul it. They can pass laws which will accomplish their injurious objects before they can be repealed by the Genl Legislre. or be set aside by the National Tribunals." State courts could not be counted on for this purpose, he continued. In short, "a power of negativing the improper laws of the States is at once the most mild & certain means of preserving the harmony of the system." The experience of the British system (in which the king could veto colonial and Parliament's bills), he said, showed that this was a fit power. Nonetheless, the convention voted the proposal down again, 3 ayes to 7 noes. It then adopted, by 10 ayes to 0 noes, a statement that state judiciaries must consider the pending Constitution, laws, and treaties the supreme law of the land. The Supremacy Clause and the requirement that state officials swear to uphold the Constitution, the ultimate form that this idea took, were not precisely what Madison wanted, but the convention clearly intended these provisions to serve the function he had in mind for his dear congressional veto over state laws.

Next, the delegates turned to the general issue of the executive branch's structure. Here, Madison specified that the executive must somehow be insulated from the "tendency in our governments to throw all power into the Legislative vortex." In general, he thought, "An independence of the three great departments of each other, as far as possible, and the responsibility of all to the will of the community seemed to be generally admitted as the true basis of a well constructed government."[95]

Legislative election did not serve this purpose. Yet Madison favored election of the chief executive by electors rather than directly by the people. The people were the fittest to exercise that function, Madison said, and they could be relied upon to choose someone "of distinguished Character." The problem, as he explained, was that the suffrage was more widely distributed in the North than in the South, while southern whites could not be given added weight in a popular vote for their human chattels. Having an electoral college would solve both of these problems. The idea was adopted, 6 ayes to 3 noes.

Madison noted in mid-convention that he found the task of recording the business of the assemblage to be a "drudgery."[96] Still, he said, he intended to keep it up "if no indisposition obliges me to discontinue it." By convention's end, Madison did have health difficulties.[97] Still, he soldiered on as the resident note taker. At this point, he still expected a drawn-out remainder of the work. Still, he said, he had heard no reports of unhappiness with the secrecy of the convention. That secrecy was closely guarded by the delegates, whose surviving correspondence is full of apologies to various correspondents for their inability to explain what was going on behind closed doors in Philadelphia.

Also in mid-July, Madison relayed news from Philadelphia about Pennsylvania politics.[98] The state's paper money, long trading at between 80 and 88 percent of face value, had suddenly ceased to circulate in early July. With riots in the offing, "some influencial characters" intervened and persuaded leading mercantile figures in the city to take it again. Yet, Madison concluded, it likely would never regain its former value. Alas, it looked as if Virginia was soon to try the paper money experiment again as well. These developments added urgency to Madison's desire for the new Constitution to bar states from issuing paper money.

On July 21, Madison supported a motion to associate the judiciary and executive in the veto power. This association, he held, would aid the judiciary in defending itself against Congress, aid the executive in exercising a power it might otherwise not, and aid the legislature in drafting better laws than America's republican legislatures had thus far. While some might object that this proposal threatened to give the judiciary and the executive too much power, Madison concluded, that was unlikely. The real danger in America's governmental systems seemed to lie in the tendency of the legislature "to absorb all power into its vortex." With that problem in mind, Madison insisted on "the necessity of giving every defensive authority to the other departments that was consistent with republican principles."

George Mason instantly agreed that this concept promised to "give a confidence to the Executive, which he would not otherwise have, and without which the Revisionary power would be of little avail." Other delegates, however, disliked the idea of making political actors of the judges. They insisted on the separation of powers. Madison responded to this objection by saying that it was checks and balances, not separation of powers, he wanted. Only the former could provide the defense of liberty that the latter was supposed to yield. Besides, he concluded, if allowing the executive and judiciary jointly to exercise the veto power should be discarded as violating the separation of powers, giving the executive alone that power met with the same objection. Despite Madison's reasoning, the convention rejected the proposal.

Madison's apportionment defeat changed the way he understood the proper allocation of powers among the branches. So, on July 21, he proposed that the chief executive be given the power to appoint judges unless two-thirds of the upper house disagreed with his selection. The reasons for giving the power to the executive rather than the upper house, he explained, were that a majority of the upper house would not necessarily represent the majority of the people and that to give the upper house this power "would moreover throw the appointments entirely into the hands of ye Nrthern States," which would provide "a perpetual ground of jealousy & discontent" to the South. When Elbridge Gerry objected that two-thirds was too great a requirement, Madison agreed to reduce that to a majority. When first considered on July 21, Madison's idea went down to defeat, 6 noes to 3 ayes. The convention remained committed to the idea of giving the upper house that power, with the three largest states (Massachusetts, Pennsylvania, and Virginia) once again in the minority.

That same day, Madison opposed Ellsworth's motion to refer the proposed Constitution to the state legislatures for ratification. The Constitution would make changes to the state constitutions, he reasoned, and the state legislatures were therefore incompetent to ratify it. If the legislatures ratified the convention's proposal, it would be a "*league*," but if the people did, it would be a "*Constitution*."

Madison preferred to have a constitution for two reasons: (1) a subsequent law might be enforced by judges in preference to a league, but not in preference to a constitution; and (2) the law of nations said that any breach of a league freed the other parties of their obligation, but the same was not true of breach of a constitution. Ellsworth's motion was rejected, 7 states to 3, and then Madison's idea was accepted, 9 states to 1.

Next, the convention considered how to elect the chief executive. Madison interjected the longest speech on July 25. "There are," he began, "objections agst. every mode that has been, or perhaps can be proposed." The election could be by some existing state institution, some other federal institution, some institution created specially for the purpose, or the people themselves. To have the federal judiciary elect the executive "he presumed was out of the question." To have the legislature elect the executive "was in his Judgment liable to insuperable objections."

First, congressional election of the chief executive would undermine that official's independence. Second, it would divide the legislators "so much that the public interest would materially suffer by it." Third, his desire to please the legislature would cause the chief executive to bend his administration to the legislative majority's will. Fourth, foreign powers would intrigue with legislators concerning the chief executive elections, as in Germany and Poland. He made similar arguments regarding lodging such elections in state institutions.

This left only popular election of electors and direct popular election. The former, he said, was not susceptible to the objections made against the other possibilities. However, since it had recently been rejected by the convention, it seemed unlikely to be adopted. That left only direct popular election, his favorite option. The two main objections to this mode of election, he said, were that it would be unlikely that a small-state resident would win and that the southern states would be disadvantaged by the smallness of the proportion of their population that was eligible to vote. He thought that the former objection could be addressed through some provision, and that the latter was in the process of being partially remedied by the southern states' republican reforms. Still, as a southern man, he was willing to make this sacrifice.

Gouverneur Morris of Pennsylvania addressed the first of those questions by proposing that each elector be required to cast at least one of his two votes for a person not from his own state. Madison suggested an additional security for the small states in the form of a limit on the frequency with which people from the same state could be elected. Fortunately for his later political prospects, that idea was not adopted. Had the delegates suspected that eight of the first nine presidential elections would be won by Virginians, it no doubt would have been.

On July 26, a five-man Committee of Detail (Gorham, Ellsworth, Wilson, Randolph, and Rutledge) was appointed to reconcile the various provisions on which the convention had agreed to that point, and the convention recessed to await the committee's report.[99] On Monday, August 6, the Committee of Detail brought in its report. The preamble was accepted without objection, as were the statement that the government should be called "the United States of America" and the decision that "the Government shall consist of supreme legislative, executive, and judicial powers."

The convention then took up the question of suffrage: who got to vote (and, by implication, who did not). Gouverneur Morris defended the old idea that property should be the qualification for voting. George Mason responded that a freehold, the substantial landed estate traditionally required both in England and in his (and Madison's) Virginia, need not be the standard. Echoing his 1776 Virginia Declaration of Rights, Mason said that evidence of a permanent common interest in society, such as parentage, money, or merchandise, should also suffice.

Madison said that if he thought it would be acceptable to the people when asked to ratify the Constitution, he would favor a freehold requirement. "The freeholders of the Country," he held, "would be the safest depositories of Republican liberty." Elaborating on this insight in a characteristically gloomy way, Madison went on: "In future times a great majority of the people will not only be without landed, but any other sort of, property. These will either combine under the influence of their common situation; in which case, the rights of property & the public liberty, will not be secure in their hands: or which is more probable, they will become the tools of opulence & ambition, in which case there will be equal danger on another side." Ultimately, the convention decided to leave the matter to each state to decide for itself.

Madison objected on August 8 to a proposal that representatives in the lower house be 1 per 40,000 inhabitants. He thought that the country's population growth could eventually make this far too high a ratio. Massachusetts's Gorham answered that it was highly unlikely that the western lands (that is, the region between the Appalachians and the Mississippi) would be part of the United States of America 150 years later (which is to say, by 1937). Oliver Ellsworth suggested that in that case, the Constitution could be amended to provide a different ratio of representation. Instead of that, Madison and Roger Sherman proposed to make 1 to 40,000 the maximum, rather than the minimum. The convention approved this motion without objection.

At this point, Morris delivered a long speech decrying the inclusion of slaves in the states' populations for purposes of computing the apportionment of the lower house. Slavery was abhorrent, he said, and why should slave owners be rewarded for owning slaves? Northerners are to be bound by the proposed Constitution to aid in suppressing slave insurrections, Morris objected, and the Committee of Detail proposed banning taxes on exports.

The possibility of direct taxation was very slight, he noted, because administration of such a tax would be virtually impossible, so non-slave-owning states would pay higher taxes than they ought. Why should slave owners be given these advantages, when their institution was both iniquitous and destructive?

Sherman answered that "it was the freemen of the Southn. States who were in fact to be represented according to the taxes paid by them, and the Negroes are only included in the Estimate of the taxes." Charles Pinckney, for his part, "considered the fisheries & the Western frontiers as more burdensome to the U. S. than the slaves."

Over the next several days, the convention concerned itself with the minutia of Article I, regarding the places and times of elections, the length of time during which a citizen must have been resident in his state to be eligible for election to Congress, whether congressmen should be paid by the state governments or the central one, etc. Madison and a handful of other delegates (Morris, Mason, Randolph, Wilson, Gerry, and a few others) generally spoke at length on every disputed issue.

Many accounts of the events in Philadelphia that late spring and summer of 1787 assert that the weather fatigued the delegates. They join some of the delegates, such as chilly Massachusetts's Elbridge Gerry, in judging those days "excessive hot."[100] Yet modern research shows that far from being unusually hot, "Philadelphia enjoyed a cool summer in 1787."[101] Madison, accustomed to balmy Virginia summer weather, never complained.

On August 15, Madison moved that both the executive and the Supreme Court should have a veto power—an override of either's veto requiring a two-thirds vote of each house of Congress, an override of a dual veto requiring a three-quarters vote of each house. Two delegates supported the idea, one objected to involving the judges in the legislative process, Gerry noted that this idea had been rejected before, and the convention voted down the motion by 3 ayes to 8 noes.

The next day, August 16, Mason insisted on a clause banning Congress from taxing exports. He said that he feared the northern majority would abuse the South, "or as he called them, the staple States," with such a power. Madison countered that taxing exports was a good idea, that some of the states presently did it, that this power would benefit all of the states (rather than only those with ports) if it were vested in the central government, and that the South could not complain, as it had the greatest need for naval protection. Besides, he forecast, "time [would] equalize the situation of the States in this matter." The convention decided to defer the question.

The next day, as the convention considered a motion to empower Congress to "make" war, Madison and Gerry moved to substitute "declare." This, they said, would "leav[e] to the Executive the power to repel sudden attacks." Their proposal passed, 7 ayes, 2 noes, 1 absent.

The following day, as the delegates grew increasingly frustrated with the laggard pace of their proceedings, they voted to meet from 10:00 a.m. until 4:00 p.m., six days per week, and to disallow motions for adjournment. That same day, Madison proposed several more powers to be lodged in Congress, and the convention voted to refer his proposals to the Committee of Detail.[102]

On August 21, the convention returned to the issue of export taxes, and Madison argued against a ban on them. "As we ought to be governed by national and permanent views," he held, "it is a sufficient argument for giving ye power over exports that a tax, tho' it may not be expedient at present, may be so hereafter. A proper regulation of exports may & probably will be necessary hereafter, and for the same purposes as the regulation of—imports; viz, for revenue—domestic manufactures—and procuring equitable regulations from other nations."

"As to the fear of disproportionate burdens on the more exporting States," he continued, "it might be remarked that it was agreed on all hands that the revenue wd. principally be drawn from trade, and as only a given revenue would be needed, it was not material whether all should be drawn wholly from imports—or half from those, and half from exports—The imports and exports must be pretty nearly equal in every State—and relatively the same among the different States."

Mason said that he feared a power to tax exports would be used to oppress the South, as the South would have only twenty-nine of the sixty-five representatives and five-thirteenth of the senators. His principle, borne out by the Virginia General Assembly, was that "a majority when interested will oppress the minority." This proposal, he said, seemed consistent with some delegates' evident aim of "reducing the States to mere corporations." Madison then, "as a lesser evil than a total prohibition," moved to allow Congress by two-thirds of each house to tax exports. His motion failed, 5 ayes to 6 noes. Next, the convention adopted the ban, 7 ayes to 4 noes.

On August 22, Madison was selected as Virginia's member of an eleven-man committee to report back on various provisions. The convention picked up where it had left off the day before: in a discussion of slavery's place under the planned Constitution. Mason traced "this infernal traffic" to "the avarice of British Merchants" and noted that the British government had repeatedly disallowed Virginia's colonial attempts to stop it. Slavery itself discouraged whites from immigrating and from doing labor they associated with slaves; it weakened the states when faced by foreign military threats (as during Cromwell's day and during the revolution); it "discourage[d] arts & manufactures"; and, notably, it had a "pernicious effect on manners," because "every master of slaves is born a petty tyrant."[103]

Slaves, Mason concluded, "bring the judgment of heaven on a Country. As nations can not be rewarded or punished in the next world they must be in this." He regretted that some New Englanders had become involved in the slave trade. He conceded that states had a right to import slaves, but he classed this as one of the many state rights that would be surrendered if this new Constitution were adopted.

Oliver Ellsworth of Connecticut thought that if slavery were really "to be considered in a moral light we ought to go farther and free those already in the Country." Merely to reduce imports would not hurt Virginia, where natural population increase outstripped demand. On the other hand, he said, it would be "unjust towards S. Carolina & Georgia," because "in the sickly rice swamps foreign supplies are necessary." He would leave the matter to local decision and trust that in time, the growth of the supply of poor white laborers would "render slaves useless."

The leading South Carolina delegate, John Rutledge, said that North Carolina, South Carolina, and Georgia would never adopt the Constitution "unless their right to import slaves be untouched." Charles Pinckney pointed out that far from immoral, slavery was sanctioned by the examples of Greece and Rome, France, England, and Holland. John Dickinson countered that perhaps France and England allowed slavery, but not within those kingdoms themselves. Finally, the convention decided to refer the matter to a committee, to which Madison was elected, 7 ayes, 3 noes, 1 absent. The same committee was also charged with deciding what portion of each house should be required to make tariff laws. Ultimately the committee decided that New England should have its way on tariffs, the Deep South should have its way on slave imports, and Mason should be disappointed on both.

The next day, August 23, Madison moved to allow the general government to appoint militia generals. Elbridge Gerry responded that if the state governments were to be destroyed, the executive ought to be "for life or hereditary," and there should be "a proper Senate." If the states were to continue to exist, then some power ought to be left in them. Madison replied that "as the greatest danger of disunion is the states, it is necessary to guard agst. it by sufficient powers to the Common Govt. and as the greatest danger to liberty is from large standing armies, it is best to prevent them by an effectual provision for a good Militia." Madison's motion was rejected, 3 ayes to 8 noes.

Soon thereafter, Charles Pinckney brought up an amended version of Madison's pet project of a federal veto over state laws: that a state law could be negated by a two-thirds vote of each house. The idea, Pinckney pointed out, had been accepted at first (June 8), then put aside because of the fear of large-state domination. Since the Senate was to be apportioned by state, this objection was no longer valid. Roger Sherman noted that the convention had already accepted a supremacy clause, so this provision would be redundant. George Mason asked the obvious questions: "Is no road nor bridge to be established without the Sanction of the General Legislature? Is this to sit constantly in order to receive & revise the State Laws?" John Rutledge interjected that "if nothing else, this alone would damn and ought to damn the Constitution. Will any State ever agree to be bound hand & foot in this manner. It is worse than making mere corporations of them whose bye laws would not be subject to this shackle." The convention refused to commit this idea to a committee, 5 ayes to 6 noes.

On August 24, the convention decided unanimously on a one-person executive. It then took up various proposals concerning that official's election. Madison was notably silent. The next day, the Committee of Eleven reported its provision disallowing Congress to prevent slave importations until 1800. Charles Cotesworth Pinckney proposed that 1800 be changed to 1808. Massachusetts' Gorham, party to the New England–Deep South agreement, seconded the motion. Madison objected: "Twenty years will produce all the mischief that can be apprehended from the liberty to import slaves. So long a term will be more dishonorable to the National character than to say nothing about it in the Constitution." The amendment was adopted, 7 ayes to 4 noes, and the proposal was adopted by the same vote—with New Jersey, Pennsylvania, Delaware, and Virginia voting no. The New England–Deep South coalition that had decided the tariff question here had its way again.

Next, the convention took up the Committee of Eleven's proposal to disallow import taxes on slaves. Mason noted that "not to tax, will be equivalent to a bounty on the importation of slaves." Madison objected that it was "wrong to admit in the Constitution the idea that there could be property in men." In the end, the clause referred to "such importation," as Madison desired. There was no objection.

On August 28, Madison proposed to ban the states from levying tariffs absolutely, not merely unless Congress agreed. Otherwise, he said, New Jersey, North Carolina, and other essentially landlocked states would remain at the mercy of their neighbors. His motion lost, 4 ayes to 7 noes.

On August 29, Charles Pinckney made the following motion: "That no act of the Legislature for the purpose of regulating the commerce of the U—S. with foreign powers, or among the several States, shall be passed without the assent of two thirds of the members of each House." Madison's account of Pinckney's speech has Pinckney saying that states are less scrupulous than individuals in pursuing their interests, and that a bare majority would oppress the minority if a supermajority were not required in this case.

Luther Martin seconded.

Charles Cotesworth Pinckney said that in light of the New England states' liberality toward South Carolina in the convention (here, he referred to the vote on the slave importation clause), he would be liberal toward them by opposing this measure. Another delegate called majority power in this area necessary to America's—particularly the "Northern & middle States'"—self-defense. Roger Sherman, showing Madison's influence, thought that the diversity of the states' economic interests was protection enough against the likelihood of an oppressive majority exploiting the commerce power. Still another judged that if a bare majority oppressed the South, Southerners would build their own ships and solve the problem. Yet, he favored the

proposal as likely to calm southern minds. Pinckney's fellow South Carolinian, Butler, said he would vote against the motion, despite the contrast
between northern and southern interests, in the name of "conciliating the
affections of the East."

George Mason, the first Virginian to speak on the topic on this day, said
that any lasting government must be "founded in the confidence & affections
of the people." "The *Majority* will be governed by their interests," he reasoned, and, "The Southern States are the *minority* in both Houses." He
asked, mockingly, "Is it to be expected that they will deliver themselves
bound hand & foot to the Eastern States?"

Madison, far calmer and less forthrightly parochial than his senior colleague from the Old Dominion, "went into a pretty full view of the subject."
A navigation act would hurt the southern states in the short run, he began, by
raising the rates they paid for transport. Yet it would also have advantages to
them in the form of relocation of northern seamen to the South and elimination of the long-simmering interstate hostility prompted by the states' dog-
eat-dog commercial relationships.

In addition, Madison said, northern abuse of a majority power to regulate
commerce was rendered less likely by bicameralism, the presidential veto, the
agricultural interests of Connecticut and New Jersey, the extensive agricultural areas in many states' inland territories, and the likelihood that western
states would join the Union with strong agricultural interests. The South, he
reminded his fellow Southerners, would gain greatly from the growth of
America's maritime strength. All of the southern states were vulnerable in this
regard, Madison held, particularly Virginia. The new government would facilitate development of the coasting trade, which would benefit Southerners.
Perhaps the Northeast would benefit even more, but that was no cause for
concern: the Northeast's increased tax payments would benefit everyone.

When Madison sat down, his friend and junior colleague, Governor Randolph, delivered a thunderous announcement: rejection of Pinckney's motion, he said, "would compleat the deformity of the system." Either way, "he
doubted whether he should be able to agree to" the Constitution. Pinckney's
motion suffered a 7–4 rejection, and Madison must have shuddered at the
thought of Randolph opposing the convention's product.

Pierce Butler then submitted a proposed Fugitive Slave Clause, which said that slaves escaping from one state to another must be returned to their masters. The convention accepted this proposal without objection. Madison later told his secretary that this turn of events formed part of a North-South agreement that also led to inclusion of a similar provision in the Northwest Ordinance—which was being ironed out in Congress as the Philadelphia Convention sat.[104]

Madison and Mason next spoke against a motion from Gouverneur Morris to strike out a provision of the committee's report stating that new states would be admitted on an equal basis with the old states. According to Madison, "the Western States neither would nor ought to submit to a Union which degraded them from an equal rank with the other States." Mason said that preventing migration might be wise, but since people were going to migrate, it was better to have them friends (equals) than enemies. Morris's motion to delete the provision passed anyway, 9 ayes to 2 noes.

On August 31, Madison proposed that the Constitution should take effect when seven states entitled to thirty-three House members ratified it. "This he said would require the concurrence of a majority of both the States and people." When some other delegates wanted to leave to the states to decide how each would ratify, Madison intervened to note that requiring conventions was more apt to yield a positive result. The Constitution would transfer powers from the state legislatures to the new government, he pointed out, which meant that "the Legislatures would be more disinclined than conventions." Yet if the people as source of governmental power ratified directly, "all difficulties were got over. They could alter constitutions as they pleased. It was a principle in the Bills of Rights, that first principles might be resorted to." Mason interjected that the people were used to the idea that under the Confederation, nine states were required to make major decisions. The convention adopted the proposal that nine states be required for ratification instead of Madison's proposal, 8 ayes to 3 noes.

At this point, several delegates joined Randolph in expressing their overall unhappiness with the convention's work. Maryland's Martin guessed that the people "would not ratify it unless hurried into it by surprize." Massachusetts's Gerry said that the system was "full of vices" and, said Madison, "dwelt on the impropriety of destroying the existing Confederation, without the unanimous Consent of the parties to it."

More bad news for Madison followed when Mason said that he would "sooner chop off his right hand than put it to the Constitution as it now stands." In case some pending votes went against him, "his wish would . . . be to bring the whole subject before another general Convention."

On September 5, when the Committee of Eleven reported its proposal for electing presidents, Madison made the point that he "considered it as a primary object to render an eventual resort to any part of the Legislature improbable." By that, he meant that he did not want to have the electors' inability to make a majority decision result in referral of the matter to, as the proposal stood, the Senate in many instances. His friend Randolph added that if the Constitution provided that the Senate would choose among the leading vote-getters, that body might come to dominate the executive; to Mason's mind, this threatened aristocracy. Madison proposed to have one-third of the votes be sufficient to make a candidate president without referral to the Senate. His motion lost, 2 ayes to 9 noes, after Gerry said that it would allow "three or four States to put in whom they pleased." In his notes for that day, McHenry summarized the day's discussion thus: "The greatest part of the day spent in desultory conversation on that part of the report respecting the mode of chusing the President—adjourned without coming to a conclusion."[105]

September 6 was the first day that Madison did not have "Committee service both before and after the hours of the House" in many days. It was also when Hamilton broke his long, conspicuous absence with an intervention concerning the election of the president. He "said that he had been restrained from entering into the discussions by his dislike of the Scheme of Govt in General; but as he meant to support the plan to be recommended, as better than nothing, he wished in this place to offer a few remarks."

That night, despite the convention delegates' pledge, Madison wrote to Jefferson describing the product of their work.[106] At the end of a skeletal description, Madison summarized by saying, "I hazard an opinion nevertheless that the plan should it be adopted will neither effectually answer its national object nor prevent the local mischiefs which every where excite disgusts agst the state governments. The grounds of this opinion will be the subject of a future letter." As to the likely aftermath of the convention, he predicted that people would receive the plan well. They had better, he said, or "it is hard to say what may be our fate."

On September 7, Madison and Butler would have allowed the Senate to ratify peace treaties without the president's agreement, but they lost by 3 ayes to 8 noes. Madison would have made a mere majority of the Senate requisite to ratify peace treaties, and those alone, and his motion passed by 8 ayes to 3 noes. Madison then endorsed Mason's motion to have the Committee of Eleven report a clause providing for the establishment of an executive council, with two members from each of the country's three sections. The motion failed, 3 ayes to 8 noes.

On September 8, Madison objected to empowering the Senate to try the president on impeachment. He reasoned that when joined with the House's power to impeach and Mason's language saying that the president could be impeached for treason, bribery, or "other high crimes & misdemeanors," this would enable the legislature to remove him from office for "any act which might be called a misdemeanor."[107] Yet, Madison's motion to strike out "by the Senate" met with defeat, 2 ayes to 9 noes.

When the convention on September 10 considered the Committee of Eleven's proposal (first suggested weeks earlier by Mason) that two-thirds of state legislatures should be able to call an amendment convention, Hamilton objected that this was too difficult a process, and that the Congress ought to be empowered to call a convention as well. Madison then proposed the version of Article V that finally appeared in the Constitution—which included provisions for amendment processes both initiated by and not involving Congress. Hamilton seconded, Rutledge insisted that the 1808 clause be added, and the proposal passed, 9 ayes, 1 no, 1 divided.

On September 10, Randolph made clear that he likely would refuse to sign the finished product. He certainly would unless the ratification provision said that the state conventions would be at liberty to propose amendments for the consideration of a new General Convention. Only thus could the radical changes he thought necessary, and which had been reflected in the Virginia Plan, be substituted for the drastically different proposal that the convention seemed poised to make.

When the other delegates had finished debating whether Congress's approval ought to be a precondition for ratification, Randolph interceded to lay out his grounds of opposition to the convention's handiwork. He said he disapproved of the Senate's role in impeachments; the size of the supermajority required to override a veto, the skimpy representation provided in the House of Representatives; the absence of a restriction on standing armies; the vagueness of the Necessary and Proper Clause; the open-ended power to make navigation acts; "the want of a more definite boundary between the General & State Legislatures—and between the General and State Judiciaries"; the pardon power's extent; and a couple of other provisions. The current plan, Randolph continued, "would end in Tyranny," so he wanted to allow the state conventions to propose amendments for the consideration of a second General Convention. "He accordingly proposed a Resolution to this effect," which Franklin seconded.

The sympathetic Mason recommended allowing Randolph's motion to "lie on the table for a day or two to see what steps might be taken with regard to the parts of the system objected to by Mr. Randolph." Randolph proposed that the Committee of Style and Arrangement (Madison, King, Hamilton, Morris, and Connecticut's William Johnson) consider a motion limiting the pardon power in cases of treason. With that, the convention's business of Monday, September 10, was at an end. The next day, the committee not having reported, the convention adjourned without doing any business.

On Wednesday, September 12, the Committee of Style reported its work. The convention agreed (in keeping with Randolph's objection) to reduce the override supermajority from three-quarters to two-thirds. Apparently because he considered theoretical imperfection more important than Randolph's support during the coming ratification process, Madison opposed this motion. Madison said that there were two reasons for the veto power: (1) "to defend the Executive Rights," and (2) "to prevent popular or factious injustice." State checks on legislative injustice had proven insufficient, he continued, so "we must compare the danger from the weakness of ⅔ with the danger from the strength of ¾. He thought on the whole the former was greater." Still, two-thirds was substituted for three-quarters on a vote of 6 ayes to 4 noes. Mason then proposed to appoint a committee to draft a bill of rights, which was defeated by 0 ayes to 10 noes.

The same day, the convention considered a letter to Congress explaining that in light of the "Impropriety" of vesting "the Power of making war Peace and Treaties, that of levying Money & regulating Commerce and the corresponding executive and judicial Authorities" in a unicameral body such as Congress, the convention had felt compelled to adopt "a different Organization." Although imperfect, it was "liable to as few Exceptions as could reasonably have been expected."

A North Carolina delegate moved that day for a provision guaranteeing trial by jury in civil cases. Gorham said that equity (an area of civil law in which judges presided over trials without juries) was impossible to distinguish from common law (where juries were the norm), so this could not be done. Mason granted the point and said he would second a motion to refer the need for a bill of rights to a committee. Gerry moved it, Mason seconded it, and the idea of a bill of rights again went down to defeat, 0 ayes to 10 noes. The Constitution would include no bill of rights. Immediately thereafter, Madison responded to a complaint that the Supreme Court's jurisdiction was an inadequate check on state misbehavior by noting that "a negative on the State laws alone, could meet all the shapes which these could assume. But this had been overruled."

On September 14, as the convention wound down its business with a succession of petty matters, Madison supported a motion to empower Congress to grant corporate charters—particularly to allow Congress to establish interstate canal companies. King objected that this power would be a cause of intrastate division over banks and "mercantile monopolies." Mason would have limited the power to canals alone, so the proposal was amended to that effect. Still, the proposal failed. Madison also joined Charles Pinckney in proposing a power of Congress "to establish an University, in which no preferences or distinctions should be allowed on account of religion." This too failed.

Soon after, the same Pinckney and Elbridge Gerry tried to add a statement that "the liberty of the Press should be inviolably observed." Sherman responded that it was "unnecessary" because "the power of Congress does not extend to the press." The motion failed, 4 ayes to 7 noes. Sherman's argument had won the day against the idea of a bill of rights generally, as well as against a press clause specifically.

On September 15, McHenry and Maryland's Daniel Carroll moved that states be allowed to collect tonnage duties to fund harbor clearance and erection of lighthouses. Madison replied that the question whether the draft Constitution already allowed states to do this depended on the extent of Congress's power "to regulate commerce." He thought this "vague" expression "seem[ed] to exclude the power of the States." This he judged a good thing, because "he was more & more convinced that the regulation of Commerce was in its nature indivisible and ought to be wholly under one authority." Despite Madison, the convention adopted the McHenry-Carroll amendment. Apparently the convention did not accept Madison's argument that Congress's commerce power ought to be exclusive.

That same day, Madison said he saw no reason not to allow the states to require Congress to call amendment conventions, except that procedural matters such as the quorum, etc., would have to be resolved. Such things, he said, could not be included in a constitution. Then the convention agreed without objection to the motion by Morris and Gerry to empower two-thirds of the states to call such a convention.

The day's proceedings closed with three delegates—Randolph, Mason, and Gerry—explaining why they likely would not sign the Constitution. First, summarizing the list of objections he had laid out a couple of days before, Randolph said that "the indefinite and dangerous power given by the Constitution to Congress" worried him. He proposed "that amendments to the plan might be offered by the State Conventions, which should be submitted to and finally decided on by another general Convention." Otherwise, he said, he could not sign the Constitution. This, he said, did not mean he would definitely oppose it in Virginia's ratification debate.

Mason endorsed Randolph's proposal for an amendment convention. This Constitution, he noted, "had been formed without the knowledge or idea of the people. A second Convention will know more of the sense of the people, and be able to provide a system more consonant to it. It was improper to say to the people, take this or nothing." As it was, he could support it neither in Virginia nor here, unless Randolph's proposal were adopted.

Gerry stated a series of structural objections, besides agreeing that Congress's powers were too broad and amorphous and that there needed to be a bill of rights. He, too, called for another convention.[108]

All eleven states voted no on Randolph's proposal. Immediately thereafter, all eleven voted for the draft Constitution. It being Saturday, the convention adjourned to Monday, when the engrossed (that is, written in calligraphy on vellum) document was to be signed.

When the convention reassembled on September 17, Benjamin Franklin stood ready to play his part. He had prepared a speech, he said, which his younger Pennsylvania colleague James Wilson would read for him.

"I confess," Wilson intoned, "that there are several parts of this constitution which I do not at present approve, but I am not sure I shall never approve them; For having lived long, I have experienced many instances of being obliged by better information on fuller consideration, to change opinions even on important subjects, which I once thought right, but found to be otherwise. It is therefore that the older I grow, the more apt I am to doubt my own judgment, and to pay more respect to the judgment of others. Most men indeed as well as most sects in Religion, think themselves in possession of all truth, and that whereever others differ from them it is so far error."

Later in the speech, at least according to the manuscript, Wilson read: "In these sentiments, Sir, I agree to this Constitution with all its faults, if they are such." Why? First, he said, any form of government "may be a blessing to the people if well administered," and "I doubt too whether any other Convention we can obtain may be able to make a better Constitution. For when you assemble a number of men to have the advantage of their joint wisdom, you inevitably assemble with those men, all their prejudices, their passions, their errors of opinion, their local interests, and their selfish views. From such an Assembly can a perfect production be expected? It therefore astonishes me, Sir, to find this system approaching so near to perfection as it does. . . . Thus I consent, Sir, to this Constitution because I expect no better, and because I am not sure, that it is not the best."

He would, Franklin said, keep his specific objections to himself. He had not informed the public of them during the convention, and he would not begin now. Good government depended in part upon people's opinion of the government, and so discussing the Constitution's shortcomings was apt to be self-defeating.

When Massachusetts's Gorham moved to change the requirement that "the number of Representatives shall not exceed one for every forty thousand" to read "thirty thousand," Washington rose in support. He had, the general said, sat mute through most of the convention because of his office, but he would speak on this issue regardless of propriety. Many members of the convention had been troubled by the smallness of the proposed House, and he agreed that this was one of the Constitution's faults. Although the time was late, he therefore supported this amendment. As Madison noted, "No opposition was made to the proposition of Mr. Gorham and it was agreed to unanimously."

With that, all the states agreed to the Constitution, and the delegates proceeded to the signing. Randolph, denying that his rejection of Franklin's advice represented a reflection on others' judgment, said that he expected the Constitution to fail of ratification by nine states, and that was why he would work for a second convention. He simply wanted to make the Constitution palatable. If he signed, this option would be foreclosed.

Gouverneur Morris, who had strenuously argued for population apportionment and against the pro-slavery provisions, said that he had objections to the Constitution. Still, once the Constitution was before the people, the only remaining question would be: "Shall there be a national Government or not?" It must be ratified, imperfect though it was, for "a general anarchy will be the alternative."

Hamilton pleaded with the dissatisfied to sign. "No man's ideas were more remote from the plan than his own were known to be," Madison had Hamilton saying, "but is it possible to deliberate between anarchy and Convulsion on one side, and the chance of good to be expected from the plan on the other[?]"

William Blount of North Carolina accepted Morris's argument that signing meant only that all the states agreed, not that each signatory agreed. On that basis alone, he would sign.

The high-backed chair from which Washington had presided was decorated with a carving of a sun. As the delegates other than Randolph, Mason, and Gerry signed the Constitution, Franklin "observed to a few members near him, that Painters had found it difficult to distinguish in their art a rising from a setting sun. I have, said he, often and often in the course of the

Session, and the vicissitudes of my hopes and fears as to its issue, looked at that behind the President without being able to tell whether it was rising or setting: But now at length I have the happiness to know that it is a rising and not a setting Sun."

That night the "Gentn. of Con. Dined together at the City Tavern."[109] George Washington's work was done. Ben Franklin's too. James Madison's, on the other hand, was just beginning.

Chapter 4

~~~~~~~~~~~~~~~~~~~

Ratifying the Constitution,
Part One: The Federalist,
1787–88

Madison left the convention uncertain what the outcome of the ratification process would be. He seems even to have been ambivalent about
the value of the convention's work. He wrote to Edmund Pendleton on September 20, 1787, three days after he signed the proposed constitution, giving
that eminence of the Old Dominion's politics a copy of the document.[1] Along
with it, Madison included a letter in which he said that he would not comment "either on the side of its merits or its faults. The best Judges of both will
be those who can combine with a knowledge of the collective & permanent
interest of America, a freedom from the bias resulting from a participation in
the work."

Clearly, Randolph and Mason's dissent weighed heavy on Madison's mind.
He told Pendleton that the "unanimity" of the convention should count as
much on the side of ratification as his two respected colleagues' refusal to endorse did against it. The convention had had great difficulty with the profound
problem of reconciling "stability & energy" in the federal government, on one
hand, with republicanism, on the other. In addition, he told his kinsman,
there had been great difficulty in drawing the line between federal and state

power. Even those who agreed on the goal had had a number of different ideas about how it could be reached.

The governor and the master of Gunston Hall, Randolph and Mason, found support for their position within the Virginia elite almost immediately. Congressman Richard Henry Lee had already drawn up a list of proposed amendments by September 23, and his colleague William Grayson was maneuvering within the Confederation Congress to ensure that that body would not endorse the Constitution before referring it to the states.[2] At the same time as he learned of these developments, Madison also heard that Lansing, Yates, and other disaffected New Yorkers were working assiduously to defeat the Philadelphia Convention's handiwork.

Madison had played a leading role in bringing about the Philadelphia Convention, and he played a leading role in securing ratification. His correspondence during the period when the draft Constitution was being debated in the several states put him in the center of the continental movement for the Constitution's adoption.

He also played formal roles in the process. First, he returned to the Confederation Congress in New York on September 24 to participate in that body's discussion of the matter on September 26–28.[3] Madison and his allies proposed that the Constitution be endorsed by the Congress and then transmitted to the states, while Richard Henry Lee proposed that amendments similar to some suggested by George Mason (who was not a congressman at the time) be added. Lee, Grayson, and the other opponents had their way: Congress simply sent it along. Federalists believed that they could spin Congress's plain referral to the states as an endorsement, and time would show that they were right.[4]

As soon as Congress sent the Constitution to the states, Madison wrote to his friend, Philadelphia Convention nonsigner Edmund Randolph, describing Congress's deliberations.[5] Here Madison initiated what was to be a months-long effort to persuade Randolph to support ratification. Preoccupied as he was with the constitutional reform efforts, Madison did not attend the Princeton commencement ceremony on September 26 in which he was awarded an honorary doctor of laws degree. Despite never having studied for the bar, Madison clearly deserved the award, and he actually received the diploma the following August.[6]

Randolph told Madison in a letter dated September 30, 1787, how he hoped to remedy the Constitution's defects: he wanted a second federal convention.[7] Randolph confided that he had suggested this idea to his fellow nonsigner, George Mason. Randolph envisioned the General Assembly sending the other states a call to a second convention along with Virginia's proposed amendments. In case nine other states should ratify the Constitution, Randolph said, Virginia could join the Union "under the exception of the points amended." Randolph left unclear what he meant by "under the exception of the points amended." As we will see, however, he believed that if a state's ratification was accompanied by a statement of the state's reservations or its particular understanding of what it was doing, that statement was authoritative.

Madison's friends soon began to infer that Randolph had had second thoughts and that he wished he had signed the draft Constitution in Philadelphia.[8] On the other hand, the same people saw that Mason intended to work to defeat ratification. Madison found the situation frustrating—so much so, in fact, that he received news of his younger brother William's interest in seeking public office only very tepidly.[9] Madison confided in Randolph through the winter and into the spring of 1787–1788 concerning the progress of the ratification process in the several states. He told the governor which states had strong Federalist majorities, which seemed to be leaning the other way, and what side notable Virginians seemed most likely to take. He also shared with him on numerous occasions snippets of conversation and significant newspaper articles on the matter.

Among those newspaper essays was one under the pen name "Brutus" laying out the claim that the Constitution erred in making the entire United States into one big republic in which the central government was to act directly on individuals.[10] Madison judged that this essayist argued "with considerable address & plausibility." Soon, Madison would level his biggest intellectual guns at Brutus's argument. It had to be refuted if the Constitution was to seem safe.

When the issue of ratification came before the Virginia House of Delegates, its proponents were in for a surprise. Patrick Henry confounded rumors that he would oppose it by all means when he said that not the General Assembly, but a convention of the people of Virginia must consider it.[11] Not for the last time, Henry proved himself more principled and less reckless than leading Federalists insinuated. The question whether to call a convention was to be debated in the House of Delegates beginning on October 25.

The day before, on October 24, 1787, Madison finally unburdened himself of the lengthy letter he had promised his friend Thomas Jefferson in the waning days of the Philadelphia Convention. Recall that then Madison had first described the Constitution the convention seemed likely soon to recommend to the states, and then told Jefferson that "the plan should it be adopted will neither effectually answer its national object nor prevent the local mischiefs which every where excite disgusts against the state governments. The grounds of this opinion will be the subject of a future letter."

Far from being the "father of the Constitution," then, Madison was an unhappy witness at its C-section birth. Perhaps he might be more appropriately called an attending nurse. He certainly did not think of it as his own offspring. In this remarkable private missive to his close friend and political ally, which ran to seventeen pages in the original handwritten manuscript,[12] Madison explained why.

Historians have speculated why it took Madison from September 17 to October 24 to send Jefferson a copy of the Constitution. Some infer that Madison guessed Jefferson would dislike the Philadelphia Convention's product. If Jefferson did oppose it, better not to have him do so too soon. Waiting longer would be pointless because Jefferson would have received a copy from someone else by the time he got one from Madison (as, in fact, he had).

In any event, Madison's letter recounted the entire convention for Jefferson. Its aims, he said, had been extremely difficult to reconcile—so difficult, Madison claimed, that only a participant could understand *how* difficult. Repeating a common theme of his post-Philadelphia correspondence, he told Jefferson that the "degree of concord" in the convention must have been "a miracle."[13]

Madison stressed to Jefferson that by far the most difficult problem the Philadelphia Convention had had to resolve had been the division of powers between the federal government and the states. He then explained at length why he so strenuously and persistently advocated the "negative," that is, the congressional veto over state laws.

In general, Madison held, the congressional veto would have had two good effects. First, it would have empowered Congress to restrain the states from infringing on the federal government's authority. (The problem of state infringement on federal authority, recall, had been one of the chief Federalist complaints about the structure of the federal system throughout the 1770s and 1780s.) Second, the congressional veto would have empowered Congress "to prevent instability and injustice in the legislation of the states."

Having laid out these general claims, Madison next rehearsed for Jefferson the fruits of Madison's research into the histories of ancient and modern confederacies. That research showed, Madison lectured Jefferson, that lack of power in the center had consistently led to dissolution or incapacity of confederacies. The same was true even of the American confederacy before and since the ratification of the Articles of Confederation in 1781. He laid out the arguments from the "Vices" in support of this claim. Madison lamented that while the new system would differ somewhat from the old, all three of the main institutions of the new federal government—House, Senate, and presidency—would be derived from the states and thus were likely to lose out to the states in a conflict over authority. This, Madison concluded, was why some such mechanism as the federal veto was necessary.

Madison had heard some people say that the federal judiciary would check state legislative overreaching. He found this dubious, as before a federal court could rule on behalf of an aggrieved individual in such a case, that individual would have to bear the expense of a lawsuit against his state. In addition, Madison considered it highly unlikely that a state that was willing to violate an individual's constitutional rights would defer to a federal judicial decree. All of this would lead to a federal-state confrontation, and that was one of the very contingencies the proposed Constitution was intended to prevent.

The federal veto was also necessary to vindicate individual rights against the states, he continued, and in fact this need had been even more significant in bringing the Philadelphia Convention about than had the desire to ensure that the federal government could enforce federal policies. The proposed constitution's bans on paper money and on impairment of the obligations of contracts were inadequate, as far as Madison was concerned. Their inclusion in the Constitution presumed the disposition to adopt such laws, and so the convention should have provided the federal government with a power to void laws that violated individual rights "in all cases whatsoever." (Here

Madison ironically echoed the infamous Declaratory Act of 1766, in which Parliament had claimed authority to legislate for the North American colonies "in all cases whatsoever.")

Why would making the federal government rather than the state governments the last line of defense of individual rights be a better way to protect those rights? Why, in other words, was the federal government more trustworthy when it came to rights? Here Madison conceded that his opinion was directly contrary to those of "theoretical writers," who agreed that a republican government could more likely meet its purposes in a small than in a large area. Madison thought that a republican government over a large area was more apt to defend individual rights.

Those who favor "Democracy"—direct popular participation in government—make the false assumption that the people have not only the same rights but also the same interests and the same sentiments. While that is nearly true "in the savage State," it is untrue "in all civilized Societies." In advanced societies, "distinctions are various and unavoidable." Where government protects different degrees of ability to acquire property, for example, people will unavoidably have different amounts of property. "There will be rich and poor; creditors and debtors; a landed interest, a monied interest, a mercantile interest, a manufacturing interest." All of these groups will be further subdivided in various ways. In addition, religious, political, and personal affiliations will divide the population as well. How should a majority be kept from oppressing a minority?

There are only three factors that will restrain one, he argued:

1. "A prudent regard to private or partial good, as essentially involved in the general and permanent good of the whole." This motive seldom affects individuals, and even less often restrains groups. Least apt of all to be restrained by this motive is a majority in control of the government. Such a majority will often follow the slogan that "whatever is politic is honest."

2. Respect for character. This motive force is far weaker even than regard to private or partial good, even in individuals. When it comes to groups, its influence declines as the group grows. If it is to be a break on public opinion, which is to say on majority opinion, it is a very

ineffective curb; after all, it is those whom it is supposed to restrain who say what it is.

3. Religion. Religion is an unreliable restraint on individuals. Public officials commonly take oaths, "the strongest of religious ties," and proceed to commit acts in public station that they would never consider committing in private life.

If in a republic a majority swayed by a common interest or passion can oppress a minority, what solution can be found "but that of giving such an extent to its sphere, that no common interest or passion will be likely to unite a majority of the whole number in an unjust pursuit." A larger society will be broken into a greater number of minorities, and the resulting difficulty in assembling a majority will make an added security for individual rights. "Divide et impera, the reprobated axiom of tyranny, is under certain qualifications, the only policy, by which a republic can be administered on just principles." However, if the country is too large, it may become impossible to unite the people against an oppressive government. Therefore, a happy medium must be found.

"The great desideratum in Government," Madison concluded his section of this missive to Jefferson on the proper extent of the society, is "so to modify the sovereignty as that it may be sufficiently neutral between different parts of the Society to controul one part from invading the rights of another, and at the same time sufficiently controuled itself, from setting up an interest adverse to that of the entire society." If the federal Constitution drafted in Philadelphia were ratified, Madison said, "The General Government would hold a pretty even balance between the parties of particular States, and be at the same time sufficiently restrained by its dependence on the community, from betraying its general interests."

Having explored this idea of the extended sphere, which he would soon develop at length and for public consumption in an immortal contribution to *The Federalist*, Madison returned to his general description of the Philadelphia Convention. Among other points he made to Jefferson under the category of balancing the interests of different sections was that in regard to the federal government's power over imports and exports, "S. Carolina & Georgia were inflexible on the point of the slaves."

Finally, Madison described the question of apportionment of Congress along lines acceptable to both large and small states as having caused "a greater alarm for the issue of the Convention than all the rest put together." In the end, he noted, the small states insisted on the equal vote in the Senate, and the resulting compromise left several large-state delegates extremely unhappy.

Madison told Jefferson that Randolph's refusal to sign sprang chiefly from two shortcomings in the draft Constitution: "the latitude of the general powers," and "the connection established between the President and the Senate." He said that Randolph was suggesting that the Constitution be sent to the states so that they could recommend amendments to a second convention. Randolph's opposition was "not inveterate"—unlike Mason's: "Col. Mason left Philada. in an exceeding ill humor indeed." While Randolph remained open to persuasion, Mason "returned to Virginia with a fixed disposition to prevent the adoption of the plan if possible."

Madison offered a fair account of reasons for Mason's anti-Federalism: the omission of a bill of rights was a "fatal objection," and he objected to the structure and powers of the Senate, the powers of the judiciary, the smallness of the House of Representatives, the ban on state ex post facto laws, "and most of all probably to the power of regulating trade, by a majority only of each House." Madison could not help leveling the kind of personal aspersion that would characterize much of his behavior during the ratification struggle, saying, "He has some other lesser objections. Being now under the necessity of justifying his refusal to sign, he will of course muster every possible one." Mason's home county and town had already made clear that they favored ratification, Madison confided, so that he was likely to be either excluded from the ratification convention or instructed how to vote in case he were elected to it. In general, Madison noted, Mason did not oppose vesting significant powers in the federal government. He favored the federal veto and the federal appointment of governors, but doubted that the public would accept such provisions, Madison confided. It was the particular form the proposed Constitution took that Mason disliked. In conclusion of this discussion, Madison told Jefferson what he knew of the prospects of ratification in each of the states, and he said that the project's success was likely. In Virginia, members of the newly convened General Assembly agreed that there must be a ratification convention, but the division in the ruling class made the outcome of Virginia's contest unclear.[14]

Madison thought that "the example of Virginia [would] have great weight." It would be "mortifying" if Virginia surrendered its customary position in the vanguard of the American states on this occasion—especially since nine states seemed certain to ratify, and so the rest would be left "either shifting for themselves, or coming in without any credit for it."[15]

Randolph finally informed Madison of the General Assembly's decision to call for a ratification convention in a letter written around October 29, 1787.[16] When a delegate moved that the Philadelphia Convention's instruction that each state call a ratification convention be heeded, Patrick Henry objected. The convention must be left latitude to propose amendments, he said, not charged merely with voting yea or nay. Ultimately, the House of Delegates and the Senate called for submitting the proposed Constitution "to a Convention of the people for their full and free investigation, discussion, and decision."

Madison's characteristic attitude concerning human fallibility shaped his understanding of the division within the Virginia political elite. As he put it:

> The diversity of opinions on so interesting a subject, among men of equal integrity & discernment, is at once a melancholy proof of the fallibility of the human judgment, and of the imperfect progress yet made in the science of Government. Nothing is more common here . . . than to see companies of intelligent people equally divided, and equally earnest, in maintaining on one side that the General Government will overwhelm the State Governments, and on the other that it will be a prey to their encroachments; on the one side that the structure of the Government is too firm and too strong, and on the other that it partakes too much of the weakness & instability of the Governments of the particular States. What is the proper conclusion from all this? That unanimity is not to be expected in any great political question: that the danger is probably exaggerated on each side, when an opposite danger is conceived on the opposite side—that if any Constitution is to be established by deliberation & choice, it must be examined with many allowances, and must be compared not with the theory, which each individual may frame in his own mind, but with the system which it is meant to take the place of, and with any other which there might be a probability of obtaining.[17]

In the midst of this dispute, Madison joined in his congressional delega-tion's November 3, 1787, letter to Governor Randolph.[18] In that report, Vir-ginia's congressmen lamented that Virginia was in arrears in meeting Congress's financial requisitions and that Congress had decided not to pursue further foreign loans "from motives of Honor and Justice." They had decided that it was dishonorable and unjust to take out loans that the states did not intend to service, and so "it remains . . . with the States to determine whether the Credit and administration of the Union, are to be Supported for another year, or abandoned." Among other bitter fruits of Congress's incapacity was Secretary for Foreign Affairs John Jay's rejection of Grayson's proposal that the United States of America should enter into a confederation with Euro-pean powers to stamp out the Barbary pirates. These North African pirates preyed on occidental shipping, stealing ships and cargoes and enslaving sail-ors, with near impunity, but the United States had insufficient funds to do anything about it. This matter would fester for many years.[19] In 1787, it was but one more factor prodding Madison to work for reinvigoration of the cen-tral government.

Soon thereafter, Madison communicated his willingness to serve as a del-egate to the Virginia Ratification Convention.[20] His younger brother, Am-brose Madison, inquired whether he would be willing, and Madison said that he had intended to refrain because of his sense that it was inappropriate for delegates to the Philadelphia Convention to participate in weighing the mer-its of their own handiwork. Yet Philadelphia Convention delegates seemed to be participating in the ratification dispute in every other state, so why should he forebear? His experience would enable him to set people straight con-cerning what he took to be some unfounded objections, and it would help him to explain why some of the undesirable features of the Constitution were adopted. In light of these considerations, Ambrose was authorized to make known that if Madison's friends continued to want him to serve, he was will-ing to accept election. As Madison, in Old Virginia fashion, put it, "I shall not decline the representation of the County if I should be honoured with its appointment."

At about this time, Madison was agreeing to join in writing *The Federal-ist.*[21] He essentially fell into it. The Virginian found himself in New York City because the Confederation Congress was supposed to meet. He had plenty of free time because the old Congress, in one final demonstration of the "imbecility" that drove Madison to despair, could not muster a quorum.

Under the pen name "Publius," Alexander Hamilton organized the series of newspaper editorials that posterity would know as *The Federalist* or, following a very popular edition published in the mid-twentieth century, *The Federalist Papers*. He had been even more discontented with the Constitution than Madison. Yet Hamilton saw the proposal as a marked improvement upon the Articles of Confederation. Ever the practical statesman, Hamilton did not let the perfect be the enemy of the good.[22]

In his home state of New York, however, the political stars seemed to be aligned against ratification. When Lansing and Yates abandoned the Philadelphia Convention, they said that they had not been sent to Philadelphia to replace the Confederation with a national government. Their explanation reflected the thinking of revolutionary New York's foremost political figure, Governor George Clinton.[23] Hamilton decided that with his state's political establishment arrayed against him, the best way to win ratification was by appealing directly to New York's electorate through the newspapers.

A lawyer actively engaged in a burgeoning practice would need help in this effort. Hamilton solicited New York's second most significant political figure, John Jay, who agreed to pitch in. He also asked the aristocratic Gouverneur Morris, who let his young friend know that scribbling for the hoi polloi did not strike him as a worthy activity. Morris suggested that Hamilton solicit the assistance of Rufus King, but Hamilton rejected that idea. Finally, Hamilton sought help from his political ally, former Confederation congressman William Duer.

In the end, however, Duer's contributions did not strike Hamilton as up to snuff. Conveniently, Madison, with whom Hamilton had cooperated in the effort to hold the Philadelphia Convention, happened to be in town. To what extent the two of them cooperated in sketching out the outline of what ultimately was a series of scores of essays is unclear, but it seems likely that Madison took a hand in the project from a very early stage. When Jay fell gravely ill, the task of writing the bulk of the eighty-five essays fell to Hamilton and Madison.[24]

From the perspective of history, it seems that more divided the authors of *The Federalist* than united them. Knowing of the party conflicts of the 1790s, historians tend to try to find distinctions between the future Republican chieftain and the soon-to-be founder of the Federalist Party even in the days of their closest cooperation. That is why the standard version says that Alexander Hamilton wrote Federalist No. 9 unassisted, and then James Madison wrote the all-time classic Federalist No. 10.

The most insightful essay in the entire series is that first number by Madison. Interestingly, "Hamilton's" No. 9 set the stage for it. The two articles are so closely related that it is hard to believe that Hamilton and Madison did not at least sketch out the two essays' outlines jointly.

In No. 9, Hamilton wrote that ratification of the proposed U.S. Constitution would promote "the peace and liberty of the States as a barrier against domestic faction and insurrection." The history of "the petty republics of Greece and Italy" provided a cautionary illustration of the problems that such societies were prone to. Then, in a turn of phrase that gives some support to the thesis that Madison helped in drafting at least some of the essays usually credited to Hamilton, Publius decries the "vices of government" that pocked the legacy of those bygone republics.[25]

Hamilton says that modern republicans enjoy a great advantage over people who lived in those Greek and Italian societies, because political science has progressed substantially. Among the discoveries that America's revolutionaries can deploy, he says, are the separation of powers, legislative checks and balances, good-behavior judicial tenure, and elections. With these discoveries comes the possibility that Americans can enjoy the benefits of republican government without the drawbacks from which earlier republics suffered.

Hamilton then says, "I shall venture, however novel it may appear to some, to add one more on a principle, which has been made an objection to the New Constitution, I mean the ENLARGEMENT of the ORBIT within which such systems are to revolve either in respect to the dimensions of a single State, or to the consolidation of several smaller States into one great confederacy." He then says that the subject of "enlargement of the orbit" will be considered in a later essay in the series.

Anti-Federalists had by the time Federalist No. 9 was first published, November 21, 1787, pointed to Montesquieu, the French jurist, political philosopher, and historian, in support of the idea that republican government was appropriate only to small states. Since the proposed federal constitution would establish republican government over a very extensive territory, then, it should be rejected. Hamilton answers that these Anti-Federalists are mistaken. While Montesquieu said that single states could not be enlarged too far without endangering republican government, Hamilton concedes, the Frenchman also "treats of a CONFEDERATE REPUBLIC as the expedient for extending the sphere of popular government." Through confederation of republican states, citizens of those states could enjoy both the foreign-policy advantages of monarchy and the domestic advantages of republicanism. Hamilton quotes extensively from Montesquieu on the tendency of this form of government "to repress domestic faction and insurrection" that likely would affect the constituent parts—in America, the states—if they were independent and separate.

It seems apparent that far from being successive essays in the series by Hamilton alone and by Madison alone, Federalist Nos. 9 and 10 were to some extent products of collaboration. Likely Hamilton was chief author of No. 9 and Madison chief author of No. 10, but No. 10 built on No. 9, which for its part used terminology that Madison had developed in his "Vices" before heading to Philadelphia for the Federal Convention.

Which is not to deny that No. 10 is an ingenious piece of work. Virtually every paragraph sparkles with insight. It is at once so learned and so penetrating that one can barely imagine such a thing appearing in an American newspaper today. It comes to nine pages in the authoritative edition of *The Federalist* (as the series was universally known down to 1961), and in those nine pages Madison develops an overwhelming response to the anti-Federalist insistence that ratification of the unamended Constitution would spell doom.[26]

"Among the numerous advantages promised by a well constructed Union," he begins, "none deserves to be more accurately developed than its tendency to break and control the violence of faction." Popular governments have always died of "instability, injustice, and confusion" as a result of their "propensity" to faction. A cure is much to be wished, Madison avers: "Complaints are every where heard from our most considerate and virtuous citizens, equally the friends of public and private faith, and of public and personal liberty; that our governments are too unstable; the public good is disregarded in the conflicts of rival parties; and that measures are too often decided, not according to the rules of justice, and the rights of the minor party; but by the superior force of an interested and over-bearing majority."

What is a faction? Madison says it is "a number of citizens, whether amounting to a majority or a minority of the whole, who are united and actuated by some common impulse of passion, or of interest, adverse to the rights of other citizens, or to the permanent and aggregate interests of the community." In other words, it is a selfish group seeking unpatriotically to have what it wants in violation of either individuals' or society's just expectations.

Madison here has in mind the problem, to which he pointed in his "Vices," of the unjust debtor-relief legislation adopted during and following the revolution. Individual creditors were being denied their property rights by stay laws and paper money laws, and debtor factions desiring such legislation had controlled every state's government at least part of the time.

One might resolve this problem by removing the cause of factions, Madison continues, but that would mean either eliminating liberty or giving every citizen the same opinions. The one was undesirable, the other impossible. Interestingly, Madison found the root of divergent opinions in the fallibility of human reason. Here as elsewhere, he assumed that there was one correct opinion, so that disagreement flowed from error.

Another source of divergent opinion was the diversity of faculties. Madison assumed that variety of human aptitudes would always mean unequal distribution of wealth, which would give men different interests. That too would lead them to have different opinions. Not only should government not try to prevent this, but "the protection of these faculties is the first object of Government."

"The latent causes of faction," he concludes, "are thus sown in the nature of man."

What to do about it, then? Men love their religious, political, and other opinions, speculative and practical, and they become attached to different leaders. These factors, too, divide them into factions. Where they have not had good grounds for division, "the most frivolous and fanciful distinctions have been sufficient to kindle their unfriendly passions, and excite their most violent conflicts. But the most common and durable source of factions, has been the various and unequal distribution of property." Certainly that seemed to Madison to have been the great problem giving rise to the 1780s' "crisis in republican government." The propertied and the un-propertied, the creditors and the debtors; the landed, manufacturing, mercantile, and monied; and many other such interests arise "of necessity" in advanced societies. Each seeks its own promotion, perhaps at the expense of society in general.

In fact, apportioning government's burdens and benefits among particular interests is "the principal task of modern legislation." It simply cannot be expected to be performed impartially. Where, for example, the question is the extent to which domestic manufactures will be favored to the detriment of foreign manufactures, the manufacturing and mercantile classes cannot be expected to have the same answer. Perhaps neither can be expected to decide the issue solely by reference to the public good. Unable to eliminate the causes of faction, then, Madison wants to control its effects.

"The republican principle" provides a remedy to minority faction: simply vote against the faction. A minority faction can "clog the administration" or "convulse the society," he hopefully proclaims, but not have its way under the Constitution. (Clearly, contrary to much twentieth-century commentary, Madison was not contemplating the advent of modern interest-group politics—for example, in the form of the New Deal coalition of unions, farmers, northern urban ethnics, and southern segregationists—which allows minority factions to join together and each have its way at the expense of the rest of society.)

The special problem of the day, "the great desideratum, by which alone this form of government can be rescued from the opprobrium under which it has so long labored," is "to secure the public good, and private rights, against the danger of [majority] faction." Only two ways to do so exist, he says: to prevent the advent of majority faction, and to prevent members of an incipient majority faction from organizing against the common good "by their number and local situation." The Constitution, he says, is a means of preventing potential members of majority factions from organizing such an unpatriotic coalition.

Madison begins his explanation of this claim by asserting that states consisting of "a small number of citizens, who assemble and administer the Government in person, can admit of no cure for the mischiefs of faction." There, a common interest will almost always animate the majority, which can easily recognize this state of affairs and exploit it. That is why such states have a deserved reputation for turbulence, oppression, and violent ends. One can imagine eighteenth-century readers of Publius, steeped in Plutarch, Thucydides, and Plato, nodding their heads in recollection of ancient Greek democracies' sad record.

"A Republic, by which I mean a Government in which the scheme of representation takes place, . . . promises the cure." Why? Because a republic differs from a democracy in two ways: the delegation of authority through elections, and "the greater number of citizens, and greater sphere of country," it encompasses. Elections put the power in the hands of a select group more able to identify the right path than the population at large "and whose patriotism and love of justice, will be least likely to sacrifice it to temporary or partial considerations."

Madison concedes that bad characters may insinuate themselves into the people's good graces and thus win election. He claims on two bases that this becomes less likely as the sphere of republican government is extended. First, he reasons, a more populous country will include a greater number of fit candidates for any particular office, and thus a greater chance of a suitable choice to each one. Second, as the number of votes necessary to election in a more populous country is greater than in one with a smaller population, it will be that much harder for candidates to win election on corrupt grounds rather than merit. It will be harder to buy more votes than to buy fewer.

Madison notes that expanding the number of citizens each official represents too far will "render the representative too little acquainted with all their local circumstances and lesser interests," just as reducing it too far may tend to make him too parochial. Fortunately, the Constitution finds the midpoint between the two, and then assigns only "the great and aggregate interests" to the federal, and "the local and particular, to the state legislatures."

Finally, Madison reaches the conclusion of his argument about the Constitution as an answer to the problem of faction: in a society with a smaller population, he says, there probably will be fewer parties, and thus more frequent occasions on which members of a budding majority realize that they could organize themselves into a party; in a smaller territory, it will be easier as a practical matter for them to organize themselves. On the other hand, "Extend the sphere, and you take in a greater variety of parties and interests; you make it less probable that a majority of the whole will have a common motive to invade the rights of other citizens; or if such a common motive exists, it will be more difficult for all who feel it to discover their own strength, and to act in unison with each other." Besides that, where more people must coordinate efforts in furtherance of malign motives, he hopefully observes, "communication is always checked by distrust."

So, just as a republic is better situated than a democracy to resist the tendency toward factious government, so a larger republic is better situated than a small one. In other words, the Union is better suited to the task of preventing factious government than are the individual states composing it. Congressmen will likely be more virtuous than state representatives, and they will likely be better informed than state legislators, The Union will include more potential parties than does any particular state. Obviously, the Union will be more extensive than any state. Even if a factious leader gains control of a state under the new constitution, Publius supposes, he will be very unlikely to assume such sway over the Union as a whole. Ratify the new Constitution, he says, and "a rage for paper money, for an abolition of debts, for an equal division of property, or for any other wicked project, will be less apt to pervade the whole body of the Union" than a single state. "In the extent and proper structure of the Union, therefore, we behold a Republican remedy for the diseases most incident to Republican Government."

Madison's great essay in political science and first foray as Publius arrives at a highly flattering evaluation of the potential benefits of the U.S. Constitution. It does not do what many have said it does, however: it does not promise that ratification will solve the problem of majority faction, or even that of minority faction. Throughout the essay, Madison suggests that various factors that have caused problems for other republics, including the American states, will be less threatening to the new Union. He says factious majorities will be less likely to arise under the new Constitution, that they will be less likely to recognize their majority status, and that they will be less likely to succeed in organizing themselves to take control of the federal than of a state government.

As we shall see, this is not the sole place in *The Federalist* in which Madison accepted that bad things that have befallen other societies might befall the American Union under the U.S. Constitution. There is in this life no perfect organization, no perfect moment, no philosopher's stone. His consistent message as Publius is that ratification will make it easier for an engaged citizenry to suffer the problems that societies suffer less often than in the absence of ratification; it will still suffer those problems, even under the Constitution, sometimes.

In writing No. 14, his second Publius essay, as in writing his last contribution to the series, No. 63, Madison frequently brandished his knowledge of the history of federal governments. He made frequent use of the extensive notes he had taken on this subject in the days before the Philadelphia Convention and of the new memoranda on various foreign constitutions he drafted sometime in the winter of 1787–1788.[27]

The limits of Publius's influence became clear at the beginning of Federalist No. 14, which was published eight days after No. 10.[28] There, he began by lamenting "the prevailing prejudice, with regard to the practicable sphere of republican administration." New Yorkers had not bought what Publius was selling. That is why, contrary to the usual presentation of No. 10 as a self-contained classic, Madison, in No. 14, proceeded to develop No. 10's argument further.

While esteemed writers (obviously meaning Montesquieu) had claimed that republics must be small, that objection properly only applies to democracies. That type of government cannot extend beyond the maximum distance from which the citizenry can travel to the capital for participation in government. A republic, on the other hand, can extend as far as the distance from which representatives can periodically travel to participate in government. The experience of the United States proves that they are not too large by that measure, as does that of several other eighteenth-century states with national assemblies.

The federal nature of the system also figures in Madison's defense at this point. He says that critics who have brought up Montesquieu's teaching about the proper scale of a republic have neglected the fact that the central government is to have only a few powers. If it were not to have limited jurisdiction, he says, the critics' point might be well founded. Besides, he says, the American network of roads and canals will be improved over time, and that will render communication between distant reaches and the federal capital easier. Too, he hastens to add, the most distant states will be contiguous with foreign territory, and thus more in need of the union's military benefits than other states.

Madison refers to opponents of ratification as "advocates for disunion." Here he plays a chord that had been struck by numerous Federalists before him and would continue to be struck through the ratification campaign. Madison was not alone in failing to offer the slightest evidence that his opponents wanted to break up the United States, but never mind. Within a decade, ironically, Madison would find himself ranged against advocates of stronger central authority, and then they would accuse him of disunionism in the same unjustified way as he had helped to pioneer.

Americans, Publius counsels, should shut their ears to the unhallowed call of disunion. Employing a series of turns of phrase that later would be echoed in Abraham Lincoln's second inaugural address, Madison denies that "the people of America, knit together as they are by so many chords of affection," have come to a parting of the ways. They are still one "family," still able to be "the mutual guardians of their mutual happiness," still able to be "fellow citizens of one great respectable and flourishing empire." "The kindred blood which flows in the veins of American citizens, the mingled blood which they have shed in defense of their sacred rights, consecrate their union, and excite horror at the idea of their becoming aliens, rivals, enemies." If the new federal Union will in some sense be a novelty, "the most alarming," "most wild," "most rash" of all novelties is the idea of disuniting in order to preserve Americans' rights and further their happiness.

Mere novelty should not earn the plan rejection. After all, Americans have persistently "paid a decent regard to the opinions of former times and other nations" while also respecting "their own good sense, the knowledge of their own situation, and the lessons of their own experience." The whole world will benefit from the innovations Americans have pioneered, among them that "they reared the fabrics of governments which have no model on the face of the globe." The least perfect result was the Confederation, Madison concludes, which they are in the process of revising.

Madison's next set of *Federalist* essays, Nos. 18–20, builds on Hamilton's arguments in Nos. 15–17 about the inadequacy of the Articles of Confederation. To a large degree, Madison here lays out what he learned in reviewing ancient history before he went to the Philadelphia Convention. In No. 18, he recounts the histories of several ancient Greek federations to demonstrate that they failed because of inadequate power in the center. In each case, the central government acted on the constituent states and depended on their cooperation in implementing its policies, so that in the end the members of the confederation were able to thwart the central government's aims.[29] The weakness of the central governments, Madison avers, predictably brought on internal squabbling in peacetime, which invariably invited "fresh calamities from abroad."

Any attentive reader of the series must have seen that Publius intended his lesson to have immediate topical resonance. The Federalists' argument was that because the Confederation Congress was so weak and had to rely on voluntary compliance by the states with Confederation policy, constant bickering and noncompliance had resulted. This, Federalists said, invited some powerful European state—France, Britain, Spain, or another—to intervene in American politics. Just as, say, Philip of Macedon had insinuated his quasi-Greek monarchy's influence into mainland Greek politics by dividing Greece's domestic councils, so might Americans one day awaken to see a Bourbon or a Guelph on an American throne. That doomsday scenario became even more likely, Madison added, if the unnamed Anti-Federalists' disunion schemes bore fruit, as he again adduced ancient illustrations to prove.

Madison points to the testimony of a contemporary expert, the Abbé Mably, that one of the ancient Greek confederations suffered fewer domestic disturbances than other democracies did because of the superintending role of its confederation government. Again, Madison clearly intends for his readers to see the applicability of the ancient lesson to the contest in which he is engaged: the American states could expect fewer Shays' Rebellion–like disturbances in the future if they ratified the proposed Constitution. If there were a rebellion in a state under the proposed Constitution, the story went, the federal government would have the power to intervene that it had lacked when Massachusetts was wracked by insurrection in 1786.[30]

Federalist No. 19, published on December 8, 1787, followed No. 18 by only one day.[31] Where the former had explored ancient Greek history in hopes of discovering lessons of general applicability concerning federal governments, this second entry in Madison's trilogy turned to modern examples. Along with the less important cases of Poland and Switzerland, Madison considered the history of Germany from the early part of the first millennium to the height of the Middle Ages. After its distribution among the sons of the emperor Charlemagne, Madison said, Germany gradually came to be dominated not by one emperor but by local magnates with near-total authority in their respective lands.

By 1787, Madison says, Germany had come to be essentially a federal entity, its emperor merely chief magistrate (with a legislative veto) of a realm with an independent parliament (Diet) and two supreme judicial tribunals. Here is Madison's summary of the state of the Holy Roman Empire: "The fundamental principle, on which it rests, that the empire is a community of sovereigns, that the Diet is a representation of sovereigns; and that the laws are addressed to sovereigns; render the empire a nerveless body; incapable of regulating its own members; insecure against external dangers; and agitated with unceasing fermentations in its own bowels." Strife among German states, whether involving outside powers or not, has been almost ceaseless for quite some time, and the empire's attempts to obtain men and money from member states for their common defense have been "altogether abortive." Germany has been miserable as a result, and one result is that Germany lives under a constitution to which foreign powers are parties.[32]

Meanwhile, Madison continued to receive extensive intelligence concerning the progress of the ratification battles in the separate states. To his friend Jefferson, still in France as the United States' minister to Versailles, he wrote on December 9, 1787, that most of Virginia's people and most of the General Assembly favored ratification, but it was hard to predict what effect the influence and exertions of Henry, Mason, and Randolph might have.[33] There were, he was informed, likely to be three parties in Virginia: those who favored ratification without amendments, those who insisted that amendments guarding individual and state rights precede ratification, and those (like Henry, he said) who insisted on such substantial amendments prior to ratification as would "strike at the essence of the System, and must lead to an adherence to the principle of the existing Confederation . . . or to a partition of the Union into several Confederacies." Joining Henry were former governor Benjamin Harrison and "a number of others." Whoever they might turn out to be, "Mr. Henry is the great adversary who will render the event precarious."

As he contemplated affairs in his home state, Madison grew a bit wistful. He confided to Jefferson: "It is worthy of remark that whilst in Virga. and some of the other States in the middle & Southern Districts of the Union, the men of intelligence, patriotism, property, and independent circumstances, are thus divided; all of this description, with a few exceptions, in the Eastern States, & most of the Middle States, are zealously attached to the proposed Constitution." He also found it worthy of note that "in Virginia where the mass of the people have been so much accustomed to be guided by their rulers on all new and intricate questions, they should on the present which certainly surpasses the judgment of the greater part of them, not only go before, but contrary to, their most popular leaders." The Federalist No. 10 remedy to the democratic upsurge since 1775 needed to be applied right away. Madison certainly had time to contemplate all possible events, for even by the time he joined his three fellow Virginia congressmen in writing to Governor Randolph about it on December 11, the Confederation Congress still had no quorum for business.[34]

In Federalist No. 20, which was published on December 11, Madison concluded his survey of the confederations of his day with an essay-length examination of the constitution of the United Netherlands.[35] In the late eighteenth century, the Netherlands remained a very significant power, one that had only recently been among the great powers.[36] It also had been among the chief friends of American independence[37] and was widely thought of as one of the few authentically free countries in Europe. For these reasons, the situation in the Netherlands was of particular potential interest to Madison's audience.

After describing the Netherlands' constitution and providing numerous examples of the chief executive's having ignored the supposed limitations on his authority, Madison draws the lesson that "a weak constitution must necessarily terminate in dissolution, for want of proper powers, or the usurpation of powers requisite for the public safety." This may result in tyranny, he says, as the executive assumes extraconstitutional powers and then refuses to surrender them. He hazards the lesson that tyranny has more often resulted from emergency assumption of necessary powers than from "the full exercise of the largest constitutional authorities." In other words, Madison oddly concludes that one need not worry about great grants of power to the federal government under the proposed Constitution, because large grants of power are safer than small.

In the Netherlands' case, although the constitution creates a weak government, there is always a felt need to remain united in the face of numerous hostile neighbors. Those neighbors' intrigues also nourish the Netherlands' constitutional vices. Netherlanders have four times tried to hold special assemblies to reform their constitution, but each attempt has failed. How fortunate is America to have had the Philadelphia Convention, Publius says.

In our day, one can scarcely imagine an editorial writer devoting three successive, very long columns (while a standard column length today is 800 words, Federalist Nos. 18 and 19 are both over 2,000 words long, while No. 20 is over 1,500 words long) to an examination of other countries' federal constitutions, past and present. Madison concedes that this is an unusual course for him to have taken as well. Yet here again he notes the applicability of historical lessons to current circumstances. "Experience is the oracle of truth," he says, "and where its responses, are unequivocal, they ought to be conclusive and sacred." The evidence he has adduced demonstrates that a government over governments (such as the Confederation) cannot work, that it will only lead to substitution of violence for law, of military coercion of communities for individual coercion through magistrates. What is needed, then, is a reform such as the proposed Constitution.

After publication of his fifth essay, which was the twentieth in the series,[38] Madison took a one-month break before beginning a series of twenty-two *Federalist* editorials. In the interim, his energies appear to have been devoted chiefly to coordination of the Federalist cause. At this point, he developed an argument in his private correspondence that he would make through the balance of the ratification campaign in Virginia: that Anti-Federalists did not agree among themselves about why the proposed constitution should be rejected. Since this was so, he insisted, they were not offering an alternative to ratification. Anyone who believed the Articles to be inadequate, then, must support ratification.[39]

The behavior of the General Assembly, and indeed of several other states' legislatures, in 1787–1788 strengthened Madison's conviction that a new federal constitution limiting states' power was needed. In Virginia, under Henry's and George Nicholas's influence, a law banning importation of several types of goods was adopted. In addition, the House of Delegates by a wide margin voted not to comply with the provisions of the Treaty of Paris respecting enforcement of British creditors' claims until the British withdrew their troops from the Midwest. And finally, the House repeatedly debated various forms of laws putting off enforcement of debts in Virginia courts, including a popular idea to allow repayment of loans in installments. Madison summarized these events to Jefferson by saying, "The Assembly [in Virginia] is engaged in several mad freaks."[40] In tandem with the states' declining willingness to meet their financial obligations to the Confederation, these acts constituted further grist for Madison's pro-ratification mill.

On December 20, Madison received Jefferson's lengthy missive evaluating the Philadelphia Convention's work.[41] From distant France, Jefferson offered up a very judicious appraisal. Diplomatically, he began with the elements of the Constitution that he most liked: the federal government's independence of the state legislatures, the division of the new government into three branches, the taxing power, the assignment of the foreign-policy powers to the president and Senate independently of the House, the respect accorded the principle of "no taxation without representation," the apportionment compromise between the small and the large states, congressional voting by persons instead of by state delegations, and the presidential veto all made his list.

Turning to what seems to have been his chief point in writing, Jefferson said, "I will now add what I do not like. First the omission of a bill of rights." Having read James Wilson's argument that no bill of rights was needed, because the new government would have only the powers that were delegated to it expressly, Jefferson explicitly rejected it. Not only did the proposed Constitution include clauses implying the contrary, but it also omitted the Articles' express recognition of that principle in Article II. "Let me add," he thundered, "that a bill of rights is what the people are entitled to against every government on earth, general or particular, & what no just government should refuse or rest on inference." His other objection was to the omission of term limits for any officials under the new government. That revolutionary principle, he insisted, had substantial support from the experience of history. The president, in particular, seemed likely to become an officer for life without a term limit. Not only that, but the selection of so significant a figure in so important a country would elicit foreign intervention in the American political process, so that eventually the great powers "will interfere with money & with arms."

Recognizing his friend's substantial investment both of time and of effort in the process of drafting the Constitution, Jefferson hedged a bit when it came to proposing a solution to the problems he saw. He did not know whether to prefer to adopt the charter and then amend it or to insist on a second federal convention before amending it. Besides, he conceded, Madison would have thought these matters all through, and so would have arrived at his own conclusion.

Jefferson did not realize it, but the two of them differed markedly on basic questions of political science. For Madison, the new Constitution held out the hope of strengthening the American federal center substantially. Contrast Jefferson: "I own I am not a friend to a very energetic government. It is always oppressive." Jefferson objected to the argument that Shays' Rebellion of 1786 required substantial augmentation of federal power in response. "The late rebellion in Massachusetts has given more alarm than I think it should have done. Calculate that one rebellion in 13 states in the course of 11 years, is but one for each state in a century & a half. No country should be so long without one. Nor will any degree of power in the hands of government prevent insurrections."

Despite his serious misgivings, he would join in supporting the new Constitution if it were ratified, Jefferson concluded. "After all, it is my principle that the will of the Majority should always prevail." With that in mind, he hoped that common people's education would be attended to, for that was the surest protection of liberty. For Jefferson, then, the people must be allowed to participate in government, which required their cultivation by public education; for Madison, the people's influence had been exposed as dangerous, and so their power must be hemmed in via adoption of the proposed Constitution, as explained in Federalist Nos. 10 and 14.

Meanwhile, Edmund Randolph grew increasingly uncomfortable in his position as leading Virginia nonsigner, and thus leading Anti-Federalist. At the Philadelphia Convention's end, remember, Randolph had called for a second convention. It seems that Henry and his fellows in the House of Delegates had this call in mind when they left open the possibility that the Old Dominion's ratification convention could call for such an assemblage.

Yet, as December 1787 drew to a close, Randolph confided to Madison that he feared his example might be miscast.[42] "It would give me no pleasure," he wrote, "to see my conduct in refusing to sign, sanctified, if it was to produce a hazard to the union; and if I know myself, I have no extreme ardor to acquire converts to my opinions." Still, he insisted on a second convention as the only hope for ratification in Virginia.

Reading Randolph's correspondence with Madison leaves the impression that the governor very much wanted to ingratiate himself and remain friends with Madison. Not only did Randolph repeatedly explain himself to Madison, but he warned the congressman that he needed to hurry back to Orange County from the Confederation capital of New York to ensure his election to the Virginia Ratification Convention.[43] Randolph also sent Madison a copy of the governor's letter to the Speaker of the House of Delegates explaining why he had not signed the Constitution.

In a letter of January 10, 1788, Madison finally answered it.[44] He thought that Randolph's idea of a second convention was not only unhelpful to the project of reforming the federal government, but perhaps absolutely harmful. Had Randolph joined Washington and Madison instead of Mason at Philadelphia, Madison said, the shift of his considerable political weight from the one scale to the other would have determined the outcome in Virginia. Besides that, he told Randolph, ratification's opponents disagreed about what to do instead of ratifying. Randolph's name, he counseled, had been used by Virginians favoring disunion and those favoring mere perpetuation of the Articles.

As elsewhere, Madison offered no evidence in support of his assertion that some Virginian Anti-Federalists contemplated disunion. Painting matters in the most lurid hues, Madison went on to say that Connecticut and Massachusetts Anti-Federalists included people hostile "in general to good government." They were even "suspected of wishing a reversal of the Revolution." Madison conceded that Randolph knew Patrick Henry better than he, but he hazarded that he thought Henry wanted an independent southern confederacy.

Why make all of these far-fetched claims? Madison's goal was to persuade Randolph to abandon the idea of a second federal convention. If there were a second convention, the advocates of strengthening the federal center would find themselves divided over what reforms to make. More importantly, a new convention, unlike the old, would include a substantial number of leading Anti-Federalists, all of them united in determination to gum up the works. Then, in an ingenious passage echoing his reasoning about elites in politics in Federalist Nos. 10 and 14, Madison said that there are many matters in politics about which the average person must concede his ignorance. He has to rely on those who are better informed to judge of them for him. If the proposed Constitution had been offered in the same words by an obscure individual instead of by an estimable convention, Madison guessed, "it would have commanded little attention from those who now admire its wisdom."

Madison had virtually no doubt that if Randolph, Henry, Ritt Lee, and the other few eminent Virginia Anti-Federalists had agreed that it should be ratified, the Philadelphia Convention's product would have been ratified quickly in Virginia. "A fortunate coincidence of leading opinions" in the ruling class was imperative to popular acceptance of so momentous a change as adoption of a new federal constitution, he concluded. To hold a second convention was a very powerful way to undercut confidence in the first, and thus to make the task still more difficult. In a final twist of the knife, Madison noted the recent news that North Carolina had postponed its vote on ratification, with the evident intention of following Virginia's lead. The governor's influence, in other words, could be decisive not only in Virginia, but in America generally.

The first entry in Madison's twenty-two-essay set, Federalist No. 37, was published on January 11, 1788, while the last, No. 58, appeared on February 20. These twenty-two essays all fell under the heading that Hamilton in No. 1 had called "the conformity of the proposed constitution to the true principles of republican government."[45] For our purposes, they can be organized into five groups: Nos. 37–40 on the Philadelphia Convention, Nos. 41–44 on the powers delegated to the federal government through the Constitution, Nos. 45–46 on federal-state relations (federalism), Nos. 47–51 on separation of powers within the federal government, and Nos. 52–58 on the House of Representatives.[46]

Nos. 37–40 generally take the position, first stated at the opening of Federalist No. 37, that the Philadelphia Convention gave the proposed federal government the least power that could possibly remedy the current problems in federal politics.[47] Madison then appeals to his readers as people who are open-minded on the question of ratification. He says that neither those who predetermined to support nor those who predetermined to oppose what the Philadelphia Convention had done have taken the right approach. Instead, given the consequences that will attend upon their decision, people should approach the question with "moderation" and let the evidence lead them where it may. (Here Madison takes an approach characteristic of the political culture of his home state, Virginia. We shall see Virginians' insistence on open-mindedness in public officials have a significant effect on the makeup of their 1788 Richmond Ratification Convention.)

Readers who approach the subject with the proper attitude, Publius says in No. 37, will realize that "a faultless plan was not to be expected." Yes, the Philadelphia Convention produced an imperfect product, but so would any particular, fallible person. As he had proven in essays 18–20, Madison said, other confederations provided more examples of what not to do than of what to do. Since it did not have a good model to follow, then, the Philadelphia Convention ought to be granted a certain leeway for error.

The first great problem that the Convention had to deal with was that of providing the central government adequate insulation and power ("stability and energy") while paying "the inviolable attention due to liberty, and to the Republican form." Government must have the energy to do its business and the stability that, according to Madison, experience had shown the state governments to lack.

These are very difficult aims to reconcile. "The genius of Republican liberty" seems to require that power be based on election, that terms be short, and that power be shared among numerous officials; stability requires that terms be long; energy requires that power be held "by a single hand." The matter of federalism, of the apportionment of powers between the federal government and the states, is no easier. No one has yet resolved the question which powers belong to which of the executive, legislative, and judicial branches, either. All of these matters puzzle "the greatest adepts in political science." Add to this the fact that language itself is an imperfect medium of communication, and the extent of the difficulty becomes even greater: "The use of words is to express ideas. Perspicuity therefore requires not only that the ideas should be distinctly formed, but that they should be expressed by words distinctly and exclusively apportioned to them. But no language is so copious as to supply words and phrases for every complex idea, or so correct as not to include many equivocally denoting different ideas." The absence of precise terms through which to convey even precise ideas will subject communication of those ideas to "unavoidable inaccuracy" to a greater or lesser degree "according to the complexity and novelty of the subjects defined." And, as everyone in Protestant America knew in January 1788, "When the Almighty himself condescends to address mankind in their own language, his meaning, luminous as it must be, is rendered dim and doubtful, by the cloudy medium through which it is communicated."

The ideas, minds, and words of men are imperfect for the task the Philadelphia Convention faced. "Any one of these must produce a certain degree of obscurity. The Convention, in delineating the boundary between the Federal and State jurisdictions, must have experienced the full effect of them all." In addition to the difficulties intruding to prevent the Philadelphia Convention delegates' meeting of the minds from being reflected accurately in the text of the Constitution, Madison notes, there were several factors at work in that assemblage to prevent the men from different states from ever agreeing at all. For example, when it came to allocation of power, the large states predictably would claim influence proportionate to their wealth and population, while the small ones would hold on tenaciously to the equal vote each state had under the Articles of Confederation. This disagreement likely would necessitate a compromise of some sort. Then, once a compromise had been reached, each side would enter the lists again, this time on behalf of heightened powers for those institutions in which the compromise had left them with the greatest share of influence. Madison admits that the Constitution bears out this supposition, and he concedes that here is one way in which the theoretically preferable had yielded to the practically necessary. Madison goes on to say that although he had spelled out in No. 10 some of the ways in which a multiplicity of interests in society might benefit the citizens of a large republic living under a common constitution, yet one could easily imagine that such heterogeneity had made it more difficult to draft the Constitution in the first place.

Still, despite the variety of interests represented in the Philadelphia Convention, Madison says in concluding No. 37, that august body had experienced a surprising degree of unanimity. (Here we have a clear example of Publius as propagandist: not only had one state, Rhode Island, not sent a delegation in the first place, but the majority of the New York delegation left the Convention early, which left that state without a vote through most of the proceedings. In the end, although fifty-five delegates attended the Convention at some point, only forty-two remained to the end, and of those, only thirty-nine signed. Seventy-one percent of the whole body of delegates from twelve of the thirteen states does not strike one as a surprising degree of unanimity—particularly in light of the fact that all of the delegates had gone to Philadelphia with the common purpose of somehow strengthening the central government.) For Publius, this "unanimity" demonstrated the intervention of "that Almighty hand which has been so frequently and signally extended to our relief in the critical stages of the revolution." Contrast the outcome, he says, to the Netherlands' failure on four recent occasions (as described in his Federalist No. 20) to revise their constitution through extraordinary assemblies. Either the Philadelphia Convention was surprisingly free of party animosity, or the delegates sacrificed personal and party interests to the general good.

In No. 38, Madison asks his readers to consider a scenario: a gravely ill patient consults the finest physicians. They proffer a recommendation, telling him that not only will it lead to recovery, but it will leave him better off than before. No sooner have they given him their prescription, however, than a second group of people tell him that he should ignore the physicians. They say that they disagree themselves about what he should do instead of adopting the physicians' joint recommendation, but they certainly oppose the joint recommendation. This, Madison says, is the situation American citizens face.

And here we have one of the most powerful points the Federalists made throughout the ratification campaign of 1787–1790. Perhaps their proposal was imperfect, they repeatedly said, but virtually everyone agreed that something must be done, and no one had offered a better proposal. Therefore, the Constitution should be ratified. Madison goes on to offer a long list of the various objections Anti-Federalists have made: that the proposed government will be too strong, that it will be too weak, that it will operate on individuals instead of states as societies, that state equality in the Senate is unjust, that population apportionment of the House is dangerous, that it lacks a bill of rights to protect individuals' traditional rights, that it should have a bill of rights but that the rights that must be protected are those of states as communities, etc. Some Anti-Federalist somewhere was criticizing virtually every significant provision of the proposed constitution from virtually every conceivable angle, and so the Anti-Federalists were offering no coherent critique at all.

How, then, can Anti-Federalists so vehemently oppose ratification? Why, because they never call to mind the shortcomings of the Articles of Confederation, Publius posits. From his point of view, the Articles are so defective that they demand immediate replacement; it seems to him utterly irresponsible simply to oppose the Philadelphia Convention's proposal without offering any alternative. For Madison, "It is not necessary that the [Constitution] should be perfect; it is sufficient that the [Articles of Confederation are] more imperfect."

Besides that, Madison continues, many of the Constitution's supposed imperfections are shared by the Articles of Confederation: Congress under the proposed system will have an unlimited taxing power, but under the Articles it has an unlimited power to requisition, which is binding on the states; Congress under either system can borrow abroad as much as it wants; the separation of powers under the proposed Constitution is imperfect, but under the Articles there is only one unicameral branch of the federal government, and so no separation at all; the proposed Constitution has no bill of rights, but neither do the Articles of Confederation; the president and the Senate are to have power to make treaties that will be the supreme law of the land, but the Confederation Congress can make treaties that have been recognized by Congress and most of the states to have that same status; the proposed Constitution permits importation of slaves for at least twenty more years, but the Articles permit it indefinitely.

Madison knew, in fact had long lamented, that many of the powers of the Confederation Congress were practical nullities, for the states had to cooperate in their exercise. His answer to this objection to his charges against the Articles was that it was imbecilic to proclaim the necessity to lodge certain powers in the central government, then omit to give the central government power actually to exercise them. As he had noted most forcefully in his "Vices," the Articles of Confederation did precisely that. The main virtue of the proposed Constitution was that it would not.

If Congress is not given adequate power to perform its essential tasks, as through the Constitution, Madison concludes No. 38, it must usurp them.

So, for example, the Confederation Congress has obtained extensive lands in what we now call the Midwest, it has begun to carve new states from them, it has erected temporary governments there, it has selected officials to serve in those governments, and it has established conditions on which the new states will be allowed to join the Union—all without any constitutional authority! All of this has been done by a single body of men who can borrow, spend, raise armies, and fund those armies for an indefinite period of time! Anyone who worries about the prospect of military dictatorship in the United States should look upon this situation and conclude that the Constitution is the way to substitute constitutional for unconstitutional government.

Madison heard from a member of the Virginia General Assembly that Publius's "greatness is acknowledged generally."[48] The same politician asked that Madison ensure that the remaining Publius essays be made available to Virginians and relayed the news that "the anti-constitutional Fever which raged here some time ago begins to abate." In that, at least, he was well wide of the mark.

Madison begins No. 39 by asking what a republic is. After denying that the Dutch, Venetian, or English governments of his day should be called republican, although they commonly were, he offers his own definition: "a government which derives all its powers directly or indirectly from the great body of the people; and is administered by persons holding their offices during pleasure, for a limited period, or during good behaviour. It is *essential* to such a government, that it be derived from the great body of the society, not from an inconsiderable proportion, or a favored class of it." In short, then, officials may be elected or appointed, but they must be ultimately chosen by the people; they can have whatever tenure, but it cannot be hereditary. Thus, the Venetian republic, which was governed by a small aristocracy, was not really a republic, nor was the English government republican, as its monarch and nobles all inherited offices that they held for life. The Netherlands' government, in which no official derived his authority from the people, also did not meet Madison's specifications, although every single one of the American state governments did.[49]

Every branch of the new government to be created under the proposed constitution, Madison observes, conforms to his definition of republican government. Not only that, but it prohibits granting of titles of nobility, state or federal, and guarantees republican government to every state for good measure.

Madison next turns to Anti-Federalists' objection that besides perpetuating republican government, the Philadelphia Convention should have defended federal government. Anti-Federalists had protested even during the Philadelphia Convention that the federal relationship among the states was in the process of being supplanted by a national government that, in Madison's terms, "regards the union as a *consolidation* of the States. And it is asked by what authority this bold and radical innovation was undertaken."

Madison here met head-on the chief objections Anti-Federalists had raised to the handiwork of the Philadelphia Convention. Since the states had sent delegates to Philadelphia for the purpose of proposing amendments to the Articles of Confederation, where had the Convention found authority to speak as "We, the People" and why had it felt free to recommend a completely new government, a highly centralized government, instead?

Madison laid out what today is a famous argument concerning the muddled nature of the government established through ratification of the Constitution. In some senses it was national, in others it was federal, in general it was without precedent, and overall it was necessary that it be at least what it was. So, in ratifying it, the Americans were to act as peoples of their respective states; no state's act was to bind any other state. If it had been a national government, the ratification of a majority of the people or a majority of the states would have bound the rest, but that was not to be the case under the proposed constitution. In this sense, then, it was to be a federal, not a national, government.

When it came to selecting officials under the new government, the proposed constitution was to be partly national and partly federal, Madison continued. Thus, he said, the House was to be apportioned nationally, as among one American people, which he called a national feature. (He omitted here that the representatives were to be allocated among the states and that each was to represent a district wholly within one state, which makes apportionment of the House a federal feature, not a national one.) The Senate, on the other hand, would be apportioned equally by state, which was a federal feature. Electoral College apportionment would see each state allocated a number of electors equal to its number of representatives plus its number of senators, which he calls a partly national, partly federal apportionment. "The eventual election," however, was to be made by the House, with each state allocated one vote, which was a federal feature. In most of these senses, then, the government was to be a federal government.

According to Madison, a federal government differs from a national government in that while the former operates on the states composing the federation, the latter operates on the citizens directly. Except in the federal judiciary's power to decide legal disputes among states, this government will be national, not federal. Yet, while a national legislature has a general legislative power, this government will have only a few enumerated powers, which is a classic attribute of a federal legislature. Naïvely or disingenuously (and Madison was seldom naïve), he claims that although the federal government's Supreme Court will decide questions of the boundary between state and federal authority, it will do so impartially. (What might Madison have thought of the Supreme Court's record of never ruling a federal statute unconstitutional from 1937 to 1995?) He says that there had to be some such tribunal, and that it obviously had to be part of the federal government and not a state institution.

Finally, in regard to amendment, the Constitution under consideration is neither national nor federal, but something in between: if it were national, amendment would be through a majority of states or a majority of the population. If it were federal, amendment would require the assent of every state to be bound by it. Instead, states ratify, but by supermajority rather than unanimously. Thus, Madison concludes, the proposed Constitution is a bit national and a bit federal.

Federalist No. 40 answers the even thornier question whether the convention was authorized to propose a new constitution. Madison has no choice but to admit that Congress's call to the states was for a convention to recommend amendments to the Articles of Confederation. He says, however, that the Confederation Congress also stated that an adequate national government ought to be formed. Since the two goals proved irreconcilable, he concludes, the Philadelphia Convention chose to meet the more important one at the expense of the less: it opted to propose an adequate government rather than merely proposing amendments to the Articles.

Or maybe not. Madison goes on to claim that one might opt to call the Constitution an extensive revision of the Articles. If one did, he could conclude that the convention had followed all of its instructions scrupulously. Even if he did not, "the great principles of the Constitution proposed by the Convention, may be considered less as absolutely new, than as the expansion of principles which are found in the articles of Confederation."

Warming to his subject, Madison claimed that the convention had been unanimous in pursuit of its goal of seeking a solution to the problems then confronting the country. Those, he said, had been produced by the Articles' inadequacy. Both the fact that the convention had been unanimous and the assertion that the Articles were to blame for America's besetting political problems were stock Federalist positions; both were also untrue—unless thirty-nine signers out of fifty-five delegates can be called "unanimity" and the states' omission to pay outstanding requisitions for more money than existed in the United States could be blamed on the form of their government.[50] Here Madison, man of the Enlightenment that he was, displayed an Enlightenment faith in the capacity of governmental reform to resolve a myriad of social and political problems (such as a third-rate power's difficulty in funding a revolutionary war against the leading military power in the world) that do not appear at this remove to be even slightly surprising.

Madison hints that people who indulge "ill-timed scruples" concerning the Philadelphia Convention's work are like opponents of the methods used to create republican state constitutions in days gone by: opponents not only of the means, but of the end of stronger federal union. Besides, Madison says, the sovereign people were to have the final word on any proposal the convention might make, so this criticism is ill placed. If the delegates to the convention deserved criticism for what they had done, he concludes, what is one to say of the Congress and the state legislatures that called for a convention to meet in Philadelphia without any constitutional authority to do so whatsoever? Even if no one involved in creating the proposed Constitution had authority to do what he did, Publius says, that does not mean that it ought to be rejected: "The prudent enquiry in all cases, ought surely to be not so much *from whom* the advice comes, as whether the advice be *good*."

In Federalist No. 41, Madison addresses those who have claimed that the Constitution gives the central government too much power.[51] He begins with the military powers, asking whether a power to declare war be not necessary. Of course it is. Then he takes up the Anti-Federalists' contention that an unlimited power to raise armies is dangerous. First, he avers that the nation's power to raise armies should only be limited after the corresponding power of all potential adversaries is similarly limited. He then says, hopefully, that the executive's responsibility to the people will restrain him from using the military against the people.

Publius argues that adopting the Constitution seems to be a safeguard against the kind of militarism that has beset Europe since France's Charles VII first decided to maintain a standing army in peacetime. Distant as they are from any likely aggressor, American states need not fear military aggression from any outside source; as long as they are united, they need not fear it from each other either. This is the chief reason that ongoing union is so desirable.

At the end of No. 41, Madison considers criticisms leveled by Anti-Federalists against the General Welfare Clause. Article I, Section 8 of the Constitution says, in relevant part, that Congress will have power "to lay and collect taxes, duties, imposts and excises, to pay the debts and provide for the common defense and general welfare of the United States." He rightly notes that they have claimed that this clause empowers Congress to apply tax money to any cause it argues will advance the "general welfare." Not to worry, Publius advises: "What colour can the objection have, when a specification of the objects alluded to by these general terms, immediately follows; and is not even separated by a longer pause than a semicolon?" A reasonable rule of interpretation, he goes on, will give effect to every portion of the instrument, and the claim that the General Welfare Clause empowers Congress to do whatever it wants effectively eliminates the rest of the same section. What Publius is saying is that the Philadelphia Convention had identified the powers Congress might exercise in pursuit of the general welfare, and they were the ones listed in article I, section 8. "For what purpose could the enumeration of particular powers be inserted," he asks, "if these and all others were meant to be included in the preceding general power? Nothing is more natural or common than first to use a general phrase, and then to explain and qualify it by a recital of particulars." To read the section in the critics' way, he says, "is an absurdity." Since the Articles of Confederation include analogous "general welfare" language, and since the reason for convening delegates of twelve states at Philadelphia was to make up for a shortage of congressional power, even experience proves that the General

Welfare Clause will not be interpreted in this way. The Anti-Federalists would not argue for unlimited power in the Confederation Congress in the same way as they are now criticizing the proposed Constitution, and so their error condemns itself.

Federalist Nos. 42 and 43 continue the examination of each power granted to the federal government by the proposed Constitution, with very little insight beyond that it seemed necessary for the central government to be empowered to negotiate with the Indian tribes, regulate weights and measures, etc.[52] Only the Guarantee Clause comes in for much discussion. In connection with that provision, which says that the federal government guarantees a republican form of government to each state, Madison says that it of course makes sense that the confederated states guarantee the regularity of republican government in each state, just as the states guarantee it in each county. It is in the interest of the other states, not that each state have a particular republican form, but that each state be republican, he says.

Publius's description of the regular power of constitutional amendment provided by Article V is worthy of some note. He says that the Article V provisions find a midpoint between excessive ease of amendment, which would make the proposed charter "too mutable," and a situation (like that in his home state of Virginia) in which even obvious flaws could not be remedied. Both state and federal initiation of the amendment process are possible, which means that overreaching on either side can be corrected on the other, he suggests. In reading Madison's exegesis of Article V, one is struck by the extreme infrequency with which the congressionally initiated process has been used, and by the fact that the state-initiated process has never been. Of course, Madison did not foresee—no one foresaw—that in time, amendment via Supreme Court decision would become a workaday part of the American constitutional system.

Also of particular note, especially in light of subsequent events, is No. 43's final paragraph. There, Publius considers the relationship between the states that join the union under the proposed Constitution and those that do not. Some American thinkers, such as President Abraham Lincoln, have said that the Union of American states originated long before implementation of the Constitution, that the individual states were never separate sovereign entities, and that one of the ramifications of these facts was that no state could withdraw from the federal Union. Publius, on the other hand, says that there will be no political relationship between the United States under the proposed Constitution and any nonratifying states. As he puts it, "no political relation can subsist between the assenting and dissenting states," but they still will have "moral relations"—one infers after the manner of Austria, Prussia, and German cantons in Switzerland, for example—as reunion is sought.

In Federalist No. 44, Madison addresses criticisms of the Necessary and Proper Clause.[53] Falling immediately after the list of congressional powers in Article I, Section 8, that clause says that Congress shall have power "to make all laws which shall be necessary and proper for carrying into execution the foregoing powers, and all other powers vested by this Constitution in the government of the United States." After noting that this clause had been the target of hot invective from the Anti-Federalists, Publius holds that no one could seriously deny that there had to be some such provision, and so the critics must have meant to decry the form of this clause. He says that there were four other ways that the convention might have addressed this issue: (1) copying article 2 of the Articles of Confederation by denying Congress any power not "expressly" delegated; (2) listing all the powers included in the phrase "necessary and proper"; (3) specifying the powers Congress was denied; and (4) maintaining complete silence on the issue, and thus leaving it "to construction and inference."

If they had copied Article II of the Articles of Confederation, the Philadelphia Convention's delegates would have laid the groundwork for contests within the federal Congress echoing those in the Confederation Congress on the question of the limits of Congress's "express" powers. In the end, this debate would have either denied Congress necessary powers or torn down the limitation on congressional power altogether. The history of the Articles, Publius claims, was one of constant resort to inferences; since the new Congress was to have more power than the old, members of Congress under the new Constitution would soon face a choice between betraying the public trust by doing nothing, on one hand, and seizing powers "indispensably necessary and proper," but not expressly granted, on the other.

Madison concedes that the federal Congress may well attempt to exercise more power under the cover of the Necessary and Proper Clause than that portion of the proposed Constitution was intended to delegate. The solution then would be the same as if the state government grabbed at unconstitutional authority, with the added check that state governments will be ever watchful against federal overreaching, while there is no lower-level legislature to keep an eye on the state government.

These are the highlights of Madison's examination of each of the powers of the proposed federal government and his inquiry into their extent. He concludes No. 44, and this section of the overall work, by saying, "no part of the power [delegated by the proposed Constitution to the federal government] is unnecessary or improper for accomplishing the necessary objects of the Union." For him, then, whether the proposed constitution gives the federal government the right amount of power comes down to this: "whether the Union itself shall be preserved."

As we said, Federalist Nos. 45 and 46 take up the relationship between the state and federal governments under the proposed federal constitution.[54] Publius says that opponents have erred in their focus on how ratification would affect the state governments. According to him, however, if the Union is essential to the defense of America against foreign aggression, to the prevention of interstate strife—and even war, to the stifling of faction (as defined in No. 10), and to the militarization of America, then its ramifications for the state governments must be a "preposterous" objection. The revolution, Madison says, was not fought to vindicate the states' claim to sovereignty, but to ensure Americans' peace, liberty, and safety. Perhaps the old saying is that in Europe the people were made for kings, he intones, but in America the states exist for the people, not the other way around. The people's happiness takes priority over the state governments' institutional integrity.

In fact, Publius holds that the states are far more apt to overwhelm the federal government than the federal government "to prove fatal to the State Governments." The state governments will have the advantage over the federal government in that the latter will depend on the former for its very existence, state officials will be more personally influential with the people than federal, the state governments will have more powers of local effect vested in them than will the federal, and the people are more likely to support the state governments against the federal.

Without the states' cooperation, no president can be elected. The senators will be chosen by the state legislators directly. The federal representatives will be elected by the people under the influence of the same men as make up the state legislatures. Thus, both houses of Congress and the president will have incentives to follow, rather than usurp from, the state governments. On the other hand, Publius says, the state governments will operate nearly independently of federal influence.

Besides that, state employees will greatly outnumber federal, which will heighten the state governments' relative influence. So, too, the state officials will be far more numerous than their federal counterparts, which means that their influence upon the people will be much more pervasive.

Turning from these sociological observations to hard, cold political reality, Publius toward the end of No. 45 offers one of the most famous assertions in the entire series: "The powers delegated by the proposed Constitution to the Federal Government, are few and defined. Those which are to remain in the State Governments are numerous and indefinite." The federal powers, he says, will relate mostly to foreign affairs, while state power will affect people in their everyday lives. The more efficient the federal government's military power, the less common will be the times when that power's exercise draws the people more powerfully under the federal government's sway. In this regard, furthermore, the proposed federal charter does not so much give the federal government new powers as invigorate the powers the Confederation Congress already had.

Federalist No. 46 picked up where the previous letter had left off. Madison criticizes the proposed Constitution's opponents, the Anti-Federalists, once again for apparently making the assumption that the federal and state governments would be free to usurp each other's power without any concerns about a superior. This was an error, Madison insisted, because the people would attend to their creatures' behavior and stand ready to check violations of the constitutional division of powers between the state and federal governments. The people would be more attached to the state governments than to that created by the proposed Constitution because they would be more expectant of employment under the state governments, they would be in closer contact with the state governments, they would be more apt to have friends or relatives among state employees, and the state governments would be the ones whose policies affected common citizens' daily lives. The experience of the Confederation years, during which the people demonstrated limited concern with the general government's incapacity for performing its duties and politicians generally sided with the states against the Confederation, bore this out.

Even in case superior administration made the people admire the federal government more, there was no reason to worry about its achieving a preponderance in the federal system, Publius hazarded a prognostication, because "it is only within a certain sphere, that the federal power can, in the nature of things, be advantageously administered." Even then, members of Congress itself will tend to favor the states over the center, while officials of state governments will rarely favor the federal government over the states. Even under the proposed system, the national interest likely will often be sacrificed to local interests; seldom will the opposite tendency guide members of Congress. States will have powerful means at hand for opposing even meritorious policies of the federal government, and so they can thwart their implementation. In case the federal government undertook to make "ambitious encroachments . . . on the authority of the State Governments," they would excite "general alarm." Soon, the states would coordinate resistance. Ultimately, if necessary, the revolution would repeat itself.

That leaves only the possibility of the federal government abusing its military powers for the purpose of usurpation. If it did try to establish military dictatorship, however, it would find that its professional army paled into insignificance in the face of the mighty militia forces of the thirteen separate states: thirty thousand men against five hundred thousand. In meeting such resistance, the aspiring tyrants would have to deal with the "advantage of being armed, which the Americans possess over the people of almost every other nation." If the federal government is made sufficiently dependant on the people by the proposed Constitution, it will not adopt policies aimed at subjecting them to tyranny; if it is not, then they will be able to use their state governments to defeat its usurpations.

Federalist No. 47 takes up the theme of the separation of powers, which reaches its climax in the classic essay No. 51.[55] Madison begins No. 47 by saying that the accumulation of all executive, legislative, and judicial power in the same person or people would be tyranny and conceding that if the proposed Constitution either established such a system or established a system that tended toward such an accumulation, "no further arguments would be necessary to inspire a universal reprobation of the system." He spends the rest of this five-essay set proving that the charge that the Constitution would tend in that direction is misplaced.

Madison notes that Montesquieu is the great authority on the usefulness of the principle of the separation of powers. Since England's government was the great Frenchman's idea of a model government, and since there was not in the eighteenth century a perfect separation of powers in that system, Montesquieu must not have insisted on such an abstract perfection either. Thus, where Anti-Federalists have objected that the Senate will share in some executive powers and the legislative branch will have some judicial powers, while the president will have some legislative and some judicial powers, Montesquieu's authority cannot properly be invoked to say that this is a shortcoming. Madison says that Montesquieu did not oppose giving the three departments "*controul* over the acts of each other," but instead he opposed giving "the *whole* power of one department" to the same person or people as exercised the whole power of another department. Madison quotes Montesquieu to prove that the Virginian's interpretation is valid, and he shows that the boundaries among the branches are just as permeable in the state constitutions established during the revolution as they will be under the proposed federal constitution.

In No. 48, Madison turns from proving that a perfect separation of powers was not what Montesquieu called for to his own belief that "unless these departments be so far connected and blended, as to give to each a constitutional control over the others, the degree of separation which the maxim requires as essential to a free government, can never in practice, be duly maintained." In other words, his point is that not only did Montesquieu not say what some Anti-Federalist critics of the unamended Constitution had him saying, but their point is 180 degrees from the truth.

It seems to Madison that the authors of the state constitutions have been content in most cases simply to have their handiwork declare that the three branches will be separate. They did not provide for mutual checks. In the event, pious proclamations alone did not work. In a hereditary monarchy, Publius teaches, that branch of government is perhaps the one most to be feared. In a republic, however, where the executive branch is carefully hemmed in by constitutional checks and the legislative has the people's sympathy, careful constitution writers must be more concerned with that branch. Madison then provides testimony to the truth of what he has said from the history of revolutionary Virginia, concerning which he quotes at length from Thomas Jefferson's *Notes on the State of Virginia,* and from that of Pennsylvania, which famously had the most democratic of the revolutionary constitutions. The history of both of those states shows, according to Publius, that mere declaration of the principle of separation of powers does not suffice, that mechanisms for the enforcement of that principle must be built into a constitution.

Federalist No. 49 takes up the topic of constitutional amendment. Madison's jumping-off point is Jefferson's proposal in *Notes on the State of Virginia* that whenever any two branches of the state government concur in calling for one, a state constitutional convention be held. Publius concurs that there is a powerful case to be made for empowering the people to correct situations in which the Constitution malfunctions. He denies, however, that Jefferson's mechanism is the optimal one.

For example, he says, what if two of the three branches are combining against the third, how would Jefferson's proposal correct that? Secondly, he says, "as every appeal to the people would carry an implication of some defect in the government, frequent appeals would in great measure deprive the government of that veneration, which time bestows on every thing, and without which perhaps the wisest and freest governments would not possess the requisite stability." Over time, people's support for a particular government strengthens as "the prejudices of the community" seem to support that government. Age, in other words, makes governments stronger. Amendment, then, should be infrequent.

Frequent discussion of constitutional amendments, Madison continues, also would tend to undermine the "public tranquility." It may be that Americans have succeeded thus far in reconstructing their state constitutions, but they did so in the midst of propitious circumstances. Future constitutional revisions will not often take place against a backdrop of war on American soil, confidence in American political leadership, and general enthusiasm for a particular kind of constitutional revision. Nor, he adds, will future debaters escape the influence of political party, itself prone to cause division.

Madison, the master of political rhetoric, has saved the best for last. The most important reason to oppose frequent revision, he says, is that the people will tend to upset the balance among the three branches of the federal government contemplated by the original Constitution. The reason is that "the tendency of republican governments is to an aggrandizement of the legislative, at the expence of the other departments. The judges are few and generally not widely known, and the executive officials' performance will tend to excite suspicion; the legislators, on the other hand, are numerous, widely known, and popular. They are seen as defenders of the people's rights. They have inherent advantages, then, in any conflict with either or both of the other two branches. Not only that, but in case of a constitutional convention, the legislators would be likely to win most of the seats! What use would there be in having the legislators pass on disputes among the government's branches? Even when the legislative cause did not predominate, as sometimes it would not, the amendment process likely still would turn on the influence of a few great men or of parties, and not on cool reason. Thus, occasional referral of constitutional questions to the people seems an ill-advised notion, and one that the Philadelphia Convention was wise to omit from the Constitution.

In No. 50, Madison turns from No. 49's issue—whether there ought to be periodic reference of constitutional difficulties to the people—to a similar one—whether there ought to be review of government acts' constitutionality at regular intervals. Madison finds several theoretical objections to that idea. If the interval is too long, he says, the mechanism will not restrain the government; if it is too short, all of the objections to occasional review stated in No. 49 will apply. Either way, the reviewing body will be the plaything of political parties, as he says has lately been true of the Council of Censors established under the very democratic 1776 Pennsylvania Constitution. In either case, men's passions and party commitments, not sound judgment, will form the basis of many of their decisions.

The climax to this quintet of essays, Federalist No. 51, is usually seen as ranking behind only No. 10 in the force of its argument. Only No. 78 has had more influence on American thinking about government. Publius here concludes his consideration of the general theme of checks and balances. Along the way, he also offers some of the most memorable lines Madison ever penned.

Separation of powers in some sense is essential to the preservation of liberty, Madison begins. That means that the involvement of the other two branches in selecting the officials of any of them must be limited. This principle is difficult to follow in regard to the judiciary, because judges must possess special qualifications. Besides this principle, another that is essential to the separation of powers is that each branch must have its say independently of either of the other two. In order to ensure the separation of powers, finally, the officials in each branch must have both the means and the motivation to resist encroachments upon their authority by either of the other two branches.

Madison's essay provides perhaps the richest illustration of the difference between the American Revolution and those that came after it. While Communists blithely forecast the advent of the New Soviet Man, and then killed 100 million of their own people in search of that selfless, patriotic creature, and while Jacobins gave supreme power in France to Robespierre, "the Incorruptible," whose tenure at the head of their government became a byword for slaughter of the innocent, Madison did not assume human nature's malleability. Far from it: the good student of John Witherspoon, he took office holders' selfishness for granted. He would not abolish it: he would harness it. Without egocentric officials, the proposed Constitution would not function. "Ambition," Madison says, "must be made to counteract ambition. The interest of the man must be connected with the constitutional rights of the place."

Lest his readers find that jarring, Madison adds, "It may be a reflection on human nature, that such devices should be necessary to controul the abuses of government. But what is government itself but the greatest of all reflections on human nature? If men were angels, no government would be necessary. If angels were to govern men, neither external nor internal controuls on government would be necessary. In framing a government which is to be administered by men over men, the great difficulty lies in this: You must first enable the government to controul the governed; and in the next place, oblige it to controul itself."

Madison calls his system "supplying by opposite and rival interests, the defect of better motives." He notes that one cannot give all three branches equal powers of self-defense, as "in republican government the legislative authority, necessarily, predominates." The proposed Constitution solves this problem through bicameralism, different term lengths for the two houses of Congress, and "different principles of action" for the two houses.

If the separation of powers principle is imperfectly incorporated into the new Constitution, Madison says, it is more completely adhered to than in the state constitutions. In addition, the federal system will benefit from the division of powers between the state governments, on one hand, and the federal government, on the other. As the multiplicity of sects is a protection for religious rights, the multiplicity of other types of interests is a protection for civil rights. This consideration, says Madison, recommends federal government to all friends of republicanism. The very magnitude of the federal Union is itself a guarantee of Americans' freedom: "the larger the society, provided it lie within a practicable sphere, the more duly capable it will be of self government. And happily for the *republican cause,* the practicable sphere may be carried to a very great extent, by a judicious modification and mixture of the *federal principle.*" And thus ends Madison's classic essay on the separation of powers.

Publius's essays Nos. 52–58, the final set in this long group by Madison, consider the proposed United States House of Representatives.[56] This set of essays kicks off a number of essays on the general subject of the structure of particular parts of the federal government. The House comes under consideration first because it is the subject of the proposed Constitution's first structural section. In No. 52, Madison first says that the length of representatives' terms must be appropriate to maintenance of "an immediate dependence on, & an intimate sympathy with the people." He then considers the question of the length of representatives' terms from a comparative point of view. In England, he notes, the Crown has never been required to call a new Parliament more often than every three years, and at the time he wrote the requirement was every seven. Given the degree of freedom the English have enjoyed even under their septennial system and with the various imperfections of their unwritten constitution, he concludes, biennial elections promise to make the American representatives highly responsive to the people's will. Madison here demonstrates a real facility for rhetoric: the Anti-Federalists' complaint was that the Philadelphia Convention had ignored the American revolutionary tradition of annual elections, and Publius compares the proposed Constitution's provisions regarding the House of Representatives not to the analogous provision of an American state's constitution, but to the seemingly only marginally relevant tradition of the House of Commons.

After comparing the proposed House of Representatives' terms to those of members of the British House of Commons, Madison next compares them to those of colonial representatives in the United States. In colonial times, he says, American representatives' terms ranged from one to seven years. The colonies' history offers no proof that biennial elections are too infrequent, he says: Virginia led the way in resisting Parliament's policies of the 1760s and 1770s, and Virginia stood foremost in promoting the Declaration of Independence, yet it was Virginia that had septennial elections. Choosing representatives every other year, then, cannot be too infrequent. Additional safety in this term is offered, Madison concludes, by the fact that the House of Representatives will have a substantially smaller share of the federal government's power than is possessed by the House of Commons within its government or was possessed by the colonial legislatures within theirs.

Madison continues on the same line in No. 53. Beginning with the then proverbial statement that "where annual elections end, tyranny begins," he disputes the point. First, he asks why the change in the seasons should be correlated with a governmental imperative. Then, he notes that Connecticut and Rhode Island traditionally had semiannual elections, while South Carolina's were biennial. Might one conclude, then, that those New England states were four times as free as, or substantially better governed than, the Palmetto State?

There is another consideration that mitigates in favor of longer terms for federal representatives, Madison says: the greater diversity of conditions and interests of which federal officials will have to take account. So, for example, he offers up the federal government's proposed responsibility to regulate trade among the several states. Surely anyone involved in formulating trade policy for the entire country will have to have a cursory knowledge, at least, of the various ports, trade centers, products, and other relevant attributes of all the states. Clearly he will need a longer term to master these than he would have needed to master those of his native state—with which he likely would have been familiar even before assuming state legislative office.

In Federalist No. 54 comes Madison's famous passage offering a defense of the notorious Three-Fifths Clause. By the terms of that clause, each slave counted as three-fifths of a person both for purposes of taxation and for purposes of representation. One could see that they should count for purposes of taxation, Publius said, but what of counting them for representation?

Recall that Publius was the fictitious author of a series of newspaper editorials directed at a New York audience. Although there was still slavery in New York, that institution was regarded even in February 1788 (when No. 54 first appeared) as a primarily southern institution. Madison therefore pretended to be a New Yorker enunciating a southern argument when he wrote, "We subscribe to the doctrine, might one of our southern brethren observe, that representation relates more immediately to persons, and taxation more immediately to property, and we join in the application of this distinction to the case of our slaves. But we must deny the fact that slaves are considered merely as property, and in no respect whatever as persons. The true state of the case is, that they partake of both these qualities; being considered by our laws, in some respects, as persons, and in other respects, as property." So, Madison says, in having to work for another, in being susceptible of physical punishment at the will of another, and in being under the physical constraint of another, the slave is treated as property; in being the object of the state's physical protection and in being held responsible for the violence he commits against others, he is treated as a person. The Constitution is in step with the laws of the states, Publius's hypothetical Southerner concludes, in treating the slave as neither fish nor fowl. In fact, he says, only on the basis of their being treated partly as property can they be denied a full share in representation, as the Three-Fifths Clause denies it to them.

Madison asks whether it is not inconsistent to expect the South to agree that each slave should count as a person for purposes of taxation, but that he should not count at all for purposes of legislative apportionment. According to Publius, this would degrade the slave even further than did the state laws enslaving him, for they accorded him at least some human personality. To the objection that the states do not count slaves in apportioning the legislatures, Publius answers that every state deprives some persons among its citizens of the vote, and that the apportionment laws vary from state to state. Any uniform federal rule about this would have been subject to the objection that some people who were omitted from state apportionment tables are being counted by the federal government. Everyone must accept, then, that there are interstate compromises in the proposed Constitution that will bear on different states in different ways. And finally, Madison's hypothetical Southerner says, wealth ought to have its weight in the public councils, and providing some heightened representation for owners of slave property is a kind of proxy for giving the wealthy extra representation. The Southerner-as-New-Yorker-as-Southerner notes that in New York's 1777 state constitution, only substantial landholders are permitted to vote, so the principle should not strike New Yorkers as odd. Publius concludes his extensive consideration of a hypothetical Southerner's defense of the Constitution's apportionment provisions by saying, "I must confess, that it fully reconciles me to the scale of representation, which the Convention have established."

In essay No. 55, Madison responds to the complaint that the House of Representatives will be too small to afford adequate representation. That might be true, he concedes, if the Congress were to have a general legislative power; since it will have only a few enumerated powers, however, it need not have a very large membership. In addition, he says, Americans would not periodically reelect sixty-five to one hundred men who proved bent on subjecting America to a tyranny. Perhaps men are often depraved, but they also sometimes exhibit virtues, and "Republican government presupposes the existence of these qualities in a higher degree than any other form." If men were so bad as some Anti-Federalists seem to assume, only despotic government would do for them.

Federalist No. 56 takes up the related assertion that the House of Representatives will be so small that its members cannot be familiar with all the interests of their constituents. Madison's answer is that while representatives need to be familiar with their constituents' situations, "this principle can extend no farther than to those circumstances and interests, to which the authority and care of the representative relate." Where only grand national objects are to be within the legislator's cognizance, then, he need not have thorough comprehension of every minute local problem. Taking up one of the great objects of Congress's concern, federal taxing measures, Madison holds that "a skilful individual in his closet, with all the local codes before him, might compile a law on some subjects of taxation for the whole union, without any aid from oral information." He reasons similarly on the other great powers confided to Congress.

Federalist Nos. 57 and 58 take up the questions, also repeatedly raised by the Anti-Federalists, of the likelihood that the elite will dominate the House and that the House will seldom be expanded to keep pace with America's growing population. Publius disposes of the former easily, asking whether elected officials of distinguished backgrounds are not the type of representative one would hope to see in such a position. If such a man overthrew republican government, he would be an "elective traitor," and there is no evidence in America's experience with officials elected on a statewide basis (for example, the governors of New York) that they would tend to do any such thing.

On the question of expansion of the House, Madison's arguments seem a bit strained now. He could not know that the number 435 would be frozen in 1913. As far as he was concerned, the House obviously would be expanded as the population of the United States grew. This is one of the two purposes of the decennial census required by the proposed Constitution, he says. Nowadays we think of that as an apportionment-related provision, but for Madison it was an expand-the-House provision too.

Second, Madison says, state legislatures have generally grown along with states' populations, and state legislators have not objected. Third, he argues, the large states will have every motivation to argue for the expansion of the House, as they are likely to be such measures' main beneficiaries; too, they will have abstract right on their side, and people will realize that. New states will join them, as their populations are apt to expand more quickly, on a proportional basis, than those of the older states. If the Senate will not concur, the House—dominated by populous states—can withhold money bills until the Senate goes along.

Madison concludes his discussion of the House of Representatives by noting a paradox: if a legislative assembly becomes too large, he claims, it will become more oligarchic. That is, where there are many legislators, the real decision-making authority tends to reside in a few. The reason is that where there are many legislators, a greater proportion of them have weak capacities. Men of that type are more easily swayed than the truly able. "Ignorance" becomes "the dupe of cunning; and passion the slave of sophistry and declamation."

Here Madison let it lie for a week, as Hamilton contributed three Publius essays on the proposed Constitution's technical provisions regarding regulation of elections. Madison's final contributions to *The Federalist*, essays 62 and 63, were published on February 27 and March 1, 1788.[57] Their subject is the Senate, and the two essays together form one extended consideration of that body's structure. Madison says that the chief issues needing examination in relation to the Senate are senators' qualifications, legislative election of senators, apportionment by state, the number and term of senators, and the Senate's powers.

Madison/Publius says that the nine-year state residency requirement provides a happy medium between excluding immigrants and hasty admission of them, and thus offers an opportunity to exploit their talents while avoiding infiltration of the federal government by agents of foreign powers. The age minimum for senators, thirty years (five more than for a representative), is calculated to ensure that senators have extensive experience and stable character, while men that age will also likely have overcome any prejudice in favor of their countries of origin that might still influence younger men.

The mode of electing senators chosen by the Philadelphia Convention, as we have seen, was election by state legislatures. As we have also seen, Madison opposed this mechanism strenuously virtually throughout the Philadelphia Convention, and indeed long after the convention's close. His October 24, 1787, letter to Thomas Jefferson spelled out some of his concerns. The distinction between what Madison wrote as Publius and what he candidly believed is perhaps nowhere better illustrated, then, than in that portion of Federalist No. 62, in which he says of election by state legislatures: "It is recommended by the double advantage of favouring a select appointment, and of giving to the state governments such an agency in the formation of the federal government, as must secure the authority of the former; and may form a convenient link between the two systems."

In plain English, what Madison is saying in referring to "a select appointment" echoes his idea about the elevating effect of larger districts in No. 10: letting legislatures elect senators will result in selection of a more elevated group to those offices than would popular election, even from districts as large as the states alone. Second, in saying that giving the states "an agency in the formation of the federal government, . . . must secure the authority of the former," Publius is asserting that the legislative election of senators will serve as a defense mechanism for the states.

In regard to the equality of the states in the Senate, Publius says that we should not look to theory, but to "a spirit of amity" and "mutual deference," for an explanation. This feature of the proposed Constitution is indeed objectionable to the larger states (recall that Madison is writing for a New York audience), but ratification will put the large states closer to population apportionment in Congress (with one house apportioned that way) than it was under the Confederation (in whose unicameral Congress all states have the same vote). Besides that, he says, giving each state an equal voice in the Senate respects the state's "residuary sovereignty," and the large states ought to be no less solicitous than the small of doing that. All of the states want to avoid "an improper consolidation of the states into one simple republic."

An overlooked advantage of this structure occurs to Madison as well: it will make it more difficult for proponents of bad legislation to have their way. Their legislative coalition will have to take in not only a majority of the population, but a majority of the states. Madison concedes that this dynamic will impede adoption of useful legislation as well, but he considers the overall effect more benefit than curse, as "the facility and excess of law-making seem to be the diseases to which our governments are most liable."

Madison first defends senators' number by saying (seemingly irrelevantly) that officials in a republic too often forget their obligations to their constituents, and bicameralism is a powerful corrective to this tendency. Both houses are far less likely, his reasoning goes, to be carried away by selfish sentiments simultaneously. Next, he says that a Senate is a good idea because a less numerous body is far less likely to be swept up in mob passions than a larger one. What he has in mind here is not today's Senate, which is larger by far than the original House, but the Senate of 1790, with its twenty-six members. Such a body ought to have long terms, Madison adds, to help it to resist the gales of popular whim.

Men of long tenure have greater opportunity to obtain familiarity with the intricacies of public issues, Madison avers. Adoption of ill-wrought laws has been one of America's great problems since the onset of the revolution, and long terms are a useful corrective to bad legislation. "Good government" must have two attributes, he says: "first, fidelity to the object of government, which is the happiness of the people; secondly, a knowledge of the means by which that object can be best attained." The Constitution's provisions regarding the Senate tend to provide the latter, and thus the former as well.

Stability in the Senate will help to establish stability in the laws and policies of the federal government, according to Publius, which will have a positive effect upon the foreign relations of the country. As things stand, America's character (by which the revolutionary generation meant its national personality) was untrustworthy. Such countries are apt to have few allies, and in their weakness will attract enemies, he continues. In fact, he says, America's current situation bears this assessment out, because it receives "no respect" from friendly nations and "derision" from its enemies.

The internal effects of instability in government are even worse, instructs Publius: laws so voluminous that they cannot be read, so incoherent that they cannot be understood, so often changed that they may be revised or repealed before they are promulgated, and so inconstant that one cannot keep up with the changes. Madison sees class bias in this kind of system, for only the few can know what the law is, while the many are required to abide by it too. He also thinks it dampens business activity, since investment is less likely when the legal framework of business cannot be predicted with confidence.

In the last paragraph of this essay, Madison returns to a subject he had taken up in discussing the proposed Constitution's amendment procedures in Federalist No. 49. Public attachment to government is undermined when the laws are as mutable as they have been. It reduces that "attachment and reverence which steals into the hearts of the people" with time.

In No. 63, Madison begins by noting that a stable institution like the proposed Senate can give a nation a certain character. It can also take advantage of the knowledge to be gleaned by examining the experience of other nations. Too, a small, stable body can be held responsible in a way that a large group of officials elected to short terms cannot. As Madison explains, many lines of public policy have effects that develop over a long period of time, and members of such a body as the Senate can be held to account for them in a way that members of an institution like the House cannot. Senators' longer terms can also empower them to resist fleeting popular fancies that should be resisted, which is something the House will not be able to do. And inclusion of a body like the Senate will compound the difficulty of organizing the kind of faction against which Publius warned in No. 10; even the considerations offered in that essay do not close the book on the problem of majority faction, and so additional guards against it are appropriate. "Abuses of liberty" are rather more the problem of the United States than "abuses of power," and the Senate is a safeguard against abuses of liberty. Other republics have had senates, and they have not proven oppressive; in Britain's civil war, in fact, the defeat of the king led to the complete elimination of the House of Lords by the victorious House of Commons. It is from that direction that the chief danger is to be feared in the proposed federal system, as well. In case the people found that the Senate had opted to pursue the abrogation of the Constitution, they, in league with the House of Representatives, could reduce the Senate to its constitutional role in the same way as the Commons had destroyed the Lords.

Chapter 5

~~~~~~~~~~~~~~~~~~~~~~

Ratifying the Constitution,
Part Two: The Richmond Convention,
1788

When, having done his part to secure ratification in the Empire State, he left New York for Virginia, Madison knew that he faced a difficult task. Many of Virginia's leading men stood foursquare against the Constitution. As the Philadelphia Convention had progressed, he had received word that Patrick Henry likely would oppose its product. Then, at the convention's end, Edmund Randolph and George Mason had opted not to sign.

Randolph had been a leading framer, even presenting the Virginia Plan to the convention, and he was the incumbent governor of the Old Dominion. His objection to the Constitution as written came as quite a blow. Perhaps even more significant, however, was Mason's refusal to sign. George Mason had been the chief author of the 1776 Virginia Declaration of Rights and Constitution, and he was widely understood to be the leading Virginia authority on such matters.

Not only had Mason not signed, but he had pledged to drum up opposition to the Constitution. While Madison had lent his hand to writing *The Federalist,* Mason had gotten the jump on him back in the Old Dominion. In a widely circulated pamphlet, he had explained why the Constitution must be amended before it was ratified.

Randolph, for his part, adhered to the more ambiguous position he had adopted at the Philadelphia Convention's end. The day after that conclave closed, he sent a copy of the Constitution to his kinsman, Lt. Governor Beverley Randolph, with a note saying that the absence of his and Mason's signatures from the document should not lead to the conclusion "that we are opposed to its adoption."[1]

From New York came word of a split among Virginia's congressmen similar to that among its Philadelphia Convention delegates: Edward Carrington and Henry Lee favored ratification, but one-time president Richard Henry Lee was "forming propositions for essential alterations in the Constitution," while interim president William Grayson "dislikes it, and is, at best for giving it only a Silent passage to the States."[2] Madison, who hoped Congress would endorse it in sending it on to the states, must have grimaced. When he resumed his seat in Congress, Madison joined Carrington against Lee and Grayson. Ultimately, despite objections that the Philadelphia Convention had violated Article XIII of the Articles of Confederation, Congress's resolution for a convention, and several states' legislative instructions to delegates by doing more than proposing amendments to the Articles, Congress forwarded the proposed Constitution to the states without commentary.[3]

Nevertheless, Richard Henry Lee launched a strenuous campaign in favor of amending the Constitution prior to ratifying it. Building on a theme he had developed in Congress, he insisted upon a bill of rights.[4] Pointing to the General Welfare Clause, Lee guessed that the Constitution ultimately would be read as justifying virtually anything Congress wanted to do. Add that to the Supremacy Clause, and he thought that a bill of rights was essential to the preservation of the rights for which Americans had so recently fought.

Lee also thought that the Constitution should be amended to expand the House of Representatives and to separate the president, vice president, and Senate. These amendments had to be adopted before ratification. Lee was adamant: "Nor can a good reason be assigned," he said, "for establishing a bad, instead of a good government, in the first instance; because time may amend the bad—Men do not choose to be sick because it may happen that physic may cure them."

On October 7, Mason sent a letter to Washington including his objections to the Constitution.[5] An amended version of notes he had made during the Philadelphia Convention, this document essentially repeated complaints Mason had raised then: there was no declaration of rights, and the Supremacy Clause meant state declarations would be unavailing; the House was too small; the Senate had money powers, although it did not represent the people; the combination of legislative and executive powers in the Senate endangered liberty; the federal judiciary would swallow up the state judiciaries and thus allow the rich to oppress the poor; the president lacked an executive council, which meant he would be led by the Senate; and the vice president, in limbo between the Senate and the executive branch, was a dangerous personage— besides which he would give one state three Senate votes, which was unfair.

In addition to these objections, Mason also went public with his Philadelphia Convention prediction that the Commerce Clause would empower the eight northern states to abuse the five southern. There would be a tendency for Congress to read almost anything into the Necessary and Proper Clause, which threatened both states' and individuals' rights. Also as in Philadelphia, Mason underscored the error of the prohibition on bans of slave imports until 1808. "Such Importations," he fumed, "render the United States weaker, more vulnerable, and less capable of defence." Ultimately, he forecast, the Constitution would yield "a Monarchy, or a corrupt oppressive Aristocracy."

Washington did not take Mason's opposition well. To hear him tell it, neither did his and Mason's home county.[6] Besides, the general told Madison, Mason had "rendered himself obnoxious in Philadelphia" by attempting to persuade some state legislators there to oppose the Constitution. At the same time as he relayed this information to Madison, Washington also let slip that he thought Randolph regretted not having signed the Constitution.

Meanwhile, Governor Randolph on October 15 had formally presented the Constitution to the General Assembly. The House of Delegates took the matter up on October 25, when it voted to call a convention. The Senate concurred on Halloween.[7] As James Monroe later explained, the convention was scheduled for June 1788 so that Virginia might mediate among the states in case they disagreed, and so that Virginia could take other states' decisions into account if they had not disagreed.[8] Battle lines began to harden right away, as Governor Randolph's neighbors dropped plans for a ceremonial reception upon learning that he had not signed the Constitution.[9]

Madison considered Mason's arguments against the Constitution rather weak.[10] He also pointed out that Mason had not raised them all in Philadelphia, and that some of them were indeed either contrary to what Mason had said in Philadelphia or simply nonsensical. It was, Madison said, Mason's "temper which produced his dissent." On the other hand, Madison confided, Chancellor Edmund Pendleton was in favor of ratification, and Patrick Henry's verdict remained unknown. The campaign seemed to be going well, as "reports . . . from different quarters continue[d] to be rather flattering."

Within a few days, however, Henry had come down solidly against ratifying the Constitution until it had been amended.[11] Thus, the situation going into the convention was clear: several leading figures in Virginia's political elite—Mason, Henry, "Ritt" Lee, Grayson, and others—opposed ratifying without first amending. (Mason, however, not only disavowed any intention of breaking up the union,[12] but said that he would accept this Constitution if it was the best to be had).[13] Governor Randolph was undecided. And Madison could call upon Pendleton and, most importantly, invoke the name of Washington in the unamended Constitution's support.

It was on October 24 that Madison finally got around to reporting on the outcome of the Philadelphia Convention to Jefferson. Here, as we have seen, he unburdened himself concerning the Constitution's shortcomings, particularly the absence of a federal veto over state laws. Recall his conclusion that "the danger of encroachments" of the states upon federal authority would remain strong even if the new constitution were ratified, that even the fair-minded must sometimes have difficulty discerning the line between central and state authority, and that therefore "some such expedient as I contend for" was necessary. Some might say that the federal judiciary could rein in the states, he reasoned, but it would be better to prevent a new law from going into effect than to negate it afterward. A federal veto would also allow the new government to check state oppressions of local minorities, which was always going to be a problem. Those things being said, Madison also updated Jefferson concerning Mason's role in Philadelphia and since and the state of things in Virginia.

By November 18, Madison had begun to worry. From his post in New

York, the Virginia news did not seem good. As Madison put it, "All my informations from Richmond concur in representing the enthusiasm in favor of the new Constitution as subsiding, and giving place to a spirit of criticism."[14] Still, he thought that proponents of ratification remained in the majority.

Just in case, however, he began on that day to seek distribution of *The Federalist* in the Old Dominion. Enclosing copies of the first seven essays, he told Washington that their subject was "the importance of the Union." In light of what he had heard about the tack opponents of ratification might take in Virginia, he thought that perhaps the series could have a positive effect there too.

The series appeared in dribs and drabs in Virginia's scattered weekly newspapers from November 1787 to mid-January 1788.[15] At that point, seemingly in anticipation of the publication of numerous entries in the series in pamphlet form, the Virginia newspaper publication dried up. Finally, the first volume (thirty-six essays) became available for purchase in Norfolk on April 2 and in Richmond on April 23. The second volume (including the other forty-nine essays) came on the Virginia market on June 4 (Norfolk) and June 11 (Richmond). Besides that, numerous Virginians purchased the set directly from New York and had it shipped to Virginia.

Not only was the New York series circulated among Virginia's elite, but the newspapers were chock-full of editorials pro and con (mostly pro) ratification. In the wake of numerous letters from politically active and informed correspondents all over Virginia, Madison summarized matters this way: "My information leads me to suppose there must be three parties in Virginia. The first for adopting without attempting amendments. This includes Genl. W—and ye. other deputies who signed the Constitution, Mr. Pendleton—(Mr. Marshal I believe)—Mr. Nicholas . . . &c &c. At the head of the 2d. party which urges amendments are the Govr. & Mr Mason. These do not object to the substance of the Governt. but contend for a few additional Guards in favor of the Rights of the States and of the people. I am not able to enumerate the characters which fall in with their ideas, as distinguished from those of a third class, at the head of which is Mr. Henry. This class concurs at present with the patrons of Amendments, but will probably contend for such as strike at the essence of the System, and must lead to an adherence to the principle of the existing Confederation, which most thinking men are

convinced is a visionary one, or to a partition of the Union into several Confederacies. Mr. Harrison the late Govr. is with Mr. Henry. So are a number of
others." Madison admitted he was unsure about the positions of several of
these people, but then added confidently that, "Mr. Henry is the great adversary who will render the event precarious. He is I find with his usual address
working up every possible interest, into a spirit of opposition."[16]

No doubt wishing that Virginia's ruling elite had divided similarly, Madison observed that while some of the middle and southern states were equally
divided, almost all eminent New England men favored ratification. (Here he
seems conveniently to have left Rhode Island out of his description.) "It is
not less worthy of remark," he said, "that in Virginia where the mass of the
people have been so much accustomed to be guided by their rulers on all new
and intricate questions, they should on the present which certainly surpasses
the judgment of the greater part of them, not only go before, but contrary to,
their most popular leaders." He accounted for this supposed trend of average
Virginians toward Federalism by reference to popular exhaustion with "the
vicicitudes, injustice and follies which have so much characterised public
measures" and popular desire for "some change which promises stability &
repose."

In other words, when the hoi polloi are upset with the status quo, you
cannot beat something with nothing. Whether Madison's opponents would
accept his diagnosis and propose an alternative to immediate ratification remained an open question. So, indeed, did the matter whether average Virginians would believe that Patrick Henry really wanted to break up the
Union into numerous regional confederacies.

Toward the end of 1787, Madison received unwelcome news: Col. Thomas
Barbour, an Orange County neighbor, was working to defeat Madison's elec-
tion to the ratification convention.[17] Friends counseled that Madison return to
Virginia to thwart this effort.

Governor Randolph published his self-justifying objections to the Constitution on December 27, 1787.[18] The impression they leave is mixed. On
one hand, Randolph clearly loved public acclaim; on the other, he wanted
the public's respect as well. Thus, protestation that "I disdain to conceal the
reasons for withholding my subscription" was joined to a concession that the
governor was "affecting no indifference to public opinion, but resolved not to

court it by an unmanly sacrifice of [his] own judgment." He justified his course by saying that a new constitution was rendered necessary by the imperfection of the old, and that neither a breakup of the Union nor the advent of new, regional confederacies could be tolerated.

He wanted, and the country needed, "a consolidation of the union, as far as circumstances will permit." That is why the convention had written the Constitution. It pained him not to have signed it, despite the signatures of three of his Virginia colleagues—all bosom friends of his. The reasons he gave came down to these: he thought amendments were necessary, he thought they would be impossible without a second convention, and he thought the people of Virginia likely to reject the Constitution without them. Therefore, he said, disunion was highly possible, and he did not want to be party to causing it. The amendments he wanted would have established proportional representation in the Senate, a supermajority requirement for tariff legislation, presidential term limits, limits on the presidential appointment power, a clearer line between congressional and state legislative power, limits on the Senate's treaty power, limits on the judicial power, and a few other things. Even without amendments, he concluded, the Constitution should be adopted, because the Union was essential to American liberty.

Far from the Anti-Federalist blast many had expected, then, Randolph's letter showed that with or without amendments, he would vote to ratify. As one proponent of ratification summarized its effect, Randolph's "letter against the Constitution is the best thing that has appeared in favor of it."[19]

Madison, meanwhile, stayed on in New York. There, he helped coordinate interstate efforts at ratification, as for example by asking Washington to tell friends in Massachusetts that he favored ratification.[20] He continued to receive warnings, however, that some in Orange County opposed him.[21] He must return home to guarantee that he would be chosen for the Richmond Convention. As to Virginia, Madison continued to try to persuade Governor Randolph to come out foursquare in favor of the Constitution.

When he had digested Randolph's explanation of his behavior in Philadelphia, Madison told him that if only Randolph had come out for ratification, there would have been virtually no opposition in the Old Dominion. Henry "would either have suppressed his enmity, or been baffled in the policy which it has dictated." One result of Randolph's course has been, Madison said, that opponents of ratification in various states have claimed the mantel of Randolph's name for programs antithetical to Randolph's aims. "In this State," Madison wrote of the New Yorkers, "the party adverse to the Constitution, notoriously meditate either a dissolution of the Union, or protracting it by patching up the Articles of Confederation." New England Anti-Federalists had "a repugnancy in general to good government," and some wanted nothing less than "a reversal of the Revolution." Madison conceded that Randolph knew Henry better than he, before he added that he had long thought that Henry wanted "a Southern Confederacy." If only the leading lights of Virginia had all joined in support, few common people would have opposed it.

Madison set out at last for Virginia in early March.[22] By then, although five states had ratified, the campaign's progress was mixed. Rhode Island stood strongly opposed, as did New York, and Massachusetts's ratification had come narrowly. Despite his having downplayed its significance, Madison cannot have been happy with the Bay State's form of ratification, which included proposals for several amendments. New Hampshire's convention had met and broken up without a conclusion, and the picture in the Old Dominion remained unclear. To top it all off, here he was having to make his way to Orange County lest his candidacy for ratification convention delegate be rejected.

Patrick Henry's influence was strongly felt.[23] There might be a possibility of aligning the Federalists who favored immediate ratification and the Federalists who favored pushing the question of amendments to the precipice of rejecting the Constitution against whatever Anti-Federalists actually wanted to reject the Constitution. Federalists calculated that among the elite, they were in the majority. Yet the common people had been so strongly stirred against the Federalists that the outcome was uncertain. Henry's argument that Virginia could hold out for amendments against nine, or even all twelve, of the other states seemed a dangerous gambit to his opponents, but the run of Virginians found it appealing.

The elections to the Richmond Convention took place in March 1788.[24] The General Assembly waived the rule making congressmen, judges, and other officials ineligible for legislative election, and so numerous such people— including Madison—ran for seats. Most won. Prominent men who did not run or did not win included Washington, Jefferson, Beverley Randolph, Richard

Henry Lee, and a few others. The most prominent men elected were Edmund Randolph, Patrick Henry, George Mason, Edmund Pendleton, and Madison himself. As James Monroe put it, "Few men of any distinction have fail'd taking their part."[25]

Madison rushed home in time to arrive in Orange County on March 23.[26] On his arrival, he said, he had "the chagrin to find the County filled with the most absurd and groundless prejudices against the fœderal Constitution. I was therefore obliged," he continued, "at the election which succeeded the day of my arrival to mount for the first time in my life, the rostrum before a large body of the people, and to launch into a harangue of some length in the open air and on a very windy day."

Apparently Madison's neighbors were more impressed by his performance on March 24 than he was with the imperative to offer it: he and another Federalist won the election "by a majority of nearly 4 to one. It is very probable," he lamented, "that a very different event would have taken place as to myself if the efforts of my friends had not been seconded by my presence." The Federalists' chief Virginia strategist had won a substantial electoral victory, but only on the strength of the type of democratic behavior to which he would have preferred not to descend.

Another of the chief proponents of immediate ratification would be Albemarle lawyer George Nicholas. Short (five feet, seven inches tall) and "deformed with fat," Nicholas was once caricatured—to Madison's intense amusement—as "a plum pudding with legs to it."[27] Yet Nicholas came from an eminent political dynasty, and he possessed a very acute mind. He also had already lit upon a promising argument: that the Constitution only granted the new government the powers "expressly" delegated, and that Virginia would ratify on "the plan of the Massachusetts convention."[28] That plan called for appending proposed amendments to the ratified Constitution on the understanding that the first congress would take them up.

If Federalists followed this line of attack, Nicholas averred, the only real danger to ratification came from Kentucky's delegates. (Kentucky was still part of Virginia in 1788.) Those westernmost Virginians feared that the new government would bargain away their access to the Mississippi River, which was their economic lifeblood. Nicholas encouraged Madison to seek election to the next General Assembly so that he could aid in putting the new Constitution into effect; surely the states' cooperation would be necessary, and Madison's presence would help offset Henry's likely hostility.

Madison replied that he would gladly write to Federalists in Maryland and South Carolina with the warning that if they followed New Hampshire's example (recessed their ratification conventions without ratifying), it would have a negative influence in Virginia.[29] He also said he would write to Kentuckians to counteract the effect that the Mississippi question was having there. (As Madison understood it, the Constitution would empower the central government to wring a positive outcome from Spain, while the Articles left the Confederation Congress essentially impotent.)[30]

Madison also confided in Nicholas concerning his fears of a second federal convention. The first had nearly failed, he said, and likely would have if its members had realized what their constituents thought of the matter. Conditional amendments or a second convention would mean further delay, and that would empower opponents of reform to defeat the entire movement. In fact, a second convention would likely include delegates from more than one state who came intending to thwart efforts to propose anything at all. Finally, Madison told Nicholas that Madison could not seek a seat in the General Assembly, as Virginia law banned plural officeholding, he was already a member of Congress, and there was no authority to which he could resign that office.

On another front, Madison continued to work to bring Governor Randolph into the Federalist fold. Seeing Randolph's sensitivity to public (and elite) opinion, Madison stressed his take on the Anti-Federalist campaign.[31] Not only did he reiterate the rumor that Henry was willing to risk a breakup of the Union in the name of prior amendments, but he told Randolph that Mason's "licentiousness of animadversion . . . no longer spare[d] even the *moderate opponents* of the Constitution." And who might those be? Randolph could easily guess that he took pride of place among the Anti-Federalists' targets. Madison hoped that his friend would get the message and join the team.

Randolph responded by echoing Madison to the effect that those who advocated amending the Constitution before ratifying it might be playing "a higher game."[32] He echoed Nicholas in "believing that personal irritation has roused some to enlarge their original views of opposition." He also said, in a phrase pregnant with later developments in his thinking, that having too many states ratify without amendment would frustrate the scheme of prior amendment. In these last few weeks before the June date of the ratification convention, Madison must have realized that the governor would be in the fold when it counted.

Exclusive of Kentucky's delegates, whose views remained unknown, Virginia seemed likely to have a small majority in favor of simple ratification.[33] As Madison summarized matters, "The superiority of abilities at least seems to lie on that side." (Here, he mistakenly classed Monroe as a tepid friend of the unamended Constitution.) Madison had already divined, as early as April 22, what the Anti-Federalists' strategy would be: "The preliminary question will be whether previous alterations shall be insisted on or not?" If yes, Virginia would either adopt a conditional ratification or call for a second convention. As Madison saw it, either of these outcomes would endanger the Union. A call for previous amendments could not reasonably be expected to entice the many states that had already ratified to reconsider in deference to Virginia, he thought, while a second convention was unlikely to achieve the same "spirit of compromise" that had yielded a good outcome to the first.

Virginia, he thought, was geographically divided. The Northern Neck had elected a pretty uniformly Federalist group of delegates. The Southside counties were overwhelmingly opposed. The area in between was a checkerboard. "The Counties between the blue ridge & the Alleghany have chosen friends to the Constitution without a single exception." Counties between there and Kentucky were mostly Federalist. "Kentucky it is supposed will be divided."

Meanwhile, Washington began to give out the Federalists' new party line.[34] "That the proposed Constitution will admit of amendments," he wrote, "is acknowledged by its warmest advocates." Yet, a program of prior amendment amounted to a program of rejection, because advocates of prior amendments had no common amendment program. In essence, men from different parts of America wanted different amendments to serve their own local interests, and they would be unable to secure agreement to such amendments from other parts of the country. People who understood how difficult it had been to cobble together this Constitution, he concluded, could not support this program.

On May 8, New York's governor, George Clinton, wrote to Governor Randolph suggesting that the two of them establish communication regarding the way their states should proceed on the question of ratification.[35] Clinton, whose official position and political strength in the Empire State combined to make him the most powerful Anti-Federalist in the country, obviously hoped that the Old Dominion's recusant governor would push for prior amendments. Rather than strike up such an exchange, however, Randolph undertook a different gambit: he kept Clinton's letter secret until after Virginia's convention.

Randolph first laid the letter before Virginia's Council of State, an appointive cabinet that the governor chaired, in accordance with Virginia's 1776 constitution. He asked the council whether it regarded the communication from Governor Clinton as public or private. Despite Clinton's saying that, "As I have no Direction from the Legislature on the Subject of your Communications, your Excellency will be pleased to consider this Letter an expression of my own Sentiments," the Council classed it as public. With that excuse, Randolph decided to hold it for presentation to the General Assembly when next that body met. Coincidentally, the next session was due to start on June 23. Due to the traditional delay in attaining a quorum, the House of Delegates' speaker did not lay Randolph's several communications before it until June 24. It did not hear this letter from Clinton to Randolph until June 26—the day after the Richmond Convention ratified the Constitution without amendments.

Meanwhile, leading Federalists had become considerably more sanguine—at least for public consumption. Washington, for one, let out that he thought the Federalists had a decided majority of the delegates, because the elections had come out better than Federalists could have hoped.[36] In private, however, the Federalist high command was not nearly so sanguine. Nicholas, soon to move to Kentucky, told Madison that he was "much alarmed" by what he had heard of the elections there.[37] He asked Madison for a written explanation of the reason why the Mississippi navigation would be more securely available to Kentuckians under the Constitution than it had been under the Articles. Madison replied with a very lengthy letter laying out the reasons why he considered it highly unlikely that the Mississippi navigation would be sacrificed.[38]

Madison began by noting that a very important person (one supposes John Jay, his coauthor on *The Federalist*) would not again support the idea of trading off access to the Mississippi for Spanish commercial favors. He also noted that the proponents of surrendering the right to use the Mississippi argued that since the Confederation could not vindicate the right, the trade they had in mind amounted to getting "something for nothing." Under the Constitution, this would no longer be a relevant argument.

Important as that was, however, Madison's chief reliance here was on the increased sense of common purpose that would naturally flow from adoption of tighter bonds of union. Besides that, "the protection and security which the new Government promises to purchasers of the fœderal lands" would encourage migration westward. With migration would come statehood, which would empower Westerners to defend themselves in Congress. They would have relations in the East, who would oppose ceding their interest in the Mississippi navigation.

Westward migration would also, Madison speculated, give people in the old thirteen states a selfish interest in retaining the Mississippi navigation: the federal government would repay the revolutionary debt in part through sale of western lands, whose value would depend largely on access to New Orleans. So much the better for Westerners' interest in ongoing access. "On these considerations principally," Madison concluded, "I ground my opinion that the disposition to cede the Mississippi will be much less under the new than it may be under the old system."

Besides these factors, Madison thought the structure of the proposed government would make it even more unlikely to cede the navigation. The president, for one, would have personal incentives not to incur the disgrace associated with having been responsible for giving up national rights. The House, which though not involved in making treaties would control the money needed to implement them, might be an obstacle to such a treaty. And the new system would certainly facilitate the positive act that Westerners really needed, which was enactment of a treaty guaranteeing their access to the great river. The Confederation Congress, everyone knew, had had no luck at all in seeking that objective.

After sharing these reflections, Madison went on for several additional closely written pages to describe some other considerations that ought to impel Westerners to support ratification. Chief among those was the need to remove British troops from their western bases. The Treaty of Paris obliged

Britain to withdraw them, but only American compliance with that treaty would bring this happy result. American compliance consisted chiefly in making it possible for British creditors to collect their American debts in American courts, and that meant that there needed to be federal courts. Absent ratification, no such courts would be created, and the Indians would continue to be prompted by the British among them to attack western settlers.

As Madison laid out his reasoning, whether in regard to the Mississippi navigation, in relation to the British posts, or on some less important question, he displayed the power of his astonishing intellect for Nicholas to see. Here as before, Madison's mind clearly had grasped all the issues surrounding the main question: whether and why the western counties' delegates should favor ratification. It would take a forceful case indeed to overmatch him. Nicholas, for his part, would serve as the chief spokesman for Federalism, because he was by far the most powerful debater on Madison's side.[39]

The convention was scheduled to open on June 2, 1788, in Richmond.[40] That day, the convention unanimously elected Edmund Pendleton its president. So great was the assembled crowd of spectators that the delegates voted to adjourn until 11:00 a.m. the next day, when they would reconvene at Richmond's New Academy, "a Spacious and Airy Building" of adequate capacity. The convention met for six days a week from June 2 to June 27, first from 10:00 a.m. to 4:00 p.m., but beginning halfway through, from 9:00 a.m. to 5:00 p.m. One exception came during the violent thunder and hailstorm of June 13 (a very dramatic scene that will be described below), when the convention adjourned from 1:00 p.m. to 2:00 p.m. In the convention's last five days, the special session of the General Assembly (of which sixty-two convention delegates were members) commenced, and then the convention accommodated its start time to the Assembly's.

On June 3, the convention first heard the congressional resolution calling for state conventions, the Constitution, the letter from Philadelphia Convention President George Washington, resolutions from the Philadelphia Convention, and relevant General Assembly resolutions. It then agreed to George Mason's motion that no votes be taken until the convention had considered the proposed Constitution section by section. (Federalists thought they had won a victory here, but as it turned out, Mason's motion reflected the Anti-Federalist strategy of delay.) From June 4 to June 25, the convention considered the Constitution in Committee of the Whole, which was chaired by Federalist George Wythe (June 4–21), Anti-Federalist Benjamin Harrison (June 23), and Federalist Thomas Matthews (June 24–25).[41]

The record of the convention is thorough, though not entirely perfect.[42] The fellow who kept the record of debate in shorthand noted that he sometimes had difficulty hearing the speakers. Recording Madison's contribution was often hard, he said. Madison wrote in 1827, "I find passages, some appearing to be defective, others obscure, if not unintelligible, others again which must be more or less erroneous. These flaws in the Report of my observations, may doubtless have been occasioned in part by a want of due care in expressing them; but probably in part also by a feebleness of voice caused by an imperfect recovery from a fit of illness, or by a relaxed attention in the Stenographer himself incident to long & fatiguing discussions. Of his general intelligence & intentional fidelity, no doubt has been suggested."

The editors of *The Documentary History of the Ratification of the Constitution,* a treasure trove of information on the ratification process in all the states, highlight the stenographer's accomplishment. His records "hold a unique place in Virginia history and the history of the debate over the ratification of the Constitution," they rightly advise. "Never before had the debates of a deliberative body in Virginia been published; and no more complete and informative set of debates exists for any of the other state conventions." They might have added that no such record of James Madison in action is available anywhere else, either. Even the records of the Philadelphia Convention pale in comparison.

The convention opened on June 2. The venerable Edmund Pendleton, former chairman of the Revolutionary Committee of Safety and a known Federalist, won unanimous election to the presidency. He presented a characteristic Virginian address. As he had when elected to the same position in the convention that drafted the Virginia Declaration of Rights and the Virginia Constitution in 1776, and as George Washington would when inaugurated as president of the United States in 1789, Pendleton said that he was not up to the job, was struck by the honor, and hoped that his fellow delegates would indulge him when he erred.[43] As he put it, "My wish to have been excused From this appointment . . . *proceeded* . . . From a Consciousness of decline in my Mental powers, and my bodily infirmities, conspiring to render me unable to discharge the *duties*." (Part of what he meant was that he was unable to stand during the debates, as presiding officers in Virginia legislative bodies customarily did, following the English example.)[44]

Although he was a Federalist, Pendleton's understanding of Virginia's relationship with the other states was characteristically Virginian. "We are met together on this Solemn Occasion," he intoned, "as Trustees for a Great people, the Citizens of Virginia, to deliberate & decide upon a Plan proposed for the Government of the United States, of which they are a *Member*." The "Great people" was not a component of an American people, but was itself a people.

When the convention met the next day, Tuesday, June 3, George Mason proposed that it consider each provision of the Constitution "clause by clause, before any general previous question be put." Madison agreed. Mason's motion then won unanimous agreement.

The following day, June 4, the real fireworks began. After some preliminaries, including the convention's going into Committee of the Whole (in which Wythe, not Pendleton, would preside), Patrick Henry asked that the clerk read the acts of assembly appointing Virginia delegates to the Annapolis and Philadelphia conventions. His implication was that the delegates to those conventions had gone beyond the powers confided to them by the General Assembly. Pendleton stated that since the Philadelphia Convention had referred the Constitution to Congress for the people's consideration, Congress had referred the Constitution to the states for their consideration, the General Assembly had called elections for this convention, and the people had elected the members of this convention to consider ratification, it was improper to consider the extent of the Philadelphia Convention's powers. Henry withdrew his motion.

The clerk then read the Preamble and the first two sections of Article I. George Nicholas, for the Federalists, delivered a lengthy address defending the structure of the House of Representatives. He said nothing at all about the Preamble, which, like other preambles, was to be merely explanatory of the document's purpose. When he had finished, Patrick Henry made his first speech.

Henry was easily the most popular man in Virginia politics. He had been elected to five terms as governor and would have been governor in 1788 if he had wanted to be.

He had made his debut in Virginia politics by pleading the side of beleaguered Virginia taxpayers in a 1763 lawsuit known as the Parsons' Cause. In his debut as a member of the House of Burgesses in 1765, he once again had pled the case of Virginia taxpayers, this time with his 1765 resolutions against the Stamp Act. With those resolutions, which Henry introduced in his first week as a burgess, Henry bucked both the cousinocracy that ran the Old Dominion and the authority of the king.

Anyone who attempted to enforce the Stamp Act in the colony would be considered an enemy to his majesty's colony, Henry's screed said. Only Virginia's General Assembly had the right to tax Virginians, he thundered, and the kings of England had always said so.

By all accounts, Henry was a hypnotic speaker. His oratory was at once sermonic and fiery. One could not help but be swept up in the mighty river of persuasion that Henry could unleash. Thomas Jefferson, who frequently butted heads with Henry in Virginia politics, enviously recalled having sat through one of his performances.[45] He found that he could not help but agree, and feel the pounding surge of the undercurrent pull him along, as Henry spoke. When the speech ended, however, it dawned on Jefferson that he did not agree at all, and he could only marvel at Henry's oratorical power.

In Richmond in June of 1788, Henry was in his glory. Perhaps Mason, in a move worked out with the absent Ritt Lee weeks ahead of time, had won the convention's agreement to consider the Constitution clause by clause. Henry, for his part, was not going to be bound by that. He spoke more than any other two orators put together, and his oratory rocked the assemblage.

"The public mind," Henry's first speech began, "as well as my own, is extremely uneasy at the proposed change of Government." Why? "I consider myself," he said, "as the servant of the people of this Commonwealth as a centinel over their rights, liberty, and happiness. I represent their feelings when I say, that they are exceedingly uneasy, being brought from that full state of security, which they enjoyed, to the present delusive appearance of things."

George Nicholas had just asked that the delegates in Richmond, like those in Philadelphia, keep their dispute among themselves.[46] Nicholas's request reflected the same assumptions about the elite nature of Virginia's politics that were reflected in Madison's confiding to Randolph that if only the few most prominent non-Federalists among Virginia's leaders had come out for ratification, the common people would have followed. Henry was having none of it.

Nor was he buying the Federalist argument, widely broadcast by Madison in correspondence, private conversation, and *The Federalist,* that republican government had come to a crisis in 1788. As far as the American Demosthenes was concerned, the Virginian revolution was a success, whatever the few untrustworthy conspirators among Virginia's Philadelphia Convention delegates might say.[47] As he put it, "A year ago the minds of our citizens were at perfect repose. Before the meeting of the late Federal Convention at Philadelphia, a general peace, and an universal tranquility prevailed in this country;— but since that period they are exceedingly uneasy and disquieted."

Henry went on. "I conceive the republic to be in extreme danger." The problem lay not in inadequate federal power, but in "a proposal to change our government." Virginians' rights were in play, and "If a wrong step be now made, the Republic may be lost forever." Henry wanted the participants in the Philadelphia Convention to explain themselves. What dangers had they faced, and why had they proposed "an entire alteration of Government."

No doubt glancing at Randolph and Madison, Henry continued. "And here I would make this enquiry of those worthy characters who composed a part of the late Federal Convention." They had formed "a great consolidated Government, instead of a confederation." Repeating the standard Whig line that "the danger of such a Government is . . . very striking," Henry said that he had "the highest veneration for those Gentlemen." Yet, he demanded to know, "What right had they to say, *We, the People. . . .* Who authorised them to speak the language of, *We, the People,* instead of *We, the States?* "Then, cutting right to the point, he said, "If the States be not the agents of this compact, it must be one great consolidated National Government of the people of all the States." He would demand an explanation, he said, "even from that illustrious man [George Washington], who saved us by his valor."

Having asserted his respect for the premier Virginia Federalists, Henry next prepared the ground for all his later attacks. Federalists had betrayed Virginians' expectations before, he was saying. They were not to be trusted:

"That they exceeded their power is perfectly clear." Why take such momentous steps? Massachusetts had had its Shays' Rebellion, yes, "but here, Sir, no dangers, no insurrection or tumult, has happened—every thing has been calm and tranquil."

Henry had denied the basic presupposition of Madison's course of behavior: that there was a crisis before America's leading men that must be met with desperate measures. He said that the people of Virginia were happy with their republic, that the threat before him came from the Federalists themselves.

Madison and his friends might well dread the effect of Henry's oratory upon the convention. One Federalist wrote a week into the Richmond conclave that Henry's "eloquence and oratory far exceeded my conception."[48] "Madison's plain, ingenious, & elegant reasoning is entirely lost" among the class of delegates most susceptible to Henry's persuasion, he said. Those were "the ignorant people," and they were abundantly represented in the convention.[49]

In Henry's wake came Madison's friend, Edmund Randolph. Madison had known of the governor's wavering since the September 17 Philadelphia signing ceremony, and a few of Madison's friends were aware of it. Yet many must have expected Randolph to join Henry and George Mason, his fellow nonsigner, in leadership of the Anti-Federalists. Anticipation must have filled the room.

If Patrick Henry was the leading example of the new breed of men who had risen to prominence in the revolutionary movement, Edmund Randolph was a different type of cat altogether. The convention included men named Harrison and Bland, Madison and Cabell, Custis and Carrington, Nicholas and Lee—the flower of Virginia's bluebloods. None of their lineages, however, matched that of Edmund Randolph, son of the last colonial attorney general, cousin of the last colonial speaker of the Burgesses, descendant of many a burgess and councilor. When Thomas Jefferson, whose mother was a Randolph, wrote his autobiography, he went on at length about his father's family. Finally, he said in passing that of course his mother was a Randolph. No elaboration was required.

Edmund Randolph was not only a Randolph: he was tall, handsome, polished, and graceful. A portrait shows a man with a solid face and deep, dark eyes. His house was located right in the center of the colonial capital, Williamsburg. He had been the leader of Virginia's Philadelphia Convention delegation. And he was the incumbent governor.

As he rose to speak, Madison was about to chalk up a signal strategic victory.

Randolph said that never in peacetime had any other nation been brought "to agitate a question, an error in the issue of which, may blast their happiness."[50] He had followed his conscience, not any urge for popularity, to this point, he said, despite the fact that "to be moderate in politics, forbids an ascent to the summit of political fame." Then he came to the climax: "I come hither regardless of allurements; to continue as I have begun, to repeat my earnest endeavours for a firm energetic government, to enforce my objections to the Constitution, and to concur in any practical scheme of amendments; but I never will assent to any scheme that will operate a dissolution of the Union, or any measure which may lead to it."

Perhaps Madison had persuaded him. Perhaps Randolph believed that insisting on prior amendments as a condition of Virginia's ratification would run the Union aground.

Randolph explained that "with me the only question has ever been, between previous, and subsequent amendments." Now, he believed that "the postponement of this Convention, to so late a day, ha[d] extinguished the probability of the former without inevitable ruin to the Union, and the Union is the anchor of our political salvation; and I will assent to the lopping of this limb (meaning his arm) before I assent to the dissolution of the Union."

To Henry, Randolph responded that the Philadelphia conclave had created a new government instead of merely proposing amendments to the Articles because experience had proven the Articles entirely inadequate. "This necessity," he said, "was obvious to all America." As to Henry's objection that the Philadelphia Convention had no right to refer to "We, the People," Randolph dismissed it as "one of the least and most trivial objections that will be made to the Constitution." Finally, still insisting on the complete rightness of his course, Randolph said, "I refused my signature, and if the same reasons operated on my mind, I would still refuse; but as I think that those eight states which have adopted the Constitution will not recede, I am a friend to the Union."

That, recall, was the argument that Madison had pressed upon Randolph.

Mason next roamed across the Constitution finding various objections. This left time for only a brief statement from Madison that he would happily join Mason in "any conciliatory plan." June 4, 1788, had been a good day for the Federalist cause.

That night, Madison wrote to Rufus King and George Washington.[51] He was in a celebratory mood. "The Govr. has declared the day of previous amendments past, and thrown himself fully into our scale," he exulted. "M-s-n & H—y appeared to take different and awkward ground, & the federal party are apparently in the best spirits."

The following day, June 5, set the pattern of proceedings through most of the balance of the convention. First, two Federalists responded to Henry's more notable claims of the day before. Then, Henry took the floor for more than two-thirds of the day's recorded proceedings.[52] Henry pitifully asked whether concern for the preservation of liberty was *"old fashioned,"* then he recalled his role in the days of the Stamp Act to his colleagues' attention. People had said that his integrity had failed him, he noted, but "23 years ago was I supposed a traitor to my country." Other Virginians, he was sure, shared his concern.

Henry ranged far and wide, identifying shortcomings—threats to liberty— in many unrelated provisions of the Constitution. So, for example, where Article I said the number of representatives would not exceed one for every thirty thousand people, Henry asked whether one representative per state might not meet that requirement. He also called attention to the great expense to be associated with "maintaining the Senate and other House in as much splendor as they please" and the "extravagant magnificence" in which the president would be kept. In the end, "the whole of our property may be taken by this American Government, by laying what taxes they please, giving themselves what salaries they please, and suspending our laws at their pleasure."

Henry also made two points that went to the heart of America's revolutionary heritage. One was that the Constitution's delegation of power to call the militia into federal service left the states with no means of self-defense in case the federal government became oppressive. The other was that the foremost rights of Virginians, which they had inherited from their English ancestors, stood at risk under this new system.

At the end of that bravura performance, Henry made clear what his strategy would be. Virginia, he said, could reject the Constitution pending amendments even in case it were put into effect. In case it did, "what is to be the consequence, if we are disunited?" Would not the other states still accept Virginia's men and Virginia's money? Why not hold off and see how the new government worked?

Trademark appeals to the spirit of the revolution, love for inherited rights, and the days of the Stamp Act crisis, joined to insistence that Virginia could stand on its own—these were powerful arguments that Madison and his allies would have to answer. But not that day.

Friday, June 6, was dominated by the Federalists. Randolph led off with another in what was to become a long string of assertions of the ethical rectitude and political disinterestedness of his behavior: "Conscious of having exerted my faculties to the utmost in [my country's] behalf; if I have not succeeded in securing the esteem of my countrymen, I shall reap abundant consolation from the rectitude of my intentions: Honors, when compared to the satisfaction accruing from a conscious independence and rectitude of conduct, are no equivalent. The unwearied study of my life, shall be to promote her happiness. As a citizen, ambition and popularity are no objects with me."[53] Even now, one winces to read it. The more forcefully Randolph insisted that he had not been trying to gauge Virginia's domestic political winds, the less persuasive his assertions seem.

Besides that, Randolph's very long performance had two notable components. First, he reiterated his key assertion, which was that since eight states had already ratified, and since it was unlikely that having ratified without prior amendments, they would accept a Virginian insistence that amendments precede implementation of the Constitution, Virginia faced a simple question of union or disunion. Second, Randolph answered Patrick Henry's overriding contention that suspicion must color one's appraisal of public men's motives. "I confess," Randolph conceded, "that a certain degree of it is highly necessary to the preservation of liberty; but it ought not to be extended to a degree which is degrading and humiliating to human nature; to a degree of restlessness, and active disquietude, sufficient to disturb a community, or preclude the possibility of political happiness and contentment." In a summary of his own stance, he averred, "Wisdom shrinks from extremes, and fixes on a medium as her choice."

In direct response to Henry, Randolph said that Virginia could not exist independently of the Union. He insisted that the Confederation had failed to provide the states with adequate defense, either of their commerce or against invasion. It had failed even to defend itself against state transgressions, and so it needed to be replaced. If the moment was lost, he concluded, the Union would be lost for good.

Madison followed.[54] Interestingly, although he allied himself with Randolph, he first distinguished himself from the governor. "I shall not attempt," Madison began in tones barely audible, "to make impressions by any ardent professions of zeal for the public welfare. We know the principles of every man will, and ought to be judged, not by his professions and declarations, but by his conduct; by that criterion I mean in common with every other member to be judged." Not for Madison repeated flowery declarations of disinterestedness or prolonged public ruminations on his own motives and virtues. (Besides the immediate contrast with Randolph, in reading this statement one thinks of the contrast between his friend Thomas Jefferson's careful sketch of his gravestone and selection of the achievements to be listed thereon, on one hand, and Madison's complete omission to designate any type of gravestone at all, on the other.)

Having drawn this contrast, Madison then highlighted another. His target was Patrick Henry. "We ought not to address our arguments," the weak, nearly inaudible Madison said, "to the feelings and passions, but to those understandings and judgments which were selected by the people of this country, to decide this great question, by a calm and rational investigation." Perhaps heat suited the firebrand of 1765, Madison meant, but what was needed now was careful, cool development of reasoned argument. Madison could not hope to match Henry in the art of swaying an audience, so he would not try. Rather, he would let the merits of his case speak for themselves. As he put it, "I hope that Gentlemen, in displaying their abilities, on this occasion, instead of giving opinions, and making assertions, will condescend to prove and demonstrate, by a fair and regular discussion."

Henry had begun by saying that the Virginia people were tranquil in the enjoyment of their rights when the Philadelphia Convention first met. Madison asked, "If this be their happy situation, why has every State acknowledged the contrary? Why were deputies from all the States sent to the General Convention? Why have complaints of national and individual distresses been echoed and re-echoed throughout the Continent? Why has our General Government been so shamefully disgraced, and our Constitution violated? Wherefore have laws been made to authorise a change, and wherefore are we now assembled here?"

Madison's speech took up all of Henry's arguments, demolishing each one in turn. Thus, where Henry had lamented that the federal government would have power to call out the militia, Madison noted that the alternative would have been to give the president a standing army to meet any contingency—surely an inferior option. Where Henry had said that one must suspect officeholders of a disposition to establish tyranny, Madison followed up on Randolph's insistence that suspicion could be carried too far; after all, Madison added, freedom had usually fallen prey not to officeholders but to "internal dissentions."

Madison answered Henry's insistence that this was to be a "consolidated," not a "federal" government at great length. "I conceive myself," he said, "that it is of a mixed nature." Here, he took up the argument he had previously developed at length in Federalist No. 39. Thus, in regard to ratification, the Constitution would be the work of the people, but not one great American people; rather, it would be the act of the people in each of the states, each state acting for itself. Any state that did not ratify the Constitution would not be bound by it. The Senate would be apportioned by state, but the House would be apportioned by population. Most powers were left in the states, but the federal government could exercise those that were "enumerated"—it had "Legislative powers on defined and limited objects, beyond which it [could not] extend its jurisdiction." In short, it was not a consolidated government.

Henry said some of the powers granted to the new government would be dangerous. Madison answered by asking whether they were necessary. The power to tax was necessary, because in wartime government had to have money in hand. As to the idea that the great powers of the new government would ultimately allow it to overwhelm the state governments, Madison called his audience's attention to the modes of election to Congress: members of the

James Madison.
(Charles Willson Peale, 1783, Library of Congress)

Patrick Henry was the greatest orator of the American Revolution. Henry's dominance of Virginia politics helped spur Madison to seek federal reform, which Henry did his best to steer in a direction distasteful to Madison. *(Lawrence Sully,* Patrick Henry *[1736–1799], Mead Art Museum, Amherst College, Amherst, Massachusetts, Bequest of Herbert L. Pratt [Class of 1895], accession no. 1945.115)*

At first his ally, then his collaborator, and finally his antagonist, the Federalist chieftain Alexander Hamilton played a prominent role in Madison's political career. *(Giuseppe Ceracchi,* Alexander Hamilton *[c. 1793], item no. 1928.18, Collection of the New-York Historical Society)*

So frequent were Madison's visits to Monticello that the room in which he and Dolley usually stayed is still called by his name. *(Madison Room, Monticello/Thomas Jefferson Foundation, Inc., Photography by Robert C. Lautman)*

John Randolph, Jefferson's cousin, began the Jefferson administration as House majority leader, but his distrust of Madison led him to break with the Republicans and form his own Old Republican party, the Tertium Quids. *(University of Virginia)*

Although not a beauty, Mrs. Madison was commonly called buxom and vivacious. She turned those qualities, along with her many family connections, to good political use. (*Gilbert Stuart,* Dolley Madison, *1804, White House Historical Association [White House Collection]*)

This image of Madison captures his reserved, cerebral personality better than any other portrait for which he sat. *(Gilbert Stuart,* James Madison, *1804, Colonial Williamsburg Foundation)*

President Jefferson relied heavily on his secretary of state for advice on diplomatic, political, and constitutional questions. *(Gilbert Stuart,* Thomas Jefferson, *1805, Colonial Williamsburg Foundation)*

Jefferson's Swiss-born treasury secretary, the longest-serving Cabinet officer ever, oversaw the implementation of the domestic program laid out in Jefferson's First Inaugural. Yet, as Madison's treasury secretary, he pushed behind the scenes for congressional legislation extending the charter of Hamilton's bank. *(*Albert Gallatin by Rembrandt Peale, from Life, *1805, Independence National Historical Park)*

Madison's home, Montpelier.
(The Library of Virginia)

This image captures the physical decline and the mental acuity notably characteristic of Madison in old age. *(Chester Harding, James Madison, 1829-30, National Portrait Gallery, Smithsonian Institution)*

With James Monroe in the chair, Madison here addresses an assemblage including future president John Tyler, Chief Justice John Marshall, John Randolph of Roanoke, and Governor William Branch Giles. *(George Catlin,* Virginia Convention of 1829-30, *Virginia Historical Society)*

Madison gravestone, Montpelier.
(The Montpelier Foundation)

House would depend on the local influence of men such as those in state offices, and so would be unlikely to strike up conflicts with them; senators would be elected by the state legislators, and so would be even more unlikely to try to undermine state government, "the source from which they derive their political existence." Besides, "I hope the patriotism of the people will continue, and be a sufficient guard to their liberties."

Nicholas followed. Here, Madison's coadjutor opined that in delegating powers, a happy medium must be sought: not only must the peril of granting too much power be avoided, but so, since government was necessary, must the peril of granting too little. The former error led to oppression, yes, Henry was right about that. The latter, however, would cause the government "to moulder and decay away."

The next day, Saturday, June 7, the Committee of the Whole first heard from a less prominent man, Francis Corbin, before settling in for long speeches by Randolph, Madison, and Henry. For anyone who had not tired of him yet, Randolph began by noting in refutation of Henry's insistence that the Confederation was adequate that "I have given the full effusions of my soul, in my attempt to prove the futility of that opinion."[55] He then went on to lament that as Henry dominated the proceedings, "The system under consideration is objected to in an unconnected and irregular manner. Detached parts are attacked without considering the whole."

One of the topics Randolph considered in this speech was Henry's objection to the smallness of the proposed House of Representatives. Randolph here merely echoed Madison's argument, in Philadelphia, Federalist No. 10, and correspondence, concerning the benefits of larger districts.

The problem of faction was more likely, Randolph said, to appear in large bodies than in small. Therefore, "I would rather depend on the virtue and knowledge of some few men, than on ever so many." Not precisely a Madisonian point, but then, Randolph explained that with Virginia divided into only ten U.S. House districts, each man elected "must be really the choice of the people: Not the man who can distribute the most gold: for the riches of Croesus would not avail." Lest his audience miss the point, Randolph elaborated by saying that "the extension of the sphere of election to so considerable a district, will render it impossible for contracted influence, or local intrigues, or personal interest to procure an election."

Who would be elected to office under the new Constitution, if not demagogues of great local influence? "Greater talents, and a more extensive reputation will be necessary, to procure an election for the Federal, than for the State representation." Some had objected that the rich and well-born would dominate the new government, but "Is it not notorious that virtue and ability have been preferred generally here to riches and connections?" One can only guess how effective this warmed-over Madisonian argument was in persuading undecided delegates.

Randolph closed with a few words on the necessity of vesting a taxing power in the central government. Citizens of ancient confederations and modern, he said, had suffered from the "imbecility of their Governments" in the absence of a taxing power. With this last bit of borrowed rhetoric, Randolph then handed off the task of developing the argument to Madison himself.

Madison took up the task, which had been developed at length in *The Federalist,* of proving Randolph's assertion with historical evidence.[56] First, he offered the American case: "Can Congress," he asked, "after the repeated unequivocal proofs it has experienced of the utter inutility and inefficacy of requisitions, reasonably expect, that they would be hereafter effectual or productive? Will not the same local interests, and other causes, militate against a compliance?" The only way to correct the problem, Dr. Madison insisted, was to administer the cure.

What cure was that? As Madison told it, "The uniform conclusion drawn from a review of ancient and modern Confederacies, is, that instead of promoting the public happiness, or securing public tranquility, they have, in every instance, been productive of anarchy and confusion; ineffectual for the preservation of harmony, and a prey to their own dissentions and foreign invasions." Even stronger ones, such as the ancient Greek Amphictionic League, proved the point. He also explained how the Achaean League, the Holy Roman Empire, the Swiss Confederation, and the contemporary government of the Netherlands had experienced similar problems. Mere confederation, without a power in the central government to tax the people directly, simply would not do.

America would be drawn into war again someday, Madison cautioned. When that happened, the Confederation would not be able to defend the American peripheries. That was why at the moment of his retirement as commander in chief, General Washington (here, Madison followed the convention of referring to Washington not simply by name, but by reference to his military service) had "publicly testified his disapprobation of the present system, and suggested that some alteration was necessary to render it adequate to the security of our happiness."

Madison accepted Henry's insistence "that national splendor and glory are not our objects." However, he added, the Confederation's inadequacy cried out for remedy. Foreign governments would not enter into treaties with the Americans because of its feebleness. Since the world knew that the Confederation could not bring the states into compliance with the Treaty of Paris, America was missing out on the advantages it might reap via new treaties with other foreign powers. Not only that, but the moral obligation to requite France for its abundant help now that it faced crying need of its own ought to impel America to act. The Confederation, in the face of these needs, had virtually no fiscal resources.

Patrick Henry next reclaimed the stage, which he kept through the rest of the day.[57] His chief contentions were directed at Randolph. First, he noted that Randolph had publicly expressed strong disapprobation of the Constitution. What had changed to make it acceptable, even necessary, now?

During the war, Henry noted, Vermont had bid defiance to all thirteen states. Maryland alone had refused to ratify the Articles of Confederation for four years. "These two states, feeble as they are comparatively to us, were not afraid of the whole Union. Did either of these States perish? No, sir." Virginia could exploit their example. It could hold out until the Constitution was amended appropriately.

Henry found an illustration of the revolutionary maxim that men were not to be trusted with power near at hand. As both Randolph and Madison listened, he held that, "When we trusted the great object of revising the Confederation to the greatest, the best, and most enlightened of our citizens, we thought their deliberations would have been solely confined to that revision. Instead of this, a new system, totally different in its nature and vesting the most extensive powers in Congress, is presented. Will the ten men you are to send to Congress, be more worthy than those seven were? If power grew so rapidly in their hands, what may it not do in the hands of others?"

Henry also turned Madison's historic illustrations against him. With a form of government similar to the Articles of Confederation, Henry noted, the Netherlands had become outstanding in the world not only for their fleets, armies, science, and affluence, but also for their liberty. "Sir, they acquired these," Henry warmed to his topic, "by their industry, œconomy, and by the freedom of their Government." The explanation of the rise of so small a country of so few people to such a station of eminence in the world was "Liberty, Sir, the freedom of their Government."

Henry closed by asserting the chief points underlying the Anti-Federalist argument: that there needed to be a bill of rights, and that the federal government should be constrained by the limits of the powers expressly conferred upon it by the Constitution. "Implication in England has been a source of dissention," he said. "The people insisted that their rights were implied: The Monarch denied the doctrine." Turning to the American example, this voice of the revolution recalled that "thirteen or fourteen years ago, the most important thing that could be thought of, was to exclude the possibility of construction and implication." A bill of rights was necessary, then, "indispensably necessary," and it should include "a general positive provision . . . securing to the States and the people, every right which was not conceded to the General Government."

With that, the Convention adjourned until Monday.

Monday, June 9, marked a milestone. That day, William Grayson (the former acting president of Congress who played a prominent role among Anti-Federalists in the Richmond Convention), George Mason, and Patrick Henry wrote to John Lamb of New York.[58] Lamb had undertaken correspondence with Virginia, New Hampshire, Pennsylvania, Maryland, North Carolina, and South Carolina Anti-Federalists on behalf of those of the Federal Republican Committee of New York, an Anti-Federalist group. Their goal was to cooperate in putting off ratification until amendments had been affixed.

Grayson and Mason both told Lamb that the outcome of the convention could not yet be predicted because the delegates were so evenly divided.[59] Henry added the observation that this did not reflect the feeling of Virginians in general, who opposed the Constitution by a margin of four to one.[60] Henry added that North Carolina opposed the Constitution strongly, and that the Virginia committee would send Lamb's committee the bill of rights and amendments his Virginian correspondents intended to propose. The draft amendments included a mélange of the Virginia Declaration of Rights, points on which Mason had been defeated in Philadelphia (such as a requirement of a two-thirds majority in each house of Congress for any tariff law), and some proposals calculated to appeal to marginal delegates (such as one requiring a three-fourths majority in each house for ratification of any treaty ceding any American territorial, fishing, or navigation claim, on which more below).

In the end, these machinations had little impact. The New York committee responded to the Virginian communications only on June 21. Although it was sent by a fast ship, that communication did not arrive in Richmond in time to affect the deliberations.

On that same Monday, June 9, only three delegates—Patrick Henry, Edmund Randolph, and Henry Lee—addressed their fellows. The great majority of the proceedings were taken up by Patrick Henry, who again ranged across the Constitution in quest of provisions and omissions dangerous to Virginians' liberty.[61] Most significantly, he dusted off the issue that Anti-Federalists hoped would win them the votes of the Kentucky contingent: the Jay-Gardoquì negotiation over the Mississippi navigation.

As Henry told the story, seven state delegations to the Confederation Congress had voted to surrender American access to the Mississippi for twenty-five years. Under the new Constitution, unlike under the Articles, that would be sufficient. He also inquired at great length how Governor Randolph could have changed his position from one of strong opposition to that of one of the leading proponents of immediate ratification. Henry mockingly said, "I had the highest respect for the Honorable Gentleman's abilities. I considered his opinion as a great authority. He taught me, Sir, in despite of the approbation of that great Federal Convention, to doubt of the propriety of that system." In sum, "When I found my Honorable friend in the number of those who doubted, I began to doubt also. I coincided with him in opinion. I shall be a staunch and faithful disciple of his."

Repeatedly turning to mockery of Randolph, Henry also at one point alighted on Madison's argument about the uniqueness of the form of government laid out in the Constitution. Recall that as in Federalist No. 39, so here, Madison had laid out the argument that the government was to be national in this way, federal in that, national and federal in this, federal and national in that, and so on. "What signified it to me," he asked, "that you have the most curious anatomical description of it in its creation? To all the common purposes of legislation it is a great consolidation of Government." Bereft of legislative authority in all but "trivial cases" and deprived of "the right of having arms in your own defence," the people ought to "Abolish the State Legislatures at once." As he saw it, "we have the consolation that it is a mixed Government: That is, it may work sorely on your neck; but you will have some comfort by saying, that it was a Federal Government in its origin."

Toward the end of his address, Henry noted that, "I am constrained to make a few remarks on the absurdity of adopting this system, and relying on the chance of getting it amended afterwards." He called it being bound hand and foot, for the sake of being unbound. He recast it as entering a dungeon, for the sake of getting out. "Human nature," he said, "never will part with power. Look for an example of voluntary relinquishment of power, from one end of the globe to another—You will find none." "I should be led to take that man to be a lunatic," he concluded, "who should tell me to run into the adoption of a Government, avowedly defective, in hopes of having it amended afterwards."

Henry Lee followed.[62] His blustery address's highlight was his insistence that Patrick Henry erred: citizens' liberties would be perfectly safe under the new Constitution. As Lee told it, "It goes on the principle that all power is in the people, and that rulers have no powers but what are enumerated in that paper. When a question arises with respect to the legality of any power, exercised or assumed by Congress, it is plain on the side of the governed. *Is it enumerated in the Constitution?* If it be, it is legal and just. It is otherwise arbitrary and unconstitutional."

Lee then repeated James Wilson's by now famous argument that while under the state governments the people had only the powers expressly retained, the federal government would have only the "certain defined powers." A bill of rights, then, was "folly."

At this point, Edmund Randolph unloaded on Patrick Henry.[63] Randolph claimed that he had explained his change of position clearly by reference to the fact that eight states had already ratified the unamended Constitution. Therefore, he had concluded, Virginia could not expect amendment to precede implementation, whatever it might do. Henry had responded, he said, by "aspersions" and "insinuations" that Randolph "disdain[ed]." Angrily, he thundered, "His asperity is warranted by no principle of Parliamentary decency, nor compatible with the least shadow of friendship; and if our friendship must fall—*Let it fall like Lucifer, never to rise again.*" In ringing denunciation, Randolph proclaimed that, "if I do not stand on the bottom of integrity, and pure love for Virginia, as much as those who can be most clamorous, I wish to resign my existence."

When Henry rose to assert that he had not intended "to wound the feelings of any Gentleman," Randolph did not accept. "Were it not for the concession of the Gentleman," the governor retorted, "he would have made some men's hair stand on end, by the disclosure of certain facts." Henry asked Randolph to explain himself, and Randolph ignored him. Randolph said that he had told his constituents before the Henrico County elections that he favored the Union strongly, and that he had never told them he would oppose ratification.

Turning to Henry's many historical references, Randolph disputed them at length. Randolph noted that if Virginia insisted on previous amendments, it would lose its influence in constituting the Congress and the executive. Without a role there, he noted, Virginia would have little say in drafting the amendments. (No one needed to have spelled out for him that if Virginia did not help choose the executive, it also would not be able to provide the first president—George Washington.)

Besides that, Randolph continued, Henry was wrong to say America needed a bill of rights. England had one, yes, but in England, the king "could trample on the liberties of the people, in every case which was not within the restraint of the Bill of Rights." America needed no such provision. "Six or seven States" had no bills of rights. In fact, as Randolph understood it, the judges might hold it superior to the Constitution, so that, "A Bill of Rights . . . is quite useless, if not dangerous, in a republic."

Randolph still believed that the Constitution needed to be amended. As he put it, "I will join any man in endeavouring to get amendments." However, that goal must be sought "after the danger of disunion is removed by a previous adoption." Ratify, then amend—just as Madison had said. Virginia needed the Union, if only because "our negroes are numerous, and daily becoming more so."

Madison and Nicholas were both absent that Monday due to illness.[64] As

Madison explained in a letter to Hamilton that night, the "Heat of the weather" had afflicted him with "a bilious attack."[65] To Rufus King, he explained that same night that, "I have been for two days & still am laid up."[66] Madison's weakness would affect his performance from time to time through the rest of the convention.

Tuesday, June 10, Madison had recovered from his illness sufficiently to return to the convention,[67] which heard more of Randolph's critique of Henry's performance and got first impressions of James Monroe and John Marshall.[68] Particularly noteworthy was Randolph's insistence that the freedoms of speech, press, and religion were not endangered. "Every power not given [to the General Government] by this system is left with the States," he said. "No power is given expressly to Congress over religion," so that one was secure. He reasoned similarly regarding the others. In addition, again borrowing arguments that Madison had made in correspondence, in Philadelphia, and in Federalist No. 10, Randolph explained the protection that a multiplicity of religions among the populace would provide: "I am a friend to a variety of sects," he explained, "because they keep one another in order." With so many of them, both in Congress and in the country at large, an "infringe[ment] of religious liberty" would be impracticable.

John Marshall, in his first speech to the convention, insisted that the new government must be adopted to render America secure. The rulers of some cantons in the Swiss Confederation had been bought off by foreign governments, he said, and the lesson was applicable to the American case. America's Confederation could not protect American commerce against foreign navies' depredations, as any adequate government must do. He would not accept Monroe's hopeful forecast that America would not soon have war again. "It imports not what system we have," Marshall lectured, "unless it have the power of protecting us in time of peace and war."

Finally, George Nicholas rose again.[69] He lamented that although the convention had sat for eight days, the irregular mode of proceeding had prevented it from accomplishing much. He also protested, "It is a fact, known to many members within my hearing, that several members have tried their interest without doors [that is, made their case to the people], to induce others to oppose this system." Could any believe that the fruit of Virginia, elected to exercise their judgment and wisdom, would be thus swayed? He hoped not.

Henry, Nicholas said, had proclaimed that ratification would deprive Virginians of the benefits of their Declaration of Rights. Yet the Declaration of Rights said that the majority had a right to reframe its government when necessary. Henry said that ratification would cost the western counties. Yet were not the western counties in need of military protection—which the Confederation could not provide? Would not people in the West like the British to leave their western posts? The British had responded to such demands by insisting that America first comply with the treaty requirement that British creditors be enabled to collect their debts in American courts—which the Confederation could not make the states facilitate. When it came to the Mississippi navigation, Nicholas held that force and treaty were its only guaranties, and that the Confederation could give Westerners neither. They must favor ratification, then.

Most interesting of Nicholas's arguments was his answer to Henry's warnings about the breadth of the Necessary and Proper Clause. Found in Article I, Section 8 of the Constitution, that clause says that Congress will have power to adopt such laws as shall be "necessary and proper" to put the listed specific powers into effect. Nicholas insisted that this clause granted no new powers, but merely entitled Congress to do what it needed to do to exercise the listed powers. "Suppose," Nicholas said, "it had been inserted at the end of every power, that they should have power to make laws to carry that power into execution; Would this have increased their powers? If therefore it could not have increased their powers, if placed at the end of each power, it cannot increase them at the end of all. This clause only enables them to carry into execution the powers given them, but gives them no additional power."

Nicholas applied similar reasoning to the Anti-Federalist argument concerning the need for a bill of rights. In England, he pointed out, the people had only enumerated rights; under the Constitution, the new government would have only the enumerated powers. "Is the disputed right enumerated? If not, Congress cannot meddle with it. Which is the most safe?" In fact, the Constitution would be analogous to the English Bill of Rights, only better: each provided for regular sessions of the legislature and against suspension of laws, but while the English Bill of Rights banned armies in peacetime without Parliament's consent, the Constitution banned military appropriations longer than two years even in wartime.

In conclusion, Nicholas commented that this government would "suit almost any extent of territory." Perhaps reflecting Madison's influence, he cited Montesquieu's dictum that only a confederate republic provided a "safe means of extending the sphere of a Republican Government to any considerable degree."

Wednesday, June 11, found Madison back before the Committee of the Whole, with George Wythe presiding.[70] First, Madison opined, "I presume that vague discourses and mere sports of fancy, not relative to the subject at all, are very improper on this interesting occasion. I hope," he continued, "these will be no longer attempted, but that we shall come to the point. I trust we shall not go out of order, but confine ourselves to the clause under consideration. I beg," he pled, "Gentlemen would observe this rule."

He then developed an argument that the power of direct taxation in lieu of the Confederation's requisitions, a power that had been much denigrated by Anti-Federalist speakers such as Henry, Mason, and Monroe, was absolutely necessary. Without it, he insisted, the government could not "protect the community." In light of the state of relations between France and Britain, he continued, recurrence of war between them was not unlikely. In case it came to that, Britain would seize American ships at sea and in port, and America would need direct taxes to repel the British.

Requisitions led to separate deliberations about compliance in the thirteen separate states, Madison said. In case this new Constitution were ratified, there would be only one deliberation, and in Congress, "No local views will be permitted to operate against the general welfare."

Madison also considered the objection, raised by numerous Anti-Federalists, that ten Virginians in the House of Representatives would not be sufficient to devise an appropriate taxation scheme. "I confess," he said, "that I do not see the force of this observation." Each of ten districts would include at least one man with adequate information for the task. He would be able to take his knowledge with him. Besides, although there were many more than ten delegates in the House of Delegates, "the business . . . devolves on a much smaller number." In fact, "It will be found that there are seldom more than ten men who rise to high information on this subject."

Besides that, Madison continued, the people's state of informedness was improving every day. That trend would continue. Members of the new Congress would have the information of the state governments at hand. Here

Madison reverted to what he had said of the benefits of extending the sphere before: representatives drawn from large districts, he intoned, were less prone to "treachery," because "undue influence" was harder to employ in a large district and the voters were more independent. The proof was to be found in the experience of the United Kingdom, whose rotten boroughs—parliamentary districts with extremely small populations—were notoriously corrupt, while its large districts traditionally produced champions of freedom.

Madison pooh-poohed James Monroe's prediction of a coalition among the three branches of the new government against the states. The representatives would have strong local connections and be answerable to state legislators because of the legislators' influence. Additionally, as during the revolution, Americans would feel greater attachment to the states than to the new government. Finally, the states would preponderate because they would employ so many more people than the general government. "I may say with truth," Madison confidently predicted, "that there never was a more economical Government in any age or country; nor which will require fewer hands, or give less influence." Monroe had it backwards, and the danger was that the states would impede implementation of federal policy.

The general government had mainly wartime powers regarding "external objects," while the state governments affected "those great objects which immediately concern the prosperity of the people." The new government would have essentially the same powers as the Confederation, except that they would now be effective, not merely nominal.

When Madison finished his argument, he reiterated that he hoped his colleagues would begin to respect the rule they had agreed to at the beginning of the convention by proceeding clause by clause instead of referring to provisions at random.[71] Henry responded that both sides had taken up whatever arguments they liked, and that he thought that was the best mode. Madison replied that he did not want to impede the convention's full consideration of the Constitution, but that he thought the rule provided the best route. George Mason then said that he had not spoken much, but he believed that ranging across the Constitution would work best, so that was what he would do.

Mason argued that the legislators in the new government would be drawn chiefly from among the rich and well-born. He said that they could not be as familiar with Virginians' situation as were the 160 members of their own legislature. He decried the absence of a bill of rights, because the Supremacy Clause meant that the new government's acts would be superior to Virginia's Declaration of Rights. As to George Nicholas's assertion that the North's population advantage would soon turn to the South's advantage, Mason compared it to an argument that "we should cheerfully burn ourselves to death in hopes of a joyful and happy resurrection!"

Mason objected to several Federalists' references to domestic safety. The Constitution, he averred, did not advance Virginians' safety; rather, "It authorizes the importation of slaves for twenty odd years, and thus continues upon us that nefarious trade. Instead of securing and protecting us," he pointed out, "the continuation of this detestable trade, adds daily to our weakness." Besides that, nothing in the Constitution prevents the northern and eastern states from meddling with slavery as it already existed. Slavery as it already existed should have been protected by the Constitution, he concluded.

"We ask such amendments," Mason held, "as will point out what powers are reserved to the State Governments, and clearly discriminate between them, and those which are given to the General Government, so as to prevent future disputes and clashing of interests." Grant them, and Anti-Federalists would support the government. Absent them, "we can never accede to it."

Mason denied that he and his allies wanted disunion. In fact, he said he did not know anyone who wanted disunion. "We acknowledge the defects of the Confederation," he said, "and the necessity of a reform. We ardently wish for an Union with our sister States, on terms of security." He would explain precisely what amendments were needed at another time, along with why subsequent amendments were "perhaps utterly impracticable."

Madison would repeat his call for regular order before the day's end.[72] Then the convention adjourned. That night, Madison explained to a correspondent both where he thought matters stood and what he understood Anti-Federalists' strategy to be.[73] At present, Federalists seemed to have a majority. Anti-Federalists, on the other hand, were playing on the local interests of particular delegates to swing them into opposition. This might defeat the Constitution. If not, Anti-Federalists could delay a final vote long enough to drive the delegates, concerned with the incoming crop, horridly hot weather, and impending session of the General Assembly, to recess the convention.

Over the next two days, June 12–13, the convention considered the issue of the Mississippi navigation. Numerous delegates spoke on the matter, laying out the Confederation Congress's posture in regard to Spanish insistence that Spain alone control the river and considering whether Kentuckians' right would be more or less secure under the proposed Constitution.

William Grayson, recently acting president of Congress, offered his opinion that it would long be in the interest of the northern states to surrender the navigation.[74] Doing so would stop the rapid migration of people to the West, which would allow the northern states to maintain their superiority of population. Under the new Constitution, two-thirds of Senate members present could ratify a treaty; two-thirds of a quorum would be ten members; therefore, five states could make a treaty to surrender the Mississippi. (Since seven states' delegations had recently voted to empower John Jay to bargain away the navigation, this was quite a daunting prospect.) Grayson's conclusion was that the West was safer under the Articles of Confederation, which required nine states to ratify any treaty.

Edmund Pendleton answered Grayson with the commonsense point that in cases of great moment, senators from all the states could be expected to attend. Then, he said, the Constitution's two-thirds requirement for ratification would amount to nine states' Senate delegations—as under the Articles. Besides, Pendleton continued, the president would represent the entire country, not a region, and he would have to approve a proposed treaty as well. In addition, Pendleton joined other Federalists (such as Madison) in adjudging successful treaty negotiations far more likely under the more stable, respectable system under consideration.

Madison's first entrance into this debate came on its first day, June 12.[75] He contradicted much of what had already been said. For example, he noted that it had been the southern states, not the northern, that had first proposed trading the Mississippi navigation for Spanish military aid during the war. At that time, the northern states had opposed the idea. Yes, the sides had later been reversed, but the proposal had been for only a temporary surrender of the right—and that joined to ultimate vindication of Americans' claim to access. Madison thought it likely that the West would be peopled by both northern and southern migrants, so that senators from both the North and the South would rush to the Mississippi navigation's defense. In addition,

Madison complicated these calculations by pointing out that Connecticut, Delaware, New Jersey, and part of New Hampshire were not "carrying" states at all. Therefore, they should not be reckoned among the bloc of states apt to want to trade the navigation for commercial considerations.

Madison had a rare occasion to make a second speech on the same day.[76] Then, unusually for him, he made flat declaratory statements about the prospect of the Mississippi navigation under the Confederation: "I will undertake to say, that [no treaty] *will* be formed under the old system, which will secure to us the actual enjoyment of the navigation of the Mississippi. Our weakness precludes us from it. We *are* entitled to it. But it is not under an inefficient Government that we shall be able to avail ourselves fully of that right." In the short term, the Constitution was necessary to guarantee Kentuckians' right; in the long term, their burgeoning population would enable them to exercise it despite any foreigners' efforts to the contrary.

The next day, June 13, Nicholas kicked things off by insisting that the convention return to regular order: taking up the Constitution clause by clause.[77] Henry objected that he would prefer to continue to discuss the Mississippi issue. In response to Henry's call for "a faithful statement of facts," Madison answered that if Henry meant that Madison's statement had been false, he was mistaken. Madison declared that he had always opposed temporary surrender of the Mississippi navigation, and Henry Lee added that Congress had always opposed the idea. In fact, Lee said, "they earnestly wished to adopt the best possible plan of securing it."

James Monroe, who had been a congressman at the time, then proceeded to explain the events in Congress that had led to John Jay's being given authority temporarily to barter away the river passage.[78] William Grayson, also a former congressman, followed with a speech insisting that the East had wanted to sacrifice the West's rights in hopes of perpetuating the East's population advantage.[79]

Madison then intervened again.[80] He thought this issue irrelevant to the matter at hand, he said, but he had to correct others' interpretations of events and others' forecasts. If the North was to be the carrying section, Madison reasoned, it would have a greater interest even than the South in maintaining American access to the Mississippi. After all, the Mississippi was to be used as a route to the sea, for exporting goods, which would be carried on northern ships. Besides that, northern population was migrating westward as well as southern, and that too would link the North firmly to the West.

Madison continued that surrender of access to the Mississippi was "repugnant to the law of nations." Temporary surrender had been contemplated by seven states in wartime, yes, but no one had thought of forfeiting the right permanently. Grayson contradicted him, pointing again to the East's purported desire to dominate the Union ever after, and added that friends to the idea had told him they intended to revive the project.[81] Patrick Henry asked whether Madison's insistence that the House would be able to block implementation of such a treaty did not give the lie to Madison's talk of checks and balances, and then Nicholas asked how an attempt by the Confederation Congress to negotiate away the Mississippi navigation for a term of years could support Henry's insistence that keeping the Confederation was the way to preserve American access to the river.[82]

The next day, June 14, the convention considered several minor provisions. Repeatedly, individual delegates asked Madison—as a participant in the Philadelphia Convention—to explain them. Madison patiently elucidated these minutiae, and he repeatedly responded to minor objections by noting that it was "impossible to devise any system agreeable to all."[83]

The day's events strike the reader now, as they struck interested observers then, as tedious. Gouverneur Morris, sitting in the galleries, waxed poetic:

> *Extempore at the Convention in Virga*
> *The State's determined Resolution*
> *Was to discuss the Constitution*
> *For this the Members come together*
> *Melting with Zeal and sultry Weather*
> *And here to their eternal Praise*
> *To find it's Hist'ry spend three Days*
> *The next three Days they nobly roam*
> *Thro ev'ry Region far from Home*
> *Call in the Grecian Swiss Italian*
> *The Roman [Russian?] Dutch Rapscallion*
> *Fellow who Freedom never knew*
> *To tell us what we ought to do*

> *The next three Days they kindly dip yee*
> *Deep in the River Mississippi*
> *Nine Days thus spent eer they begin*
> *Let us suppose them fairly in*
> *And then resolve me gentle Friend*
> *How many Months before they End*[84]

At one point, Madison had an opportunity to state his general political faith. He had heard, he said, many people say that one side was more confident, the other more distrustful. He didn't deny it, but hastened to add that where power was necessary, prudence required that it be given. "I profess myself," he enthused, "to have had an uniform zeal for a Republican Government. If the Honorable Member, or any other person, conceives that my attachment to this system arises from a different source, he is greatly mistaken. From the first moment that my mind was capable of contemplating political subjects, I never, till this moment," George III's one-time subject concluded, "ceased wishing success to a well regulated Republican Government. The establishment of such in America was my most ardent desire."

The problem Americans faced was "the tendency of a relaxation of laws, and licentiousness of manners." Historically, trends like that led to anarchy, then despotism. "I can see no danger," he gushed, "in submitting to practice an experiment which seems to be founded on the best theoretic principles." Patrick Henry replied that he could barely believe Madison wanted to trust Virginia's liberty to an experiment. Madison's answer[85] was that America's situation verged on anarchy, and the Confederation's weakness was tantamount to a dissolution. "Is it not agreed upon all hands, that a reform is necessary? If any takes place, will it not be an experiment as well as this system?" Henry admitted that the Confederation was defective, Madison continued, and any change he could propose would be an experiment too.

The obviously fatigued delegates must have rejoiced that the next day was a Sunday.

The following day, Monday, June 16, found Madison disputing Henry's characterization of the new government's proposed militia power.[86] Every government had to have force in hand, Madison noted. The South, due to its "situation and circumstances," had a greater interest than other states in ensuring that the central government have the requisite power.

Again and again, Henry raised the specter of arbitrary government. Again and again, Madison calmly refuted Henry's warnings. At one point, amid various contentions over sundry provisions, the reporter noted, "A desultory conversation ensued."[87] Then, Mason, Henry, and Grayson argued that the reservation of all powers not granted to the central government by the Constitution must not rest on implication.[88] Mason asked what it would hurt to make this point explicit by an amendment, and Grayson noted that inclusion of an explicit provision to that effect in the Articles seemed to contradict the idea that one could take the idea for granted. So, he continued, did the inclusion of provisions barring Congress from conferring titles of nobility and from suspending the writ of habeas corpus except in certain circumstances; why would these provisions have been included, Grayson asked, if one could not have inferred from some other clause that Congress had these powers?

Meanwhile, Madison found himself beset by illness once again.[89] He explained that evening that "to day have a [bit?] of relapse. My health is not good, and the business is wearisome beyond expression." Whether by "wearisome" he meant "fatiguing" or "tedious" is unclear.

The next day, Tuesday, found Madison in an uncomfortable position. Mason kicked things off with a short, sharp speech criticizing the Constitution's provision that Congress could not ban slave imports until 1808.[90] Mason had argued against this clause in Philadelphia, and he remained unreconciled. As he put it, "I would not admit the Southern States [meaning Georgia and South Carolina] into the Union, unless they agreed to the discontinuance of this disgraceful trade." Not only did the Constitution perpetuate imports, he said, but it provided no protection for the slavery that already existed.

Madison's answer, too, was brief, and it contested what Mason said at both points.[91] First, Madison claimed that Georgia and South Carolina would not have agreed to the Constitution absent the 1808 clause.[92] That clause, Madison noted, was temporary—and in fact was an improvement upon the Confederation, which did not empower Congress ever to ban slave imports. Virginia could maintain its own ban on slave imports.

Besides that, Madison boasted, the Constitution *did* provide increased protection for the slave property that Virginians already held. With its Fugitive Slave Clause, the Constitution would require states into which fugitive slaves fled to return them to their masters. The Articles included no such provision, he noted, and so fugitives were not presently being returned, but were rendered free by their arrival in free states.

In the Philadelphia Convention, Madison noted, South Carolina and Georgia delegates had responded to Mason's complaint by saying that bans on slave imports raised the value of slaves Virginians already held. Really, they said, Mason's argument was self-interested. "I need not expiate on this subject," Madison closed. "Great as the evil is, a dismemberment of the Union would be worse." If separated from the United States, South Carolina or Georgia might well seek a league with a major European power, and that outcome must be avoided. Later in the day, Madison responded to Anti-Federalist arguments that the taxing power might be used against slavery with the calculation that not only were the five more southerly states devoted to slavery, but Connecticut, New York, and New Jersey had significant holdings, and thus were "safe" on that issue, as well.[93]

Madison's performances on June 17 were uncharacteristically brief and, it seems, labored. The stenographer repeatedly reported that week that his voice was inaudible.[94] Apparently he was very unwell. Yet he soldiered on. Opponents' dilatory and repetitious meanderings through unconnected provisions gave the impression that Madison and his coadjutors, chiefly Nicholas and Randolph, were having the better of the argument. That must have been heartening.

Randolph's course continued very odd. Clearly, his position as a nonsigner who now advocated ratification before amendment left him rhetorically vulnerable. He did not enjoy the advantage Mason, Henry, and other Anti-Federalists had taken of his weakness. On June 17, he once again spoke as one not thrilled to have to advocate instant ratification.[95]

He did that by arguing against the Anti-Federalists' inferences concerning the powers the Constitution granted to Congress. Virginia, he reasoned, had no choice but to delegate powers to the Confederation. It had done so. On the other hand, its state constitution did not say anything about the powers granted to the state government. Why? Because all power was granted. Under the proposed Constitution, "its powers are enumerated." Surely, he concluded, the implication was that "it has no power but what is expressly given it."

Here Randolph had hit upon the phraseology that he would push through the rest of the convention—ultimately with Nicholas joining him.[96] Having laid out this argument, Randolph next showed how the exceptions to Congress's legislative power in Article I, section 9—the limitation on the power to suspend the writ of habeas corpus, for example, and the prohibition of ex post facto laws—did not presuppose a general legislative power, but merely restricted powers expressly delegated. No actual bill of rights was necessary, Randolph (echoing Publius) said, because "the express enumeration of its powers" was the strongest possible security for American rights against the federal government.

He closed his speech by asking again whether Virginia should expect the states that had already ratified the Constitution to repeal their ratifications in deference to Virginia's insistence that the Constitution must be amended first. He concluded that the risk of disunion if Virginia followed that path was simply too great, while the risks it would take by demanding subsequent amendments were slight. Pressed to say more about his objections, Randolph said, "I considered that our critical situation rendered adoption necessary, were it even more defective than it is."[97]

The debates of June 18 produced little of lasting interest. William Grayson for the Anti-Federalists and Madison on behalf of the Federalists did reckon that day that the Federalists likely still had a very narrow majority.[98] As Madison told it, the narrowness of the division might induce some Federalists to vote to adjourn without deciding. The outcome lay in the balance.

The following day, June 19, saw the Committee of the Whole discuss the treaty power at great length. In the end, Madison intervened to say that he understood the treaty power to be limited to the purposes for which it was being granted.[99] "I do not conceive," he held, "that power is given to the President and Senate to dismember the empire, or to alienate any great essential right." (Here, he may have nodded in the direction of the Kentucky delegates, who were still concerned about the Mississippi navigation.) To enumerate the purposes for which the treaty power might properly be used would be impossible, Madison thought, but that did not make the broad statement conferring the treaty power unsafe.

Mason, Henry, and company were consistently suspicious. Madison countered that American officials could be expected to act in their country's interest. Britain lodged the treaty power in its monarch on this same theory, and he did not seem to have disappointed his country on that score. Madison also accepted a fellow Federalist's assertion that the Supremacy Clause made treaties superior to state laws, but not to federal ones. To calm the fears of those who thought the president might sell out the national interest, Madison noted that the impeachment power would enable Congress to rein him in. Even if he persuaded part of the Senate to abet him, one-third of that body's number would be replaced every other year, and so he could be impeached soon enough. At the end of the speech, once again, the stenographer protested that Madison had become inaudible.

In the regular order of the convention, George Nicholas next stood up and introduced the judiciary article of the Constitution, Article III. When he had finished, George Mason objected that the variety of types of jurisdiction conferred by the Constitution upon the federal courts left virtually nothing for state courts to do.[100] This was no accident, Mason asserted, as some men in the Philadelphia Convention hoped for "one national consolidated Government" over all of America.

Madison demanded that Mason explain himself. Since others might think Mason meant to impugn all of the delegates to the Philadelphia Convention, Madison said Mason should name names. Mason replied that no, he had not meant to imply that Madison desired any such outcome. He said that while "many gentlemen in Convention" were of that contingent, Madison had told him privately that he did not want it. None of the Virginians, Mason said, had ever advocated it. Madison said he was satisfied with this explanation.

Still much bothered, Mason said that he would prefer to see the federal courts' appellate jurisdiction confined to the law, despite Article III's language about appellate jurisdiction over facts.[101] Mason roamed at large through the judiciary article, showing that various elements were objectionable. Madison, at day's end, briefly replied that where a phrase with a settled meaning was used, all of its elements were implicit.[102] The example he gave was that the right to trial by jury had always included a right to peremptory jury challenges, and so it would under the Constitution as well. He would return to the subject the next day, he promised.

The following day, Friday, June 20, was destined to be the convention's last Friday. Madison took the floor early and delivered a long address on Article III, the judiciary article.[103] He explained that there needed to be a supreme court to maintain uniformity of application of federal treaties, that the same court had to have jurisdiction over cases between two states and cases between a state and a citizen of another state (in which only the former, not the latter would be the plaintiff), and so on. Madison's mode of presentation was dispassionate, his approach reasonable. He frequently allowed that there might be objections of various kinds, and he described how they might be addressed. Thus, for example, where Anti-Federalists had expressed concern over the idea that federal courts might hear appeals as to fact, Madison said Congress would be able to prevent it by appropriate legislation. (In the end, Congress did.)

Toward the end of his presentation, Madison summed up the course the Anti-Federalists in the convention had taken: "I have observed, that Gentlemen suppose, that the General Legislature will do every mischief they possibly can, and that they will omit to do every good which they are authorised to do. If this were a reasonable supposition, their objections would be good." Was it a reasonable supposition? Madison denied it. "I go on this great republican principle," he said, "that the people will have virtue and intelligence to select men of virtue and wisdom. Is there no virtue among us?—If there be not, we are in a wretched situation. No theoretical checks—no form of Government, can render us secure. To suppose that any form of Government will secure liberty or happiness without any virtue in the people, is a chimerical idea." If there was, on the other hand, the people would select fit rulers. "So that we do not depend on their virtue, or put confidence in our rulers, but in the people who are to choose them."

Several other speakers addressed this article that day. Notable among their claims was John Marshall's assertion concerning the limitations on congressional power.[104] "Has the Government of the United States power to make laws on every subject?" he asked. "Can they go beyond the delegated powers?" Obviously not, he continued: "If they were to make a law not warranted by any of the powers enumerated, it would be considered by the Judges as an infringement of the Constitution which they are to guard. . . . They would declare it void." The judiciary, according to John Marshall, would police the line between Congress's few powers and the sea of power not included in the Constitution's enumeration. Along the same line, Marshall reiterated Madison's assertion that states could not be defendants in federal court in suits brought by citizens of other states.

Meanwhile, off the floor, the caucusing—and nose counting—continued. Madison judged that Federalists had a majority "of 3 or 4 or possibly more."[105]

Madison's next and last major effort of the Richmond Convention came the following Tuesday, June 24.[106] That day's proceedings began with a short speech by George Wythe in favor of ratification before amending.[107] Wythe said Virginia ought to join the several other states that had proposed specific amendments, and he proposed an instrument of ratification saying that the new government would have only the powers the Constitution gave it.

Having sat virtually silent through a couple of days' discussions, Madison here gave a sort of valedictory address. Picking up on themes that he, Hamilton, and Jay had developed in *The Federalist* (notably in Hamilton's No. 1 and Jay's No. 2, but elsewhere as well), Madison noted the world-historic significance of the moment. "Nothing has excited more admiration in the world," he pontificated, "than the manner in which free Governments have been established in America. For it was the first instance from the creation of the World to the American revolution, that free inhabitants have been seen deliberating on a form of Government, and selecting such of their citizens as possessed their confidence, to determine upon, and give effect to it." If the state constitutions excited foreigners' respect, Madison said, completing the task of devising a suitable federal system would impress them even more.

As in Philadelphia Benjamin Franklin had urged his colleagues to put aside petty objections in pursuit of the greater good, so here Madison assumed the role of senior statesman. (With his many historical and philosophical lectures, Madison had struck the pose of a wise uncle throughout. As we have seen, Federalists and Anti-Federalists alike had often ceded the point.) "We must calculate the impossibility that every State should be gratified in its wishes, and much less that every individual should receive this gratification," he observed, commonsensically. "It has never been denied by the friends of the paper on the table, that it has its defects." Yet, those defects were minor, and they might be negated in time.

To expect the other states, perhaps nine of them already, to retract their unconditional ratifications in the name of meeting Virginia's demand for previous amendments, Madison continued, was unreasonable. "Virginia has always heretofore spoken the language of respect to the other States, and she has always been attended to." She should not change her course now. If the Anti-Federalists had their way, and if the other states agreed to amend, all of them would have to take up the question again. There was no telling how that would turn out. Given the difficulty the Philadelphia Convention had had in drafting the Constitution, it could not be taken for granted that amendments would be agreed.

Insofar, Madison said, as Patrick Henry's proposed amendments "are not objectionable, or unsafe, so far they may be subsequently recommended. Not because they are necessary, but because they can produce no possible danger, and may gratify some Gentlemen's wishes. But I can never consent to his previous amendments, because they are pregnant with dreadful dangers."

With that, Madison yielded the floor to his foremost antagonist. Patrick Henry, the voice of the revolution, then had his last chance to impress his fellow delegates. He did not disappoint.

Henry had shown himself in the convention to be what he had always been, all the way back—as he had pointed out more than once—to the Stamp Act crisis of 1765–1766. He was the great guardian of Virginians' self-government and inherited rights. He was also an orator without parallel, one who could cause hair to stand up on the necks even of his most devout opponents.

An account given by Federalist delegate Archibald Stuart proves the point.[108] Henry concluded his speech by calling attention to "the awful dangers" attendant upon their vote. "I see *beings* of a higher order," Henry thundered, "anxious concerning our decision." "Our own happiness alone is not affected by the event—All nations are interested in the determination. We have it in our power to secure the happiness of one half of the human race. Its adoption may involve the misery of the other hemispheres." The stenographer noted that at this point, a severe storm broke up the convention. As Stuart told it, Henry took advantage of the storm, "rising on the wings of the tempest, to seize upon the artillery of Heaven, and direct its fiercest thunders against the heads of his adversaries." The Committee of the Whole broke up until the storm had passed. Henry's work was done.

George Nicholas's last speech to the convention followed the recess. It was perhaps the most pregnant with future import of all. This powerful co-adjutor of Madison's, the representative of Thomas Jefferson's hometown in the convention and soon to be first attorney general of Kentucky, held that the instrument of ratification should allay Anti-Federalists' fears.

In voting whether to ratify, the convention would not be asked, "All for ratification, say 'Aye.' All opposed, 'Nay.'" Rather, they would be presented a resolution on which to vote. That resolution, drafted by a committee that Wythe had chaired, asserted that the central government would have only the delegated powers, and that those could be reclaimed whenever they were perverted to the people's oppression. As Nicholas put it, it said "that every power not granted thereby, remained at their will," so that "no danger whatever could arise" from the kind of federal overreaching about which Mason, Grayson, and particularly Henry had warned over and over again.

Henry, in particular, had insisted that federal officials would read every ambiguity in the Constitution, real or imagined, in such a way as to empower the central government still further. In time, he held, the result would be a tyranny. Mason held that the result must be either an aristocracy or a consolidated monarchy. Governor Randolph had warned of similar results, back when he leaned against ratification before amendment.

As Nicholas told it, however, the instrument of ratification made all these warnings obsolete. "The Constitution cannot be binding on Virginia," he said, "but with these conditions." Here Nicholas, astute lawyer that he was, gave a little sermonette on the law of contracts. "If thirteen individuals are about to make a contract," he explained, "and one agrees to it, but at the same time declares that he understands its meaning, signification and intent, to be, what the words of the contract plainly and obviously denote"—in this case, that the new government would have only the powers the Constitution listed—"that it is not to be construed so as to impose any supplementary condition upon him, and that he is to be exonerated from it, whensoever any such imposition shall be attempted—I ask whether in this case, these conditions on which he assented to it, would not be binding on the other twelve? In like manner these conditions will be binding on Congress. They can exercise no power that is not *expressly granted* them" (emphasis added).

Here, in the convention's waning moments, Nicholas repeated the explanation of the Constitution that had been offered at various points by John

Marshall, Edmund Randolph, Edmund Pendleton, and James Madison, besides Nicholas himself—that is, by virtually every significant Federalist spokesman. The only people who had denied it, who had considered this principle an inadequate defense of Virginians' liberties, were Anti-Federalists such as Patrick Henry, William Grayson, and George Mason, each of whom had called for making the principle explicit.

At that point, an obscure delegate endorsed Henry's call for a suite of amendments.[109] The delegate said he could not vote for ratification until assured that amendments protecting Virginians' historic rights would be recommended. Madison answered that he would not oppose any safe amendments, but that he thought "a solemn declaration of our essential rights . . . unnecessary and dangerous." "Unnecessary," he explained, "because it was evident that the General Government had no power but what was given it, and the delegation alone warranted the exercise of power—Dangerous, because an enumeration which is not complete, is not safe." He preferred the "general negation" that Wythe had proposed: a general statement that the new government had only the few powers the Constitution gave it.[110]

John Tayler answered that the recommendations for amendments being circulated among Federalist delegates did not address the real problems Anti-Federalists had with the Constitution.[111] They said nothing about direct taxation. They said nothing about limitations on federal judicial power. "Gentlemen," he concluded, "hold out the idea of amendments which will not alter one dangerous part of it." Threats of Algerine attacks and disunion if the Constitution were not ratified unamended did not persuade him, Tyler said. The question had come down to one between "previous and subsequent amendments," and the reason to disbelieve in the latter was that "we have granted power." That another convention would be dangerous was "only their assertion." "The wisdom of Great-Britain gave each State its own Legislative Assembly, and Judiciary, and a right to tax themselves. When they attempted to infringe that right, we declared war. This system violates that right." That was why he adjudged the Constitution "dangerous to the liberties of my country."

Henry followed, lamenting that Federalists on one hand promised subsequent amendments and on the other declared them unnecessary.[112] Then, Randolph, awkward to the last, swore once more that he would vote "aye" only because disunion seemed the sole alternative.[113] Next came the votes: for proposing amendments to the other states prior to Virginia's ratification: 80 ayes, 88 nays. On ratifying the Constitution without first amending it: 89 ayes, 79 nays.[114]

The convention then selected a five-man committee to prepare an instrument of ratification. Its members included Randolph, Nicholas, Marshall, Francis Corbin, and Madison—perhaps the five most vocal Federalists in the convention. This committee reported a form of ratification saying that the new government of the United States would have, as Nicholas had explained, only the powers "granted thereby" and that "the powers granted under the Constitution, being derived from the people of the United States may be resumed by them whensoever the same shall be perverted to their injury or oppression."[115] Madison had explained this to Hamilton as "some plain & general truths that can not affect the validity of the Act."[116] This was true as far as it went. Time would show, however, that the explanation of the Constitution sold by Randolph, Nicholas, and the other Federalist leaders had been very significant indeed.

That night, Madison wrote Hamilton, Rufus King, and Washington with the happy news.[117] He was clearly exhausted. Still, Hamilton had badgered him repeatedly to relay the good tidings as soon as possible, and Madison hoped they might help New York's embattled Federalists achieve a similar result in their convention.

On Friday, June 27, the convention adopted a set of proposed amendments for transmission to Congress.[118] Besides a bill of individual rights, this group of proposals included Anti-Federalist favorites such as a two-thirds requirement for tariff bills to pass Congress, a proposal that requisitions precede taxes, and various other structural changes. Federalists proposed striking the requisitions amendment from the list, and Madison voted "aye," but the Convention retained it, 65 ayes to 85 noes. With that, the convention thanked President Pendleton for his service, Pendleton thanked them for their accolade, and the convention was over.

That night, a group of disgruntled Anti-Federalists convened in the Senate chamber of Jefferson's Virginia capitol.[119] George Mason proposed that it issue a written address to Virginians critical of the Constitution. One account has Patrick Henry insisting that Anti-Federalists acquiesce in their defeat. Madison's version, on the other hand, has Henry joining Mason in urging resistance. In any event, Harrison, Taylor, and others spoke against the idea, which Mason then withdrew. Madison thought that the assemblage's adoption of the address would probably have done mischief. Either way, opposition to the new Constitution among leading Virginians had not died yet. Soon enough, it would come back to bite Madison.

Chapter 6

Inaugurating the Constitution, 1788–1800

Ratification of the U.S. Constitution marked a tempered success for James Madison. He had devoted months to the task of bringing the Philadelphia Convention into being. He had coordinated a private campaign to persuade General Washington to attend. He had taken the lead in composing the Virginia Plan. He had helped make the U. S. Constitution markedly different from the Articles of Confederation.

In the wake of the convention's adjournment on September 17, 1787, Madison had worked tirelessly to shepherd the proposed Constitution first through the Confederation Congress, then through the state ratification conventions. Before leaving New York for Richmond, he had joined Alexander Hamilton and John Jay in authoring *The Federalist*, a series of pro-ratification newspaper essays destined to have a significant effect on American constitutional history. He had also worked assiduously to persuade his longtime friend Edmund Randolph to put aside his objections to the Constitution and his desire to amend it first and join Madison in advocating immediate ratification. In Virginia's own convention, with Randolph serving as the chief spokesman for ratification, Madison had also been—insofar as his health allowed—a principal spokesman for ratification. Friend and foe alike admired Madison's performance, both because of his characteristic mastery of all the issues and because of his adeptness at parrying opponents' objections.

Yet he was discontented with the Constitution. He thought that, absent the federal veto of state laws and with the Senate elected by the state legislatures, it was doomed to failure. Still, Madison could not rest. As before, he determined to make the best of things, always looking toward further reform where it seemed indicated.

Madison's performance over the past two years had won him continental renown—among certain people. Among others, he was viewed as the key figure in a coalition that had deceived the state legislatures into sending delegates to Philadelphia with the task of proposing amendments to the Articles, when in fact they had intended to substitute the national Virginia Plan for the Articles all along. Where Madison saw the Constitution as likely to fail because it was not a completely national one, his critics thought it national enough to augur the end of the American republican experiment.

George Washington responded with great anxiety to the news from New York.[1] Taking the matter up while the Richmond Convention still sat and voting on it soon after the Virginians adjourned, New York's ratification convention voted both to ratify (by the very narrow vote of 30–27) and to call for a second federal convention.

Washington's response was to press Madison to enter the General Assembly. Only having Madison there, he thought, could defeat Patrick Henry's likely move for a second convention. Madison stayed in New York.

Unfortunately for him, chief among the enemies he had made in the effort to write and ratify the new Constitution were Virginians, such as former governor and longtime House of Delegates speaker Benjamin Harrison and, more notably, the undisputed kingpin of Virginia politics, Patrick Henry.

Since the Constitution empowered the state legislatures to elect senators, Madison would be at Henry's mercy. Henry had his way, as Madison placed a distant third: 98 votes for Richard Henry Lee, 86 for William Grayson, and only 77 for Madison. Virginia's first two senators, Grayson and Lee, had both agreed with Henry that the Constitution should be amended before it was ratified. Both, presumably, would favor a second convention.

Madison thought Henry wanted more than that. "The defects which drew forth objections from many quarters," he wrote, "were evidently of little consequence in the eyes of Mr H.ry. His own arguments proved it. His enmity was levelled, as he did not scruple to insinuate agst the *whole System*; and the destruction of the whole System, I take to be still the secret wish of his heart."[2]

For his part, Madison held that amendments should be adopted, but not by a second convention.[3] For one thing, some states would oppose a convention so strongly that they would reflexively oppose any amendment it might propose. For another, it would be easier to have Congress propose amendments than to follow the process in Article V of the Constitution for convening another meeting like the one at Philadelphia. Finally, another convention would include members with extreme views on both ends of the political spectrum, enflame the public mind, and produce nothing conducive to the general good. He had seen how the first convention had worked, and he did not want to hazard a second—which, too, would undermine the impression of the American republic's stability left in European capitals by the success of the recent ratification campaign.

Chastened by his electoral defeat, Madison agreed to stand for the House of Representatives. Here, again, his prospects were dimmed by Henry's opposition: exercising its new power to draw congressional districts, the General Assembly had drawn a map that put Montpelier in the same district as James Monroe's house.

Monroe was, like Randolph, one of Madison's regular political correspondents. In the Richmond Convention, however, Monroe had stood behind Henry, Mason, and Grayson in the second rank of Anti-Federalists. He also had voted "nay" on the ultimate question. Because Monroe had been an authentic hero in the revolution—suffering a significant wound in Washington's great victory at Trenton—and had established a respectable legislative record in both Virginia and Congress, his opposition would be formidable.

Madison did not worry overmuch about his electoral prospects. Nor did his political friends. Their logic was that if Madison were not elected, he would be available to assume the helm of one of the executive branch departments.[4] In either event, his skills would not go to waste.

If Madison wanted to be elected, correspondents warned him, he would have to come back to Orange County. "Calumnies of Absent characters," including Madison, were the opposition's favorite tactic, and Madison's presence would "shrink into nonentity almost—those now aspiri[ng] Assassins."[5] His opponents there had made headway in asserting that Madison could not be trusted to favor amendments. Henry had even gone so far as to say that Madison held "that not a letter of the Constitution" should be altered.[6]

To head off the campaign against him, Madison decided that he had to return to Virginia. He left New York in mid-December 1788. He visited Washington at Mount Vernon en route.[7]

At this point, Madison received several letters from Jefferson insisting that a bill of rights be added.[8] He told his friend that he liked the idea of amending the Constitution to safeguard rights, but held that "the revisal . . . be carried no farther than to supply additional guards for liberty, without abridging the sum of power transferred from the States to the general Government."[9]

Madison resented having to campaign against Monroe.[10] The two of them traveled from courthouse to courthouse in their district, addressing assembled voters on the issues of the day. At one point, they attended a Lutheran service together and then spoke outdoors, resulting in a case of frostbite for Madison.[11] Madison still retained his skepticism about the efficacy of bills of rights, but he had decided that they could "if pursued with a proper moderation and in a proper mode . . . serve the double purpose of satisfying the minds of well meaning opponents, and of providing additional guards in favor of liberty."[12] Seemingly placated, Madison's neighbors chose him for the House of Representatives by a margin of 1,308 to 972 votes.[13] In retrospect, Madison was certain that his presence had been essential to his victory.[14]

His election put Madison in an excellent position to influence the start of the new government. So did his friendship with Washington. The historian of the Washington-Madison friendship, Stuart Leibiger, entitles his chapter on this period "Washington's 'Prime Minster,'" and it seems apt to think of Madison that way.[15] Madison, he shows, drafted Washington's—the new government's—first inaugural address.[16] The four-page speech took Washington twelve minutes to deliver.[17] If brevity is the soul of wit, Washington (and his ghostwriter, Madison) certainly outwitted their successors in our own day.

Madison advised Washington concerning appointments to top posts in the executive branch and to the courts. Other pressing topics surrounding the new government's creation were grist for their mill as well. Most pressing, perhaps, were the Mississippi navigation and the fate of Kentucky (long among Madison's preoccupations); federal finance (also a subject that had consumed Madison) did not rank far behind. Not only that, but for the first six months of the government's existence, when "Washington and John Adams . . . constituted the entire executive branch, . . . Washington regularly sought Madison's advice about relations with Congress, etiquette, appointments, and policy."[18]

George Washington lacked the intellectual brilliance of a Madison. Fortunately, he knew it. More fortunately, his ego did not bristle at relying on able counselors to guide him. Recognizing that his every step would mark the bounds of precedent, he leaned on Madison for support. House and Senate colleagues recognized Madison's special combination of talent and experience as well. Thus, the stage was set for one of the really odd exchanges in American or, one imagines, world political history.[19]

After Washington delivered the inaugural address that Madison had drafted, Madison drafted and the House unanimously adopted a response. Washington then had Madison draft a response to the House's response, which was soon joined by a different response, also drafted by Madison, to the Senate's answer to the inaugural. So, Madison had drafted the inaugural, the House response, and President Washington's answers to the House and Senate responses![20] Washington and Madison saw themselves as establishing precedents that future administrations and Congresses would follow, but nothing like that has happened since.

Then Congress turned to business. Among its first acts were statutes creating the executive branch departments—State, Treasury, and War—and confirmations of Washington's appointments to the secretaryships. Madison helped Washington settle on Jefferson, Hamilton, and Henry Knox to fill those positions. Edmund Randolph, longtime attorney general of Virginia before he became governor, framer, and ratifier, seemed perfectly qualified to be attorney general in Washington's administration, particularly in light of his having long been Washington's personal attorney.

Turning to substantive matters, Congress requested that Hamilton recommend steps it might take to set the United States' finances on a sound footing. Hamilton responded with a series of state papers laying out such proposals. Many observers, within the government and outside it, found Hamilton's program awkwardly evocative of British policy.

Hamilton proposed in late 1789 that the federal government assume responsibility for all state debts. The burden borne by the states in funding the revolution was really a national burden, Hamilton and his allies reasoned, and so the nation might pay it. Besides, it would be far easier for the federal government to impress foreign creditors as creditworthy if there were only one federal government, not thirteen states and one federal government, paying America's creditors.

Of course, before the federal government could assume responsibility for the states' debts, a question would have to be answered: should the debt be extinguished, or merely funded? If it were extinguished, the goal would be to repay the principal. Then one day there would be no more debt. If the debt were only funded, provision would be made for payment of the interest, but extinguishing the debt would come later—if ever. Hamilton opted for funding.

The ideas of assumption and funding provoked screaming opposition, particularly from the South. After all, southern states had generally retired their debts, and why should they join in paying the North's? Besides that, Americans had before them the example of Britain. Madison and his fellows found that example distasteful.[21]

In Britain, Sir Robert Walpole had at the beginning of the century controlled the Bank of England. Through the instrumentality of a funded debt, he had been able to manipulate wealthy men who owned government bonds to do Walpole's bidding. Control of wealthy politicians' money had so empowered Walpole that his position as chancellor of the Exchequer, an analog of the American position of secretary of the Treasury, had morphed into that of prime minister.

British critics charged that Walpole controlled the House of Commons through this corrupt mechanism.[22] Shocked by the prospect of such a thing Americans feared Hamilton might try the same. Madison, recorder of Hamilton's monarchist, Anglophile speeches in the Philadelphia Convention, took pride of place among them.

One hostile historian has Madison and other Virginia congressmen opposing assumption out of a combination of state interests and "a deep-seated prejudice against everything the program implied."[23] One person's strong conviction, it seems, is another's "deep-seated prejudice." Whatever his motivations—and perhaps they were mixed—Madison had a counterproposal: discrimination.[24]

Pay the foreign debt at face value, he said. As to domestic creditors, however, "Give the present holder a bond equal to the highest market price it had reached; give the original holder a bond equal to the difference between that and the original face value." Hamilton shot this proposal down by noting that to adopt it would be to announce that the U.S. government was going to break its faith at the first opportunity; such a move was likely to ruin American credit.[25]

The House finally voted to extinguish the foreign debt and to fund the domestic. American bondholders, in other words, would remain creditors of the federal government for the long haul. They thus would continue to be dependent upon that government, and particularly upon the treasury secretary— just as in England.

When the question of assumption came up for a vote, Madison proposed that not only the outstanding debt, but the revolutionary debt that the states had already retired, should be assumed. He and Hamilton might have been expected to find a way to agree to this, because it would mean that the large share of its wartime expenditures that Virginia had already financed would now be reimbursed out of the federal purse, while from Hamilton's point of view, it would mean additional domestic creditors of the federal government.

The two sides could not agree, however. That is when Thomas Jefferson became involved.[26] According to Jefferson, he walked out of Washington's house one day in the midst of this congressional debate, and there stood Hamilton. Pacing back and forth, appearing uncharacteristically disheveled, Hamilton made quite a sight. When Jefferson asked what was wrong, Hamilton laid out the whole story.

His assumption bill was hung up in the House, the New Yorker said. If it did not pass, the government's new financial scheme would come crashing down. American credit would suffer a severe blow, as would the new government. Arguably, the chief motive for having the new Constitution would be thwarted.

Jefferson had an answer. Come to my house tomorrow, he offered. Jefferson would invite Madison to join the two of them for dinner, and they could, "by some mutual sacrifices of opinion . . . form a compromise which was to save the Union."

The compromise might involve another issue then pending in Congress: the location of the United States' permanent capital. The question had frequently drawn members' attention when Madison was serving in the Confederation Congress, and it divided members of both houses in the new Congress's early months. As Jefferson told it, Madison insisted that assumption be joined to federal reimbursement to states that had already substantially retired their war debts. Once Hamilton had accepted that stipulation, the Virginians agreed to persuade two Virginia congressmen to cease voting against assumption. For his part, Hamilton said he would get Pennsylvanians to vote for the permanent capital to be on the Potomac (as long as the interim one could be in Philadelphia). Madison would not vote for assumption, but he would "not be strenuous." By the time the congressional term ended in August, then, the twin measures in this "Compromise of 1790" had been adopted.

Jefferson later called this the biggest mistake of his public life.

Madison, recently chastened by events in Virginia, must in these earliest months of the new federal government have kept careful tabs on public opinion back home. Although he had long favored centralizing control of American finances to a greater extent than under the Articles of Confederation, Hamilton's measures disturbed him. And other Virginians as well.

Patrick Henry, for one. Although he had headed off full-scale opposition to the Constitution in the wake of the Richmond Convention, the "American Demosthenes" remained highly skeptical of the new system.

Less surprising than Henry's readiness to protest federal measures, however, was that of Virginians who only recently had been full-throated advocates of ratifying the Constitution without first amending it. Thus, for example, Henry Lee, a famous Continental Army officer and member of that very prominent patriot family, came to doubt the wisdom of his 1788 position almost the moment the new government came into being. There he was in 1790, then, joining Henry in sponsoring a General Assembly resolution in protest.[27]

Henry's resolution, adopted by the House of Delegates the day he introduced it (November 3, 1790) and passed by the Virginia Senate six weeks later, put the federal government on notice. Adopting precisely the same mechanism as he had used in 1765 to whip up opposition to Parliament's Stamp Act, Henry labeled Hamilton's bill for federal assumption of state debts "repugnant to the Constitution, as it goes to the exercise of power not *expressly* granted to the general government." Why "expressly"? Because that was the promise that Randolph and George Nicholas had made in Richmond: the federal government would have only the powers, in Randolph's words, "expressly delegated."

Seventeen days after Henry introduced his resolution, a General Assembly committee reported an address on the vector of Washington administration policy in general. It said that Hamilton's measures closely tracked the English system, which the committee said was responsible for corrupting both houses of Parliament and the English courts. Hamilton's policies could subordinate agriculture to other economic interests, it continued, and "change . . . the present form of the federal government." It went on to say that Virginia had ratified the Constitution only on the understanding "that every power not granted was retained" by the states, and the power to service the states' debts (assumption) certainly was not among the granted powers.

Virginia's ruling elite had bought the moderate Federalists' explanation of the U.S. Constitution. They insisted upon it. Shortly, so would Madison.

Meantime, back in Congress, Madison had taken steps to shore up his political position back home. Other congressmen might be driven by the need to create the executive branch agencies and to establish a federal judiciary. Madison, for his part, kept calling their attention to the several states' requests for constitutional amendments.[28]

True, he never had come to think of them as strictly necessary. In fact, Madison did not consider a bill of rights desirable in itself. Its chief utility, he thought, would be to allay the fears of moderate men such as his friend Jefferson and his esteemed acquaintance Mason.

Thus, Madison announced to the House on May 4, 1789, that he would commence discussion of amendments on May 25.[29] He had already laid the groundwork for this initiative by including a general endorsement of the project in Washington's inaugural address.[30] Reflecting Madison's conception of desirable amendments, Washington had said that the amendments should be those "rendered expedient . . . by the nature of the objections which have been urged against the System, or by the degree of inquietude which has given birth to them." Washington's (and Madison's) conception of the proper role of the president in the legislative and amending processes shaped his disavowal of any intention to descend to particulars; that would be up to Congress. Washington had closed this portion of the address by saying that what he had in mind were amendments that did not significantly impair the powers of the new government, but that reflected "a reverence for the characteristic rights of freemen, and a regard for the public harmony."

When Madison had drafted his proposed amendments, he ran them by the president.[31] "As far as a momentary consideration has enabled me to judge, I see nothing exceptionable in the proposed amendments," Washington responded "Some of them . . . are importantly necessary, others, though . . . not very essential, are necessary to quiet the fears of some respectable characters and well meaning Men. Upon the whole, therefore . . . they have my wishes for a favorable reception in both houses." One historian of the process says that Madison later marshaled support for his amendments by showing this letter to hesitant congressmen.[32] No doubt that was precisely the outcome that Washington had in mind in writing it. After all, politicians in those days commonly wrote out their sentiments so that the recipients could share them around.

When May 25 came, Madison, seeing how overwhelmed the House was with more pressing business, moved to delay the discussion by two weeks.[33] Then, on June 8, he introduced his proposals. He recognized the House was still busy, he said. He did not intend an exhaustive discussion. Rather, he wanted to show the people that the subject was being pursued. This might "stifle the voice of complaint, and make friends of many who doubted [the government's] merits." If he had thought it practicable, he would for these reasons have made amendments "the first business we entered upon."

After some angry debate on the subject of taking up the matter, Madison spoke again to suggest the appointment of a select committee to consider the topic and to report proposed amendments. His reasons for insisting on this, he said, had to do with quieting the public mind. A majority of Americans had supported the Constitution, but not all. Amendments could show that the Constitution's advocates "were as sincerely devoted to liberty and a republican government, as those who charged them with wishing the adoption of this constitution in order to lay the foundation of an aristocracy or despotism." Besides that, it might remove some citizens' fears that there were those who wanted to deprive them of "the liberty for which they valiantly fought and honorably bled."

Since there were many citizens who would become supporters of the government if only they were satisfied on this one score, Madison continued, the Federalists ought to meet their demands "on principles of amity and moderation . . . and expressly declare the great rights of mankind secured under this constitution." In addition, he held it likely that Rhode Island and North Carolina, which still had not ratified the Constitution and thus remained outside the new Union, would join if "those securities for liberty" that they required were provided.

Finally, Madison said, amendments could provide further bulwarks for liberty. In that sense, "We have . . . something to gain, and, if we proceed with caution, nothing to lose." He did not contemplate, he said, reopening the question of what powers were properly lodged in the federal government. He would not propose any amendment he did not authentically desire to see adopted.

Madison then laid out the changes to the Constitution that he considered desirable. His assumption was not that amendments would be tacked onto the end of the document, as we have come to expect. Rather, he contemplated having changes made to the Constitution's body. Thus, for example, the proposed amendment providing for grand jury indictments in criminal proceedings was to be inserted into Section 2 of Article III (the judiciary article).

In general, Madison's proposed amendments are familiar to us either as components of the Virginia Declaration of Rights or as provisions of the Bill of Rights (the first ten amendments) and the Twenty-seventh Amendment. Thus, he would have changed the Preamble to say, as the Virginia Declaration of Rights began by saying, that all power is originally in the people, that government is instituted for their benefit, and that they are entitled to change or replace it when it no longer serves their purposes. He also proposed preliminary versions of the Establishment Clause, the Free Exercise Clause, the Second Amendment, the criminal-law provisions of the Fifth Amendment, and the Ninth Amendment assurance that the omission to name a right in the Constitution would not be read as denying that that right must be respected.

Madison also envisioned a separation of powers amendment, one guaranteeing that no branch would ever exercise the powers vested in another. Interestingly, Madison's version of what became the Tenth Amendment read, "The powers not delegated by this constitution, nor prohibited by it to the states, are reserved to the States respectively." As we shall see later in this chapter, Madison distinguished between "state" as referring to state governments and "states" as referring to sovereign people of each state. His formulation, then, was devoid of the ambiguity of the Tenth Amendment's added-on final clause, "or the people thereof." Madison pointed out that several states' ratification conventions had recommended amendments to this effect, and he said that he understood this principle to underlie the Constitution.

All of these are restrictions on the power of the federal government. The exception is his proposal that Article I, Section 10's list of things states would no longer be allowed to do be expanded by the addition of this statement: "No state shall violate the equal rights of conscience, or the freedom of the press, or the trial by jury in criminal cases." Here, the federal government would have been given more power than it had before, as federal officials likely would somehow have been empowered to enforce this language. To expand the powers of the federal government had not been the aim of anyone calling for constitutional amendments in the state ratification conventions, nor certainly were Rhode Island and North Carolina holding off on ratification until federal power was first expanded. Notably, this provision was the one substantive Madison proposal that Congress did not adopt and send to the states for their ratification.

After itemizing the amendments he contemplated, Madison hurried to explain himself. "The first of these amendments," he said, "relates to what may be called a bill of rights." Perhaps his colleagues knew that Publius had held a bill of rights unnecessary, even dangerous. Madison continued, "I will own that I never considered this provision so essential to the federal constitution," he admitted, "as to make it improper to ratify it, until such an amendment was added." With Mason, Jefferson, Randolph, and other friends and acquaintances no doubt in mind, Madison explained, "I always conceived, that in a certain form . . . such a provision was neither improper nor altogether useless."

Madison next pointed out the chief difference between American and

British provisions in favor of rights. In Britain, he noted, rights were reserved against the monarchy. In the United States, on the other hand, the legislatures predominated and were "under the least controul"; that was why bills of rights tended to be limitations on them, not on executives. A greater difficulty in the United States, however, was in restraining a majority determined to abuse a minority. For that reason, it was majorities, not executives or legislatures, that must be restrained.

No doubt with Patrick Henry's declamations against "paper checks" in the Richmond Convention ringing in his ears, Madison conceded that "it may be thought that all paper barriers against the power of the community, are too weak to be worthy of attention." Still, he held, the mere existence of statements of the significance of individual rights tended to teach the people to respect them—and thus "to controul the majority from those acts to which they might be otherwise inclined."

In the ratification debates, several prominent Federalist spokesmen—James Wilson and Alexander Hamilton among them—had held that bills of rights were entirely unnecessary. Since the federal government would have only the powers the Constitution "enumerated, and it follows that all that are not granted by the constitution are retained . . . a bill of rights cannot be . . . necessary." Madison again admitted that "these arguments are not entirely without foundation." Still, he held, even though that was true, the federal government would have a degree of discretion in implementing even the enumerated powers, and so a bill of rights might prove useful. The example he gave was that the federal government might consider it necessary and proper to issue general warrants—hated instruments of arbitrary British power in colonial times—to collect taxes. For that reason, a reservation of a right against unreasonable search and seizure could be useful.

In closing, Madison said that he did not believe that any of his ideas would "endanger the beauty of the government in any one important feature." If amendments could win the Constitution new admirers without losing it any, "we act the part of wise and liberal men to make such alterations." As the discussion progressed, Connecticut's Roger Sherman objected to Madison's plan in a general way.[34] To insert the proposed amendments into the Constitution's main text, he strenuously insisted, would undercut the Constitution. After the amendments, the document would no longer be the one that George

Washington (and Madison, and Sherman) had signed in Philadelphia. The amendments should be affixed at the end. Madison finally agreed.

The House, seemingly persuaded by Madison's arguments concerning the urgency of amendment, sided with him, not with his several critics, and referred the matter to the Committee of the Whole. It also put off the climactic debate until July 21.[35]

Meanwhile, Madison learned that his initiative had already begun to yield the fruit he hoped for. From "foreign" North Carolina, for example, came word that "the honest part of our Antifederalists have publickly expressed great satisfaction on this event."[36] If amendments could be proposed by Congress prior to the upcoming reconvening of the North Carolina ratification convention, the Federalist cause seemed apt to benefit. Virginia Anti-Federalists, too, seemed to have been swayed in Madison's direction—just as Madison's critics in Congress expected.[37]

When July 21 rolled around, Madison asked that the Committee of the Whole take up the amendments.[38] Instead, the House appointed a select committee of one member per state, which reported on July 28. On August 13, its report was taken up. Madison once again said that he thought the House owed it to the people to consider these proposals, "to secure those rights which they are apprehensive are endangered by the present constitution." He spoke in favor of amending the Constitution's main body, but said he considered the idea inessential.

The House devoted eleven days' attention to the proposed amendments.[39]

As the debate proceeded, Madison rose periodically to offer explanation of the committee language and to advocate proposals he considered essential. So, for example, he said that an early version of the First Amendment's religion clauses meant that "congress should not establish a religion, and enforce the legal observation of it by law, nor compel men to worship God in any manner contrary to their conscience."[40] Still devoted to his ratification-period perspective, he added that, "whether the words were necessary or not he did not mean to say," but he did offer that people commonly feared that the Necessary and Proper Clause might be extended to allow people to interfere with religion in exercise of some power that Congress had been expressly delegated.

On two occasions, Madison found his opponents' arguments agitating.

First, Representative Thomas Sumter offered up a harsh appraisal of the entire amendments project: far from substantial, he said, the amendments under debate were "little better than whip-syllabub, frothy and full of wind, formed only to please the palate."[41] They were, he concluded, "like a tub thrown out to a whale, to secure the freight of the ship and its peaceable voyage."

The twenty-first-century reader is to be excused for not knowing exactly what this combination of metaphor and simile meant. The expert will owe familiarity to a tale by Jonathan Swift and a perusal of the dictionary. Let us just summarize by saying that the first comparison had to do with an eighteenth-century delectation, the second to a technique used by whalers of centuries gone by to keep their prey from destroying their ships.

Neither one was exactly flattering.

Madison would not let the charge pass. As he noted, his opponents had charged him and his allies with "act[ing] without candor." He asked members who knew whether the amendments under consideration were not the ones most widely demanded by Anti-Federalists during the ratification dispute. He had vowed in the Richmond Convention that he would seek their adoption, and here he was. He would not advocate structural amendments, he said, because he considered them unlikely to garner the requisite degree of support to secure congressional passage and state ratification. If he did not want amendment, he would be recommending precisely that type of amendment; as it was, he was sponsoring amendments he authentically favored.

Madison privately confided that the vow to sponsor amendments in the First Congress accounted for Federalists' success in securing ratification, at least in Virginia.[42] In fact, "In Virginia it would have been *certainly* rejected" without that promise, he said. Not only that, but without this pledge, Virginia's largely Federalist House delegation would have been dominated by critics of the Constitution, and failure to follow through would throw the Virginia General Assembly even more firmly into the hands of the Constitution's opponents. Conversely, if Congress recommended amendments, "It will kill the opposition every where."

On August 17, the House took up the provision concerning state infringement of "the equal rights of conscience," freedom of speech, freedom of the press, and the right to trial by jury in criminal cases.[43] Fearful that the proposal would be rejected, Madison described this as "the most valuable amendment on the whole list." If the federal government should be restrained on these scores, he said, so ought the state governments. The House retained the amendment.

Thomas Tucker of South Carolina moved in the House to insert the word "expressly" into the language that became the Tenth Amendment.[44] Madison objected, explaining that "it was impossible to confine a government to the exercise of express powers." Ultimately, the House rejected Tucker's motion, 32–17. Since, as we saw when considering the Richmond Convention, prominent Federalists in Virginia and several other states had already assured the public that the principle for which Tucker was contending was implicit in the Constitution, it is hard to say what effect this vote should be understood to have.

When finally the list came from the Senate, Madison's favorite amendment had been rejected. So had his proposals regarding the Preamble. Since Senate proceedings were then secret, we do not know the grounds of these acts. We do know, however, that Robert Morris—longtime ally of Madison's in the Confederation Congress—scoffed at the entire concept of amendment, attributing Madison's effort to Virginia political imperatives.[45] Another former Philadelphia Convention colleague, Senator Pierce Butler of South Carolina, wondered whether Madison could have been sincere in advocating them, in light of their "milk-and-water" (that is, largely rhetorical) content.

Representative Fisher Ames of Massachusetts offered up a curt appraisal of Madison in the midst of the Bill of Rights debate.[46] "I made two speeches," he wrote, "the latter in reply to Madison, who is a man of sense, reading, address [meaning good work habits], and integrity, as 'tis allowed." Then came the negatives: "Very much Frenchified in his politics. He speaks low, his person is little and ordinary. He speaks decently, as to manner, and no more. His language is very pure, perspicuous, and to the point. Pardon me, if I add, that I think him a little too much of a book politician, and too timid in his politics, for prudence and caution are opposites of timidity." How did one account for this timidity? "He is not a little of a Virginian," Ames explained, "and thinks that state the land of promise, but is afraid of their state politics, and of his popularity there, more than I think he should be." Yet, all things considered, "He is our first man."

Soon thereafter, the same colleague reflected on Madison further: "Madison is cool," he wrote, "and has an air of reflection, which is not very distant from gravity and self-sufficiency.[47] In speaking, he never relaxes into pleasantry, and discovers [that is, displays] little . . . warmth of heart. . . . His printed speeches are more faithful than any other person's, because he speaks very slow, and his discourse is strongly marked. He states a principle and deduces consequences, with clearness and simplicity." In summation, Ames held that, "I think him a good man and an able man, but he has rather too much theory, and wants that discretion which men of business commonly have. He is also very timid, and seems evidently to want manly firmness and energy of character."

Most of the amendment provisions that Madison wanted were included in the twelve proposals that survived the Senate. He was among three representatives appointed to a conference committee to work out the final language with the Senate. It was in the conference committee that the religion clauses received their final, Madisonian forms.[48] The House adopted the committee report on September 24, 1787, by a vote of 37–14. The Senate followed the next day.

Virginia's senators emerged from this process highly dissatisfied. William Grayson judged the twelve proposals "good for nothing," while Richard Henry Lee scoffed that "when the thing done is compared with that desired, nothing can be more unlike."[49] Their powerful ally, Patrick Henry, could not prevent the Virginia House of Delegates from ratifying the amendments, though George Mason's nephew defeated what now are the First and Seventh Amendments in the state senate; they were too weak, he insisted. In conference committee, the house refused to go along with the senate's action, and so the entire suite of amendments went down to defeat.

When next the matter came up, the General Assembly approved all twelve proposals. President Washington thus had the pleasure of announcing that Virginia had ratified, and thus that the first ten amendments had been adopted. For his part, Henry said simply that "Virginia had been outwitted." Since the vote in the ratification convention had been so close, the implication that the commonwealth would not have ratified if it had known what amendments the First Congress would adopt may have been accurate.

While the adoption of the Bill of Rights now strikes us as a very important development, at the time it seemed far less momentous. Remember, several of Madison's congressional colleagues had thought his proposals "a tub to the

whale." Even his friends, it seems, tended to agree. When Secretary of State
Thomas Jefferson sent a letter containing word of ratification to the state governments, he got to that matter only after first noting adoption of "an Act
concerning fisheries" and "an Act to establish the post office."

Among the other matters that Congress had been considering while the
Bill of Rights gestated was that old concern of Madison's: finance. Arguably,
the Confederation government's dependence on the state governments for
funds was the reason the U.S. Constitution had come into being. Hurriedly,
congressmen had focused their attention on exercising the federal government's financial powers.

Washington's point man, Alexander Hamilton, had strongly nationalist
financial views. As an immigrant and an Anglophile, he knew neither the
strong local prejudices of most of his colleagues nor their aversion to British
forms. Congress's requests that he propose financial measures elicited brilliant state papers making clear what that meant.

His proposal that the federal government assume the states' debts, as we
have seen, won quick approval. In addition, it stirred the roiling political
waters in Virginia, where Henry Lee wrote that the vector of Hamilton's
policy made Patrick Henry a "prophet."

Besides that, in December 1790 Hamilton called for Congress to levy a tax
on distilled liquor and to charter a national bank.[50] The whiskey excise, as it
came to be called, passed easily, but the bank proposal led to a notable constitutional dispute in the House, and then to an epochal one in the cabinet.

In the House, Madison rose to state a strong constitutional objection to
Hamilton's Bank Bill. As we have seen, Madison had joined with Hamilton,
Robert Morris, and others in Confederation days in support of a national
bank. Now he shifted his ground.

The Senate had already adopted Hamilton's bill when it came up in the
House.[51] Hamilton had explained his proposal in a lengthy report, and the
Senate had taken a month to debate it before adoption on January 20, 1791.
When it came before the House, the distrust that Virginians, notably Jeffer-
son and Madison, had begun to nurse for Hamilton came boiling over. As
Madison explained, he opposed Hamilton's emulation of England because
"the genius of the Monarchy favored the concentration of wealth and influ-

ence at the metropolis." Hamilton, one inferred, was an aspiring Walpole who had to be headed off at the first pass.

Madison focused upon the constitutional aspect of Hamilton's bill.[52] As he explained, "he had reserved to himself . . . the right to deny the authority of Congress to pass it. He had entertained this opinion from the date of the constitution. His impression might perhaps be the stronger, because he well recollected that a power to grant charters of incorporation had been proposed in the general convention [meaning the Philadelphia Convention] and rejected." (In fact, as we have seen, Madison had supported that proposal on September 14, 1787.)

The question, as he saw it, was whether "the power of establishing an *incorporated bank*" was "among the powers vested by the constitution in the legislature of the United States." The Constitution granted only some few powers, he said. This had been, according to Madison, conceded by friend and foe alike. "In controverted cases, the meaning of the parties to the instrument, if to be collected by reasonable evidence, is a proper guide."

Here, Madison had first apparently contradicted, then conceded a point he had made as Publius years earlier. *The Federalist* repeatedly asserted that the state ratifying conventions' understanding would be binding, but Madison had led off here by referring to events in the Philadelphia Convention. Finally, however, he came around to reliance upon the understanding of "the parties to the instrument"—which is to say, the ratifying conventions.

With this as predicate, Madison listed the only three constitutional provisions that he thought might form the basis of a claim to congressional power to incorporate a bank: the General Welfare Clause, the grant of power to borrow money, and the Necessary and Proper Clause. He slapped the first— "Congress shall have power . . . to lay and collect taxes to pay the debts, and provide for the common defence and general welfare"—aside by noting that since the bank bill "laid no tax whatever," it could not even arguably apply.

More ticklish than his textual argument here was the matter of precedent. Recall that while in the Confederation Congress, Madison had voted to establish a national bank. "This was known . . . to have been the child of necessity," he insisted, and "never could be justified by the regular powers of the articles of confederation." The Confederation Congress had met this objection at the time by calling on the states to incorporate the bank, which they clearly had the power to do.

As to the second possibility—the power of Congress to borrow money—Madison again had a ready reply. "Is this a bill to borrow money?" he asked. More aptly, it could be called a bill "creating the ability, where there may be the will, to lend." Congress had no such power.

Finally, he came to the Necessary and Proper Clause. Patrick Henry, George Mason, and other skeptics of central government authority, as well as hesitant Federalists such as Edmund Randolph, had feared that this clause would be twisted to empower Congress to do essentially whatever it wanted. Madison must have heard their arguments, and his own assurances to the contrary, in his mind as he answered this contention they had told him to expect.

Madison began by saying that whatever the Necessary and Proper Clause positively meant, it certainly could not be given a construction "that would give an unlimited discretion to Congress." Thinking that he was only stating the obvious, Madison went on to say "Its meaning must, according to the natural and obvious force of the terms and the context, be limited to means *necessary* to the *end,* and *incident* to the *nature* of the specified powers."

Turning to the arguments made by the Bank Bill's advocates, Madison held that "the essential characteristic of the government, as composed of limited and enumerated powers, would be destroyed: If instead of direct and incidental means, any means could be used, which in the language of the preamble to the bill, 'might be conceived to be conducive to the successful conducting of the finances; or might be *conceived* to *tend* to give *facility* to the obtaining of loans." These terms, Madison noted, were not interchangeable with "necessary" and "proper." If the Necessary and Proper Clause were read as giving Congress whatever power was "conducive to . . . success" or might "tend to give facility" to government's operations, congressional power would be extended markedly. So, for example, Congress might conclude that profit would be useful to the accumulation of money, and so it might "incorporate manufacturers."

As he warmed to the subject, Madison's logic reached a crescendo:

To borrow money is made the *end* and the accumulation of capitals, *implied* as the *means.* The accumulation of capitals is then the *end,* and a bank *implied* as the *means*. The bank is then the *end*, and a charter of incorporation, a monopoly, capital punishments, &c. *implied* as the *means*. If implications, thus remote and thus multiplied, can be linked together, a chain may be formed that will reach every object of legislation, every object within the whole compass of political economy.

Madison next went through the enumerated powers and showed that some of them were more closely related to others of them than chartering a bank was to borrowing. If the Necessary and Proper Clause was to be read as the Bank Bill's proponents said it was, there would not have been a need for so many powers to have been enumerated.

The Constitution assumed, Madison concluded, that no "great and important power" could be exercised by Congress unless it was "evidently and necessarily involved in an express power." Since "it cannot be denied that the power proposed to be exercised is an important power," and since it was not expressly delegated, it had not been granted to Congress.

Madison noted that some might say the federal government had all powers that governments necessarily had. Here, he said, they would err. For example, if the Constitution had not granted the federal government power to make treaties—a power necessary to government—the only remedy would have been an amendment. The power to incorporate a bank not only had not been delegated, but was not necessary to the government.

Madison next turned to proving that the Constitution had been ratified on the understanding he was offering. Thus, for example, Federalists had responded to their opponents' demands for a bill of rights by saying that the powers not granted by the states through the Constitution had been retained by the states. "On any other assumption," he said, "the power of Congress to abridge the freedom of the press, or the rights of conscience, &c. could not have been disproved." Besides that, he noted, Federalists had insisted in several states' ratification conventions (he cited language from the Constitution's chief proponents in Pennsylvania, Virginia, and North Carolina, but there were several others) to this effect. In further validation of his argument, Madison pointed to the Tenth Amendment, then pending before the states for ratification. That amendment said, "The powers not delegated to the United States by the Constitution, nor prohibited by it to the States, are reserved to the States respectively, or to the people." What clearer proof could one want?

To pass this law would bring down upon the members of Congress who had been Federalists in the ratification dispute the charge that they had made one argument before ratification and behaved the opposite way after. It would be "usurpation . . . leveling all the barriers which limit the powers of the general government, and protect those of the state governments." This would tend to destroy "the main characteristic of the constitution." The House should therefore defeat the bill.

A couple of days later, Madison's colleague Roger Sherman of Connecticut asked him in writing whether he did not agree that Congress had power "generally of regulating the Finances."[53] Sherman, like Madison a significant framer, wrote that the question was "Is a Bank a proper measure for effecting these purposes." Madison inserted "a necessary &" before "proper."

Madison had a final opportunity to speak against the bank bill on February 8.[54] In response to a colleague's assertion that the House ought to respect the Senate by conceding the validity of that body's implicit judgment that the Bank Bill was constitutional, Madison outlined the relationship among the branches of the federal government. If they got into the habit of deferring to whichever of them had passed on a question first, he said, the benefit of having independent branches would vanish.

In the days intervening between his first major effort against the Bank Bill and this one, Madison had heard Hamilton's House allies deploy a new argument: that the Preamble to the Constitution granted powers. Madison lectured the House that "the preamble only states the objects of the confederation, and the subsequent clauses designate the express powers by which those objects are to be obtained." In case others were desired, Article V provided mechanisms for amendment.

Despite Madison's objections, the bill passed the House by 39 to 20.[55] Washington received it on February 14. So powerful was Madison's argument against the bill's constitutionality that Washington, having heard of it, required all four of his Cabinet members to submit first oral, then written opinions on the subject. In common with the five presidents who followed him, Washington conceived of the veto power as intended to allow the president to keep Congress within its constitutional limits, and only in case a bill was unconstitutional would he veto it.[56] Attorney General Randolph, chief proponent of the enumerated-powers argument in the Richmond Convention, agreed with Madison. Henry Knox took the opposite position. The Cabinet's chief members, Jefferson and Hamilton, submitted two of the great state papers in American history.

Jefferson's memorandum on the Bank Bill is usually considered as the first and last words on the subject, from a strict construction, states' rights point of view.[57] Yet, while stated with characteristic Jeffersonian force, it said basically nothing that Madison had not already said. Jefferson began by positing, as Madison had in the House, that the Tenth Amendment stated the underlying principle of the Constitution—which meant that the enumeration of powers defined the limits of Congress's discretion. He insisted that in order to come under the Necessary and Proper Clause, a legislative act must be both "necessary" and "proper." The bank bill, the secretary of state concluded, failed both of these tests, and therefore should be vetoed.

Washington, impressed, asked Hamilton for a written response. Hamilton gave his chief the most cogent argument for a liberal, or loose, construction of the Constitution ever penned. All conceded, he said, that the Constitution grants powers not only explicitly but implicitly. The question then became which powers were implicitly granted.

Looking at the list of congressional powers in Article I, Section 8, Hamilton saw several related to the economy. There was no institution other than Congress that could regulate the economy. Only Congress could decide what was "necessary and proper" to the achievement of that end. Besides that, Jefferson was wrong: in everyday English, "necessary" did not always mean "*strictly* necessary," but sometimes meant useful, conducive, or otherwise helpful.

The Constitution did include prohibitions on Congress, notably in Article I, Section 10. Chartering a bank was not among the acts that were prohibited. Where the ends were legitimate, and the means were not prohibited, he concluded, the means—in this case, chartering a bank—were constitutional.

Washington agreed and signed the bill.

By this point, members of the House who had consistently stood with Madison on a range of issues had begun to refer to themselves as "the republican interest." Hamilton's actions, and his explanation of the Constitution as granting the federal government virtually unlimited power, had roused great fear among a significant number of people. Some of them, like Madison, had spent years in alliance with Hamilton to augment the powers of the central government.

These people did not go the whole way with Hamilton, however. They called themselves "republican" to distinguish their position from Hamilton's. In the eighteenth century Anglophone world, if one was not republican, he was likely monarchist. The Republicans had taken their moniker to imply that Hamilton intended to remake America's republican federal Constitution along British lines; the combination of his statements on the matter and the tendency of his initiatives as secretary of the Treasury cinched their certainty that Hamilton was a monarchist bent upon remaking America. Madison seems certainly to have feared as much, although he was never as angry at Hamilton as Jefferson was.

Hamilton had come to rely on John Fenno's *United States Gazette* as a mouthpiece for the administration.[58] Three days after Washington signed the bank bill into law, Madison and Jefferson asked poet Philip Freneau to come to Philadelphia and set up a Republican paper. When Jefferson (corruptly?) gave Freneau a translator's post in the State Department to supplement his newspaper income, Freneau agreed.

Experienced political penman that he was, Madison took to the newspapers in late 1791 in opposition to Hamilton. Between November 19, 1791, and December 20, 1792, Madison wrote eighteen anonymous essays for the *National Gazette*.[59] The essays' topics included consolidation, which Madison called "the high road to monarchy"; parties, in which he dropped the conventional opposition to the existence of parties that had marked his thought as recently as Federalist No. 10; and the French Constitution of 1791, which Republicans strenuously defended. Each of these essays took a nakedly partisan position, opposed to Hamilton and, through Hamilton, to the Washington administration.

By the time the series wound down, these essays were far less scholarly and more popular than the Publius pieces of five years earlier. A representative column, "The Union. Who Are Its Real Friends?" appeared in the March 31, 1792, *National Gazette*. It began with six statements of who were not real friends to the Union and concluded with five statements of who were. So, for example, "Not those who study, by arbitrary interpretations and insidious precedents, to pervert the limited government of the Union, into a government of unlimited discretion, contrary to the will and subversive of the authority of the people. Not those who avow or betray principles of monarchy and aristocracy, in opposition to the republican principles of the Union." And, "*The real* FRIENDS *to the Union are those* . . . who are friends to the limited and republican system of government, the means provided by [the authority of the people], for the attainment of [liberty]." This short piece ended, "In a word, those are the real friends to the Union, who are friends to that republican policy throughout, which is the only *cement* for the Union of a republican people; in opposition to a spirit of usurpation and monarchy, which is the *menstruum* most capable of dissolving it."

Through the decade, Madison occasionally contributed to other Republican outlets, as well. So, for example, he wrote a lengthy essay for *Dunlop's American Daily Advertiser* in October 1792 defending Jefferson's actions in regard to Freneau.[60] In that piece, to no great credit, Madison pooh-poohed the idea that Freneau's State Department appointment and his newspaper were somehow related. He also denied that Jefferson had anything to do with the newspaper.

Setting up a Republican paper and occasionally providing it and other papers with copy were not Jefferson's and Madison's sole contributions to the mobilization of the Republican interest, what historians now call the "Jeffersonian Persuasion" or the Jeffersonian Republican Party. Rather, by the middle of the decade, the Republicans would be both an elite political faction and a full-fledged popular movement.[61] Public processions, public dinners, popular speakers, and competing holidays (the Fourth of July—associated with Jefferson—for Republicans, and Washington's Birthday—akin to British celebrations of the king's birthday—for Federalists) pulled the common man into the fray. Across the country, "Democratic-Republican societies" mobilized in opposition to Hamilton and the administration.

Republicans also celebrated particular dates associated with milestones of the French Revolution. The anniversary of French forces at Valmy, for example, won annual celebration. Of course, the other side could be expected to respond. It could hardly be coincidental that President John Adams, Washington's Federalist successor, signed the Alien and Sedition Acts into effect on July 14, 1798.

American attitudes toward the French Revolution developed as the French Revolution did. While Jefferson served as minister to France (1784–1789), America's friend, Louis XVI, realized that he needed substantial new income to service his debt—much of it accrued in support of American independence. In order to reform France's financial system, he called the first of several assemblies. America's friends, including the marquis de la Fayette, played a prominent role in these early phases of what ultimately would be the French Revolution.

Jefferson enthusiastically supported French reform. It seems that he provided la Fayette with American materials that made their way into the French Declaration of the Rights of Man and Citizen, for example. Jefferson hoped things would go further. La Fayette kept Washington in the know in the process, as well, which accounts for the fact that even today, the key to the Bastille adorns the mantle over the fireplace in the dining room at Mount Vernon.

European monarchs' reaction to events in France differed markedly from Americans'. As Louis was first reduced to the status of a constitutional monarch, then made a virtual prisoner, then dethroned and imprisoned, his brother kings and his brother-in-law the Holy Roman Emperor became increasingly unhappy. They determined to restore Louis. On September 20, 1792, a motley French force repulsed invading Prussian forces at Valmy.

As the Prussians were esteemed Europe's finest army, the continent was astonished. The next day, the revolutionaries proclaimed that France was a republic. On January 21, 1793, they beheaded Louis. Ten days later, France declared war on Great Britain, the Netherlands, and Spain.[62]

These developments caused severe strains within Washington's administration. Jefferson exulted in the democratizing tendency of French events. As he saw it, America should remain supportive of the French for three reasons. First, France had helped America achieve its independence. The United States of America would not have been able to do so without French assistance, as everyone who had been involved in the Revolutionary War knew. Second, France was the world's other great republic, and it was beset by monarchies—including the British monarchy. Third, Jefferson argued, America's mutual defense pact with France put the nation under legal obligations as powerful as the moral ones. Under the law of nations, if America did not live up to those obligations, France would be entitled to exact compensation by seizing American ships, taking American territory, or carrying out whatever other measures might be reasonable. Since foreign policy was the secretary of state's portfolio, Jefferson had reason to expect Washington to heed his advice.

Hamilton took a diametrically opposed position. The treaty of 1778 had been with Louis XVI, the secretary of the Treasury responded. Louis was now deceased, and his killers ruled France. Their course was increasingly bloody, both within France and without. America should not want to be associated with it.

Besides that, Hamilton feared that America's finances, highly dependant on tariff revenue, would be seriously affected by renewed conflict with Britain. As during the colonial era, 90 percent of American trade was with the former colonial power, so confrontation would mean a mammoth disruption of American trade. Less trade meant fewer imports, which meant less tariff revenue.

Finally, Hamilton said, America could not much affect matters anyway. To stick our nose into it would only result in a bloody nose without helping France significantly. Better to remain neutral and reap the benefits of providing agricultural products to both sides.

Secretary of War Knox agreed with Hamilton, while Attorney General Randolph sided (though far less vituperatively) with Jefferson.[63] Washington decided to issue a proclamation keeping America out of the war, but to avoid the word "neutrality." Use of that word, Jefferson believed, would possibly give France license to attack the United States, as it would arguably mark an American refusal to live up to the mutual defense treaty of 1778.

Washington issued what came to be called his Neutrality Proclamation in early June 1793. France responded by dropping its former restrictions on American trade with French colonies in the Caribbean. The British protested, noting that since 1756 their position had been that trade that was illegal in peace was also banned in war. In other words, Britain refused to allow America to circumvent British interdiction of French trade.

Madison objected to the Neutrality Proclamation on several grounds.[64] His position would soon become Republican orthodoxy. (Indeed, Virginia was staunchly Republican from the moment the Republican Party began to coalesce around Madison in the House.) From Virginia, Madison wrote Jefferson on June 19, 1793, that the proclamation "wounds the National honor, by seeming to disregard the stipulated duties to France. It wounds the popular feelings by a seeming indifference to the cause of liberty. And it seems to violate the forms & spirit of the Constitution, by making the executive Magistrate the organ of the disposition the duty & the interest of the Nation in relation to war & peace," which were Congress's responsibility. Madison fretted that Washington had unwittingly fallen under the influence of "Anglomany," by which he meant that Hamilton seemed to have won the president over in this as in most other things.

Soon after, Madison elaborated this argument against the Neutrality Proclamation in a series of newspaper articles.[65] Madison wrote these articles in response to Jefferson's begging him, "For god's sake, my dear Sir, take up your pen, select the most striking heresies, and cut him to pieces in the face of the public. There is nobody else who can & will enter the lists with him."[66] Madison joined Jefferson and other Republicans in thinking this series necessary because Hamilton ("Pacificus") had been attacking their position in print. Citizen Edmond Charles Genet, the new French minister to the United States, publicly mocked Washington's Neutrality Proclamation by commissioning Americans as French officers and giving letters of marque to American ship's captains. If this were allowed to continue, the British could not fail to consider these as acts of war by the U.S. government. In the end, Jefferson insisted that the bumptious Genet be recalled and that France send a new minister. Adopting the pen name "Helvidius," Madison concerned himself chiefly with the constitutional point. Making foreign policy, he said, was for Congress, not the president, and so the Neutrality Proclamation had been a usurpation. The idea that it was for the executive branch to make treaties and declare war was derived from *"British commentators,"* as those powers appertained to the king under the British constitution.[67]

The Republicans had by this point organized a trial run at a national political campaign, with some success.[68] In mid-1792, Jefferson and Madison had met with New York's governor, George Clinton, to sound him out on his willingness to take the role of vice presidential candidate. The three men had no illusions about defeating John Adams for the post, but they thought they might organize a Virginia–New York alliance for later use. Clinton ran well in New York, Virginia, North Carolina, Georgia, and South Carolina, thus laying the ground for later efforts.

At about the same time, Washington came to Madison with what must have been a surprising request: to draft a farewell address.[69] Washington had grown tired of the dissension in his cabinet and the roiling popular politics in the country, particularly in the form of the Democratic-Republican societies and the critical newspapers, and he wanted to retire. Madison took up the task, dashing off a suitable "valedictory."[70] In his cover letter, however, Madison said that he could not refrain from reiterating his view (previously expressed in person) that the country required "one more sacrifice, severe as it may be," of its first citizen. For Washington to continue in office, Madison said, was an "inestimable advantage."

Having heard similar pleas from Madison, Jefferson, and Hamilton, Washington in the end acquiesced. As soon as he did, Jefferson and Hamilton told him that they intended to depart. The ongoing feuding over virtually all major matters had exhausted their patience as well.

Jefferson left the cabinet in 1793. Madison, holding down the Republican fort during his friend's temporary retirement, finally married in 1794.[71] He had spent the winter congressional session of 1793–1794—the first since Jefferson's retirement—in new lodgings, and one historian supposes that he was "perhaps lonely." Dolley Payne Todd's congressman uncle had been a colleague of Madison's. The young widow was a relative of Martha Washington, who not so subtly encouraged the match. Her taking wedding vows from an Episcopal priest distantly related to Madison meant Dolley's expulsion from the Quakers, her father's faith. Although few people were in attendance at the wedding, his parents not among them, Madison seems to have been married "happily ever after."

The chief political development of Washington's second term was the fracas over the Jay Treaty.[72] In 1795, Chief Justice John Jay returned from England with a treaty it had been hoped would square away the main issues between the two Anglophone powers. Among those were the removal of British forces from their inland posts in the United States, American compliance with the Treaty of Paris in regard to British creditors' access to American courts, enforcement of the provision for compensation of slave owners whose slaves had fled with or been taken by the British forces when they evacuated North American posts, American access to British markets in the Caribbean, and—most inflammatory of all—the end of the British practice of impressment.

Washington and Jay (an abolitionist) did not want to push the issue of slave owners' compensation, as they found the issue morally distasteful. The British, mercantilist to the core, had no incentive whatsoever to give the Americans greater access to British colonies, and the United States had nothing to give the British in return. As long as American courts remained effectively closed to British creditors, Britain would not likely withdraw from its forts in today's Midwest—and John Jay and Washington privately agreed that Britain's position was reasonable.

The chief issue about which the Americans were concerned, impressment, did not seem any more tractable than those. Impressment was the name given to the British practice of stopping American ships at sea, questioning the sailors, and conscripting those who were determined to be British into the Royal Navy on the spot. Britain found itself in another major war with France, and it had to man its navy. Without its navy, it would soon succumb to France. Although Americans would continue to chafe under impressment for decades, the British did not abandon the practice until after Waterloo—which, of course, was not brought on by American effort.

Working with such a weak hand, Jay came back to America with a disappointing treaty. Impressment would continue, slave owners would go uncompensated, British forces would vacate the Midwest (as they had been obligated to do under the Treaty of Paris), and only small American ships would be allowed into British colonial ports. This last was something, but not what Republicans were insisting upon. Still, British traders would continue to dominate the Indian trade. What really outraged Republicans, however, was a final provision pledging the two countries not to try to coerce each other through economic legislation.

Washington kept the treaty secret for a while and then submitted it to the Senate. Although Senate rules required that the communication from the president remain secret, a Republican senator slipped the treaty to a newspaper editor, and soon a huge flap developed. Jay, ever imperturbable, wrote that he could have walked from one end of the country to the other by the light of his burning effigies.

For the Republicans, Jay's treaty offered a new opportunity to tag Federalists as Anglophile to a fault. This treaty amounted to a renunciation of America's French alliance, they hollered. France, predictably, saw things in much the same way. Still, other than mobilizing their supporters and guaranteeing that John Adams, not John Jay, would succeed Washington as the Federalists' pick for president, nothing much came of Republican opposition to the Jay treaty.

Late in 1796, fed up with the political wars and exhausted from years of top-level service, Washington decided definitely to retire. In 1792, thinking of retirement had prompted him to have Madison draft a farewell address. By 1796, so distant had they become that Madison had no part in the process. Instead, Washington turned to Hamilton and Jay for assistance.

Madison, for his part, recruited a presidential candidate: Thomas Jefferson. And for vice president, up-and-coming New York lawyer-politician Aaron Burr. As far as we can tell, Madison played no part in the actual organization of the campaign. Burr, on the other hand, worked hard in New York to put his state into the Republican column. Burr well might have been disappointed, even aggrieved, then, when some of the Republican electors threw away their second ballots so that Jefferson would have more votes than Burr.

In those pre–Twelfth Amendment days, electors cast two votes each. The first-place winner became president, while the second-place candidate won election as vice president. The Republican high command, centered in Virginia, realized that the outcome might be close, so it took precautions. The Republican Party, Jefferson confided to Madison, represented the "Southern interest."[73] Burr, unlike Republican eminences such as Jefferson, Madison, John Taylor, William Giles, and others, was no plantation owner. When Burr decided to campaign in New England, where Jefferson seemed unlikely to garner any electoral votes, Virginia Republicans feared that Burr would sneak past their man and become vice president under Adams. What to do? The manager of Jefferson's effort, himself a Virginian, suggested that half of Virginia's electors cast their second votes for New York's governor, George Clinton, instead of for Burr.

In the end, Virginia Republicans' betrayal of Burr went even further than that: while Jefferson received 20 of a possible 22 electoral votes from Virginia, Burr reaped only 1. When the electoral votes were tallied, John Adams became president with 71 Electoral College votes, Jefferson ran second with 68, and Burr was a weak fourth, with only 30. Four years later, this result would have significant repercussions.

For Madison in 1796, the result was quite gratifying. His friend Jefferson had nearly won and might be expected to succeed to the chief magistracy when Adams vacated the post. Madison contentedly retired from public office when Congress adjourned in 1796. Yet he could not steer clear of the partisan fighting of the Adams administration.

The central issue, as it had been since he first came of age, was foreign policy. More specifically, John Adams's presidency coincided with the French Republic's final determination that it was not going to brook further American refusal to live up to the moral and legal obligation to take a pro-French position in international affairs.

Since the Jay Treaty, at least, and effectively since Washington's inauguration, the United States had tried to avoid becoming embroiled in Europe's affairs. Washington's farewell address laid down as a principle that America ought to steer clear of foreign entanglements. Americans generally thought that involvement in military conflict would undermine republicanism, so they wanted to stay out of it.

In 1797 and 1798, France stepped up its depredations against American shipping. At home, meanwhile, Democratic-Republican clubs up and down the Atlantic Coast protested the Federalists' supposedly supine foreign policy. Federalists could not help but notice that recent immigrants, hailing mainly from Ireland and francophone territories on the European mainland, tended to align with the Republicans.

In Richmond in 1797, a federal grand jury indicted Virginia Republican congressman Samuel Cabell for seditious libel. His supposed offense lay in criticizing President Adams in a letter to his constituents. Vice President Jefferson drafted a petition calling for the impeachment and trial on treason charges of the members of the federal grand jury.[74] The charge should be treason against Virginia. The Commonwealth, he reasoned, had never delegated the federal government power to restrict elected officials' right to communicate freely with their constituents. Governor James Monroe told Jefferson that the petition should be addressed to Congress, but Jefferson insisted "that in the worsening crisis of federal authority, Virginia must assert itself to preempt the Federalists' seizing 'all doubtful ground.'" Nothing came of Jefferson's idea in the short run, but he and other Virginia Republican friends of

Madison's continued to ponder how to resist Federalist transgressions of the states' reserved powers.

The results were the immigration reform and the Alien and Sedition Acts of 1798.[75] John Adams signed the Alien and Sedition Acts on July 14, 1798, Bastille Day, and that cannot have been a coincidence. Democratic-Republicans, after all, celebrated that day as the birthday of the French Republic. The new immigration law extended to fifteen years—still to this day the longest period ever required in American history—the time an immigrant must be resident before he could become an American citizen. Perhaps these Frenchmen were going to live here, but they were not going to vote against John Adams.

The three laws comprising the Alien and Sedition Acts empowered the federal executive and judiciary to stanch political opposition. The first of them, the Alien Enemies Act, provoked little protest. It provided that the president could in time of war identify dangerous enemy aliens and imprison or expel them. Used by numerous presidents throughout American history, it remains in effect today.

The others provoked vigorous resistance.

The second, the Alien Friends Act, applied to aliens from nonenemy countries. It gave the president authority to identify aliens from countries with which the United States were not in hostilities and expel them. Finally, most notoriously, the Sedition Act made it a crime punishable by substantial fine, imprisonment, or both, not only to organize resistance to federal law, but to say anything that tended to bring the government into ill repute. The only significant federal government official not covered by the Sedition Act was Vice President Jefferson, the ranking Republican. Say whatever you liked about him, it was no crime.

John Adams made no use of the Alien Friends Act. The Sedition Act was a different story. Federal judges energetically enforced that law, winning themselves lasting infamy along the way. Justice Samuel Chase, for example, in one instance told people in Maryland that when he got to Virginia, he was going to empanel a grand jury to indict a particular writer.[76] That writer having been indicted, Chase then arbitrarily excluded evidence, harassed defense counsel, and crafted his jury instructions to ensure a conviction. Once the author had been convicted, Chase threw the book at him, giving him a long prison sentence and a heavy fine.

Numerous Republican journalists, including even major newspaper publishers, went to prison under the Sedition Act. So did a Vermont congressman. For the Republican leadership, here was a constitutional crisis. After all, if criticism of incumbents were banned, how would free elections ever take place? The chief topic in most elections, then as now, was the record of the incumbents. The Sedition Act seemed calculated to destroy republican government in America.

Republicans had several constitutional objections to the Alien Friends Act and the Sedition Act. Most significantly, they violated the Tenth Amendment's reservation of all undelegated powers to the states. The principle that Congress only had the powers "expressly delegated," which Federalists like Edmund Randolph had said was implicit in the unamended Constitution, underlay the mainline Federalist construction of the Constitution during the ratification process. The Tenth Amendment made it explicit.

A second Republican objection to these laws was that the Alien Friends Act united executive and judicial powers in the hands of the president. He was to identify dangerous aliens, and he was to expel them. The principle of separation of powers, Republicans groused, could not be any more flagrantly violated.

Finally, Republicans held, the Alien Friends Act and Sedition Act both violated the First Amendment. Arguing for a novel understanding of the freedom of speech, Republicans said that it was essentially unlimited when it came to political affairs.[77] People must be allowed to say what they would about political officials' performance, or else elections would degenerate into a hollow sham. Thus, even the Sedition Act's provision—unknown to the common law—that truth was a defense did not save the law from constitutional scrutiny.

So Madison and other like-minded people had powerful arguments. But what to do? After all, the president had signed these laws, the Congress had passed them, and, since both presidents had been Federalists, every member of the federal judiciary supported them, most vociferously.

Every branch of the federal government was hostile.

But in the federal system, the federal government is not the sole actor.

There are also the state governments. And at least one state, the most populous one, Virginia, was friendly to the Republican cause. It had, indeed, always elected staunchly Republican congressional delegations and Republican General Assembly majorities. Might Virginia step into the breach, as it had in the days of the imperial crisis?

John Taylor of Caroline, Edmund Pendleton's nephew and political protégé, certainly thought so. For years he had been urging Madison, Jefferson, and anyone else who would listen to deploy the state governments against the federal government. So far as he was concerned, the new government would establish its own personality in its first years, and so it must be watched especially carefully.

While one of their own, George Washington, presided and other prominent Virginians—Jefferson, Madison, Randolph—played prominent roles, Virginians had been hard to bestir. As late as June 4, 1798, Jefferson wrote Taylor not to be overly hasty. Yes, the vice president said, Massachusetts and Connecticut (meaning the Federalists) made stern task-masters, but Americans' attitudes toward them would change once the tax bill for the Federalists' naval and military buildup of that year had to be paid. Forty days later, Adams signed the Alien and Sedition Acts. Suddenly, finally, the mainstream of the Republican Party took a strongly Taylorite turn. In 1790, it had been Patrick Henry and Henry Lee who warned that exercise of powers not expressly granted to the federal government by the Constitution was usurpation, and that usurpation would not be tolerated. Now, Madison and the vice president led the way.

But secretly.

In summer 1798, Jefferson, Madison, and other prominent Republicans seem to have met at Monticello, Jefferson's Albemarle County estate, to plot strategy and draft resolutions. I say "seem" because we are not certain: in light of the Sedition Act and the jailing of so many prominent Republicans, even including a congressman, these men kept their acts essentially secret. Jefferson, for one, left us over thirty thousand documents in his own hand, but he saved very few letters from that year. Madison's correspondence for 1798 is relatively sparse as well. Why? They feared that association with these anti–Alien and Sedition Acts manifestos might give the Federalist administration an opportunity to throw even them into prison.

If the federal government would not heed Republicans' pleas, the state legislatures would. Virginia's, of course, but what other? Jefferson thought North Carolina's, but an ally noted that his relatives in Kentucky assured him that this strategy would be well received west of the Blue Ridge. So Kentucky it was.

Jefferson drafted what came to be called the Kentucky Resolutions of 1798, while Madison wrote the Virginia Resolutions. The public did not know of Madison's role until years later, when Taylor, confronted in a newspaper dispute, said that Madison, not he, had written them; knowledge of Jefferson's role came later, as well.

The two documents had similar outlines.[78] The Virginia Resolutions began by saying that Virginia would "maintain and defend the constitution of the United States, and the Constitution of this state, against every aggression, either foreign or domestic," and that it would "support the government of the United States in all measures, warranted by [the Constitution of the United States]."

The most important of the Virginia Resolutions, the third one, bears reproducing in full:

> That this Assembly explicitly and peremptorily declare, that it views the powers of the federal government, as resulting from the compact to which the states are parties; as limited by the plain sense and intention of the instrument constituting the compact; as no farther valid than they are authorised by the grants enumerated in that compact, and that in case of a deliberate, palpable and dangerous exercise of other powers not granted by the said compact, the states who are parties thereto have the right, and are in duty bound, to interpose for arresting the progress of the evil, and for maintaining within their respective limits, the authorities, rights and liberties appertaining to them.

The resolutions went on to lament the federal government's tendency to expand its own powers by construction and to hold that this tendency would ultimately mean the end of republican government in America.

Besides that, the resolutions noted, the Alien Friends and Sedition Act embodied "palpable and alarming infractions of the constitution." The first of them, they said, "exercise[d] a power no where delegated to the federal government" and violated the principle of separation of powers. The Sedition Act, for its part, exercised a power not granted to the federal government by the Constitution, but took up one "expressly and positively forbidden by one of the amendments thereto." In doing so, that act "ought to produce universal alarm," for it prevented the criticism of public officials, "which has ever been justly deemed, the only effectual guardian of every other right."

Virginia's legislators next reminded the other states that the Old Dominion had "by its convention which ratified the federal constitution, expressly declared, 'that among other essential rights, the liberty of conscience and of the press cannot be cancelled, abridged, restrained or modified by any authority of the United States" and that Virginia had joined other states in insisting on the Tenth Amendment's adoption.

In the following resolution, its last, Virginia asked other states to join it in saying "that the acts aforesaid are unconstitutional." When John Taylor of Caroline introduced the resolutions in the House of Delegates, they here went on to call the offending federal statutes "not law, but utterly null, void and of no force or effect." It was at Madison's instigation that this language was dropped, and this excision has led some historians to say that the Virginia Resolutions were less stark and strident than Jefferson's Kentucky version with its reference to "nullification." It may well be that Madison understood his editing to have that effect. As to the General Assembly, however, the record of the House of Delegates debates shows clearly that Taylor agreed to this deletion because he and other proponents of the Virginia Resolutions understood "unconstitutional" to include "not law, but utterly null, void and of no force or effect." The latter, so far as they were concerned, was mere redundancy; it could be dropped if Madison disliked it.

The Virginia Resolutions, like their Kentucky counterparts, closed with a direction to the governor to relay them to the other state governors for transmission to the legislatures and to Virginia's members of Congress. The resolutions included repeated assertions of filial amity, and sending them to the other governors followed logically.

The result? From states to Virginia's south, silence. From more northerly climes, a torrent of abuse.

In 1799, then, Kentucky responded with a second set of legislative resolutions, the Kentucky Resolutions of 1799. Possibly outlined but certainly not written by Vice President Jefferson, these resolutions said that Kentucky loved the Union for the limited purposes for which it was created, and that Kentucky would be among the last states to secede. Lest you think this a moderate position, consider: although secession had been mentioned in private and in public by some second-tier Virginia Republican leaders (Taylor and Representatives William Giles), never before had it been part of an official position. In that context, the Kentucky Resolutions of 1799 must be seen as a shot across the Federalist bow.

Virginia responded to Federalist criticisms of its 1798 resolutions as well. Madison came out of retirement to enter the General Assembly, where he authored the Virginia *Report of 1800*. This pamphlet-length report took up every one of the criticisms of the resolutions in depth, elaborating on the Republicans' constitutional argument in detail. Not content simply to attack the Alien and Sedition Acts, Madison ranged across the entire decade of Federalist dominance of the federal government. Among his targets were the Bank Bill, the Neutrality Proclamation, and other such federal usurpations.

The most common state criticisms of the Virginia and Kentucky resolutions asserted that the state legislatures had no rightful role in interpreting the U.S. Constitution and that the people, not the states, had created the federal government. In regard to the latter, Madison explained what his opponents must surely have known: that the word "states" had different meanings. One might use the word "state" in reference to the territory of a state, as in, "Tomorrow I'm going to the state of New York." Alternatively, one might use the word "state" in reference to the government, as in, "The state of Connecticut taxes people to support the Congregational church."

The third definition was crucial. It referred to the sovereign people of a state, as in, "The state of Virginia ratified the Constitution." Madison said that it was in this sense that Republicans claimed the states had ratified the Constitution. The fact was indisputable.

Madison, Jefferson, and their fellows did not expect their manifestos to persuade die-hard Federalists to vote Republican in 1800. Their hope was to move the population at large. And they did not expect constitutional arguments to be the chief reasons that the people opted for Jefferson rather than

Adams, and Republican congressional candidates rather than Federalists, in 1800. Rather, Jefferson counseled that "land tax, stamp tax, increase of public debt," and war would lead Americans to abandon Hamilton's party in favor of Jefferson's.[79]

Once again, Jefferson ran with Aaron Burr as running mate. Madison energetically coordinated Jefferson's presidential candidacy, sometimes dragging Jefferson along. And in the end, the Jeffersonians triumphed. Not only did Jefferson and Burr win the presidency and vice presidency, but Federalists were swept from their majority status in both houses of Congress, never to return.

Madison agreed to sit at Jefferson's right hand. In the Jefferson administration, Madison would head the cabinet as secretary of state. Since Jefferson was a widower, Dolley Madison would serve as White House hostess, carving out an important role not to that point known in the United States.

Chapter 7

Secretary of State, Then President, 1800–17

Both Federalists and Republicans pulled out all the stops in attempting to win the election of 1800. Republicans in control of the Virginia General Assembly, for example, changed the way their state's electoral votes were allocated. Rather than having them elected on a district basis, which would have risked giving John Adams some Virginia electoral votes, they adopted a law drafted by Madison establishing a winner-take-all system.

Federalists in New York, on the other hand, came up with a different strategy. After Aaron Burr's campaigning shifted the New York legislature from the Federalist to the Republican column, Alexander Hamilton proposed a Madisonian move. He wrote to Governor John Jay saying that Jay should have the lame-duck majority in New York's legislature assemble to give Adams the election.[1] This extraordinary step was justified, in Hamilton's estimation, by the imperative "to prevent an *Atheist* in Religion and a *Fanatic* in politics from getting possession of the helm of the State."

Hamilton confided to Jay that Hamilton knew the Republican Party better than Jay did. Some of them, Hamilton said, advocated "the overthrow of the Government by stripping it of its due energies," while others would push America "to a Revolution after the manner of Buonaparte." In case this seemed overheated, Hamilton insisted that he "sp[o]k[e] from indubitable facts." So the legislature should move New York in the opposite direction from that in which Madison's gambit had moved Virginia's: from statewide selection of presidential electors to their selection on a district basis.

Hamilton insisted that "the reasonable part of the world" would approve Jay's action. Perhaps it would have, but John Jay did not approve. Instead, he filed Hamilton's letter away after noting that it recommended a measure for party purposes that it would not become the governor to take. Unbeknownst to anyone, John Adams's, and thus Thomas Jefferson's and the country's, fate would turn on John Jay's very strong sense of ethics. Some have described Thomas Jefferson as the "Negro president" because the Three-Fifths Clause provided the margin of his 1800 victory; they might as easily have called him the "chicanery president," because Madison's clever exploitation of the Electoral College can be said to have accounted for the post-1800 Republican ascendancy as well.[2]

When the Electoral College votes were counted, the Republican nominees for president and vice president led President John Adams by three electoral votes. Federalist rule would end.

But who would succeed Adams? Nowadays, electors cast votes for presidential and vice presidential tickets. The top vote-getter for president, if he has a majority in the Electoral College, wins the presidential election, while the top candidate for vice president, if he has a majority of electoral votes for that office, wins the vice presidency. Thus works the procedure established by the Twelfth Amendment, which was ratified in 1804.

But why should there have been an amendment to the original system under which Washington and Adams were elected in 1789? Why does our current system date only to 1804?

Because of the outcome in 1800–1801.

At this remove, in both time and culture, the crisis atmosphere that surrounded the election of 1800 is difficult to recover. Members of both parties had speculated for years that there would not be a normal election in 1800.[3] Republicans feared that Federalists would instigate a coup, and vice versa. The Sedition Act's energetic enforcement underlay Republican fears, while Federalists' concerns centered on the Virginia and Kentucky resolutions, the Virginia Report, and the militia preparations undertaken by Virginia as the election approached. As leading Federalists put it, a military takeover of the mid-Atlantic states would come once Republicans had finished "render[ing their] militia[s] as formidable as possible, and supply[ing their] arsenals & magazines."[4] Jefferson touted Hamilton as "our Bonaparte" and dreaded the "political salvation" he might inflict.[5]

Prior to the Twelfth Amendment, each elector had two votes. The top vote getter became president and the runner-up served as vice president. One awkward possibility under that old system was the one that actually obtained in 1797–1801: the president's chief political opponent, in that case Thomas Jefferson, could be runner-up in the Electoral College, and thus serve as his vice president. The other glaring shortcoming of the system was the one that struck in 1801: that the top two vote-getters might tie.

Everyone knew that Thomas Jefferson, not Aaron Burr, was the Republicans' choice for president. Yet, the two had the same number of electoral votes. Therefore, according to the provisions of Article II, Section 1, Clause 3 of the Constitution, the House of Representatives would choose between them. Each state, regardless of population, would have one vote. Voting would continue until either Jefferson or Burr won the votes of a majority of state delegations.

Before the voting began, Republicans knew that they controlled eight of sixteen delegations, while Federalists had six, and two were equally split. To secure a majority vote, then, might not be easy. Leading Federalists discussed the option of preventing a majority. Some thought that in case there were no majority, the president pro tempore of the Senate or the Speaker of the House—both Federalists—would succeed John Adams.[6] Federalist House members even met in caucus to discuss this option, but they broke up without adopting it as a party goal.

Virginia's governor, James Monroe, long a close ally of Jefferson and Madison, wrote of the possibility of Federalists' elevating someone other than Jefferson to the presidency that "if the union cod. be broken, that wod. do it." Jefferson, as vice president, realized that he could prevent one of the options Federalists were discussing from ever arising: if he attended every session of the Senate, no president pro tempore would be elected, and so no such person could be elevated to the presidency in the event of a House deadlock. So he did, and none was.[7]

Madison came up with last-ditch contingency plans.[8] As he told Jefferson, in case the Federalists prevented the people's choice from assuming the presidency, Republicans could bide their time until Congress reconvened in December 1801, when the new Republican majority could award Jefferson his office. Alternatively, Madison said, Jefferson and Burr could jointly issue an extraconstitutional call for Congress to meet sooner; the theory here was that since one of them would become president, the two of them together could legitimately (if extralegally) convene the federal legislature. Jefferson apparently preferred an alternative approach broached by Albert Gallatin. Gallatin's idea was that the Republicans ought to accept acts undertaken by whomever the Federalists put into power before the December 1801 session of Congress, so long as those acts were "not immediately connected with Presidential powers." Then, when the Congress convened, it could install the rightful victors in the election: Jefferson and Burr.

Federalists generally determined that they would either elect Burr president over Jefferson or prevent any election at all. So things continued through thirty-five House ballots. At that point, however, Representative James Bayard—Delaware's sole member—changed his mind. His reasons are unclear: some would say that he reached a backstairs agreement with Jefferson not to eliminate the navy altogether, while others insist that no such agreement was reached. In any event, Jefferson was finally elected. Burr, who had served willingly as the Federalists' cat's paw, was ruined in the Republican Party before the new administration had even begun.

Jefferson was inaugurated on March 4, 1801. He took the oath of office from Chief Justice John Marshall. Marshall had been appointed by John Adams in the last days of Federalist dominance. Like Jefferson, Marshall was the son of a Randolph mother. He would prove Jefferson's most successful foe. As the new chief executive loathed public speaking, his first inaugural was hard to hear.[9] Yet that most memorable of presidential inaugurals laid out the program Republicans had developed in the 1790s in the poetic way in which Jefferson almost always wrote.

First, in the time-tested Virginia manner, Jefferson deprecated his own abilities. He followed with a ringing assessment of the diplomatic setting of his administration. America was, in the new president's assessment:

A rising nation, spread over a wide and fruitful land, traversing all the seas with the rich productions of their industry, engaged in commerce

with nations who feel power and forget right, advancing rapidly to desti-
nies beyond the reach of mortal eye. . . .

He would feel overwhelmed with the magnitude of the task before him, Jefferson continued, if he were not aware of the "resources of wisdom, of virtue,
and of zeal" that would be provided to assist him by the other high officials of
the government. He hoped the Congress would help him in his task.

Next, with a nod to the defeated Federalists, Jefferson said what he hoped
would result from his party's victory. The contention that had marked the
recent election, the Republican chieftain held, might mislead a foreigner.
Americans would "bear in mind this sacred principle, that though the will of
the majority is in all cases to prevail, that will, to be rightful, must be reasonable." Where there had been acrimony, Jefferson called on his compatriots to
"unite with one heart and one mind," to "restore to social intercourse that
harmony and affection without which liberty and even life itself are but dreary
things."

Jefferson lauded his countrymen (and, implicitly, Madison and himself)
for having "banished . . . the religious intolerance under which mankind so
long bled and suffered," but he implored them not to believe that "every difference of opinion is . . . a difference of principle." Hopefully, he told his audience, "We have called by different names brethren of the same principle.
We are all republicans—we are all federalists." For Jefferson, as indeed for
Madison, "the Republicans [were] the nation."[10] The 1790s behind them,
Americans would now find their natural consensus: "If there be any among
us who would wish to dissolve this Union or to change its republican form,
let them stand undisturbed as monuments of the safety with which error of
opinion may be tolerated where reason is left free to combat it."

The era of Hamilton thus rhetorically behind him, Jefferson pivoted toward the future. "Some honest men" feared that America's government was
"not strong enough," that republicanism carried that defect. Yet, he said, the
government had been a success thus far. Fears were only "theoretic and visionary." For himself, "I believe this, on the contrary, the strongest government on earth. I believe it is the only one where every man, at the call of the
laws, would fly to the standard of the law, and would meet invasions of the
public order as his own personal concern."

Prodded on by Madison, Jefferson was going to stake his presidency on this idea. Because the populace would run to help in time of war, no peacetime military establishment to speak of was necessary. Therefore, the Federalists would soon be obliterated. As he put it later in the address, Jefferson held that "a well-disciplined militia" was the "best reliance in peace and for the first moments of war, till regulars may relieve them." Firm believers in the Whig dogma that a large military establishment and republican government were ultimately irreconcilable, Madison and his friend the president decided that an army and a significant navy could be dispensed with. Even in the midst of a world war, they would substitute the slogan of "a well-regulated militia" for military preparedness. That would suffice. First Jefferson's, then Madison's presidency would show how wrong they were.

Having repealed the Federalists' military buildup, the new Jeffersonian majority would be in position to repeal their taxes too. As Jefferson put it, Republicans would bring "a wise and frugal government, which shall restrain men from injuring one another, which shall leave them otherwise free to regulate their own pursuits of industry and improvement, and shall not take from the mouth of labor the bread it has earned."

When it came to foreign policy, Jefferson's prescription was by this point predictable. His immortal formula was "peace, commerce, and honest friendship, with all nations—entangling alliances with none."

Still in the Whig line, Jefferson pointed to the primacy of agriculture in America's economy. "Commerce" was important as "its handmaid." He listed several basic constitutional ideas to which Republicans were committed, including the primacy of the state governments ("the surest bulwarks against anti-republican tendencies") and various individual rights, and concluded by positing that these were the ideas for which "the blood of our heroes" had been shed. Truly, Republicanism was Americanism in the eyes of the new president.

We do not know that Madison played any role in drafting this first Republican inaugural address. It would be unsurprising if he had. Leaving aside the characteristic Jeffersonian felicity of language, there was nothing in it that one might not have found in a Madison composition. Even if Madison had no role in it at all, he would over the following sixteen years endeavor, first as the number two man in the executive branch and then as number one, to implement it in its entirety.

The first momentous decision of the new Republican administration cannot have seemed very significant at the time. John Adams had in his last days in office appointed several men to new federal judicial posts.[11] John Marshall, serving as secretary of state to the outgoing president even though he had already assumed the center seat on the Supreme Court, had to deliver the new judges' commissions. In the crush of work, he did not deliver them all.

There matters stood when Madison first found his way to his new office. As Jefferson explained near the end of his life, the president decided that those of the "midnight judges" whose commissions had not been delivered would never receive them. Without those commissions, they could not take their new posts.

One appointee to a minor post had a different idea. The Supreme Court, as William Marbury told it, should order Madison to give him his commission. The president had nominated him to the post, the Senate had confirmed the nomination, and so he was entitled to his commission. Far from discretionary, the duty to deliver his commission was mandatory. The constitutional process of appointment had already been completed.

So argued the plaintiff's counsel in *Marbury v. Madison* (1803), perhaps the most famous judicial decision in American history.[12] Chief Justice Marshall took the opportunity to make far more of the case than simply a dispute over an insignificant local office in Washington City. In the two years between Jefferson's (and, one infers, Madison's) decision to withhold the commission and the Supreme Court's decision, the Jefferson administration and its congressional allies had taken a substantial step against the federal judiciary. They had repealed the Judiciary Act of 1801. Among other things, that meant the elimination of several judgeships. Marshall thought that a violation of the Constitution's provision to federal judges of "good behaviour tenure."

Marshall had wanted to resist that repeal, but his colleagues judged the idea unwise.[13] Still, his anger with Jefferson and Madison shaped his opinion in *Marbury*. The structure of Marshall's opinion for his apparently unanimous court is completely unlike what one would expect. In the American judicial system, state courts can hear cases involving any kind of law, federal or state, but federal courts can only hear federal cases. Thus, federal courts routinely begin their decisions by explaining the basis of their jurisdiction over the case at hand.

Marshall in *Marbury,* however, took up the jurisdictional question last. Before he got to that, he first answered two other questions: whether Marbury had a right to his office, and whether there was a legal remedy. Yes, he said, Marbury did have such a right. The Constitution required only nomination by the president and confirmation by the Senate, which had already been granted. Yes, he added, there was a legal remedy: a writ of mandamus, the kind of technical legal order that Marbury was requesting.

Then, finally, Marshall took up the jurisdictional matter—the question whether the Supreme Court had power to hear this case. He decided that it did not. Although the Judiciary Act of 1789 purported to give the Court power to entertain suits for writs of mandamus, Marshall explained, that provision of the act was unconstitutional. The reason was that Article III, Section 2 of the Constitution says, in part, "In all Cases affecting Ambassadors, other public Ministers and Consuls, and those in which a State shall be Party, the supreme Court shall have original Jurisdiction. In all the other Cases before mentioned, the supreme Court shall have appellate Jurisdiction." In trying to give the Court original, rather than appellate, jurisdiction over suits for writs of mandamus, the Court held, Congress had exceeded the limits of its power.

Ingeniously, Marshall had found a way to upbraid Jefferson and Madison for their behavior, to claim the power of judicial review for his court, and to leave the executive branch no way to respond. Without an order to Madison, which Madison would have ignored, there was no opening for the president to put Marshall in his place. While some lower federal courts had already claimed the power of judicial review in previous cases, this was the first time the Supreme Court staked a claim to that power.[14] That is why it is the most famous case in American history. James Madison won, but he cannot have been too pleased with his victory.

As the Supreme Court considered *Marbury,* the judicial branch had come under fire in the House of Representatives. There, District of New Hampshire Judge John Pickering was the target of an impeachment proceeding.[15] The House of Representatives voted to impeach him on the ground that he frequently appeared in court drunk. No, his defense counsel insisted in his Senate trial, Pickering was not a drunk: he was senile. Or perhaps insane. Neither one of which, his defense counsel roared, was a "high crime" or "high misdemeanor."

According to the English precedents on which the Constitution's impeachment provisions are based, incapacity certainly was a high misdemeanor. The Senate, befuddled by this incorrect argument, convicted and removed Pickering anyway in March 1804. The same day as Pickering was convicted, the House was initiating the more momentous impeachment of Justice Samuel Chase.

Chase was the picture of a hanging judge. In one instance, he had as a circuit judge identified a man he wanted indicted, convicted, and sentenced; pushed a grand jury to indict him; and conducted a completely rigged trial. In that trial, he had cut off defense witnesses' testimony, mocked defense counsel to the jury, and otherwise made clear what outcome he wanted. When all was over, he had sentenced the defendant to the punishment Chase had determined upon weeks before.

As the leading authority on American impeachment noted, if anyone ever deserved to be impeached and convicted, it was Justice Samuel Chase. Yet, once again, defense counsel asked the question: what are "high crimes" and "high misdemeanors"? Some senators seem to have been swayed by the argument that an unindictable offense was not a "high crime" or "high misdemeanor"—that is, not the kind of action for which the Constitution provided the remedy of conviction in the Senate and removal from office.

In addition, defense counsel argued that Chase was really being punished for his political views. Here, they exploited the fact that besides determining trials' outcomes before even impaneling a grand jury, Chase was in the habit of delivering plainly partisan attacks on Republicans (including Jefferson) from the bench. In the end, Chase was spared conviction. There was talk that John Marshall was to have been the next target—as his baldly political behavior in gratuitously lecturing Jefferson and Madison in *Marbury v. Madison* arguably had earned him. Under the English precedents, abuse of judicial office for political purposes was ground for removal from office. Yet the lamentable Chase acquittal left that question forever unanswered.

Perhaps the most unsavory element of the Chase trial in the Senate was that Vice President Aaron Burr presided. Not only had Burr been persona non grata among Republicans throughout his tenure in that office because of his collusion with Federalists in resolving the electoral impasse with Jefferson. By the time the Senate's Chase proceedings began, Burr was also under indictment for having shot Alexander Hamilton to death in a duel.[16] Madison left no record of his response to the death of his close collaborator-turned-partisan enemy. As the duel resulted in part from the defeat of Burr's bid for the governorship of New York, it wrote *finis* to the political career of the man who, along with Jefferson and Madison, had founded the Republican Party, the one who had secured victory in the pivotal New York legislative elections of 1800.

Jefferson and Madison did not publicly associate themselves with the impeachment campaign. In fact, the House counsel in the Chase Senate trial, Jefferson's cousin John Randolph, believed that the White House had hung him out to dry. Still, both Jefferson and Madison would regret that the judicial branch now felt free to write Hamiltonianism into "constitutional law."

By the time these events transpired, however, Jefferson's political success had been ensured by a diplomatic coup no one expected. It boiled down to one word: Louisiana.

In early 1803, Jefferson and Madison dispatched James Monroe to France. His assignment: to purchase New Orleans and the area immediately surrounding it. As Monroe's superiors understood it, New Orleans was the key to the West's economic future. If denied access to the Gulf of Mexico through New Orleans, farmers in the Ohio and Mississippi river valleys would be deprived of foreign markets. In those days before refrigeration and railroad, their crops would be worthless.

So New Orleans must be bought.

The need became urgent in November 1802. That was when Secretary of State Madison got word that Spain had closed New Orleans to American commerce.[17] America's agent in New Orleans also notified Madison that the Spanish did not intend to provide an alternative place at which American goods might be deposited.[18] In other words, the Mississippi was being closed off to Americans, precisely as Patrick Henry had feared would happen fifteen years before.

The secretary of state and his chief responded by sending Monroe to Paris, where Robert Livingston had been trying to pry the Crescent City from French hands since 1801. Napoleon Bonaparte, the French first consul, had had no interest in selling the city. To the contrary, his hope was to make New Orleans the center of a revivified French North American empire.

But now things were different. Madison and Jefferson both refused American aid to the army Napoleon sent to reconquer Saint Domingue, and that failed in its task.[19] It was ravaged by tropical diseases that killed even Bonaparte's brother-in-law, the commanding general. With the Peace of Amiens drawing to a close, Napoleon realized that war with Britain and its coalition partners would likely resume. North America, the New World generally, was no longer on his radar; as he put it, British naval superiority meant that Louisiana was "already lost."[20] Monroe's arrival in France could not have been better timed.

Napoleon's foreign minister, the wily Charles Maurice de Talleyrand-Périgord, shocked Monroe by replying to his offer to purchase New Orleans by asking whether Monroe would like to buy all of Louisiana. The French territory of Louisiana was far more expansive than today's state. It stretched from the Mississippi River to the Rocky Mountains, with the then-Mexican province of Texas to its south and a northern boundary inside today's Canada. Careful not to seem overly enthused, Monroe jumped at the offer.

Madison, meantime, had sent Monroe and Livingston instructions to seek a British alliance in case the French overtures proved unavailing.[21] Imagine, then, the excitement of the president and his secretary of state at the news Monroe ultimately sent them. Instead of war against a military genius, a whole North American empire, for a song! The greatest land deal ever!

News of the gift from the diplomatic gods arrived on July 14, 1803—ironically, the fifth anniversary of John Adams's signing the Alien and Sedition Acts.[22] Madison happily relayed Jefferson's "entire approbation" of Livingston's and Monroe's exceeding their instructions, which only extended to the purchase of New Orleans and West Florida (what are now the coastal portions of Alabama, Mississippi, and part of Louisiana). Pregnant with later difficulty was the lack of clarity concerning the new western boundary of Florida, which would cause friction between the United States and Spain for years to come. Still, Madison's letter to his subordinates in France was downright exuberant.

Yet President Jefferson had a mixed reaction. On one hand, the news from Monroe was too good to be true. Who could believe it: the area of the United States doubled, for only $15 million. His favored scheme of political economy, in which the vast majority of Americans farmed for a living and depended on no one, could be continued for generations to come.[23]

On the other, he thought the Louisiana Purchase was unconstitutional.[24] For such a constitutional purist as he, this was no minor consideration. Indeed, Madison had played a leading role in establishing Jeffersonian Republican constitutional orthodoxy, in the Richmond ratification convention, in the House, and as author of the Virginia Resolutions of 1798 and *Report of 1800*. One might have expected Madison to join Jefferson in proposing to amend the Constitution to empower the federal government to incorporate foreign territory into the Union, then.

Secretary of the Treasury Albert Gallatin told Jefferson that he saw no constitutional difficulty in acquiring territory, and Jefferson at first agreed. He initially distinguished between the acquisition (constitutional) and the admission to the Union (unconstitutional). In the end, however, Jefferson said that the Constitution authorized neither.

Madison drafted an amendment saying, in part, "Louisiana as ceded by France is made part of the U. States. Congress may make part of the U.S. other adjacent territories which shall be justly acquired." It is hard to tell from this whether Madison shared Jefferson's scruples about the contours of the treaty power the Constitution granted the president or the need for an amendment. Certainly the language of Madison's proposed amendment implies that power to obtain Louisiana already existed. Virginia's Senator Wilson Cary Nicholas pointed out to Jefferson that the Constitution's provision permitting admission of new states did not include a limitation to territory already possessed, but Jefferson replied that he did not think it safe to read that provision broadly.

While this matter was pending with Jefferson and the cabinet, a letter from Minister Livingston arrived.[25] The French, he said, "think we have obtained an immense advantage over them." As he understood it, "Be assured that were the business to do again it would never be done." Thus prodded, Jefferson swallowed his misgivings. His chief achievement as president—and Madison's as secretary of state—won easy Senate ratification.

As Madison departed for Montpelier for the summer, a new carriage that he had ordered arrived in Washington. "The body was glassed all around, with complete Venetian blinds, light-colored cloth and handsome lace, 'coachman's seat in circular form, wheels boxed.' The lamps held candles instead of oil. Each door carried a silver 'M.' Dolley Madison soon became a familiar figure in this striking outfit (built in Philadelphia at a cost of $594)."[26] No American citizen or foreign diplomat, whatever his background, would be able to miss the fact that the secretary of state was a very wealthy Virginia planter. His wife, at least, made sure of that.

Possession of Louisiana was transferred to the United States on December 20, 1803. Napoleon's minister in Washington judged that this guaranteed Jefferson's reelection. Thanks to the Twelfth Amendment, submitted to the states by Congress at the behest of Jefferson's ally, Senate John Taylor of Caroline, in October 1803, there would be no 1800-style chance for the Federalists to try to thwart the will of the electorate. From then on, electors would cast separate votes for president and vice president.

Even as Jefferson was riding a newfound popularity to a second term, however, difficulties were brewing within the Republican Party. They arose out of a combination of combustible personalities with two issues: the judicial impeachment campaign and the Yazoo scandal.

The latter grew out of a dispute over Georgia's inland lands.[27] Colonial Georgia extended all the way to the Mississippi River, and by 1802, Georgia was the only one of the original thirteen states that retained all of its colonial land claims. In 1795, the state legislature had sold a substantial portion of its inland lands—most of today's Alabama and Mississippi—to private buyers. In 1796, it had repealed those sales. Much consternation ensued, particularly among the New Englanders who had purchased land from the original speculators. As the Republicans were weak in New England, Jefferson appointed a postmaster general who was a leading investor.

The chief river through what is now Mississippi is the Yazoo, so the whole matter came to be known as the Yazoo scandal. Madison, along with Gallatin and Attorney General Levi Lincoln, was appointed by Jefferson to a commission to resolve the issue in 1801. As senior secretary, Madison headed the commission. The commissioners on April 26, 1802, sent to President Jefferson its agreement with Georgia.[28] By its terms, Georgia ceded to the United States its claims west of today's Georgia in exchange for the federal government's payment of $1,250,000; confirmation of the land claims of everyone settled in the ceded land by 1795; extinguishment of all Indian land claims within today's Georgia; and eventual elevation of the ceded lands to statehood.

Madison's name was first among those of the cabinet officials who had negotiated this agreement. It seems that Gallatin actually bore responsibility for the terms, but never mind: the political fallout would land mainly upon Madison. The matter formed grist for litigation all the way down to the Supreme Court's decision in *Fletcher v. Peck* (1810).[29] In the medium term, its chief effect was to precipitate the break between John Randolph of Roanoke, Jefferson's cousin and one-time House majority leader, and Jefferson's administration. Not Jefferson, nor Gallatin, but Madison was the target of Randolph's ire.

The Yazoo lands thicket was a tangled one indeed. Investors had bought titles, grants had been revoked, investors had sold their titles, and so on. As it turned out, all but one member of the 1795 Georgia legislature—all but one!— had been bribed by the land companies. That was why the land had been sold for next to nothing. So the legislature revoked the sale. Then sold again.

Whatever the commissioners agreed to do, however much they decided to pay, and regardless to whom, someone was going to feel aggrieved. Randolph espied corruption. The result was the formation of the Tertium Quids, a group of Republican stalwarts who insisted that the Jefferson administration behave as chastely in power as Republicans had criticized Federalists for not being in the 1790s.

Yet, despite the Quid schism, Jefferson could not be kept from reelection. His Federalist opponents, South Carolina's Philadelphia Convention framer, General Charles C. Pinckney and Massachusetts's framer, Rufus King, had not much to offer. With lower federal taxes, lower spending, no Alien and Sedition Acts, the Louisiana Purchase, and a much-improved economy (the fruit of America's foreign policy), what could the Federalists offer? The vote in the Electoral College had Jefferson and George Clinton, 162 to Pinckney and King, 14.[30] Only Connecticut, Delaware, and two Maryland electors went Federalist. Even Massachusetts joined the Republican parade. It seemed that Jefferson's prognostication was correct and the age of partisan politics was soon to end.

But Jefferson, like Washington before him, encountered far more difficulty in his second term. In his first term, overseas events beyond his control had redounded to his benefit, as Napoleon was persuaded by hints of an Anglo-American alliance to sell Louisiana and Americans enjoyed the benefits of trading with both sides in the Napoleonic Wars. In his second, the British and the French alike would decide that rather than letting the Americans trade with both sides, they preferred the United States to trade with neither.

One should not have the impression that for James Madison, service as secretary of state was always a serious matter.[31] Consider, for example, the point in late 1805 when Madison found himself needing to entertain both a delegation of Indian chiefs and an ambassador from the Bey of Tunis, Sidi Suliman Mellimelli. The Indians included "tall, exotic Sauks, Sioux, and Osage chiefs sent from the Missouri country by Lewis and Clark." Mellimelli, on the other hand, was to be treated in the traditional Middle Eastern way: provided with concubines. Madison, tongue in cheek, noted that he had hired one "Georgia a Greek," and put the matter down to "appropriations to foreign intercourse." The course of American foreign policy over the next decade would give that note a particular irony.

Meanwhile, Madison took the lead in formulating the Jefferson administration's response to the belligerents' naval policies. His hope and expectation was that if threatened with loss of access to American agricultural products, each of the great powers would toe the line. He devoted extensive energy after the resumption of war in 1805 to trying to make this forecast come true.

If today it seems somewhat absurd to persevere in an embargo on Cuba that has been going on, to eject Communists from power, since 1959, two hundred and ten years ago the recent record of economic coercion was quite different. In the 1760s, after all, American colonists had pressured Great Britain into repealing the Sugar Act, the Stamp Act, and most of the Townshend Acts chiefly through what amounted to private embargoes.

Yet things were different in the years after 1805. In that year, Britain, through its smashing victory at Trafalgar, established its absolute domination of the seas. France, for its part, in 1805 at Austerlitz, in1806 at Jena-Auerstädt, in 1807 at Friedland, and in 1809 at Wagram, made itself undisputed master of the Old Continent.

Militarily, the great powers had achieved a stalemate. Napoleon could not get at Britain because of the latter's naval supremacy. Britain could not confront Napoleon on land. A trade war was the predictable outcome.

But any trade restrictions one belligerent might impose upon the other would have a major flaw: the Americans' continued access to both sides' ports. What to do?

Britain confronted the question first. In April 1805, George III's government resuscitated its Rule of 1756. Under that directive, his majesty's government did not recognize as neutral any trade that would not have been allowed in peacetime.[32] Thus, for example, the United States could not carry goods between Spanish ports in the Caribbean and France if the United States had not been allowed access to those ports in peacetime.

Madison found this policy infuriating. Like Jefferson, he hoped to see a day when all nations, belligerent and neutral, would be subject to the law of nations in all their behavior. The British made no claim that their policy complied with the law of nations. In fact, they forthrightly flouted it. As the *Edinburgh Review* lamented, "many people have been lately seduced into a contempt of the whole idea of the rights of states." Americans, predictably, agreed.

So concerned was the secretary of state that he wrote and published an entire pamphlet on the subject.[33] That work, *An Examination of the British Doctrine, Which Subjects to Capture a Neutral Trade, Not Open in Time of Peace,* was written and published by Madison in 1806. Although it appeared anonymously, Madison made no attempt to conceal his authorship.

The gist of Madison's argument was that just as in peacetime no two countries' trade was subject to the control of any other, so, "Between the nations not engaged in the war, it is evident that the commerce cannot be affected at all by a war between others." Through 151 pages in his published papers, Madison exhausted the subject (if not his readers' patience), proving dispositively for anyone who cared that the Rule of 1756 was inconsistent with the law of nations. The leading historians of the subject say that Madison's treatise formed the foundation of "the subsequent development of international legal thought."

In the House of Representatives, Joseph Nicholson offered up a Non-Intercourse Bill.[34] This bill would establish higher duties on British goods and restrictions on British ships' access to American ports. Patterned on Madison's proposal to Congress of a similar measure in 1794, it passed overwhelmingly—but not before John Randolph of Roanoke took it as the occasion to break with the Jefferson administration in hopes of elevating Monroe, not Madison, to the presidency in 1809. The break was precipitated, it seems, by a combination of rejection of Randolph's candidacy for the post of ambassador to Britain and the administration's adoption of a policy of resistance to British measures.

All of which affected British policy not one iota. A theory of neutral rights was one thing. National survival was another. As far as the British were concerned, the latter had precedence over the former. As Jefferson later put it in regard to a completely different matter, "Justice is in one scale, and self-preservation in the other."[35] For men of the Enlightenment, self-preservation was man's first priority. Theoretical justice came second.

The British government would interdict American trade with Europe. And, besides that, it would continue its policy of impressment. Under that policy, British warships stopped American ships at sea and forced any sailor adjudged British into the Royal Navy on the spot. It is hard to say which was a greater affront to American sovereignty, the trade policy or the impressment policy.

The United States sent James Monroe and William Pinkney to Britain to negotiate a resolution of the outstanding issues in that bilateral relationship. Madison instructed them that they must resolve the question of impressment. In fact, as Madison himself defined it, this was a narrow issue.[36] Britain confessed that American territorial waters were off limits to impressment efforts, while the Americans conceded that Britain could impress within its own territorial waters. Madison also granted that virtually all American ships on the high seas ultimately would end up in Britain, which means that they would pass through waters in which the Americans recognized Britain's right to impress. The question whether Britain might impress them en route to British seas, then, was chiefly academic, but Madison insisted that high seas impressment must be abandoned by the British as a component of any treaty.

At the end of 1806, Monroe and Pinkney signed a treaty intended to resolve

various outstanding issues between the two countries.[37] Matters concerning
Canada, American trade with the East Indies, and the American right to
trade between the belligerents and their colonies were resolved in a way the
Americans quite liked. For their part, the Americans stipulated that they
would not for ten years adopt a policy either of nonimportation from or non-
exportation to Great Britain. Finally, the Americans vowed not to accept
Napoleon's Berlin Decree of 1806: his policy that ships trading with the British would be lawful prize.

Although it was likely the very best treaty that was to be obtained from
Britain at the time, Jefferson and Madison had long since made an end to
impressments a nonnegotiable condition of any British treaty. In addition,
Jefferson refused to buy the provision concerning the Berlin Decree. As far as
he was concerned, it amounted to a commitment to take Britain's side in a
trade war with France. Even though the British had agreed informally to be
more careful in the execution of their impressment policy, and despite their
having made the point that it was a hostile act for the U.S. government to allow bona fide Britons to sail in American merchant marine ships, Jefferson
and Madison rejected the Monroe-Pinkney Treaty early in 1807 without even
submitting it to the Senate.[38]

Madison's and Jefferson's ideological commitment, their naïve appraisal
of America's place in the international system, was nowhere more evident than
in Madison's explanation of the president's decision. Monroe and Pinkney
should renegotiate the treaty, he said, with special attention to the imperative
that impressments end. America was in a particularly strong position, he
lectured; loss of American grain "would be an evil which no provident Counsels would neglect to guard against, by any measures equitable in themselves,
or even by concessions neither dishonorable nor materially injurious."
Clearly, abandonment of impressment fell into that category, by Madison's
calculation. American agricultural products were to the British "the means
of existence." If the British were only "provident," they would concede the
point.[39]

Monroe took umbrage at this decision. His personal and professional
friendship with Madison, dating back a quarter century, would stand in abey-
ance for several years—until he came to President Madison's rescue nearly a
decade later.

As spring 1807 dawned, American politics were rocked by a stunning episode.[40] The HMS *Leopard*, a British warship, hailed the American frigate *Chesapeake* at Hampton Roads, just where the Chesapeake Bay meets the Atlantic Ocean. To the dismay of civilians watching from the shore, the *Leopard* responded to the *Chesapeake*'s refusal to allow British officers aboard by firing on its prey. Twenty-one Americans were killed or wounded, three American sailors were impressed into British service, and a firestorm swept up and down the Atlantic seaboard.

Americans insisted on abandonment of the Virginian administration's foreign policy. What Americans wanted was war. As Madison put it, "the spirit excited throughout our nation, by the gross attack on its sovereignty, is that of the most ardent and determined patriotism."[41]

The British had even before the *Chesapeake-Leopard* incident responded to Napoleon's measures by banning trade among enemy ports.[42] Since America was essentially the only neutral plying the waters of Napoleon's continental empire, this measure amounted to a British attempt to stifle America's carrying trade. These Orders in Council struck Madison as hostile measures. They also seemed to him clearly inconsistent with the law of nations, as he had laboriously explained in his pamphlet.

Precisely such circumstances had driven the Federalists into war preparations in 1798. Should Republicans now follow their partisan enemies in jacking up taxes and expanding the army and navy? Jefferson, Madison, and their congressional allies cast about for an alternative. What they found was the embargo.

On December 22, 1807, Jefferson's signature on congressional legislation launched America on an experiment in economic coercion.[43] Since neither of the great belligerents would allow America to trade unmolested, fine: America would not trade with anyone. American ships would be allowed only the coasting trade—trade among the states.

Jefferson explained that the Embargo Act would enable Americans to pay off their debt and preserve their strength. The most jaundiced historian of his administration comments, "How the United States could pay its debts and clear its revenues with only minimal revenues from imports Jefferson did not say." Time would show that whatever the president meant, he had gravely miscalculated.

The embargo proved virtually impossible to enforce. Over the course of its life, frustration with its inefficacy led the administration to ask Congress for greater and greater enforcement power. Ultimately, the embargo contributed, one might even say "led," to the formation of what Harvard history professor Henry Adams, the great-grandson of John Adams and author of the most influential account of Jefferson's administration, called "a British party" in the United States.[44]

The reason was that the embargo was so clearly contrary to the economic interest of New England. Besides which, as from the beginning, the New England Federalists tended to sympathize with Britain in the great world struggle with Napoleon. These two mutually reinforcing factors, together with the overwhelmingly Virginian origins of the federal government's Jeffersonian leadership, both in the Congress and in the executive branch, pushed New England into resistance.

As resistance grew, as smuggling from the New England states into Canada became more brazen, Republicans countered by giving Jefferson more draconian enforcement powers. Jefferson requested such powers in April 1808, only four months into the embargo.[45] Jefferson found it almost impossible to stop the international trade without interfering with the coastal trade, because a ship bound for another state was indistinguishable from a ship headed overseas.

Jefferson commanded Secretary of the Treasury Albert Gallatin in May 1808 to begin wide-ranging enforcement.[46] What kind, he could not say: "I think it is impossible to form precise rules," the president wrote. "After a number of cases shall have arisen, they may probably be thrown into groups and subjected to rules." Jefferson told Gallatin to consider "the power of detention" as "the panacea" and to "use it freely." "Consider me as voting for detention" in every doubtful case, Jefferson instructed. With tariff agents in every port, Gallatin was the cabinet officer who could make Jefferson's word bite. He did not have to like it.

In time, entire states came near rebellion. The arbitrariness of Jefferson's enforcement did not help matters. Madison, for his part, stayed clear of the enforcement effort—which, after all, did not fall within his bailiwick. Eventually, not only Gallatin, but also Secretary of the Navy Robert Smith expressed unhappiness with the president's policy.[47] Gallatin finally counseled

Jefferson that Congress needed to give him further powers. "Congress must either invest the Executive with the most arbitrary powers and sufficient force to carry the embargo into effect, or give it up altogether," he wrote.[48] To judge by his phrasing, perhaps Gallatin hoped that his chief would give it up altogether. Jefferson chose to be arbitrary.

John Randolph of Roanoke, in the House of Representatives, thundered on the unconstitutionality of Jefferson's course. The power to regulate commerce, he insisted, was not a power to destroy it.[49] Here, Jefferson's cousin was a perfect Jeffersonian. Yet, Jefferson was not. As the ultra-Federalist historian Henry Adams put it, "no one could doubt that under the doctrine of States-rights and the rules of strict construction the embargo was unconstitutional. Only by the widest theories of liberal construction could its constitutionality be sustained." Yet, this was not quite right: as we have seen, one of Madison's goals for the U.S. Constitution in 1787 had been to empower the federal government to conduct trade wars of exactly this type. The power to regulate commerce with foreign nations arguably extended to an embargo power.

Because the alternative was war. And war meant the abandonment, if only temporarily, of the Republican scheme of political economy. It meant concentration of power in the executive. It meant higher taxes. It entailed more manufacturing. It might mean an end to elective government. And so, Republicans held, it was to be avoided.

Despite the fact that the economic consequences of the embargo bore very greatly upon Americans north and south, Madison breezed to election as president in 1808. The Federalists were a mere sectional party now, and although Monroe did not try to dissuade Randolph from raising his name as an alternative to Madison's, Monroe gained very little support even in their home state. Madison's election in 1808 was easy, but it was won with very little enthusiasm. The superannuated George Clinton was the Republicans' number two, as he had been in 1804, for want of an alternative. Pinckney and King received 47 electoral votes, Madison and Clinton got 122.

Meanwhile, in Europe, the embargo was a flop. Napoleon saw it as chiefly an anti-British act, as even without it the United States could not have traded with the Continent. John Armstrong, America's representative in France, wrote Madison on August 30, 1808, "Here it is not felt, and in England . . . it is forgotten. I hope," he said, "that unless France shall do us justice we will raise the embargo, and make in its stead the experiment of an armed commerce."[50]

By the time Jefferson left office, his embargo was a forlorn failure. All adjudged it to be. Rather than change the policy himself, Jefferson simply stepped aside. In an era when presidents were inaugurated on March 4, Jefferson wrote on November 13, 1808, "On this occasion I think it is fair to leave to those who are to act on them the decisions they prefer, being to be myself but a spectator. I should not feel justified in directing measures which those who are to execute them would disapprove. Our situation is truly difficult. We have been pressed by the belligerents to the very wall, and all further retreat is impracticable."[51]

Gallatin wrote Jefferson two days later to insist that he must make a decision: either the embargo must be enforced completely, he said, or there must be a war. Jefferson, for his part, dithered. He insisted that he would play no part in further decision making, but he also exerted himself to ensure that the embargo was not formally ended before he left office.[52]

Madison, with Gallatin's assistance, concocted a new foreign policy in the last days of the Jefferson administration.[53] As he would have had it, America would have dropped its embargo in favor of a new nonintercourse act. That act would have provided that America would trade with neither of the belligerents, Britain or France, until one of them abandoned its hostile trade regulations; at that point, America would trade freely with the belligerent that had adopted an America-friendly trade policy, while it would maintain nonintercourse toward the other belligerent. The U.S. government, under this plan, would also grant letters of marque and reprisal against whichever belligerent(s) maintained its hostile regulations.

In Congress, the proposal to issue letters of marque and reprisal (in effect, government licenses for private ship owners to prey on hostile ships) went down to defeat. Repeal of the embargo became law, with Jefferson's signature, on March 1, 1809. Trade with the British and the French was prohibited, pending repeal of their hostile policies, but without the letters of marque and reprisal, not much would come of this. In fact, no one expected the new nonintercourse policy to be enforced.

James Madison took the oath of office as the fourth president of the United States three days later, on March 4, 1809. The diminutive new president must have seemed particularly slight beside the two Randolph cousins, Jefferson and Marshall, each of whom was nearly a foot taller than Madison.

Madison's inauguration was a watershed. He was the first president who had not been a member of the Second Continental Congress, the intercolonial assemblage that raised an army and made war for independence. He was the first president who had not played a major role in the American Revolution. He was the first president who did not command others' attention the moment he entered the room.

James Madison Jr. was also the first "junior" among the presidents. Quiet and introspective like his friend Jefferson, he was also seen as the second-in-command of the Virginia Republican Party. When he entered upon the task of the president, Madison found the country's public affairs in a very sad situation. The chief line of Jefferson's foreign policy, whose conception owed so much to the former secretary of state, had failed utterly. Yes, the Louisiana Purchase would redound to Americans' benefit for centuries to come, and yes, Jefferson and Madison had exploited the opportunity presented to them by events in Europe to make clear to France that Louisiana must be sold. Yet, the embargo had inflicted wartime pain upon Americans of all sections, and for what? In the end, for nothing.

The first inaugural strikes one now as classic Madison.[54] It sounded all the classic Republican themes that Jefferson had brought up in his immortal inaugural in 1801. Yet it did so in the characteristically forgettable Madison way. Thus, for example, where Jefferson had memorably called for a foreign policy characterized by "peace, commerce, and honest friendship with all nations, entangling alliances with none," and had hopefully opined that "we have called by different names brethren of the same principle. We are all republicans. We are all federalists," Madison intoned the following single-sentence paragraph:

> To cherish peace and friendly intercourse with all nations having correspondent dispositions; to maintain sincere neutrality towards belligerent nations; to prefer in all cases, amicable discussion and reasonable accommodation of differences, to a decision of them by an appeal to Arms; to exclude foreign intrigues and foreign partialities, so degrading to all Countries and so baneful to free ones; to foster a spirit of independence

too just to invade the rights of others, too proud to surrender our own, too liberal to indulge unworthy prejudices ourselves, and too elevated not to look down upon them in others; to hold the Union of the States as the basis of their peace and happiness; to support the Constitution, which is the cement of the Union, as well in its limitations as in its authorities; to respect the rights and authorities reserved to the States and to the people, as equally incorporated with, and essential to the success of, the general system; to avoid the slightest interference with the right of conscience, or the functions of religion so wisely exempted from civil jurisdiction; to preserve in their full energy, the other salutary provisions in behalf of private and personal rights, and of the freedom of the press; to observe œconomy in public expenditures; to liberate the public resources by an honorable discharge of the public debts; to keep within the requisite limits a standing military force, always remembering, that an Armed and trained militia is the firmest bulwark of Republics; that without standing Armies their liberty can never be in danger; nor with large ones, safe; to promote by authorized means, improvements friendly to agriculture, to manufactures and to external as well as internal commerce; to favor, in like manner, the advancement of science and the diffusion of information as the best aliment to true liberty; to carry on the benevolent plans which have been so meritoriously applied to the conversion of our aboriginal neighbors from the degradation and wretchedness of savage life, to a participation of the improvements of which the human mind and manners are susceptible in a civilized state: As far as sentiments and intentions such as these can aid the fulfillment of my duty, they will be a resource which can not fail me.

Difficult though this 375-word beauty is to follow in writing, it must have been simply impossible for the assembled audience to make heads or tails of as they heard it, or perhaps we should say "witnessed it," being delivered in his faint voice by an "extremely pail" Madison who "seemed scarcely able to stand."[55] No wonder, then, that this speech goes essentially unmentioned in histories of the United States.

Yet, for those of us who are concerned to understand the course of Madison's presidency, the first inaugural contains much meat—and not least in this pivotal paragraph. Madison paid extensive attention in the rest of his speech to America's place in the world in the midst of the French Revolutionary and Napoleonic wars. "The present situation of the world is indeed without a parallel," he held, "and that of our own Country full of difficulties." This was particularly unfortunate, he continued, in light of the fact that the Americans had profited so handsomely from their role as neutral carriers of both sides' commerce prior to the recent promulgation of competing exclusionary policies by the belligerent powers.

Sounding every bit the author of a disquisition on the rights of neutrals, Madison also pointed out that America's policy had been just and respectable. "Posterity at least [would] do justice" to these facts. Napoleon and his British opponents, on the other hand, certainly would not. Madison lamented that "principles of retaliation have been introduced, equally contrary to universal reason, and acknowledged law." Still, come what might, he was certain that "the determined spirit and united Councils of the nation" would vindicate American rights in the end.

Then came the lengthy paragraph set out above. Most notable there, other than the extremely ponderous writing, is the pervasive and thoroughgoing naïveté. Madison's vow "to prefer in all cases, amicable discussion" over warfare must have elicited nothing but contempt from the great warrior prince of the modern age, and Napoleon's British antagonists must have found it particularly frustrating. He laid out the Republican doctrine that the Constitution must be maintained "as well in its limitations as in its authorities," and in regard to "the rights and authorities reserved to the States and to the people." Along with highlighting the freedoms of religion and of the press, Madison restated his fateful devotion to the Jeffersonian nostrum "that an Armed and trained militia is the firmest bulwark of republics"—even to the point of lecturing his audience that "without standing Armies their liberty c[ould] never be in danger."

The next-to-last paragraph of his address found Madison laying encomia upon his august predecessor, friend, and political benefactor. He was happy to see Jefferson retire bearing "the benedictions of a beloved Country, gratefully bestowed for exalted talents, zealously devoted, thro' a long career, to the advancement of its highest interest and happiness." As at John Adams's inauguration in 1797, the contrast between the retiring chief and the ascendant deputy did not inspire hope. John Adams had not been George Washington, and James Madison was not Thomas Jefferson.

Lastly, Madison noted the reassurance he took from the prospect that he would be aided in his work by the citizenry and other officials. His chief reliance, he closed, would be upon "the guardianship and guidance of that Almighty Being whose power regulates the destiny of nations."

Ceremonial occasions did not showcase Madison's abilities. Far from it. Madison was at his best in mastering large bodies of data, in synthesizing extensive bodies of information, in wrestling measures through parliamentary assemblies. In the earliest days of his administration, however, he failed at precisely such a task.

The Jefferson administration's three chief officers, the president, the secretary of state, and the secretary of the treasury, had led the Republican opposition in the 1790s. They then had worked well together through the third president's two terms.

With the president's retirement and Secretary of State Madison's elevation, it made sense to Madison that Secretary of the Treasury Gallatin should move into Madison's old position. His plan met defeat in the U.S. Senate.

There, Madison's fellow Virginian, William Branch Giles, and Gallatin's fellow Pennsylvanian, Michael Leib, along with Senator Samuel Smith of Maryland, undertook to thwart Madison's effort to promote Gallatin.[56] Leib seems to have been motivated primarily by disappointment over patronage matters in Pennsylvania, where he and Gallatin were rivals. Giles, for his part, felt himself slighted by the prospect of Gallatin's elevation; as one historian put it, "Giles was alone in thinking himself the proper secretary."[57]

Madison did not confront the opposition and try to push Gallatin's nomination through. It seems likely that had he done so, he would have had the number two man he wanted. Instead, Madison established at the outset of his administration that he could be cowed. In time, poor personnel choices came to Madison more out of omission to fight than as a result of desire to avoid political infighting. In short, Madison surrendered preemptively on the Gallatin question, and he would do so again.

Most momentously, the military cabinet posts—secretary of war and secretary of the navy, which then were both cabinet-level positions—went to people with virtually no claim to the jobs. The Department of the Navy would be headed by a physician, William Eustis, who had served two terms as a congressman, while the Department of War's chief was former South Carolina governor Paul Hamilton. Perhaps Madison considered these selections inconsequential, because he intended for the United States (to borrow his words) "to cultivate peace by observing justice, and to entitle themselves to the respect of nations at war, by fulfilling their neutral obligations, with the most scrupulous impartiality." If it came to war, the country would learn to its injury, Madison's boast of "clean hands" would count for little.

Besides these two, Madison also appointed Robert Smith, brother of Senator Smith, as secretary of state. This would mean that Madison served as his own secretary of state; in time, it would put him in the position of having to fire his top cabinet officer.

Given Jefferson's essential resignation in his administration's last days, and in light of Madison's high position in that regime and of the fact that Gallatin was already cooperating with him in prodding the president in the Monticellan's final weeks as president, the Madison administration marked very slight policy or political change from its predecessor. Madison's chief concerns would be in the area of foreign policy throughout his two terms, and that foreign policy would be a continuation of the one he and Jefferson had followed since 1801—arguably since the early 1790s.

The Madison administration could be seen as simply a continuation of the Jefferson administration, with one notable exception: Dolley Madison.[58] Mrs. Madison, or "The Presidentess," as one contemporary called her in those pre–Mary Lincoln/"First Lady" days, carved a special role. While James was cerebral, soft-spoken, physically unimpressive, and somewhat retiring in large groups, his wife was none of the above.

The most basic advantage of the Dolley Madison alliance for James was familial: two of Dolley's brothers-in-law were congressmen, and a third was a Supreme Court justice.[59] In addition, her cousin Edward Coles served as Madison's private secretary while he was president.

Besides that, Dolley Madison made it her mission to establish a truly republican society in Washington, D.C.—an elite social life appropriate to the new form of government. Where George and Martha Washington had tried holding stilted levées on a weekly basis, and where Jefferson had gone so far in the opposite direction as to seat guests at state dinners in what he called "pell-mell" fashion, Dolley Madison found a way to host nonpartisan, perfectly republican social events in the White House.

President Madison, atypically of men of his rank and time, turned this over to Dolley. Where Jefferson had conducted politics chiefly by hosting small dinner parties, almost always of the like-minded and exclusively male, Dolley's affairs were mixed. Where Jefferson had been at pains to avoid the image of the slave owner as president, both at the White House and at Monticello, Dolley stationed a slave at each dinner guest's side.

One contemporary observer thought in 1807 that Secretary of State Madison's chief advantage over fellow potential president Vice President George Clinton was that, "The secretary of state has a wife to aid his pretensions. The vice president has nothing of female succor on his side. And in those two respects [the wife and the social events], Mr. Madison is going greatly ahead of him."[60]

Once James became president, Dolley continued in contributing social support to his political endeavors. For example, it was she who initiated what is now the long-standing tradition of the Inaugural Ball. So dominant was she in the Madison household that at state dinners, she took the chair at the head of the table![61] Dolley came to be called "Queen of Washington City," and while she never endorsed the title, "she affirmed the appellation constantly."[62]

In ancien régime France, even the office of attending to the king as he performed the most brute bodily functions was an honor. In republican Washington, Dolley Madison had her hand on the lever of access. James Madison attended her weekly salons, and he must have been involved in drawing up invitation lists, but one had the impression that they were all Dolley.

Of course, we have seen that Madison knew how to use George Washington's prestige and Thomas Jefferson's reputation. There is no reason to doubt that his hand helped guide Dolley Madison's planning as well. But "helped guide" is not "guided"; Dolley took a prominent part—as we shall see.

The first significant development in the area of foreign policy was the arrival in Washington of a new British minister, David Erskine, who brought fabulous news: the policy of economic coercion had succeeded.[63] Britain had decided to change its policy, dropping the Orders in Council that interfered with neutrals' (meaning Americans') shipping. Madison ought to have ascertained that the British cabinet approved his agreement with Erskine. He did not take time to do that. Instead, on April 19, 1809, Madison issued a proclamation saying that beginning on June 10, trade with Britain was once again legal.[64]

The initial public response was extremely positive. Madison's stock rose even in Federalist Connecticut. Madison dared hope that Napoleon would follow his enemy Albion by rescinding his anti-American decrees. Jefferson wrote to Madison to crow that, "The British ministry has been driven from its Algerine system."

As one historian noted, "It all seemed too good to be true, and to Madison's dismay, it was too good to last." It took a while before word reached Whitehall that Erskine had made this arrangement with Madison without insisting on his superiors' one stipulation: that the British be allowed to enforce America's policy against American ships' trading with France. The British government decided to disavow Erskine's work in mid-May, but word of the decision did not make its way across the Atlantic to Madison until early July.

Madison was crestfallen. Especially troublesome was a rumor that not pure policy considerations, but a slip of the pen explained the British decision.[65] As the story went, George III had seen a comment by then Secretary of State Madison concerning the *Chesapeake-Leopard* incident. In insisting that the *Leopard*'s captain ought to be punished by the British government, Madison was supposed to have written, "while he [Madison] forbears to insist on further punishment of the offending officer, he is not the less sensible of the justice and utility of such an example, nor the less persuaded that it would best comport with what is due from His Britannic Majesty to his own honor." Supposedly, George III upon reading that had told his ministry that "he would not ratify anything in which he was so personally insulted."

The full significance of this story, if it was true, was gargantuan: the Jeffersonian foreign policy's chief element had been on the verge of success, but a characteristic Jeffersonian Republican dig—the kind of gratuitously offensive thing that Madison and his friends had said and written about Federalists and foreign monarchists every day for nearly two decades—had derailed it on the very verge of success. What might have been suitable in a squib penned for Freneau's newspaper struck with a completely different impact when placed before the king of England.

The end result was the War of 1812.

Madison faced ticklish legal and constitutional questions. The Non-Intercourse Act had empowered the president to rescind that policy whenever one of the belligerents had earned America's trade friendship by meeting American requirements. Madison had been entirely within his rights in doing so. Yet, the act said nothing about what the president could do if after he had revoked sanctions on one power, that power decided to keep its trade restrictions after all.

Arguably, the stickler's way to handle the situation would have been to call Congress into session and ask it to adopt a new statute reimposing nonintercourse on the British. Madison opted simply to reimpose the policy on his own initiative. The new British minister, Francis James Jackson, likely prodded him in that direction. Jackson had essentially accused the president to his face of colluding with Erskine. Jackson asserted that both Erskine and Madison had realized that the British government would never agree to drop its Orders in Council without providing for the Royal Navy to enforce America's policy of nonintercourse with France on the high seas.

Madison, livid, told Jackson to communicate with him only on paper. When he heard that Jackson had made similar insinuations to other people, Madison had his secretary of state relay the message that no further communication from Jackson would be accepted. So Madison was back where he had started: waiting for the British to abandon impressment in the name of trade with America—waiting for Britain to do something it would not, could not do.

Meanwhile, both Jefferson and Joseph Story, Madison's Supreme Court appointee, said that they thought that Madison's conduct in connection with the revivification of the nonintercourse policy toward Britain was unconstitutional.[66] Republican presidents had come into the habit of violating the Constitution where foreign policy was involved, it seems.

Foreign policy complications continued to mount. So, for example, the nonintercourse law was due to expire at the close of 1809. What to do? Nathaniel Macon, the Old Republican Speaker of the House, proposed continuing to exclude French and British ships but allowing importation of French and British goods on other nations' ships. That proposal was defeated. Substituted for it was "Macon's Bill Number 2," not actually written by Macon, which provided that trade with the major belligerents would be restored until such time as one or the other revoked its hostile policy concerning American trade. At that point, the bill continued, the non-importation policy would be resuscitated in relation to the other country. So, for example, if France revoked its ban on American trade with Europe, America would restore its old policy of nonintercourse in regard to the United Kingdom.

Just as Madison had foolishly taken Erskine's offer as representing the policy of the British cabinet without bothering to verify that fact, so now he made a similarly foolish decision. When Napoleon responded to Macon's Bill Number 2 on August 2, 1810, by saying that he would suspend his ban on neutral trade with the Continent as long as America had resumed nonintercourse with the United Kingdom by then, Madison invoked the provision of the law allowing him to restore nonintercourse with the United Kingdom. You can guess what happened next: Napoleon never actually revoked his policy. Madison was out on a limb, having revived nonintercourse with Britain without obtaining any compensating change of French policy. Besides that, he had impressed British public opinion that, just as the British had always believed, Madison was pro-French. The bookish president was no match for the emperor of the French. Surely Napoleon and Talleyrand had a laugh or two over that one.

For Americans, this was not a laughing matter. Rather, as the French had hoped, it had pushed the new republic quite a way down the road toward war with Britain. Ironically, that war would come even as Britain—unlike France—complied with the terms of Macon's Bill Number 2.

The midterm congressional elections of 1810 have long been noted for having brought into public life a new class of men. Those men, dominated by "War Hawks" (a disapproving John Randolph's name for them) such as Henry Clay and John C. Calhoun, rode into public life on the issue of confrontation, preferably military confrontation, with Britain. Calhoun, for one, had made his first public speech in the immediate wake of 1807's *Chesapeake-Leopard* incident.[67] Like Madison, these men essentially ignored French offenses against American rights in their fixation on British misdeeds. Like the president, they held that Britain had instigated the problem of the belligerents' offenses against neutral rights.[68] Little protest, then, resulted from Napoleon's omission to reverse the Berlin and Milan decrees.

As the country careened toward a military conflict for which it was not at all prepared, Republican dogma ran up against hard, cold reality. Alexander Hamilton, recall, had persuaded Congress to charter the first Bank of the United States. One of his goals was to use that bank in aid of servicing the debt accrued during the Revolutionary War. Even as war with one or both of the belligerent powers seemed increasingly likely, the twenty-year charter granted to Hamilton's bank in 1791 was due to expire.

President Madison had led the corps in Congress that argued against the Bank Bill in 1791 on the basis of its unconstitutionality. He and Secretary of State Thomas Jefferson had been so worried over that and similarly British-inspired initiatives that they had organized the Republican Party to oppose Hamilton's stewardship of the federal government.

In 1811, however, things looked a bit different. Albert Gallatin, the secretary of the treasury upon whom Madison relied for economic and other advice, favored rechartering the bank. Just as Hamilton had said, the Bank of the United States provided a ready source of loans when the government's revenues fell short of its obligations. Perhaps it had benefited city dwellers and financiers more than farmers, Gallatin held, but it should be perpetuated. He said as much in a formal report of March 3, 1809.[69]

Rank-and-file Republicans remained opposed. So did Vice President Clinton. Since 1787, he had feared that the new Constitution would be abused by officials determined to grab more power than they ought to have; if he had had his way, New York's ratification convention would have thwarted Madison's attempt to lodge significantly greater powers in the new government. At the height of his anti-Hamiltonian maneuvering, Madison had joined Jefferson in steering Clinton into their Republican Party. Now those chickens came home to roost.

The bill to recharter the bank came up for a Senate vote in early 1811. At that point, it failed by a single vote in each house—with the vice president casting the decisive vote in the Senate.[70] Clinton's vote is especially noteworthy because Madison had come to favor recharter. He favored it, but not publicly and not strongly.

If Madison favored such a measure, why did he not say so? The answer seems to lie in Madison's concern for his own reputation. Political opponents had long criticized Madison for political inconsistency, and one historian holds this concern for his reputation responsible for Madison's silence.[71] Even though Madison refrained from public statements in support of recharter, the Baltimore *Whig* ran an extensive commentary on April 18, 1810, laying bare the gravity of Madison's about-face.[72]

As the pseudonymous letter writer insisted, if, despite his earlier forceful arguments against the bank charter's constitutionality, Madison now took the opposite position, he risked making the Constitution into "a nose of wax." Madison was "committed in a thousand ways" in regard to the first Bank Bill; to sign such a bill now would mean that his "fame [would] be blasted forever." Flummery about the question's being "*settled*" would expose him to "eternal odium and reproach." Only "corruption's soul-dejecting arts" could account for such a spectacle. If Republicans had expelled the Federalists on the basis of constitutional arguments only to abandon those arguments once in office, politics was "nought but a contest for loaves and fishes,—an ignoble squabble between *ins* and *outs*."

Madison would have been more than human if he had wanted further criticism like that—particularly since he did not have a substantial answer other than "I changed my mind." The matter likely is not that simple, however. Madison, like Washington before him, did not believe that the president should play the leading role in the legislative process. He may have thought that privately relaying his position to members of Congress was as far as he should go.

The congressional maneuvering against Gallatin on the bank issue pushed Madison to a decision: he wanted a new secretary of state. Robert Smith would never have been appointed in the first place had not his brother, Senator Samuel Smith, joined with Giles and Leib to thwart Gallatin's elevation to the position of secretary of state. Secretary Smith had been saying privately and not so privately that Madison had been bamboozled by Napoleon, and Madison did not much appreciate such backbiting within his own official family. Besides that, he had a superior candidate for the job close at hand: James Monroe.

Monroe and Madison's falling-out over the Monroe-Pinkney Treaty had given Jefferson, ever attentive to his friends' friendship, unhappiness. Booting Smith out of the State Department, Madison happily replaced him with Monroe. In light of the extremely complicated state of America's foreign relations in the spring of 1811, Madison had a chief secretary upon whom he could rely just in time. Among the usual trade-related issues, with France, Britain, and various North Africa Barbary states were complications arising from the revolutions roiling Spanish colonies in North America. Madison, like Jefferson before him, hoped to exploit the hiatus in Spanish authority by seizing control of West Florida—essentially the coastal regions of Alabama, Mississippi, and the portion of Louisiana that lies east of the Mississippi River. In late 1810, Madison had sent American troops into West Florida, but the attempt fell through.

Of course, foreign policy and what might be called "court politics" were not Madison's only official concerns as president. For example, he on February 21, 1811, sent the House of Representatives a veto message elucidating the meaning, in the eyes of its chief draftsman, of the First Amendment's Establishment Clause.[73] Congress had passed "an Act incorporating the protestant Episcopal Church in the Town of Alexandria in the District of Columbia." Alexandria, located in the territory ceded to the federal government by Virginia, had of course formerly had an Episcopal establishment. That meant that various social-welfare functions, such as provision for the blind and the retarded, were performed by the local parish vestry.

An Alexandria congressman first presented the Alexandria Episcopalians' petition for incorporation in December 1810, and Congress passed the bill through both houses on February 8, 1811. The bill regulated selection of the parish's minister, as well as establishing several other internal rules for the congregation. It would have insulated the parish even from the authority of the Episcopal Church generally. The bill would have made those regulations matters of civil law, rather than of the church's internal organization. It also "vest[ed] in the said incorporated Church, an authority to provide for the support of the poor, and the education of poor children of the same; an authority, which being altogether superfluous if the provision is to be the result of pious charity, would be a precedent for giving to religious Societies as such, a legal agency in carrying into effect a public and civic duty."

In short, Madison held, the bill violated the Establishment Clause. The House considered Madison's objections on February 23, 1811. It decided against overriding his veto.

Madison clearly thought it important that he put on the record his understanding of the Establishment Clause. Jefferson had never, in eight years as president, sent a bill back to Congress with a veto message. Madison's Alexandria Episcopal Church Veto Message was brief, but it said all that needed to be said.

Four days later, Madison wrote Emperor Alexander I of Russia to inform him that the American minister was being recalled.[74] John Quincy Adams seemed to Madison a good selection for the Supreme Court—for reasons that are not immediately clear. Adams had been a Federalist, his father took pride of place among all living Federalists, and so Minister Adams ought not to have struck Madison as a potentially reliable Jeffersonian voice on the Supreme Court. Madison turned to Adams after first appointing a candidate who refused the post and then nominating a candidate whom the Senate rejected. Adams too ultimately rejected the post.

Only three days later, Madison had another opportunity to call the Establishment Clause to Congress's attention.[75] This time, the issue was "an act for the relief of . . . the Baptist Church at Salem Meeting House, in the Mississippi Territory." He vetoed it, objecting to the provision that set aside land for the Baptists. He explained that "the Bill, in reserving a certain parcel of land of the United States for the use of said Baptist Church, comprizes a principle and precedent for the appropriation of funds of the United States, for the use and support of Religious Societies," and thus that it violated the Establishment Clause. Perhaps surprisingly, North Carolina Baptists wrote to Madison to laud him for his actions.[76]

By year's end, Madison would have his Supreme Court appointee: Joseph Story of Massachusetts.[77] Like John Quincy Adams, Story was a Republican of the New England stamp. That is why Thomas Jefferson warned Madison against appointing him.[78] Over time, Story would come to be John Marshall's right-hand man, second only to the chief justice in his energetic advocacy of a Hamiltonian reading of the Constitution from the high bench and, as law professor at Harvard, without peer in academic advocacy of the anti-Jeffersonian creed. Before the Madison administration ended, Story would have authored his most significant opinion, claiming for Congress constitutional authority to give the Supreme Court appellate jurisdiction over state supreme courts.[79] If we assume that a president's goal in appointing a Supreme Court justice is to further his own reading of the Constitution, Madison's appointment of Joseph Story may be the most spectacular flop in appointment history.

The same day as Story's, the Senate confirmed Madison's nomination of Gabriel Duvall to join the Supreme Court in place of Samuel Chase. Thus, Madison's two appointees joined the Court at the same time in 1811. Duvall had been a nonentity before joining the Court, and he made virtually no mark as a justice.

Madison sent his annual message to Congress on November 5, 1811.[80] Having persevered in the Jefferson-Madison foreign policy of economic coercion for many years, and having seen his hope that it would succeed disappointed by each of the great powers in turn, Madison finally reached for the alternative: military preparation. He told Congress that he had done the things the law allowed him to do, including marching the army toward the Northwest to confront the Indians, repositioning naval assets to guard the coast, and taking other such moves. The time had come, however, when Congress had to do more. Madison described measures taken by France and Britain, then urged, "With this evidence of hostile inflexibility in trampling on rights which no Independent Nation can relinquish; Congress will feel the duty of putting the United States into an armour, and an attitude demanded by the crisis, and corresponding with the national spirit and expectations." He wanted the army expanded. The belligerent whose behavior had elicited this response, he made clear, was Britain. (Madison had mused that war on both belligerents could be justified, but he decided that such a war would cost America its access to European ports. That was too great a price to pay.)[81]

Congress did not distinguish itself over the following months in implementing Madison's recommendations. Madison, for his part, hung back from intervening to prod the legislative branch in the direction he preferred; such matters, his constitutional vision told him, were confided to the Congress, not to the executive branch.

Still, Madison believed by mid-1812 that he had no other choice. Britain would not change its policy of impressment and commercial restriction. Therefore, on April 1, 1812, he confidentially proposed to Congress that it adopt a "general embargo" for sixty days.[82] In the event, Congress enacted a ninety-day embargo.[83] The provision of thirty extra days sprang, according to Madison, from the desire of some senators to use the embargo as leverage in negotiation instead of as time to clear the seas of American shipping in the runup to war.[84] The British minister, Augustus Foster, asked Madison whether he was to understand that the embargo meant war. "Oh! No, Embargo is not war," Foster reported Madison as having responded. Yet, Foster continued, Madison held that America would be justified in warring on Britain, because Britain was warring on America.

Soon after his annual message, Madison could present to Congress news of a military victory in the Northwest.[85] At least, the public was told it had been a victory. William Henry Harrison, governor of the Indiana Territory, had fought a battle at Tippecanoe.[86] There, his men cut down followers of Tecumseh and the Shawnee Prophet in the Prophet's absence, destroying their chief town.[87] As Madison summarized, "It may reasonably be expected that the good effects of this critical defeat and dispersion of a combination of savages which appears to have been spreading to a greater extent, will be experienced not only in a cessation of the murders and depredations committed on our frontier, but in the prevention of any hostile incursions otherwise to have been apprehended." Madison did not describe the event as a great victory by Harrison. Still, in time, Harrison would ride it to the White House nonetheless.

Madison's use of the word "savages" betrayed a certain conception of the Indians. Rude children of the forests, the story went, they did not think much for themselves. Rather, they tended to be guided by Europeans. Predictably, then, Americans understood the events in Indiana Territory to reflect British attempts to manipulate the Indians against the Americans from Canada.[88] This only further steeled the United States to make war on its neighbor to the north.

Madison knew that America remained unprepared for the fight.[89] Still, he judged, "It had become impossible to avoid or even delay war, at a moment when we were not prepared for it, and when it was certain that effective preparations would not take place, whilst the question of war was undecided." Seeing Congress dither, in other words, Madison decided to push the legislative branch to more resolute action by recommending a declaration. He concluded "that it would be best to open the war with a force of a kind and amount that would be soon procured, & that might strike an important blow, before the Enemy . . . could be reinforced."

Madison took two passes at a war message to Congress. The first, which he ultimately rejected, traced British hostility all the way back to 1783.[90] The version that he ultimately presented to the legislature began by confining its attention to events of great magnitude commencing with resumption of war after the dissolution of the Peace of Amiens in 1803. The first point on which Madison relied was British persistence in the practice of impressment. Second was the offense the Royal Navy had given to American sovereignty by prowling in American territorial waters and there attacking American ships (most famously, of course, in the *Chesapeake-Leopard* incident).

Third, Madison pointed to British seizure of American ships at sea. Next, Madison moved to British interference in America's trade with France and its allies. Madison explained this policy by saying that Britain aimed simply to sweep America from the seas so that it could monopolize the trade itself: "She carries on a war against the lawful commerce of a friend, that she may the better carry on a commerce with an enemy." Even when notified that if the British ceased to impose upon American shipping, America would choose war with France, Britain had retained its policy.

Madison noted the temporary agreement achieved via Erskine. His reading of it: that the cabinet's disavowal of Erskine's position must result from "a spirit of hostility to the commercial rights and prosperity of the United States." In the very next paragraph, he blamed the problem with Indians in the Northwest on British interference as well.

Madison almost could not believe that the British failed to behave as he hoped they would behave. Besides "moral obligations" and America's "friendly dispositions," the British government should at least have been affected by Britain's interest in access to "the invaluable market of a great and growing Country, disposed to cultivate the mutual advantages of an active commerce." But it had not.

And so, Britain was in "a state of war against the United States," while America was in "a state of peace towards Great Britain." He found the Constitution had "wisely confided to the Legislative Department of the Government" the question "whether the United States shall continue passive under these progressive usurpations, and these accumulating wrongs." France's course had been one of offense as well, and he would, he said, inform Congress of the results of ongoing consultations with Napoleon's government.

The House passed a declaration of war on June 4, 1812, by a vote of

79–49. In the Senate, the debate consumed several days, and war was voted only 19–13; several Republican senators voted no.[91]

Ironically, while war was being declared in Washington, D.C., the chief irritant between Britain and the United States was being removed in England.[92] It was on June 17 that the Orders in Council were withdrawn, and less then twenty-four hours later that the five-year-old naval policy to which Madison had so strongly objected, both as secretary of state and as president, was removed. In the *Times* of London, the editor said, "We are most surprised that such acts could ever have received the sanction of the Ministry when so little was urged in their defence." At the other end of Europe and two days after that, Napoleon on the precipice of his fateful Russian campaign "issued the first bulletin of his Grand Army."

America thus found itself at war with the greatest naval power in the world. It did so fully aware of its own unpreparedness. From the top down, and with the notable exception of the conflict at sea, the American war effort would prove a debacle.

Early in the war, Madison issued a public call for a day of prayer and fasting.[93] The president advised that the prayers to be presented to "the Sovereign of the Universe, and the Benefactor of mankind" on that day follow the pattern of traditional Christian liturgies: first, praise God; second, acknowledge our wrongdoing; third, ask forgiveness and seek "His assistance in the great duties of repentance & amendment"; and finally, ask God's help in the war—whether on the battlefield, in the public councils, in foreigners' minds, or in their hearts. Most notably, perhaps, he wanted Americans to ask God to inspire in other nations "a reverence for the unerring precept of our holy religion, to do to others as they would require that others should do to them."

This proclamation received wide circulation.[94] From north to south, it was published in newspapers and in a stand-alone form. Madison in time decided that such official calls for prayer violated the Establishment Clause because "they imply a religious agency, making no part of the trust delegated to political leaders." No doubt he would have insisted, if asked, that he had been perfectly consistent on this score all along.

A president's responsibility in wartime, as Madison understood it, is to ensure that Congress has the information necessary to making good policy decisions—to raising a full complement of troops, providing the necessary naval forces, and obtaining the requisite supplies. He must put the right men in command, and then he must oversee the making of military policy.

Madison compiled a decidedly mixed record in the War of 1812.

Most significantly, he went into the war with unqualified men in the top civilian posts, the war and navy secretaries. Of more moment, however, was the U.S. government's—that is, ultimately, Madison's—failure to establish an appropriate military strategy.

Across the Atlantic, Napoleon I had by 1812 completely remade military strategy.[95] In his campaigns of 1805 and 1806, in particular, he had demonstrated that the leading principle of strategy was to identify the key to the opponent's array, to concentrate one's forces upon it, and to destroy it. In his most successful campaigns, those of Austerlitz (1805) and Jena-Auerstädt (1806), Napoleon had destroyed his opponents' armies. He had abolished the Holy Roman Empire, and, if he had desired to do so, he could have wiped Prussia off the map.

In his message to Congress in November, Madison told Congress that it ought to bolster America's military academies. Jefferson had put considerable effort into establishing a professional officer corps with West Point as America's military academy. Yet America's chief warriors and president gave no indication in the War of 1812 that they had learned anything from Napoleon's example.

The grand strategy was to seize Canada and then to use it as a bargaining chip for wringing from Britain the commercial and naval concessions the Republicans had long desired. Those concessions, the president had insisted for nearly twenty years, must be granted. Common morality and the law of nations, as well as Britain's interest, demanded it. American strategy for achieving those ends could not easily be expected to yield that outcome.

Oddly enough, Madison's decision to take Canada by force represented a mutation of his long-held theory that Britain could be brought to heel through economic pressure.[96] Grabbing Canada, he believed, would force Britain—which relied on Canadian timber for ships' masts—to concede the merits of America's case without a full-scale war. Call it "economic coercion by other means."

Madison had arrived at the key insight that America must strike quickly, before Britain had a chance to prepare a defense. But how? Where? The highest officials of the government were essentially unconcerned. As Secretary of State James Monroe confided to a friend, "My candid opinion is that we shall succeed in obtaining what it is important to obtain, and that we shall experience little annoyance or embarrassment in the effort." The Speaker of the House, Henry Clay, agreed, holding that "the militia of Kentucky are alone competent to place Montreal and Upper Canada at your feet."[97]

The strategy America adopted was anything but Napoleonic. Under the leadership of generals almost entirely lacking in initiative, the U.S. Army would implement a plan devised by General Henry Dearborn. That plan envisioned a three-pronged offensive against Canada, with one American force invading eastward from Detroit, one bound for Montreal, and the final embarking between Lake Erie and Lake Ontario. The three were to be launched simultaneously, to exploit the American advantage in manpower in the war's earliest stages.

This strategy suffered from three basic flaws. First, its successful implementation would require coordination across a large area despite great difficulty in communication; second, it would require that all three forces be commanded by generals determined to make headway, whatever obstacles they might encounter; and third, it did not concentrate the United States' force against the chief strategic objective.

The American force at Detroit, numbering just over three thousand men, came under the command of revolutionary veteran William Hull. When faced with the enemy, Hull—who had recently suffered a stroke—dissolved into drunken blathering and crouching in the corners of his fort. The British threatened him with Indian slaughter if he did not surrender. In the end, Hull did surrender the fort. By the time the army went into winter encampment, a detachment under the command of James Winchester found itself forced to yield to Indians at the Raisin River, and "sixty of the Kentucky militiamen were butchered by drunken Indians."[98]

In the east, things did not go markedly better.[99] Under the command of another revolutionary veteran, Henry Dearborn, the federal forces in that theater failed even to coalesce. New England in general opposed the war effort, as was made perfectly clear by the refusal of the governors of Connecticut, Rhode Island, and Massachusetts to provide militiamen to participate in the planned invasion of Canada. Besides that, forces at other points in the East were not assigned leaders, and so dissolved. When Dearborn made arrange-ments for an armistice with the British commander in Lower Canada so that he would have time to assemble his army, the British thought that perhaps the Americans were trying to end the war. Madison told him to hurry up and in-vade, and the militiamen—famously—took their leave. They said that the Con-stitution did not empower Madison to use militia to invade Canada.

New York's militia, meanwhile, did decide to cross into Canada. Part of the detachment was captured, and its commander resigned. The rest of the militia melted away. When Dearborn at last led an invasion of Canada in mid-November, the regular army troops fired on the militia, and the whole army retreated back into the United States of America. By the time they went into winter quarters, then, America's fighting men had done little to validate Secretary of State Monroe's prediction that the conquest of Canada would be easy.

At sea, meanwhile, some intrepid American captains shocked the Royal Navy and the British public with a series of victories. The British had long since established complete command of the seas with their crushing victory over the combined French and Spanish fleets at Trafalgar; no one had thought that the Americans would be able to face them down.

Yet despite their early successes, America's warships were pitifully few. Of ships of the line, the multidecked floating fortresses with ranks of can-nons made famous by many a Hollywood movie, Britain had 191 and Amer-ica had . . . zero.[100] Of the next class down, frigates (approximately thirty to fifty guns each), Britain had 245 and America had 7, of which 6 would see service in the war. America might have fielded a more imposing naval force, if not for Jefferson's infatuation with so-called gunboats—essentially, narrow rowboats, each of which had one small cannon mounted in the front. While captains such as Stephen Decatur achieved notable isolated successes, and while the Americans ultimately did clear the Great Lakes of British ships, by war's end the Americans' remaining frigates were forced by the overwhelm-ing British numerical superiority to stay in port.

Despite the military situation, Madison won reelection in 1812.[101] The country did not display any notable enthusiasm for Madison. Federalists found themselves reduced to supporting a Republican dissenter, DeWitt Clinton, the nephew of the late Vice President George Clinton. (George had died in

April.) At one point, Federalists thought they would reduce the president's reelection prospects by coordinating a boycott of Mrs. Madison's weekly White House social events, but the Republicans attended them to a man, and the Federalist maneuver collapsed. Their campaign for the office failed as well. Madison's Electoral College margin was very narrow, 128–89. In fact, had Pennsylvania gone for Clinton, the election would have as well.

Madison's performance as president seems not to have changed in consequence of his 1812 electoral chastisement. The war dragged on.

The amateurish performance of the U.S. Army and militia, and particularly the general officers, in 1812 had wasted the element of strategic surprise on which Madison's plan to seize Canada depended. Events beyond his power to affect them worked further in that winter to change the military equation. By the end of winter 1812–1813, Napoleon's invasion of Russia had degenerated into an absolute disaster. Hundreds of thousands of French and French-allied soldiers never returned from that country. It was the beginning of the end for the French First Empire, which spent the balance of the War of 1812 on the strategic defensive. Although Russia's Alexander I, grandson of an Enlightened monarch, was a sincere friend of the United States, his triumph over the French would mean the elimination of the chief factor keeping Britain from focusing its military resources against the United States. On the other hand, if the war with France should end, Madison's concerns with British policy—chiefly its Orders in Council and impressment—likely would become moot.

As 1813 opened, Britain began to reinforce its Canadian forces. Madison booted his secretary of war, William Eustis, in propitiation of popular revulsion at the army's 1812 missteps, and replaced him with a marginally less incompetent figure, John Armstrong of New York.[102] On the bright side, Commodore Oliver Hazard Perry cleared Lake Erie of British ships (an accomplishment still reflected in the demilitarized state of the Great Lakes).[103] "We have met the enemy," Perry famously wrote, "and they are ours." Besides that, the army, under Dearborn, succeeded in taking York, Ontario.

Having taken York (later known as Toronto), the question became what to do with it. Dearborn had no idea. Some American soldiers violated orders by looting homes and prominent public buildings, including St. James Church and the local library.[104] Next, someone—it is not known who—burned the

Parliament buildings, seats of Upper Canada's legislative, executive, and judicial branches of government. Although burning those two buildings was not Dearborn's idea, the subsequent torching of the home of General Roger Sheaffe, the British commander, was. As if that were not enough, Dearborn took the parliamentary mace and General Sheaffe's snuffbox when he departed.

The British would not forget.

In February 1813, Madison accepted Emperor Alexander's offer to mediate the conflict.[105] Alexander, besides a friend to the United States, stood as Britain's chief anti-French ally, and so had good reason to want the Anglo-American conflict wound down. Madison named Gallatin and Federalist senator James Bayard of Delaware, the man most responsible for resolving the Jefferson-Burr impasse in the House in 1801, to join Minister Adams in St. Petersburg for the negotiation. As in the Erskine affair and in suspending the nonintercourse policy against Napoleon, Madison here waited neither for confirmation that Britain had accepted Alexander's mediation nor for his appointments' confirmation. This opportunity ran aground in June 1813, unfortunately, on the shoal of Republican opposition to the Gallatin nomination in the Senate. That was all right, however, because Britain did not accept the Russian emperor's offer.

Madison's second inaugural address, which he delivered on March 4, 1813, found him focused entirely on the war. America had delayed declaring it far beyond the time when Britain actually began to make it, he insisted, reprising a theme of his first such address four years before. Americans' behavior in war obeyed the dictates of law and morality, unlike their opponents'. Americans could rightly object to the British government's decision to sic "the savages" upon them using "the hatchet and the knife, devoted to indiscriminate massacre," whom the British had "allured . . . into their service" and taken into battle "eager to glut their savage thirst with the blood of the vanquished and to finish the work of torture and death on maimed and defenseless captives." Britain had even sunk so far as to attempt to disunite the United States, "to dismember our confederated Republic." Happily, Madison held, this strategy would fail. America remained willing to negotiate an end to the war, but the end must be honorable.

Of particular note in Madison's address was the passage in which he laid out the constitutional and ideological nature of the war between Britain and its quondam colonies.[106] Britain, he said, persisted in forcing into its naval forces former British subjects who had legitimately emigrated to the United States. In effectively denying the possibility of emigration, one reads between the lines, Britain denied the legitimacy of America's claim to sovereignty.[107] It denied the possibility of America's existence as a separate country. It denied that the American Revolution could occur. Americans were at war, then, for the very idea of America.

In any event, the British preferred to negotiate with the United States directly. Madison selected Gallatin (now former treasury secretary), Adams, Henry Clay, Bayard, and former minister to France Jonathan Russell for the task. The negotiation would take place at Ghent. In the meantime, however, calamity befell.

Madison decided on the ground of Britain's interest in negotiating not to undertake the energetic Canadian campaign that Armstrong had conceived for 1814.[108] Repeated border setbacks had not burnished the army's image by the time spring 1814 rolled around; in fact, as the *Times* of London summarized the American war effort, "The world has seen President Madison plunge into a war . . . and conduct it with the most entire want of ability."

Meanwhile, the U.S. government found itself in the same fiscal situation as it had faced when Madison was in Congress thirty years and more before: entirely strapped for funds, printing money to make up for the inability to borrow adequate money. Some people pushed for Congress to charter a second bank of the United States, but Republicans in general resisted. Auspiciously, Leib's appointment to the postmastership of Philadelphia removed him from the Senate, and Giles found himself in bad odor with the Virginia General Assembly—and thus likely to join his fellow leader among Senate Republican thorns in Madison's side as an ex-senator.[109]

On March 31, 1814, Madison proposed repeal of the latest embargo measures. Only British trade would remain illegal. This gambit apparently came in response to the news that Napoleon's position was irretrievable, and Madison's estimate that Britain was to rule Spain and Germany, leaving America to face Britain alone.[110] On April 14, Madison signed repeal into law. Madison's long experiment with economic coercion, recognized by Jefferson as a failure at the end of his presidency five years earlier, had finally been abandoned by Madison as well. Perhaps now the fires of separatism in southern New England could be tamped down.[111]

At this point, the Orders in Council had been forsworn, America's policy of economic coercion had been abandoned, it was clear that the United States was not going to conquer Canada, Napoleon's Continental System had been smashed by the Russian winter, and impressment seemed likely to be consigned to the scrap heap of history in the medium term, if not sooner. Why, then, did the war continue?

There are two great forces in human history: boredom and inertia. By mid-1814, at the latest, the continuation of the War of 1812 was a product of the latter.

At about this time, the Yazoo Scandal finally came to an end.[112] Madison, at Jefferson's command, had tried to paper over the conflicting claims of Georgia citizens, investors, and American taxpayers, to no avail. In 1810, in *Fletcher v. Peck,* the Marshall Court had weighed in against the commission's solution and in favor of a more complete victory for investors. With Randolph out of the House—he had suffered defeat in the pro-war wave that swept the nation in 1812, and so was absent for one term—a $5 million bill to resolve the issue passed through Congress. Madison, happy to see the matter resolved at last, signed it. Here, too, New England should have been placated.

Unfortunately for the Americans, Napoleon abdicated his French throne in April. Madison years later recalled having calculated that Napoleon's unpredicted collapse had upset all reasonable expectations; had that not happened, he insisted, the British would have concluded the War of 1812 in 1812 or 1813 on conditions congenial to the United States.[113] Madison's point was that he should not be held responsible for what actually happened in 1814.

An unfriendly chronicler described matters a bit differently. As Henry Adams began the relevant chapter of his monumental *History of the United States During the Administrations of Thomas Jefferson and James Madison,* "For two years Washington stood unprotected; not a battery or breastwork was to be found on the river bank except the old and untenable Fort Washington. . . . A thousand determined men might reach the town in thirty-six hours, and destroy it before any general alarm could be given."[114] Yet, despite this fact of geography, and despite the ease with which it might have been protected, Washington remained unprotected.

The problem was not that the situation had escaped notice. Madison told Secretary of War Armstrong to see to the problem beginning in May, but Armstrong sloughed the matter off. His judgment was that there was no military objective at Washington, and so the British would not bother with it. "Baltimore is the place, sir," he told Madison; "that is of so much more consequence."[115] Hearing rumors of a British invasion, Madison became more concerned to provide for the defense of the District of Columbia. Characteristically, however, he seems never to have given Armstrong an absolute command to set up earthworks and take other defensive measures at the capital.

The first wave of British strikes came in New England in April.[116] Already then, Virginians reported seeing tall sails in Chesapeake Bay. Brigadier General William Winder, charged by Madison with the task of defending Washington, called up fifteen thousand militia from Maryland, Virginia, and Pennsylvania. Armstrong negated his orders, except insofar as six thousand from Maryland were involved.

Even as reports of British incursions into coastal Maryland began to arrive, Armstrong refused to respond to them by sending requested equipment.[117] Madison intervened to override Armstrong. All the way down to August 22, Madison accepted Armstrong's insistence that a large force was not really bound for Washington. That night, to his dismay, the president stood corrected.

That was when Madison heard that a British army was en route to the capital, and he went out to attend to his own force opposing it.[118] Secretary Monroe had personally ridden out as a scout—yes, James Monroe, the top official in Madison's cabinet, who had joined the Continental Army in 1776, himself rode out to find the enemy—without managing to locate the British. Absurdly, the citizens of Washington, D.C., decided to take matters into their own hands and began to erect defense works themselves. Hearing of this development, Armstrong sent an engineer to help them at it.

An American force of nearly two thousand men under Winder's command shadowed the British all day on August 22 without undertaking to impede their approach to the capital. Winder continued to insist that the British were bound for Annapolis.[119]

On August 24, all became clear. Winder roused Madison from breakfast at the White House with the news that the British had set out for Bladensburg. Winder, it seems, had become overwhelmed with the prospect of battle. He ordered five hundred men to destroy a bridge, a hundred times as many as were needed. Madison intervened to send several hundred sailors and five naval guns to join Winder's army. Armstrong did nothing. Madison ordered Armstrong to go to Winder and help him with troop dispositions. Armstrong went but did not help.

On the field of Bladensburg, the nearly six thousand militiamen and several hundred sailors under Winder's command outnumbered their invading foes. Almost immediately, two thousand men were ordered to retreat without shooting. Monroe attempted to countermand those orders, but could not be heard in the din. Virtually all of the militiamen simply fled—thus earning the battle the name the Bladensburg races. Here, in the failure of the militia to defend the federal capital, was Republican military policy in its full glory. One wonders whether the paeans to republican militias in his own or Jefferson's first inaugural came to Madison's mind. For some reason, Winder at this point made his chief contribution to the battle: he ordered the sailors, whose guns dominated the Washington road, to retreat. The route to the District of Columbia lay undefended.

By nightfall, the British had reached Washington. They burned the Capitol, they burned the White House, they burned the executive offices, and they destroyed the presses and type of the *National Intelligencer*—the newspaper that served as the government's official organ.[120] York, Upper Canada, had been avenged in full.

In the leadup to his capital's sacking, James Madison had coolly headed into Washington. He instructed his cabinet secretaries that they should meet at nearby Frederick, Maryland, if the capital were seized. Dolley Madison, still in the White House, saved James's papers and the famous Gilbert Stuart painting of George Washington before she fled the city, thereby earning herself a reputation as quite the intrepid woman.[121] In the wake of the British, Madison gave Armstrong a brief dressing-down. Armstrong resigned his post. Madison drew Monroe into that job too. Madison came under intense heat for his conduct of the war after the fall of Washington, which of course as the capital had gigantic symbolic significance. However, its military significance was very slight. The war dragged on.

The British force that had been launched upon Washington next descended upon Baltimore, where Fort McHenry's resistance would be immortalized by Francis Scott Key. At the same time, the British plan to invade through New York State was thwarted by the U.S. Navy.

In November 1814, Madison's second-term vice president, fellow Philadelphia Convention framer Elbridge Gerry, died. Gerry had been unwell, so his passing away cannot have come to Madison as a surprise. In those days before the Twenty-fifth Amendment, Madison would be without a vice president for the remainder of his term.

Finally, on Christmas Eve 1814, the negotiators in Ghent signed a treaty to end the war. The British agreed to the status quo ante bellum—that is, to restoration of the condition that existed before the war began. There would be no avowed end to impressments, no explicit British concessions concerning the rights of neutrals . . . in short, no American gains of any kind. The two parties did agree to enter into a commercial treaty as soon as possible, but that was not part of the Treaty of Ghent itself. Luckily for Madison's administration, word of the treaty made its way to Washington only after other news arrived.

On January 8, 1815, General Andrew Jackson won a smashing victory outside New Orleans. There, a seven-thousand-man army of British veterans of Wellington's Peninsular campaign commanded by Wellington's brother-in-law, Lord Pakenham, had confronted a four-thousand-man force of U.S. Army regulars, militia, and Francophone pirates commanded by Jean Lafitte. So overwhelming a victory can scarcely be imagined: the British suffered 291 killed (including Pakenham), 1,262 wounded, and 484 captured to the Americans' 7 killed and 6 wounded.[122]

While news of events at Ghent and outside New Orleans made its way to Washington, Madison had another duty. He reported to the nation the outcome of the Hartford Convention.[123] In the capital of Connecticut, a regional convention, with delegates appointed by Massachusetts and Connecticut state governments and some popular meetings elsewhere in New England, had on January 12 adopted a series of anti-Republican resolutions.

The convention had long been the brainchild of disgruntled, even seces-sionist, Federalists such as the Massachusetts senator and one-time secretary of state, Timothy Pickering. That is why Monroe contemplated sending an army detachment to Connecticut.[124] The twenty-odd men who finally partici-pated, on the other hand, were dominated by Federalists of the old stamp—cautious men contemptuous of democracy. Their report began by saying, among other things, "A severance of the Union by one or more of the States against the will of the rest, and especially in time of war, can be justified only by absolute necessity.[125] The report then followed the model of the Virginia Resolutions of 1798, which had been revealed to be Madison's handiwork by John Taylor of Caroline in 1809, in saying that the states had the responsibil-ity to "interpose" in case the federal government committed constitutional infractions.[126]

What the convention called for at the time were state laws impeding federal conscription, an agreement with the federal government empower-ing these states to undertake their own defense (and keeping some of their federal taxes for that purpose), and state establishment of state forces for this purpose. All this would be under a New England Confederation. In addition, the Hartford Convention recommended a package of seven anti-Virginia-Republican constitutional amendments: for repealing the Three-Fifths Clause, against successive presidents from the same state, for limiting presidents to one term, and for requiring a two-thirds vote in each house of Congress for adoption of any commercial restriction.[127] Separatists from out-side New England, such as Gouverneur Morris, egged the convention on.

The governors of Massachusetts and Connecticut approved the conven-tion's report, and the Massachusetts legislature endorsed it by a margin of three to one. The Massachusetts Governor, Caleb Strong, moved to secure financing for the state army. In fact, no eminent Federalists from any part of the country publicly or privately disapproved of the convention.

Arriving in Washington with the convention's demands at virtually the same time as the Treaty of Ghent arrived, former congressman Harrison Gray Otis could not gain admittance to Dolley Madison's victory celebra-tion. As Timothy Dwight, the secretary of the convention, conceded, "the Hartford Convention became [a] theme of universal calumny and re-proach."[128]

The mirror image was James Madison. Suddenly, he had become a hero. As Pennsylvania's Senator Jonathan Roberts recorded it,

> I drove to the President's. On arriving there all was still and dark. I found Mr. Madison sitting solitary in his parlor . . . in perfect tranquility, not even a servant waiting. What a contrast from the scene I had just left. I apologiz'd for my intrusion, stating that I had heard a rumor of Peace, but I apprehended it was incorrect. Take a seat, said he, & I will tell you all I know. . . . I believe there is peace, but we have not as yet the information in such form, as that we can publish it officially. . . . The self command, and greatness of mind, I witness'd on this occasion was in entire accordance with what I have before stated of the Pres[iden]t, when to me things looked so dark. I think it to be regretted that these evidences, of the solidity and Sterling worth of his character, will perhaps find no place in the history of his administration, brilliant as it must ever appear.[129]

The conclusion of the War of 1812 affected America's self-perception notably. As Joseph Story put it, "we have stood the contest, single-handed, against the conqueror of Europe; and we are at peace, with all our blushing victories thick crowding upon us."[130]

In the war's aftermath, in his seventh annual message to Congress, delivered in December 1815, Madison proved capable of learning from experience at last.[131] He moved to reorganize the militia to make it easier for the president to employ when needed. (It may be that his ideology had blinded him to the reality of the situation. Given Madison's characteristic clearheadedness, however, it seems more likely that he bowed to the Republican presidents' tradition of flattering the common man, at least a little.) He moved to maintain a substantial navy even in peacetime. He recommended the establishment of a national university. He asked that Congress maintain a protective tariff as a hedge "against occasional competitions from abroad," particularly when it came to products necessary for the country's defense.[132] Madison also called upon Congress to undertake the construction of a national network of roads and canals. These, he said, would have notable economic and political benefits. "Any defect of constitutional authority," he was quick to add, "can be supplied in a mode which the Constitution itself has providently pointed out."

Having heard this Hamiltonian wish list intoned by the House of Representatives' clerk, John Randolph of Roanoke thundered that Madison "out-Hamiltons Alexander Hamilton." It seemed to Randolph that Madison had completely abandoned the Principles of '98.[133]

Most noteworthy, perhaps, was Madison's change of position concerning a federally chartered bank. Although Gallatin had long since departed the cabinet, Madison in his December 1815 message accepted his counsel and publicly asked Congress to consider chartering a second Bank of the United States.

In Washington's first term as president, the president had presided over a debate in the cabinet concerning the constitutionality of the Bank Bill. What may strike us as surprising about this is that the bill had been proposed by Secretary Hamilton, and yet Washington pondered vetoing it. In Madison's administration, the president had sat by silently as Gallatin made known that he would like to see the Bank of the United States rechartered in 1811, and then his vice president had killed the recharter bill in the Senate.

Now, Madison called for a new bank to be chartered, and in 1816, Congress complied. He signed the bill chartering the second Bank of the United States on April 10.[134] Soon thereafter, he also signed the Cumberland Road Bill, a bill to fund construction of a route across Speaker Henry Clay's Kentucky. Seemingly, the constitutional scruples at which he had hinted in his annual message had left him.

In his final annual message, which he delivered to Congress on December 3, 1816, Madison reprised many of the previous message's highlights: he wanted a national network of roads and canals, but an amendment must precede the undertaking; he wanted a national university in the District of Columbia; he wanted Congress to legislate national militia organization so that the militia would be ready in case it was needed again; and he offered a general description of the United States' relations with foreign countries.[135]

Of particular note in this address was Madison's observation that America had been the first to ban "the transportation of the natives of Africa into slavery," which Madison coupled with a call for Congress to adopt legislation making slave smuggling more difficult. Notable, too, was Madison's suggestion that Congress relieve Supreme Court justices of the duty of riding circuit and that Congress reorganize the inferior federal courts—as had been done under the Judiciary Act of 1801, whose repeal had been one of the first achievements of the new Republican congressional majority after the Revolution of 1800. Madison, it seems, was experiencing wide-ranging buyer's remorse at the end of his term, which saw him propose to undo several Republican accomplishments. Nothing happened in that Congress, or indeed for decades to come, to correct the problem of circuit riding.

Madison's penultimate State of the Union message had been longer than any he had delivered before, and this final one came in longer still. He included at its end a long passage in a valedictory vein, in which he initially contemplated what Americans had achieved and then considered what they still could. First, he agreed with Jefferson ("We are all republicans, we are all federalists") that Americans had succeeded in erecting a Constitution proven "to contain in its combination of the federate and elective principles a reconcilement of public strength with individual liberty." This "reconcilement," he continued, insured that America both could defend its rights and would not make wars "of injustice, of ambition, [or] of vainglory." The constitutional system Americans had adopted, he concluded, guaranteed them their fundamental rights (some of which he enumerated), allowed them to improve their system as imperfections came to light, and left them free to prod foreigners to establish a more just international order through America's "appeals to reason and . . . liberal examples." America's government, in other words, bespoke "the most noble of all ambitions—that of promoting peace on earth and good will to man."[136] These contemplations, he vowed, would mark his "prayers for the happiness of my beloved country, and a perpetuity of the institutions under which it is enjoyed."

When Congress chartered the new bank, it provided that 20 percent of the bank's shares would be owned by the federal government and reserved a $1.5 million "bonus" to itself.[137] Speaker Clay, fresh off his victory in the Cumberland Road contest, and John C. Calhoun had plans for the bonus: they would spend it on a national network of roads and canals. They believed that they had Madison's support in this effort, for he had called for such a program in more than one of his annual messages—just as President Thomas Jefferson had done before him.

In his last official act as president, on March 3, 1817, Madison vetoed the bill. As he had done repeatedly as president, Madison took the opportunity to instruct his fellow citizens on the meaning of the Constitution.[138] "The legislative powers vested in Congress," Madison lectured, "are specified and enumerated in the eighth section of the first article of the Constitution, and it does not appear that the power proposed to be exercised by the bill is among the enumerated powers, or that it falls by any just interpretation within the power to make laws necessary and proper for carrying into execution those or other powers vested by the Constitution in the Government of the United States."

The power to build roads and canals did not fall under the Commerce Clause either, Madison insisted. Both knowledge of the reasons why the power to regulate interstate commerce was granted and "the ordinary import of the terms" led to this conclusion. The General Welfare Clause ("Congress shall have power . . . to provide for the common defense and general welfare") did not provide Congress this power either, because to read it as a substantive grant of power instead of as a description of the list of specific powers that immediately followed it in the Constitution would thwart the purpose of enumerating powers. If one were to read the General Welfare Clause as empowering Congress to do whatever it thought conducive to the general welfare, the line between federal and state authority would be removed, and the Supreme Court would have no role in enforcing that boundary. After all, questions of welfare were questions of "expediency," which were political rather than legal.

Even a provision such as that in the bill providing that expenditure for these purposes would depend upon the particular states' consent did not make it constitutional. Rather, the only consent of the states that could confer new powers on Congress was that necessary to the amendment process provided in Article V.

In sum, Madison held that "believing . . . that the permanent success of the Constitution depends on a definite partition of powers between the General and the State Governments, and that no adequate landmarks would be left by the constructive extension of the powers of Congress as proposed in the bill, I have no option but to withhold my signature from it," and to hope that the aims of the bill might be achieved after the requisite amendment gave Congress power to undertake such a program.

Madison's congressional allies were shocked by the veto.[139] Calhoun, learning that it was coming from Madison himself, responded that he had thought the bill to be congenial to Madison. In light of Madison's recent assent to, even advocacy of, protective tariffs, a new bank law, and the Cumberland Road, Calhoun and Speaker Clay could not have expected Madison to dust off the argument about constitutional construction that he had first elaborated in response to Hamilton's Bank Bill in 1791. If he had not thought that Madison wanted a bill like this, the Carolinian assured the president, he would not have presented Madison with "the unpleasant duty, at the very close of his administration, of vetoing a bill passed by . . . his friends." Calhoun had erred unintentionally and asked Madison to reconsider. Madison, as we have seen, refused.

The day after Madison sent the Bonus Bill Veto Message to Congress, he attended the ceremony in which his old friend and ally James Monroe succeeded him as president. Another Virginia Republican slave-owning aristocrat, not coincidentally a friend and longtime ally of Madison's, succeeded to the chief magistracy of the federal republic. Madison, elated at his liberation from presidential cares, lingered in Washington with Dolley for a couple of days, and then the two of them were off to Montpelier.

Chapter 8

An Active Retirement,
1817–36

Unburdened of public office at last, Madison joined Dolley in one last whirl of socializing. Then they headed home to Orange County.

In the nineteen years that remained to him, James Madison was politically and publicly active. For example, in 1817 he accepted a position as titular president of the Albemarle Agricultural Society (AAS), one of many county agricultural societies that came to dot the Old Dominion in that and the following decade.[1] Albemarle's leading citizen, Jefferson, Peter Minor, and the young reform advocate John Hartwell Cocke were behind the effort, which likely explains why Madison agreed to take the society's top office.

He never actually participated in the AAS's activities, other than by giving an address on May 12, 1818.[2] His performance was not generally well received, and in fact still earned him mockery over a decade later. Characteristically of Madison's written productions, it brandished extensive reading in agricultural science; unlike his political writings, it did not reflect extensive experience. Multiple Albemarle critics judged it embarrassing, though others in Madison's audience (including Thomas Jefferson, habitually Madison's friendliest critic) piled on superlatives.[3]

Madison's old friend Jefferson had undertaken years before to persuade the General Assembly to create a new public university. The College of William and Mary, Jefferson held, was too beholden to the Episcopalian Tidewater elite to serve the purpose of grounding the Old Dominion's future leaders in Enlightenment rationalism. A more westerly alternative organized on Jeffersonian lines—without formal religious instruction as an element of its curriculum—should be built.

Madison sympathized with Jefferson, saying of the omission of a chair in theology, "The Public Opinion seems now to have sufficiently yielded to its incompatibility with a *State* Institution, which necessarily excludes sectarian Preferences."[4] He also remained bound to his old captain by firm ties of friendship forged at the height of the revolution, when both had been young and promising. How easy it was for Jefferson to recruit Madison to assist him in founding the University of Virginia.

Jefferson bounced off Madison a proposed list of books that the new university's library ought to obtain. The Declaration of Independence would be required reading, of course, as would *The Federalist*. The two of them exchanged compliments about these works, one mainly Jefferson's handiwork, the other largely Madison's. Madison, Jefferson said, should compile works in theology and Christian history for inclusion in the library. Possibly Jefferson's deference to Madison in relation to religious matters reflected Madison's superior expertise. As we saw, Madison had stayed on at Princeton after graduation to pursue religious study under Dr. Witherspoon. Although his surviving papers from 1800 on provide extremely little evidence that he continued to give theology serious attention, perhaps evidence of ongoing interest could have been found in the papers that Madison had Dolley destroy after his death.

Madison replied that although theological study was not to be compulsory at the University of Virginia, still "its Library ought to contain pretty full information for such as might voluntarily seek it in that branch of Learning."[5] The catalog he offered included a complete listing of most of the early Christian writings, including most of the Apostolic fathers and a good number of the ante-Nicene fathers. Besides that, Madison hoped to see the university's collection include the Koran, Leibniz, William Penn, a smattering of English Episcopalians, and some contemporary skeptical material (including writings by Joseph Priestley). John Locke's works on religious subjects, which may have influenced Madison's thinking on church-state relations, also found their way onto Madison's list.

Besides helping Jefferson with his projected university in this way, Madison also accepted a position as one of the first members of the University of Virginia's Board of Visitors. Too, he contributed substantial funds to the school. Still, as he insisted, the project was mainly Jefferson's. Even though Madison succeeded Jefferson at the head of the school in Charlottesville upon the latter's death on July 4, 1826, it remains to this day "Mr. Jefferson's University."

Affairs in Washington would not release their grip on Madison's attentions, either. It was not long after Madison's retirement from the presidency that an obscure New York congressman, a Republican no less, launched the Missouri Crisis.[6] Residents of the Missouri Territory, many of them Virginia natives, had submitted an application for statehood.[7] Representative James Tallmadge proposed two conditions on Missouri's admission to the Union: that no additional slaves be taken to Missouri; and that all Missouri slaves be freed upon reaching adulthood.

No one had expected this controversy. They certainly did not think it would last for the better part of two years. Madison fretted lest it draw a permanent line between the sections. He thought it might ultimately mean the permanent separation of North from South.

Madison argued forcefully for the southern position in the Missouri controversy. Thus, for example, he wrote a long letter exploding the anti-Missouri congressman's contention that the 1808 Clause of Article I, Section 9 of the Constitution meant that Congress could exclude slavery from Missouri.[8] That clause says, "The Migration or Importation of such Persons as any of the States now existing shall think proper to admit, shall not be prohibited by the Congress prior to the Year one thousand eight hundred and eight, but a tax or duty may be imposed on such Importation, not exceeding ten dollars for each Person." No, Madison said, this referred not to a congressional power to regulate the slave trade among the states, but to a power to exclude importation of slaves from abroad. He found proof of this in his recollections of the Philadelphia Convention, in his notes of the Philadelphia Convention debates, in *The Federalist,* and in the Congress's omission to exercise any such power before 1819. On this last score, he noted that Congress had banned the foreign slave trade as early as Article I, Section 9, allowed. (Indeed, at President Jefferson's suggestion, it had adopted legislation doing so in 1806.)

Having disposed of that argument, Madison turned to anti-Missourians' alternative argument: that Congress had power to exclude slavery under the Territories Clause of Article IV, Section 3. That clause reads, "The Congress shall have Power to dispose of and make all needful Rules and Regulations respecting the Territory or other Property belonging to the United States." According to Madison, that section granted only power "over the Territory as property, & a power to make the provisions really needful or necessary for the Govt. of settlers until ripe for admission as States into the Union." He deduced that power to exclude slavery did not fall into that category, as Congress had never yet exercised such a power. Even if it did, however, "The power . . . is obviously limited to a Territory whilst remaining in that character as distinct from that of a State."

Madison finally added an objection not to that point mentioned. Congress, he said, had no right to elevate a new state above, or to reduce it below, equality with the other states. If the other states had been able to decide the question of slavery for themselves, then Missouri must be able to do so as well. Otherwise, since the other states had all exercised this power, it would be an inferior state. This observation led Madison to observe that while the Northwest Ordinance's exclusion of slavery from the Midwest seemed to make those states an inferior class, the question whether that exclusion was valid had not yet been decided.

In a plaintive concluding section to this letter, Madison summarized his evaluation of the Missouri contretemps. "The tendency of what has passed and is passing," he wrote, "fills me with no slight anxiety." For even-tempered James Madison, this was agitated writing. "Parties under some denominations or other must always be expected in a Govt. as free as ours." When the parties were national, "they strengthen the Union of the Whole, while they divide every part." Let them become sectional, however, and "what is to controul those great repulsive Masses from awful shocks agst. each other?"

By the following February, Henry Clay's so-called Missouri Compromise package of legislation—a bill admitting Missouri with slavery, a bill admitting the Maine district of Massachusetts as a state without slavery, and a bill prohibiting slavery from all the rest of the Louisiana Purchase territory north of 36 degrees 30 minutes north latitude—commanded the public's attention. In time, President James Monroe would accede to John C. Calhoun's advice and sign all three bills. Monroe agreed with Calhoun that the most important imperative in the Missouri Crisis was not to secure a theoretically satisfactory outcome but just to end the debate; that way, Calhoun advised, Americans might not be permanently impressed with the idea that North and South were separate and irreconcilable.

Madison did not agree.[9] As the fourth president advised the fifth, bringing in Missouri and Maine as new states at the same time was "a very doubtful policy." Madison explained that the idea was "fast spreading" that the anti-Missouri leaders' goal was not "the welfare of the slaves" but to reform the old parties. Since they had lost the political wars when founded on "political" distinctions, those leaders hoped now to redraw political lines on the basis of "local" distinctions. In other words, the real goal here was to break up the Republican Party, dividing Republicans of the North from their former compatriots of the South.

Madison went on to tell his friend the president that the Philadelphia Convention had never contemplated that the words "migration or importation" related to the interstate slave trade. He implied that leaders of the anti-Missouri movement, such as New York's Rufus King, acted in bad faith: no one who had been a member of the Philadelphia Convention, as King had, "could favor an opinion that the terms did not *exclusively* refer to Migration & importation *into the U.S.*" As to the ratification conventions, he said, Monroe himself was as good an authority as there was regarding the probable effect if the Federalists of 1788 had avowed an intention to empower Congress to prohibit the interstate slave trade into any state.

One might have objected that such a power was implicit in the existence of a federal government charged with managing unorganized territories. As a basis for this argument, one might have pointed to the Northwest Ordinance of 1787—passed when the Confederation Congress lacked even the power to regulate the international slave trade. Madison argued against this reasoning to the effect that if Congress had had the power to prohibit the international slave trade in 1787, it would not have adopted a law "preventing an interior dispersion of the slaves actually in the U. S. & creating a distinction among the States in the degrees of their sovereignty."

Madison had here adopted the most "southern," or pro-slavery, arguments. It was perhaps predictable that Madison, like Jefferson, Taylor, and other elderly Republican figures, espied a Federalist plot behind the Missouri Crisis. Senator Rufus King's prominent role in the anti-Missouri leadership gave this hypothesis great weight, as King had been the Federalist presidential nominee in both 1812 and 1816. Yet, Madison's argument concerning the Northwest Ordinance is particularly trivial; he would have done better to say that the ordinance had in this sense been unconstitutional, but that no one had recognized its unconstitutionality in 1787.

Thus advised, President Monroe asked Madison for further counsel. In response, less than two weeks later, Madison wrote his friend again.[10] Madison told Monroe that he considered a congressional exclusion of slavery from a territory unconstitutional even during the territorial phase; it certainly was beyond Congress's powers to impose such a restriction after the territory became a state. Still, he would not blame those who supported a territorial exclusion "in a conciliatory course." In other words, Monroe might well veto the Missouri Compromise on constitutional grounds—and as far as Madison was concerned, he would be in the right. Yet, if "the injury threatened to the nation" by thwarting the compromise seemed likely to be greater than that from "an acquiescence in the measure," signing the bill could be justified.

Finally, Madison turned to the behavior of the anti-Missouri leadership. "The inflammatory conduct of Mr. King surprises every one," he wrote. "His general warfare agst. the slave-holding States, and his efforts to disparage the securities derived from the Constn. were least of all to be looked for." King, Madison said, *knew* that he was misconstruing the Constitution. While anti-Missouri leaders had made much of the record of the Richmond ratification convention, he said, they had said little about the proceedings in other states. If they turned to Alexander Hamilton's speeches in New York and King's own in Massachusetts, they would find that "a sense of *equity* & a spirit of mutual concession" underlay the slavery-related provisions of the Constitution. King and Hamilton had defended the Three-Fifths Clause on that basis, he noted, and his point was that King ought to move in the same spirit now.

Monroe signed the legislation. To his and his fellow moderates' surprise, that did not end the matter. This time, the trouble originated with Missourians, who included in their state constitution a prohibition on free blacks' entering their state. Madison lamented this provision, which he considered likely unconstitutional.[11] (Here he probably had in mind Article IV's guarantee to citizens of one state the rights of citizens of states in which they sojourned.) Madison suggested that Missouri's admission to the Union be "suspend[ed]" until the offending clause was removed. If not that, he said, perhaps the provision could simply be read as applying to free blacks who were not citizens of other states.

Looking back upon the Missouri imbroglio, historians commonly call it the point at which sectional conflict in the federal system became normal. Madison did not see it that way.[12] Rather, he described American politics as marked by "occasional fevers," but held that "they are of the transient kind flying off thro' the surface, without preying on the vitals." The Missouri Crisis, he said, had been one of these.

By peculiarly unhappy coincidence, the Missouri Crisis began just as two other factors combined to make Virginia Republicans uneasy. It was in 1819 that a marked economic contraction began, and that Chief Justice John Marshall's Supreme Court handed down its decision in *McCulloch v. Maryland*.[13] Both of these impressed Virginians with the precariousness of their social and economic situation.

Marshall's majority opinion in *McCulloch* endorsed the very broad conception of congressional power taken by proponents of Hamilton's bank in 1791. Even a careless reader could not miss the debt that Marshall's opinion owed to Hamilton's memorandum to Washington.

Virginians responded with a torrent of criticism. Notable among the critics were two Virginia judges, including the chief judge of Virginia's highest court, Spencer Roane. Roane wrote a series of newspaper columns eviscerating Marshall's opinion on the basis of the original understanding. As we have seen, the Hamilton position—that the list of congressional powers in Article I, Section 8, was not exhaustive, but that Congress could exercise various other powers supposedly implicitly granted—was inconsistent with Madison's understanding in 1787–1788, not to mention that of the Virginia ratification convention majority.

That said, Roane expected Madison to agree with him. He was not disappointed. Madison expressed great exasperation that the Supreme Court had given Congress power "to which no practical limit can be assigned."[14] Here the Court had betrayed the people, Madison said: "It . . . was foreseen at the birth of the Constitution" that the line between federal and state authority would be hard to draw; still, the people had understood that there would be such a line. Marshall had said that it was for Congress to choose the means to constitutional ends, and "the avowal of such a rule would . . . have prevented [the Constitution's] ratification."

Madison remained an advocate of giving Congress the powers necessary to the health of the Union, but he would do it by amending the Constitution. He had said the same thing formally and publicly only two years before *McCulloch* in his Bonus Bill Veto Message, so it can have come as no surprise. Here, Madison waded into a controversy between the Virginia Republican leadership and the Marshall Court that had begun when he was still president, and that was not over yet.

Two years later, Roane wrote to Madison again. This time, the topic was the Marshall Court's decision in *Cohens v. Virginia* (1821), which stated that defendants in criminal cases could appeal to the Supreme Court without taking notice of the contrary policy seemingly established by the Eleventh Amendment. Roane looked to Madison for support in Virginia's dispute, and Madison responded with a mixed verdict. He lamented the Marshall Court's long-standing habit of going beyond the question at hand to deliver political discussions tending "to amplify the authorities of the Union at the expense of those of the States." In doing so, he said, the Court violated its obligation to maintain the boundary between federal and state authority. "Every deviation from it," he lectured, "in practice detracts from the superiority of a Chartered over a traditional Govt." In plain English, the difference between a constitutional government and one without a constitution (a "traditional" one) depended on enforcement of the written limits on the government's authority; absent that enforcement, there effectively was no constitution.

Lamentably, the history of the federal government did not "preclude doubts" about the future of the American system. Still, he did not believe that the Congress and the courts together could permanently usurp state power "without some change in the character of the nation." The experience of the Alien and Sedition Acts—which were instantly crushed despite the federal judiciary's connivance—showed that the structure of Congress was an adequate guard against federal usurpation. Since one house was chosen by the people and the other by the legislatures, American rights were safe.

If most of Congress's constituents favored violations of the Constitution, as Madison said they had in the Missouri Crisis and "as may again happen in the constructive power relating to Roads & Canals," the Constitution offered no way to stop them. When it came to the Court's decision in *Cohens,* Madison told Judge Roane, the proper recourse was to appeal to Congress not to exercise the powers the Court wanted Congress to have. Congress could also rein in the Court when it claimed power for itself.

Madison lamented the Court's omission to take note of the Eleventh Amendment. If a plaintiff could not sue a state in federal court, he asked, did it make more sense to think that a defendant could drag a state into federal court on appeal? Clearly, he thought not.

Yet when Roane sent him a new set of anti–Marshall Court columns a couple of months later, Madison disappointed his Virginian correspondent.[15] "On the abstract question whether the federal or the State decisions ought to prevail," the older man confided, "the sounder policy would yield to the claims of the former." It had to be that way, he said, because if it were left to each state to decide for itself matters on which it found itself in conflict with the federal government, "the Constitution of the U.S. might become different in every state, and would be pretty sure to do so in some."

Over time, Madison thought, decision of constitutional questions would tend to yield more uniformity of opinions between state and federal judges. So too would selection of abler judges in all the states. In time, federal and state judges would not differ much in their understandings at all. This was particularly significant when it came to marking "the true boundaries of power, on which must depend the success & permanency of the federal republic." Madison conceded that "I may permit my wishes to sway too much my hopes." Roane certainly must have thought so.

The economic contraction bankrupted several leading Virginians. Not least of these was Jefferson's in-law, former governor Wilson Cary Nicholas.[16] Since Jefferson had cosigned for a substantial loan, Nicholas's financial ruin entailed Jefferson's virtual bankruptcy as well. These events spurred Jefferson to devote much of his last years' energy to lamenting the misdeeds of banks and bankers (such as Nicholas), whom he accused of gambling and worse. Despite his most concerted efforts, he never got his head above water after the Nicholas fiasco.

If Jefferson's last years found him in dire economic straits, Madison's agricultural enterprises fared little better than his friend's. Unlike Jefferson, Madison was not a complete spendthrift, but he did have his worries. As he confided to Jefferson in 1826, "Since my return to private life . . . such have been the unkind seasons, & the ravages of insects, that I have made but one tolerable crop of Tobacco, and but one of Wheat; the proceeds of both of which were greatly curtailed by mishaps in the sale of them."[17] If, like Jefferson's, Madison's creditors called in their loans, he would be hard up too. Fortunately, he concluded, that seemed unlikely. Still, his debts had "swelled" enormously, and he had "been living very much throughout on borrowed means." (In fact, he would have borrowed substantially more, if the Bank of the United States had let him.)[18]

Madison traced Virginia's economic decline to several causal factors. Most prominent, in his thinking, was the opening of a huge inland empire of virgin land to American farmers. That land produced far more than the exhausted lands of Tidewater and Piedmont Virginia with the same effort, and that production drove down the price of Virginia's agricultural products. In addition, that land's appearance on the market drove down the value of Virginia lands, thus further reducing the wealth of Old Virginia.[19] Ironically, some of the land that was driving down the standard of living of Virginia planters such as the two ex-presidents had been added to the United States by the Jefferson administration's Louisiana Purchase in 1803.

That was Madison's explanation. For their part, rather than blame their economic situation on the opening of virgin land to the west and the vagaries of foreign trade, Southerners in the 1820s often highlighted the negative effects of federal policy. Jefferson did it.[20] In a number of books, John Taylor of Caroline did it.[21] And, most momentously, the South Carolina Nullifiers did it. In other words, sons of the revolution, Madison's fellows believed that there must be a political solution to their problem. He, less romantic, doubted that there was any solution.

The nullification movement came to a head in 1832–1833, when South Carolina nullified the tariff.[22] The short of Carolinians' argument was that the Virginia and Kentucky Resolutions were right: it was for states to police the bounds of federal authority, and—as the Virginia Resolutions said—states "have the right, and are in duty bound, to interpose" in case of unconstitutional and dangerous federal policies to prevent those policies from being enforced "within their respective limits [that is, territories]." But how was that to be done? The Virginia and Kentucky Resolutions of 1798, the Kentucky Resolutions of 1799, and the Virginia *Report of 1800* did not say.

Vice President John C. Calhoun did. As he explained in his "Fort Hill Address" and in the "South Carolina Exposition," in case a state legislature believed that a federal policy was unconstitutional and dangerous, it might call for election of a state convention like the one that had ratified the federal Constitution. That convention, political embodiment of the sovereign people according to Madison's Virginia *Report of 1800,* could then vote "yea" or "nay" on the question whether the offending federal policy really was the type against which the state was "in duty bound, to interpose" (as Madison had put it in the Virginia Resolutions), and it could nullify the policy—that is, declare that it would not allow that policy's enforcement within that state's territory.

In 1798–1800, as we have seen, the federal policies that prompted Republicans to enunciate the Principles of 1798 centered on the Alien and Sedition Acts. Madison remained convinced even in his dotage that Republicans' fears of the 1790s had been justified. But why were Carolinians so upset in 1832–1833?

Their problem was the tariff. Carolinians held that when Article I, Section 8, said that Congress would have power to levy imposts (that is, tariffs—taxes on imports), it meant only that it could raise money to fund the government by taxing imports. President Madison had called for Congress to adopt protection as an ongoing policy in the wake of the War of 1812, however, and to a growing extent beginning in 1824, it had been the announced policy of Congress to tax imports in order to protect domestic industries—that is, to raise prices of foreign goods in order to force American consumers to purchase competing domestic products. Revenue tariffs were constitutional, the Carolina Nullifiers said, but protective tariffs were not.

Virginia's political establishment joined in the widespread concern about the equity of protective tariffs.[23] In fact, when Henry Clay first pushed a protective tariff through Congress in 1824, not a single member of the U.S. House from south of the Potomac River voted for it. Still, it passed. In 1828, another, higher tariff—which Southerners called "the Tariff of Abominations"—passed. It was then, with the standard tariff rate at 50 percent, that Southerners grew particularly restless.

Yet they thought that ordinary politics would solve their problem. Calhoun had joined with Thomas Ritchie of the *Richmond Enquirer* and with New York senator Martin Van Buren in creating the Democratic Party to eject President John Quincy Adams from office, and he thought their man's election in 1828 would mean reduction of the tariff.[24] Disappointingly, even though the Democrats came to power in 1829, the tariff was not reduced. In fact, in 1832, it was raised still further.

At that point, the South Carolina legislature invoked Calhoun's theory. A Nullification Convention was elected. It met, and it declared that early in 1833, the tariff would be thwarted by state authority in South Carolina.

Madison met all this with growing unease, not to say panic. Within the South Carolina political establishment—strongly inclined toward secession as it was—Calhoun's position was a moderate one. We can stay in the Union without simply accepting the tariff, Calhoun advised. Outside the Palmetto State, however, it looked horribly radical. As the Marshall Court's decisions had struck Madison with the possibility of collapse of the federal system into an unlimited, "traditional" (that is, constitutionless) government, nullification looked set to yield the breakup of the Union.

Madison did agree with the protective tariff's opponents that such a policy as Clay's was inconsistent with republican government. As early as during the debate over Clay's initial 1824 proposal, he decried the tendency to convert the federal government into "a general supervisor of individual concerns."[25] In fact, he said, if "a certainty of perpetual peace, & still more, a universal freedom of commerce," could be assured, then "Government should never bias individuals in the choice of their occupation."

Since periodic war was a fact of life, Madison continued, government might decide to tax some articles in peacetime so that reduction of the tariff on them in wartime would allow the prices of those goods to remain constant in peace and war. Still, even if he conceded this, he regretted that "the patrons of domestic manufacturers" ignored the principle that "in every doubtful case, Government should forbear to intermeddle." This was especially true, he held, "where one part of the community would be favored at the expense of another." In the context of the 1820s, the suffering section was the South, while those who stood to benefit at the South's expense were the other two great sections: the North and the West.

Two weeks after penning these words, Madison had an opportunity to explain his opposition to the "American system" to that system's author, Henry Clay, himself. Clay had laid out his platform of protective tariffs, federal sponsorship of public works, and a federally chartered bank in a widely disseminated speech, of which he had sent Madison a copy.[26]

Madison told Clay that he admired Clay's eloquence, as ever. Yet, he went on to say, "The Bill, I think loses sight too much of the general principle which leaves to the judgment of individuals the choice of profitable employments for their labor & capital." Clay had said that he would by his legislation move a half-million American men off farms and into factories, and Madison disapproved.

To Madison's mind, market forces had moved people from tobacco production to wheat production, and from wheat production to cotton production. The same motives of personal interest ought to be relied upon to guide people from farming into manufacturing, if the latter became more socially useful. He conceded that there were some exceptions to the general rule, but pointed out that proponents of protection went too far in denying the utility of market signals.

Madison's argument tracked the proposals he had made in his second-term annual messages. He noted three classes of manufactures that government seemed to him justified in supporting with tariff protection: goods necessary in wartime; other items "too indispensable to be subjected to foreign contingencies"; and goods produced by what Adam Smith called "infant industries," which were industries that could be expected, if once established under tariff protection, to become self-sustaining without ongoing tariff protection. This list barely affected the general principle that Clay's notion of protection as a positive good struck Madison as a deplorable idea. Clay can hardly have found this letter encouraging.[27]

So, Madison agreed with the Nullifiers on the desirability, even the wisdom, of promiscuous protection. He disagreed with them on the constitutionality of protection.[28] As Madison noted, "every existing Commercial Nation" had used protection for "the encouraging of particular domestic occupations." Not only that, but he recalled (correctly, as we have seen) that the separate states' inability to employ the power effectively had been one reason for the creation of the federal Constitution. From the first Congress under the Constitution to the present (1827), the power had been exercised under every president. Madison thought that Virginia's recent legislative resolutions made it the only state ever to deny that the federal government had this power.

None of this proved to Madison that the tariff measures then in the air were wise. He denied that they were. However, where a particular reading of the Constitution had been settled for forty years, some overwhelming evidence should be required to show that it was incorrect. Here, he cautioned that abuse of a constitutional power did not make that power unconstitutional. "The abuse," he wrote, "cannot be regarded as a breach of the constitutional compact, till it reaches a degree of oppression, so iniquitous and intolerable as to justify civil war, or disunion pregnant with wars, then to be foreign ones."

In time, South Carolina joined Virginia in pronouncing the protective tariff unconstitutional. Madison professed shock. South Carolina, he insisted, had always been steadfastly devoted to the Union, and he found its new, radical turn surprising.[29] Most painful to Madison was Calhoun's and the Carolinians' loud invocation of his and Jefferson's federal theory.[30] Madison was at great pains to reject the idea that Virginia had ever stood for the South Carolina doctrine.

Thus, for example, in 1829, Madison described the Virginia Resolutions of 1798 as holding "that the States, as parties to the Constitutional compact, had a right and were bound, in extreme cases only, and after a failure of all efforts of redress under the forms of the Constitution, to interpose in their sovereign capacity, for the purpose of arresting the evil of usurpation, and preserving the Constitution and Union."[31] South Carolina, by contrast, "assert[ed] that in a case of not greater magnitude than the degree of inequality in the operation of a tariff in favor of manufactures, she may of herself finally decide, by virtue of her sovereignty, that the Constitution has been violated; and that if not yielded to by the Federal Government, tho' supported by all the other States, she may rightfully resist it and withdraw herself from the Union."

The problem Madison identified in South Carolina's nullification movement was that it seemed apt to make single-state nullification routine. To his mind, the Principles of 1798 were about extremities, what he called "the right to judge *in the last resort*," and not about the day-to-day.[32] To him, the tariff issue just was not important enough to justify a state in taking ultimate measures. If there were no constitutional provision for resolution of day-to-day matters, the U.S. government would not be a government, but "a mere Treaty between independent nations."

Madison's position was *not* that a single state could never conceivably have a right to stand up to the federal government alone. Rather, he insisted that "in all cases not of that extreme character, there is & must be an Arbiter or Umpire in the constitutional authority provided for deciding questions concerning the boundaries of right & power." In such everyday situations, that umpire was the Supreme Court, he concluded, citing Federalist No. 39. (Not coincidentally, Madison had written that essay.) He also claimed elsewhere that the Nullifiers had it wrong in asserting that a state could impede enforcement of federal policy while remaining in the Union.[33]

Madison feared that nullification might end in disunion.[34] (He had of course feared that the Missouri Crisis would lead to disunion as well.) "The happy Union of these States is a wonder," he enthused, "their Constn. a miracle." On the other hand, "The disastrous consequences of disunion [were] obvious to all."[35]

In 1830, Madison had an opportunity to present his concerns directly to one of the Carolina Nullifier chieftains. At the dawn of that year, Senator Robert Y. Hayne debated Senator Daniel Webster of Massachusetts on the nature of the Union, in the process fully developing the Nullifier view. Assuming that Madison would agree with his explanation of what Calhoun and his allies thought of as the Virginia Doctrine, Hayne sent a copy of his speeches to Madison. Madison took this chance to tell Hayne what he had told others: that in everyday matters, the Supreme Court was the arbiter of disputes between the federal government and states.[36]

The Carolinians' argument was that a state's nullification was authoritative unless three-quarters of the states disagreed. In that case, they said, the three-quarters had made an authoritative interpretation, and the nullifying state must choose between submitting to the majority's reading and leaving the Union. Madison pointed out that this effectively allowed minorities to amend the Constitution. In addition, Madison asked why three-quarters was magic; after all, the Constitution had been unanimously ratified, so why not require unanimity among the nonnullifying states? He knew Hayne had no effective answer.

Then again, his assertion that a single state could prevent enforcement of federal policy within its territory only in situations in which that seemed appropriate to him was not exactly calculated to win converts. Madison thought it obvious that protective tariffs, though undesirable when overindulged, were constitutional. He did not think that South Carolina had ground, then, for taking such extreme measures as nullifying.

Madison complained that he came under fire for inconsistency.[37] He had sometimes said that the Supreme Court was the final judge between the states and the federal government, he said, and on others that the states themselves were. Was this inconsistent? His answer was no, because it depended on the context: in ordinary matters, the Supreme Court filled this function, but in extraordinary ones, the states themselves had to interpose. In the same letter, he objected to John Taylor of Caroline's *New Views of the Constitution of the United States,* which said that Madison and Edmund Randolph had pushed in the Philadelphia Convention for a consolidated government.[38] Madison was at pains to disprove this assertion, including by falsely claiming that his favorite idea of 1787—the congressional veto over state laws—had been abandoned by him because of the force of its opponents' arguments.

In general, Madison was only human, in that he wanted to have been consistent even when he had not been. He wanted to have been a Jeffersonian even when at his most nationalist. It is likely that he actually remembered events that way. He had a more difficult time explaining his change regarding congressional power to charter banks between 1791 and 1816. His rationalization—that a long course of allowing such a law to remain in effect established a valid precedent for future laws of the same kind—cannot have been very persuasive even for the friendly audience to whom it was written.

After all, Hamilton's bank had been given a twenty-year charter, and the Congress and president at the time of that charter's expiration had refused to recharter it. What long train of precedents was that?

Madison also spoke out against an erroneous method of interpreting the Constitution. Some had committed the "error" of "ascribing to the *intention* of the *Convention* which formed the Constitution, an undue ascendancy in expounding it." The authoritative source, he said, was not the Philadelphia Convention but the "State Conventions which gave it all the validity & authority it possesses."

Madison's fears concerning the prospect of the Nullifiers' destroying the Union in the end led him to mischaracterize the Principles of '98. "It seems not to have been sufficiently noticed that in the proceedings of Virginia referred to," he wrote, "the *plural* [term] *States* was invariably used in reference to their interpositions; nor is this sense affected by the object of maintaining within their respective limits the authorities rights and liberties appertaining to them, which could certainly be best effectuated for each by co-operating interpositions."[39] He returned to this point repeatedly.[40] This controversy led Madison finally to express an opinion on the subject of secession, or unilateral withdrawal of particular states from the Union. It was permissible only where the other states consented or the Constitution was so abused that the seceding state was morally absolved of its adherence to it.

Madison judged that the risk of secession, and of a breakup of the Union, was increasing.[41] As long as the North and the South had disparate interests, the risk would continue. Madison was happy to note that the General Assembly in 1833 adopted a formal position "that the resolutions of 98-99, gave no support to the nullifying doctrine of South Carolina."[42] Yet, he feared that political manipulators would keep the nullification idea alive as a prelude to secession, and to the creation of a separate southern union. He would carry that fear to his grave.

One of Madison's attractive characteristics in old age was his evenhandedness toward former political foes. He did not make an exception even for the chief of them. So, for example, when President John Quincy Adams forwarded Madison documents in early 1829 seeming to indicate that Alexander Hamilton had once attended a disunionist meeting, Madison was quick to defend his one-time collaborator, later his committed opponent, against this charge.[43] Madison noted that such an assemblage would have obvious reasons to desire Hamilton's cooperation; he added, however, that "obvious considerations oppose[d] a belief that such an invitation would be accepted; and if accepted, the supposition would remain, that his intention might be to dissuade his party & personal friends, from a conspiracy as rash as wicked and as ruinous to the party itself as to the country."

Also admirable in Madison was his refusal to accept more credit than he was due. (Perhaps he thought that he was due enough.) So, for example, he refused to be referred to as *"the* writer of the Constitution of the U. S."[44] People ought to know that "this was not, liked the fabled Goddess of Wisdom, the offspring of a single brain. It ought to be regarded as the work of many heads & many hands."

In his last letter to Jefferson, shortly before his friend's death on July 4, 1826, Madison waxed nostalgic. "You cannot look back to the long period of our private friendship & political harmony," Madison wrote, "with more affecting recollections than I do. If they are a source of pleasure to you, what ought they not to be to me?" In the "weren't we great?" mode that Jefferson so loved, Madison added, " "We cannot be deprived of the happy consciousness of the pure devotion to the public good with which we discharged the trusts committed to us." Then, turning to Jefferson's fondest hope—that he would be remembered well by succeeding generations—Madison added, "I indulge a confidence that sufficient evidence will find its way to another generation, to ensure, after we are gone, whatever of justice may be withheld whilst we are here. The political horizon is already yielding in your case at least, the surest auguries of it."

And then, after a half century, their momentous friendship was gone. Gone, but never forgotten. "Take care of me when dead," Jefferson had begged his younger friend. For another ten years, Madison did.[45]

From the moment when he first saw it in 1776, Jefferson had wanted to reform Virginia's revolutionary state constitution.[46] Madison, one of its authors, had joined his friend in the quest to change it as early as 1784.[47] Finally, in 1829, reformers succeeded in assembling a constitutional convention. Madison agreed to participate.

The Virginia Constitutional Convention of 1829–1830 has been called the last great American constituent assembly. Not only Madison, but fellow former president James Monroe, incumbent chief justice of the Supreme Court John Marshall, Governor William Branch Giles, Representative John Randolph of Roanoke, future president John Tyler, and a host of lesser lights participated.

Reform sentiment centered in what then were the western counties of Virginia, which since the Civil War have been West Virginia. Population had for decades been growing quickly there, but the absence of a regular reapportionment provision from the 1776 constitution meant that they were increasingly underrepresented in the General Assembly over time. Echoing Jefferson's complaints about this situation in *Notes on the State of Virginia*, reformers insisted that whites should count equally in apportioning the General Assembly.[48]

In addition, reformers objected to the 1776 constitution's suffrage qualifications. As in England, the vote was tied to wealth. In Virginia, one had to have a substantial landed estate to be eligible to vote; reformers said that all free white men should have that right.

Madison and Monroe both entered the convention intending to find some middle way between the reformers in western Virginia and the conservative Tidewater and Southside regions in the east. Monroe said that only "contentment" between the two great sections could help Virginia vindicate its "great principles," as republics' record for longevity did not inspire confidence.[49]

Madison spoke only once at the Constitutional Convention, on the topic of the suffrage.[50] He advocated extending it beyond the traditional group, freeholders, to all housekeepers and leaseholders. In other words, instead of allowing only owners of substantial property (freeholders) to vote, Madison would have allowed other economically independent white men to vote as well.

In the notes he wrote in anticipation of staking out his position, Madison explained that improvements in agriculture must over time yield "subsistence for a large surplus of consumers, beyond those having an immediate interest in the soil." That surplus would increase as improvements continued. Their competition for labor in other lines of work would reduce them to lower and lower wages. As they have no great amount of property, their sympathy for the rights of property holders would be less and less.

How could the republic accommodate such people? Excluding them from participation would be dangerous. Therefore, everyone having "a sufficient stake in the public order," particularly "House keepers & Heads of families," should be empowered to participate. Madison would not have given the vote to "every individual bound to obey [the laws]." Although desirable in the abstract, that goal "confessedly requires limitations & modifications." Properly modified, the Virginia Constitution could last another hundred years, he hoped.

In actually delivering his speech, Madison began by noting that "the rights of persons, and the rights of property, are the objects, for the protection of which Government was instituted." They could not be separated. The right to acquire property, he held, was a natural right, and once property was acquired, "a right to protection" became "a social right."

In republics, Madison continued, majorities often overran the rights of minorities. Mere conscience, on which the naïve might have relied, was not enough to protect minorities from this tendency. Neither was individuals' interest in the long-run health of society or "the proverbial maxim, that honesty is the best policy." Rather, what was needed was "the coercive provision belonging to Government and Law." "A minority having right on its side" needed to rely upon a properly structured government to defend it in the last resort.

The minority he had in mind in 1829, Madison continued—the one whose interest had to be guaranteed in revising Virginia's constitution—was the slave-owning minority. If mere numbers governed, then slave owners might "be oppressed by excessive taxation." Slaves themselves "should be considered, as much as possible, in the light of human beings, and not as mere property," on the basis of "justice . . . humanity . . . truth . . . the sympathies of our nature[, and] our character as a people." Madison concluded that he felt the U.S. Constitution's Three-Fifths Clause as a basis of apportionment might work as well in Virginia as in the federal government.

Why would Madison take this position? How could he arrive at the conclusion that slave owners ought to be given bonus representation for their slaves, when the west's reformers were demanding the white basis?

Because quite simply, the convention seemed bound for a crackup. The great danger facing Virginia in 1829 was that the convention would fail to reach any compromise position, and that the Old Dominion would split into two states, East and West Virginia. In highlighting the federal number, Madison could point both to the experience under the U.S. Constitution and to the experience of Georgia, which used the same ratio. Far from insisting on a philosophical argument (as he had repeatedly done in the Philadelphia Convention, despite warnings from John Dickinson and others), Madison in his old age sought a happy medium.

In the end, that was what the convention found. Not the one Madison had recommended, but an extension of the suffrage and a reapportionment that gave the west greater—though not proportionate—weight in the General Assembly. Driven by Jeffersonian reformers and Tidewater aristocrats from left and right, the Old Dominion at last fixed on a Piedmont, Madisonian compromise.

Madison, again, did not envision this solution as permanent. Tidewater nabobs would drive their state further from the west's demands. Within four decades, uncompromising Virginians did indeed split their state in two.

Besides establishing the university and reforming the state constitution, another Jeffersonian ideal that Madison shared was colonization. As Jefferson had explained in his only book, *Notes on the State of Virginia,* he thought that black and white people could never live in harmony in Virginia.[51] Blacks, Jefferson reasoned, hated whites, who gave them new reasons to do so every day; whites, he held, were prejudiced against blacks and were not likely to cease being prejudiced.

Many critics nowadays say that Jefferson was a hypocrite to pronounce that "all men are created equal" while holding slaves. But this implies that he thought this situation should continue. He did not. He believed that blacks were entitled to self-government. For the practical reason just explained, however, he held that blacks could not expect self-government in Virginia. To free them there would result in a genocidal race war.

What to do? Jefferson's solution was to free them and then send them somewhere else: to colonize them. At various points, Jefferson and his friends pursued this idea in connection with Canada, the Midwest, Haiti, Missouri, and—finally—Liberia. It was during the administration of Jefferson and Madison's friend James Monroe that the small West African country of Liberia was founded as a haven for free blacks from the United States. As a result, Liberia's capital even today is called Monrovia.

Establishing such a place did not solve the problem, however. Once freed, how were the blacks to get to Africa? After all, passage by ship cost a pretty sum, and blacks were less well off than the average American.

One answer was the American Colonization Society, of which Madison was long president. That charitable organization, whose chapter in Jefferson's hometown of Charlottesville last met in the 1960s, devoted itself to raising money and political support for the project of sending free blacks from the United States to Liberia.

To us, of course, this idea seems bizarrely racist. Why deport all the blacks—or any of them? Virginians should have just freed their slaves, educated them, and established a decent, biracial society. But our reflexive counsel to the past ignores Jefferson's warning that an attempt to establish a biracial society in Virginia would precipitate a race war, in which one or the other race would be wiped out. Jefferson penned this dire warning in the 1780s. Within a quarter century, the Haitian Revolution had seen all whites in Haiti either expelled or killed. Virginians by and large believed it could happen in Virginia as well.

Where Madison diverged from Jefferson was in accounting for Virginia blacks' evident degradation. Jefferson inferred from the evidence around him that blacks must be congenitally inferior, both in mind and in body. Ever the Enlightenment empiricist, he would not believe in things he did not see. Including accomplished blacks. Passages on blacks' supposed congenital inferiority dot his correspondence and his *Notes*. He says that it is possible that slavery itself accounts for the absence of a black Homer, but then he notes that several ancient slaves achieved renown as men of letters. Polybius is the most obvious example. So, he tentatively concludes that blacks are just slow. He says he would like to be dissuaded, but then, as in the cases of Benjamin Banneker and Phillis Wheatley, pooh-poohs contrary evidence. Surely Wheatley did not really write the poems that have been attributed to her; surely Banneker did not really perform those mathematical calculations himself.[52]

Madison took the opposite tack. Likely the blacks' situation owed to slavery.

Where it was illegal to teach slaves to read, slaves tended to illiteracy, let alone lack of poetic achievement. As we saw in considering the Philadelphia Convention, Madison held American slavery to be far more repressive than its Greek and Roman counterparts; so much for the lack of an African Polybius among America's slaves.

In the 1830s, Madison thought the prospect for large-scale transportation of blacks from the United States to Africa was brightening.[53] Private manumissions (freeing of individual slaves) were becoming and would continue to become more common, he said, and the state governments were moving to facilitate colonization. The chief problem facing the colonization movement had always seemed to him to be in providing a place to which the blacks could go, not to be in securing their manumissions.

Africa seemed the obvious place for them to be sent, Madison said, and the founding of Liberia was thus "peculiarly appropriate." "Many circumstances at the present moment seem to concur," he wrote in 1831, "in brightening the prospects of the Society and cherishing the hope that the time will come when the dreadful calamity which has so long afflicted our Country and filled so many with despair, will be gradually removed, & by means consistent with justice, peace, and the general satisfaction; thus giving to our Country the full enjoyment of the blessings of liberty and to the world the full benefit of its great example."

In the 1780s, Madison had advocated federal reform in order to vindicate republicanism. Here, he worked for colonization in part from the same motive. Slavery blackened America's—and thus republicanism's—good name, and its removal would help the cause. Madison must have calculated that it would add luster to his legacy.

In 1831, Nat Turner's rebellion in Southampton County struck Virginians very close to home. A band of marauding slaves murdered dozens of white people, all but one of them children, women, or elderly, in that remote Southside county. In response, Jefferson's grandson, Thomas Jefferson Randolph, dusted off his grandfather's revolutionary proposal: gradual emancipation.

The only way to avoid recurrence of such calamities, Randolph told his fellow House of Delegates members, was to put slavery on the path to abolition. Jefferson had made the same argument in the 1770s, and scattered other

Virginians had raised the idea since. Now it would have its first serious post-revolutionary hearing.

For a year and more, the House of Delegates—the whole Virginia political class—discussed gradual emancipation. Under a gradual emancipation law, as had been adopted in New York, say, or Connecticut, slaves born after a certain date (commonly the first July 4 after the statute's enactment) became free when they reached adulthood. The reason such statutes were called "*gradual* emancipation acts" is that people already enslaved when they were adopted were never freed by them. All the emancipation was prospective. New York adopted one such act at Governor John Jay's behest in 1799, for example, and yet New York still had slaves in the 1840s.

So the idea was about as moderate as an antislavery measure could be.

Why, then, was the House of Delegates wracked by the idea for over a year? Because of the other questions it raised. First, if the slaves were to be freed, would the owners be compensated? After all, people had the right not to be enslaved, but slave owners had the right to their property. (This idea appealed very strongly to members of the Delegates, who were drawn overwhelmingly from the slave-owning class.) Where would the money come from?

Even if that question could be answered satisfactorily, it left the more difficult one: where would the freedmen live? Jeff Randolph, as Jefferson had called him, had followed his grandfather in proposing a slow end to slavery. Most Virginians followed the third president in believing a biracial society in the Old Dominion was impossible.

Slaves could be sent to Africa. If so, how would the purchase of land for them to live on in Africa be financed? If that question could be resolved, who would pay for their transportation?

A professor at the College of William and Mary, Thomas R. Dew, had a simple answer to all these questions: it was impossible. Virginia could not afford it. It could not compensate slave owners for all their slaves. It could not transport all of them to Africa. It could not buy them all land there. It could not. His pamphlet recounting and criticizing the debates in the House of Delegates struck a body blow to the colonization cause. The House of Delegates gave up on the idea, which never got a serious hearing in Virginia again.

In the wake of this defeat, Colonization Society president James Madison wrote Dew a long letter on the subject of colonization.[54] He began by saying that he was "aware of the impracticability of an immediate or early execution of any plan, that combines deportation, with emancipation; and of the inadmissibility of emancipation without deportation."

Ending slavery would be easy, he said: Virginia could just purchase all the slave girls, and soon there would be no more slaves. The requirement that they be colonized, Madison continued, complicated matters considerably. Not only must land to receive them be acquired, but so must their consent. Then, after their departure, their labor must somehow be replaced.

Madison clearly had given the matter considerable thought. He hoped that not only Africa, but also Caribbean islands might receive American expatriates. Even the inland United States, "sufficiently distant to avoid for an indefinite period, the collisions to be apprehended from the vicinity of people distinguished from each other by physical as well as other characteristics," might be appropriate receptacles. He thought that not only private manumissions but also state appropriations and even congressional designation of proceeds from land sales might help fund the effort.

Interestingly, Madison held that the freedmen's consent must be obtained before they were colonized. Their known aversion to the idea likely would fade as good reports of the first migrants' experience made their way back to the United States, Madison forecast.

Madison said that of course the replacement of the slaves' labor posed the most difficult of the problems associated with his program. Yet, the white population of Virginia was growing, farming would take less labor than planting, and Virginia plantation slavery's slow, inevitable decline in competition with virgin western lands could just as well be avoided.

Madison was no Pollyanna. He knew colonization might well fail. If it did, however, at least its proponents would have tried "the only mode presenting a chance of effecting" what he called "relief from the greatest of our calamities." Perhaps, he conceded, his hopes led him to overestimate the odds of success. He had to try.

Of great interest to Madison was the fate of his many slaves. In his will, he said of them, "I give and bequeath my ownership in the negroes and people of colour held by me to my dear wife, but it is my desire that none of them should be sold without his or her consent or in case of their misbehaviour; except that infant children may be sold with their parent who consents for them to be sold with him or her, and who consents to be sold."[55] The portion beginning with "but" was of no legal effect. Dolley Madison would be free to comply with it or not.

Madison's friend and admirer Edward Coles believed that what lay behind this confused statement of Madison's desires was an agreement with Dolley.[56] According to the famous former governor of Illinois, Madison and Dolley had agreed that Dolley would free Madison's slaves upon Dolley's death. Madison had expressed his doubts that the prejudice whites held toward blacks could ever be overcome, but he had decided that freedom should be his slaves' lot just the same. He therefore had joined Coles in concluding that they should make their way to Liberia—the destination of participants in the American Colonization Society's project.

Coles participated in the House of Delegates debate on colonization in 1831–1832. He lamented the possibility of freeing slaves in Virginia without colonizing them. Madison's nearly one hundred slaves would be difficult to colonize, especially as they included an uncommon percentage of very old ones.

Why had Madison not freed his slaves in his will? Because he wanted his wife to enjoy their service for the balance of her life. George Washington, similarly motivated, famously had provided in his will that his slaves would be free at Martha's death. What the father of his country had neglected to notice was that such a provision gave the people preparing Martha's meals, giving her water, tending her house, etc., every incentive to desire her death. She had to rid herself of the slaves right away. Other members of the Virginia elite, then, avoided providing for their slaves' freedom at their wives' deaths.

That is why Madison had left his to Dolley. According to Coles, Dolley had confirmed this story to Henry Clay, the prominent statesman. Besides that, Madison himself had told the lawyer who drew up Madison's will that "Mrs. Madison knew his wishes & views and would carry them into effect at her death." Another woman close to the Madisons confirmed for Coles that those close to Madison knew of this instruction. It was assumed to be included in "a sealed paper" seen by many close to Madison at the time of his death.

Dolley Madison began to auction off old slaves immediately after James Madison's death. She did not obey the convoluted injunctions in Madison's will about sales of children, etc. She also never freed his slaves.

An explanation of Mrs. Madison's behavior must center on the disappointment of James's forecast concerning the value of his estate. He believed that his papers would yield his beloved Dolley $100,000—in those days, a fortune.[57] It was on that basis that he allocated $12,000 of bequests to various individuals and causes.

Madison had devoted considerable effort in the last years of his life to the task of preparing his papers for publication. Among them were extensive records of proceedings in the Confederation Congress, an extremely voluminous and historically invaluable correspondence, and, most significantly of all, the most complete record of the Philadelphia Convention. Madison hoped and expected Dolley to derive a considerable sum from these documents.

She would have had to if she were to continue to live in the fashion to which she had become accustomed: as the mistress of a substantial plantation and mother of a wastrel son. Yet, it was not to be. Montpelier had long since ceased to produce adequate profit for that purpose, and the secular economic downturn through which Virginia was suffering promised no relief. More to the point, the publishing industry was in sad shape when various of Dolley's personal and political friends tried to sell Madison's papers for her as well.

Ultimately, then, she had to make do with $30,000—a magnificent sum in those days, but not a princely one. Even that amount could only be obtained by having various of the Madisons' political friends put the American people on the hook for that amount, and even then only after John C. Calhoun strenuously noted the inconsistency of a federal purchase of Madison's papers, on the one hand, with the late president's positions concerning the extent of congressional powers in the debate over Hamilton's Bank Bill, the Virginia Resolutions, the *Report of 1800,* and the Bonus Bill Veto Message, on the other.[58]

Sadly, these factors, plus the profligacy of her only son, drove Dolley Madison from Montpelier. In that development, Madison's hopes were once again disappointed.

Several months prior to his death, a weak and sickly Madison dictated "Advice to My Country."[59] "The advice dearest to my heart," he began, "and dearest in my convictions is that the Union of the States be cherished and perpetuated. Let the open enemy to it be regarded as a Pandora with her box opened; and the disguised one, as the serpent creeping with his deadly wiles into Paradise." In 1817, with his Bonus Bill Veto Message, Madison had had his constitutional valedictory; here, he hoped that his passing would prompt his fellow citizens to rededicate themselves to America.

His death finally came on June 28, 1836.[60] The slave who had shaved him every day for sixteen years shaved him as usual, a slave who had attended him for nearly seventy years brought his breakfast, and his niece asked what was troubling him. "Nothing more than a change of *mind,* my dear," he replied. As the niece recounted, "his head instantly dropped, and he ceased breathing as quietly as the snuff of a candle goes out."

Madison was buried on his ancestral estate, Montpelier. His four pallbearers included his neighbors, former governor James Barbour and Supreme Court justice Philip P. Barbour; there were nearly a hundred slaves in the funeral party. The site of his grave lies off the beaten path. One does not arrive at it by taking the main road up to the plantation house the president inherited from his father. A visitor who knows where to go, however, is free to take a look.

One finds at Madison's grave that here, as in so much else, he differed markedly from his great friend who now lies buried twenty miles away. There is no stone inscribed with Madison's preferred titles from among the long list he had earned, including Co-Author of the Constitution, Author of the Bill of Rights, Co-Author of *The Federalist,* Co-Author of the Virginia Declaration of Rights, Founder of the Republican Party, Author of the Virginia Resolutions of 1798 and *Report of 1800,* Rector of the University of Virginia, President of the American Colonization Society, and Sponsor of the Virginia Statute for Religious Freedom—not to mention all the political offices he held, mostly to great effect.

James Madison prescribed no monument at all.

For decades, his grave lay unadorned among those of some of his relatives. In the end, it was finally marked by a monument bearing the name "Madison" and the dates of his birth and death.

That is all.

Soft-spoken in life, Madison remained unassuming in death.

His legacy must speak for itself.

Notes

Chapter One *From Subject to Citizens, 1751–76*

1 William T. Hutchinson et al., eds., "Record of Birth and Baptism of James Madison, Jr.," *The Papers of James Madison: Congressional Series* (hereafter, *PJMC*) (Chicago: University of Chicago Press, 1962–1991), 1:3. Also see n. 1.

2 *PJMC*, 1:43, n. 1.

3 Douglas Adair, ed., "James Madison's Autobiography," *William & Mary Quarterly* 2 (1945), 191–209.

4 For Witherspoon's philosophy and his presidency of Princeton, Jeffry H. Morrison, *John Witherspoon and the Founding of the American Republic* (Notre Dame, IN: University of Notre Dame Press, 2005), 113–28, 45–69.

5 Ibid., 58.

6 Ibid., 152, nn. 76–77.

7 "Collegiate Doggerel," *PJMC*, 1:61–65.

8 *PJMC*, 1:66, n. 1.

9 "Notes on Salkeld," *PJMC*, 1:70–71.

10 For Bradford's biography, see *PJMC*, 1:73, n. 1.

11 JM to William Bradford, November 9, 1772, *PJMC*, 1:74–76.

12 William Bradford to JM, March 1, 1773, *PJMC*, 1:79–81.

13 JM to William Bradford, September 25, 1773, *PJMC*, 1:95–97.

14 JM to William Bradford, December 1, 1773, *PJMC*, 1:100–01.

15 William Bradford to JM, December 25, 1773, *PJMC*, 1:102–03.

16 JM to William Bradford, January 24, 1774, *PJMC*, 1:104–06.

17 *PJMC*, 1:109, n. 1.

18 JM to William Bradford, April 1, 1774, *PJMC*, 1:111–13.

19 As Madison feared, the 1774 session did not grant dissenters any relief. *PJMC*, 1:114, n. 3.

20 JM to William Bradford, July 1, 1774, *PJMC*, 1:114–16; JM to William Bradford, August 23, 1774, *PJMC*, 1:120–22.

21 William Bradford to JM, October 17, 1774, *PJMC*, 1:125–27.

22 JM to William Bradford, November 26, 1774, *PJMC*, 1:129–30.

23 JM to William Bradford, May 9, 1775, *PJMC*, 1:144–45.

24 Editors' Note and address, "Address to Captain Patrick Henry and the Gentlemen Independents of Hanover," May 9, 1775, *PJMC*, 1:146–47. I accept William Cabell Rives's claim that he took these resolutions from a copy in Madison's hand. For Rives and Madison, see Drew McCoy, *The Last of the Fathers: James Madison and the Republican Legacy* (New York: Cambridge University Press, 1989).

25 "Commission as Colonel of Orange County Militia," October 2, 1775, *PJMC*, 1:163. The information in the balance of this paragraph is found at 1:164, n. 1, and in Adair, ed., "James Madison's Autobiography."

26 On November 8, 1775, Madison was also elected a trustee of Hampden-Sydney Academy, which in 1783 would become Hampden-Sydney College. His only known effort in this regard was in helping to run a lottery in 1777. *PJMC*, 1:211, n. 1.

27 "Certificate of Election of James Madison, Jr., and William Moore," April 25, 1776.

28 Kevin R. C. Gutzman, *Virginia's American Revolution: From Dominion to Republic, 1776–1840* (Lanham, MD: Lexington Books, 2007), 24. The quotation is from Robert A. Rutland, *George Mason: Reluctant Statesman* (Baton Rouge: Louisiana State University Press, 1961), 49.

29 Hugh Blair Grigsby, *The Virginia Convention of 1776* (1855; reprinted New York: Da Capo Press, 1969).

30 JM to William Bradford, c. May 21, 1776, *PJMC*, 1:180.

31 See William Bradford, "Memorandum Book," June 3, 1776, *PJMC*, 1:184, in which Bradford noted that JM had requested that Bradford provide him information concerning both Pennsylvania and Connecticut. As we shall see, Madison's characteristic mode of preparation was to assemble relevant materials from as many jurisdictions as possible, foreign and domestic, contemporary and historic.

32 The declaration as ultimately adopted is at "Virginia Declaration of Rights," The Avalon Project, http://avalon.law.yale.edu/18th_century/virginia.asp (retrieved on August 1, 2010).

33 Editors' Note, "Independence and Constitution of Virginia," 1827?, *PJMC*, 1:175–78, at 176.

34 Editors' Note, "Committee's Proposed Article on Religion," *PJMC*, 1:173.

35 "Committee's Proposed Article on Religion," May 27–28, 1776, *PJMC*, 1:173.

36 "Madison's Amendments to the Declaration of Rights," "B," May 29–June 12, 1776, *PJMC*, 1:174; Virginia Declaration of Rights, http://avalon.law.yale.edu/ 18th_century/virginia.asp (retrieved on August 1, 2010).

37 This account is based on Gutzman, *Virginia's American Revolution*, 30–31.

Chapter Two Winning the Revolution, 1776–87

1 Madison's recollection and the House of Delegates petition are found at "Defeated for Election to Virginia House of Delegates," *PJMC*, 1:192–93, including n. 1.

2 The classic account is Charles S. Sydnor, *Gentlemen Freeholders: Political Practices in Washington's Virginia* (Chapel Hill: University of North Carolina Press, 1952).

3 *PJMC*, 1:211, n. 1.

4 Editors' Note, "Session of Virginia Council of State," *PJMC*, 1:214–16. While Madison was on the council, his Orange County neighbors again elected him to the House of Delegates. He could not serve, as the 1776 constitution explicitly banned simultaneously holding office in plural branches. "Election to Virginia House of Delegates Voided," from *Journal of the House of Delegates*, May 27, 1778, *PJMC*, 1:242.

5 See the several council-related documents in *PJMC*, 1.

6 Editors' Note, "Session of Virginia Council of State," *PJMC*, 1:214–16, states, "In no instance, insofar as any contemporary manuscript is concerned, can JM's service as a councilor be isolated from that of his fellow members."

7 "Credentials as a Delegate to Continental Congress," December 14, 1779," *PJMC*, 1:318, n. 1.

8 Articles of Confederation, Article V, Section 2, Clause 2, http://avalon.law.yale .edu/18th_century/artconf.asp (accessed on August 4, 2010).

9 JM to Thomas Jefferson, March 27, 1780, *PJMC*, 2:5–7.

10 Madison actually used the word "starving" in his next letter to Governor Jefferson. JM to Thomas Jefferson, May 6, 1780, *PJMC*, 2:19–20.

11 JM to John Page [?], May 8, 1780, *PJMC*, 2:21–22.

12 JM to Thomas Jefferson, June 2, 1780, *PJMC*, 2:37–38.

13 JM to Thomas Jefferson, June 23, 1780, *PJMC*, 2:40–41.

14 Woody Holton, *Forced Founders: Indians, Debtors, Slaves and the Making of the American Revolution in Virginia* (Chapel Hill: University of North Carolina Press, 1999).

15 George Mason to JM, August 2, 1780, *PJMC*, 2:52–54 and n. 3.

16   This and the following two paragraphs rely in part on Editors' Note, "Motion Regarding the Western Lands," *PJMC*, 2:72–77.

17   In JM to Edmund Pendleton, September 12, 1780, *PJMC*, 2:81–82, Madison stated that invigorating the government was the land proposal's aim.

18   JM to Joseph Jones, September 19, 1780, *PJMC*, 2:89–90.

19   Congress ultimately rejected the provision concerning Indian land grants. Madison's Virginia colleagues voted against him, which put Virginia in the 6-to-4 majority against. JM to Joseph Jones, October 17, 1780, *PJMC*, 2:136–37, and n. 2.

20   *PJMC*, 2:92, n. 8. The classic treatment of boardinghouse culture among politicians in the early republic is James S. Young, *The Washington Community, 1800–1828* (New York: Columbia University Press, 1986).

21   *PJMC*, 2:196, n. 3. Here and in subsequent notes, quoted materials are presented as written and without the notification "sic."

22   JM to Edmund Pendleton, September 19, 1780, *PJMC*, 2:93, P.S. and n. 2.

23   "Draft of Letter to John Jay, Explaining His Instructions," October 17, 1780, *PJMC*, 2:127–35. Although they were the product of a committee, Madison later confided that these instructions had been perfectly satisfactory to Madison. JM to Joseph Jones, November 25, 1780, *PJMC*, 2:202–04.

24   See Gutzman, *Virginia's American Revolution*, chapter 1, and, particularly, Kevin R. C. Gutzman, "Jefferson's Draft Declaration of Independence, Richard Bland, and the Revolutionary Legacy: Giving Credit Where Credit Is Due," *Journal of the Historical Society* 1 (2001): 137–154.

25   William Jay, *The Life of John Jay: With Selections from His Correspondence and Miscellaneous Papers* (1833; reprinted Bridgewater, Virginia: American Foundation Publications, 2000).

26   JM to Joseph Jones, October 24, 1780, *PJMC*, 2:144–47.

27   JM to Joseph Jones, October 24, 1780, *PJMC*, 2:144–47, n. 6.

28   JM to Edmund Pendleton, November 7, 1780, *PJMC*, 2:165–66.

29   Joseph Jones to JM, November 18, 1780, *PJMC*, 2:182–84.

30   The ultimate version of the legislation gave enlistees land plus a choice between money and a slave. The money for it was provided by a property tax, not by a tax directly on large slave owners. *PJMC*, 2:185, n. 6.

31   JM to Joseph Jones, November 28, 1780, *PJMC*, 2:209–10.

32   *PJMC*, 2:210, n. 1. Madison at the end of his life designated this passage for publication in the first edition of his select published papers.

33   Joseph Jones to JM, December 2, 1780, *PJMC*, 2:218–20.

34   Joseph Jones to JM, December 8, 1780, *PJMC*, 2:232–33.

35   JM to Joseph Jones, November 21, 1780, *PJMC*, 2:190–92.

36   JM to Joseph Jones, November 25, 1780, *PJMC*, 2:202–04.

37   For Jay's communication to Congress, *PJMC*, 2:205, n. 8.

38   JM to Joseph Jones, December 5, 1780, *PJMC*, 2:223–25.

39   Virginia Delegates in Congress to Thomas Jefferson, December 13, 1780, *PJMC*, 2:241–42.

40   "Instruction from Virginia General Assembly to Its Delegates in Congress," January 2, 1781, *PJMC*, 2:273.

41   JM to Thomas Jefferson, January 9, 1781, *PJMC*, 2:279–80.

42   JM to Edmund Pendleton, January 16, 1781, *PJMC*, 2:286–87. Soon enough, New Jersey troops did behave similarly. Virginia Delegates in Congress to Thomas Jefferson, January 30, 1781, *PJMC*, 2:300.

43   *PJMC*, 2:300–01, nn. 2 and 4.

44   *PJMC*, 3:19, n. 1.

45   "Proposed Amendment of Articles of Confederation," March 12, 1781, *PJMC*, 3:17–18 and 3:20, n. 11.

46   *PJMC*, 3:47, n. 6.

47   Jefferson's performance as governor came under legislative investigation at the end of his second and final one-year term. He was unanimously exonerated of any wrong-doing. *PJMC*, 3:338, n. 3.

48   JM to Thomas Jefferson, April 3, 1781, *PJMC*, 3:45–47.

49   JM to Thomas Jefferson, April 16, 1781, *PJMC*, 3:71–72.

50   JM to Edmund Randolph, June 11, 1782, *PJMC*, 4:333–34.

51   JM to Edmund Randolph, September 30, 1782, *PJMC*, 5:170–71. Mrs. Jefferson died on September 6, 1782.

52   Two months later, Madison moved in Congress to reappoint Jefferson to the commission to negotiate a peace. "Motion to Renew Thomas Jefferson's Appointment as Peace Commissioner," November 12, 1782, *PJMC*, 5:268. He gleefully recorded in his "Notes on Debates" that his motion "was agreed to unanimously and without a single adverse remark." December 12, 1782, *PJMC*, 5:268–69.

53   Andrew Burstein, *The Inner Jefferson: Portrait of a Grieving Optimist* (Charlottesville: University Press of Virginia, 1995).

54   "Motion on Impressment of Supplies," May 18, 1781, *PJMC*, 3:124.

55   Ibid., n. 2.

56   JM to Edmund Randolph, July 28, 1783, *PJMC*, 7:256–57.

57   Motion *in re* Jurisdiction of Congress over Permanent Site, September 22, 1783, *PJMC*, 7:357; TJ to Thomas Jefferson, September 20, 1783, *PJMC*, 7:352–54, at 354.

58   "Report on Retaliation against British," October 1, 1781, *PJMC*, 3:271–72.

59   JM to Edmund Pendleton, September 18, 1781, *PJMC*, 3:261–62.

60   *PJMC*, 3:273, n. 7.

61   Thomas Nelson to Virginia Delegates, October 5, 1781, *PJMC*, 3:275–76.

62   Edmund Pendleton to JM, October 8, 1781, *PJMC*, 3:277–79.

63   Virginia Delegates to Thomas Nelson, October 9, 1781, *PJMC*, 3:281–82, as well as, nn. 5, 6, and 7. Although in Madison's hand, this document's wording seems that of a group effort.

64   Virginia Delegates to Thomas Nelson, October 16, 1781, *PJMC*, 3:286–88. This document was in Madison's hand.

65   JM to Thomas Jefferson, November 18, 1781, *PJMC*, 3:307–08.

66   JM to Edmund Pendleton, October 16, 1781, *PJMC*, 3:289–90.

67   Virginia Delegates to Benjamin Harrison, January 8, 1782, *PJMC*, 3:18–19.

68   The following account relies on *PJMC*, 3:20–22, n. 7.

69   JM to Edmund Pendleton, January 8, 1782, *PJMC*, 3:22–23.

70   For Morris's program, see Jack N. Rakove, *The Beginnings of National Politics: An Interpretive History of the Continental Congress* (Baltimore: Johns Hopkins University Press, 1979), 297–329.

71   Virginia Delegates to Benjamin Harrison, February 15, 1782, *PJMC*, 4:65–66.

72   *PJMC*, 4:105, n. 7.

73   Virginia Delegates to Benjamin Harrison, May 14, 1782, *PJMC*, 4:235–38.

74   Jonathan R. Dull, *A Diplomatic History of the American Revolution* (New Haven, CT: Yale University Press, 1987).

75   Among numerous other documents reflecting this development, see JM to Edmund Randolph, August 13, 1782, *PJMC*, 5:49–50.

76   For Madison as advocate of adherence to the French alliance, see "Comments on Instructions to Peace Commissioners," August 2, 1782, *PJMC*, 5:15 and "Comments on Instructions to Peace Commissioners," August 15, 1782, JM to Edmund Randolph, September 24, 1782, *PJMC*, 5:158–61; for anti-French feeling, see JM to Edmund Randolph, August 5, 1782, *PJMC*, 5:20–21.

77   "Motion on Slaves Taken by the British," September 10, 1782, *PJMC*, 5:111–12. Madison's motion followed hard upon the heels of a letter from Governor Harrison to the Virginia congressmen asking that something be done about the issue of seized slaves. Benjamin Harrison to Virginia Delegates, August 30, 1782, *PJMC*, 5:90. Harrison relayed a Virginian's complaint that the approach of peace had led Britons to step up the theft of slaves, supposedly for sale in the West Indies. Harrison asked whether something might not be done about this development. Seemingly a pro-slavery measure, then, Madison's motion can be understood in a different light: being taken away from one master to be sold to another was among the worst fates a slave could suffer, as it meant permanent separation from friends and loved ones.

78   For Jay's master stroke, see Richard Morris, *The Peacemakers: The Great Powers and American Independence* (New York: Harper and Row, 1965).

79 "Motion to Inform States of Financial Crisis," May 20, 1782, *PJMC*, 4:254–55, and n. 3.

80 "Report on Mission to Inform States of Financial Crisis," May 22, 1782, *PJMC*, 4:269–70.

81 This issue dominated Madison's correspondence through the balance of his career in the Confederation Congress. See *PJMC*, 4 and 5 passim.

82 "Notes on Debates," December 6, 1782, *PJMC*, 5:371–74, at 373.

83 JM to Edmund Randolph, July 2, 1782, *PJMC*, 4:386–87; *PJMC*, 5:333, n. 32; Edmund Pendleton to JM, December 9, 1782, *PJMC*, 5:382–84, text at n. 12 and text of n. 12.

84 The protest is Virginia Delegates to Benjamin Harrison, December 31, 1782, *PJMC*, 5:477–78.

85 Benjamin Harrison to Virginia Delegates, November 8, 1782, *PJMC*, 5:257–58.

86 JM to Edmund Randolph, September 24, 1782, *PJMC*, 5:158–61. Rumors that the army would turn its weapons upon Congress circulated among prominent politicians in 1783. JM to Edmund Randolph, February 13, 1783, *PJMC*, 6:232–33.

87 Congress received petitions from army officers in 1783 and thereafter, and Madison forlornly advocated making good on the United States' pledges to them. *PJMC*, 6 passim. Yet, Virginia's refusal to support lodging a tariff power in Congress left Madison without a firm leg to stand on in advocating the soldiers' cause, as he lamented. JM to Edmund Randolph, January 22, 1783, *PJMC*, 6:55–56. For the difficulties Washington encountered, see Notes on Debates, March 17, 1783, *PJMC*, 6:348, and nn. 1 and 2 at 349.

88 Benjamin Harrison to JM, November 30, 1782, *PJMC*, 5:340–41 is one of several documents bearing out this point. For a recent study supporting the state-level figures' impression, see Keith L. Dougherty, *Collective Action Under the Articles of Confederation* (New York: Cambridge University Press, 2000).

89 "Notes on Debates," November 2, 1782, *PJMC*, 5:234–35. Madison took notes through the remainder of his congressional service.

90 Notes on Debates, June 21, 1783, *PJMC*, 7:176–78.

91 Notes on Debates, February 13, 1783, *PJMC*, 6:229–30, at 230 for this and the first quotation in the following sentence.

92 For the second quotation in this sentence, see JM to Edmund Randolph, February 13, 1783, *PJMC*, 6:232–33.

93 Introduction, *PJMC*, 6:xv.

94 Notes on Debates, April 10, 1783, *PJMC*, 6:445–46.

95 Notes on Debates, April 15, 1783, *PJMC*, 6:462.

96 Notes on Debates, January 28, 1783, *PJMC*, 6:141–49, at 143–44.

97   Notes on Debates, February 21, 1783, *PJMC*, 6:270–74, quotations at 270–71.

98   Virginia Delegates to Benjamin Harrison, April 10, 1783, *PJMC*, 6:446–48.

99   Instructions to Virginia Delegates *in re* Permanent Site for Congress, June 28, 1783, *PJMC*, 7:202–03.

100 Thomas Jefferson to JM, April 14, 1783, *PJMC*, 6:459; JM to Thomas Jefferson, April 22, 1783, *PJMC*, 6:481–82.

101 Thomas Jefferson to JM, May 7, 1783, *PJMC*, 7:23–25.

102 For this and the following sentence, *PJMC*, 7:27, n. 16; JM to Edmund Randolph, July 28, 1783, *PJMC*, 7:256–57, at 257; JM to Thomas Jefferson, August 11, 1783, and nn. 3, 4, and 5.

103 Thomas Jefferson to JM, August 31, 1783, *PJMC*, 7:298–99.

104 This last sentence relies on JM to Edmund Randolph, June 24, 1783, *PJMC*, 7:191–92, insofar as the soldiers' demands, and on Madison's correspondence as a member of Congress generally, in relation to congressional powerlessness.

105 Notes on Debates, June 21, 1783, *PJMC*, 7:176–78. As the editors of Madison's papers explain in the Editorial Note at 176, although headed "June 21, 1783," this entry cannot have been completed prior to June 26.

106 *PJMC*, 7:179–90, nn. 4, 8.

107 TJ to James Madison, Sr., August 30, 1783, *PJMC*, 7:294.

108 JM to Edmund Randolph, August 30, 1783, *PJMC*, 7:295–96.

109 JM to Edmund Randolph, August 18, 1783, *PJMC*, 7:281–82.

110 JM to James Madison, Sr., September 8, 1783, *PJMC*, 7:304.

111 Edmund Pendleton to JM, October 20, 1783, *PJMC*, 7:385.

112 JM to Edmund Randolph, July 26, 1785, *PJMC*, 8:327–28.

113 JM to Thomas Jefferson, February 11, 1784, *PJMC*, 7:418–19. Jefferson predicted, on the basis of another state's experience, that the entire package would never be adopted. Thomas Jefferson to JM, April 25, 1784, *PJMC*, 8:23–26, at 25.

114 Patrick Henry to JM, April 17, 1784, *PJMC*, 8:18.

115 Editorial Note, *PJMC*, 8:29.

116 Edmund Randolph to Thomas Jefferson, *PJMC*, 8:35, n. 1.

117 Editorial Note, "The General Assembly Session of May 1784," *PJMC*, 8:35–38, at 37.

118 "Resolution on the Revision of the Virginia Statutes," May 29, 1784, *PJMC*, 8:48–49.

119 "Resolutions on Private Debts Owed to British Merchants," June 7, 1784, and c. June 22–23, 1784, and June 23, 1784, *PJMC*, 8:60–63.

120 "Resolutions Appointing Virginia Members of a Potomac River Commission," June 28, 1784, *PJMC*, 8:89.

121 *Ibid.*, n. 1.

122   Edmund Randolph to JM, July 17, 1785, *PJMC*, 8:324–25, and n. 1.

123   JM to Thomas Jefferson, July 3, 1784, *PJMC*, 8:92–95.

124   JM to James Madison, Sr., January 6, 1785, *PJMC*, 8:216–17.

125   For Pendleton, Editorial Note, "Madison's Notes for Debates on the General Assessment Bill," *PJMC*, 8:195–97 (citing Edmund Pendleton to Richard Henry Lee, February 28, 1785).

126   JM to James Monroe, November 27, 1784, *PJMC*, 8:156–58, at 157.

127   JM to James Monroe, November 14, 1784, *PJMC*, 8:136–37.

128   Richard Henry Lee to JM, November 26, 1784, *PJMC*, 8:149–51.

129   "Madison's Notes for Debates on the General Assessment Bill," December 23–24, 1784, *PJMC*, 8:197–99.

130   Data in this paragraph come from JM to James Monroe, December 24, 1784, *PJMC*, 8:199–200, and n. 3, and from JM to Thomas Jefferson, January 9, 1785, *PJMC*, 8:222–32, at 229.

131   JM to James Monroe, April 12, 1785, *PJMC*, 8:260–61.

132   George Nicholas to JM, April 22, 1785, *PJMC*, 8:264–65.

133   JM to James Monroe, May 29, 1785, *PJMC*, 8:285–86.

134   JM to Thomas Jefferson, April 27, 1785, *PJMC*, 8:265–70.

135   "Memorial and Remonstrance Against Religious Assessments," Editorial Note, *PJMC*, 8:295–98.

136   "Memorial and Remonstrance Against Religious Assessments," c. June 20, 1785, *PJMC*, 8:298–304.

137   JM to Thomas Jefferson, August 20, 1785, *PJMC*, 8:344–46, at 345.

138   This account is based on Editorial Note, "Bill for a Revised State Code of Laws," *PJMC*, 8:391–94. Further detail on Madison's strategy can be derived from JM to James Monroe, December 9, 1785, *PJMC*, 8:436–37.

139   "Act for Establishing Religious Freedom," October 31, 1785, *PJMC*, 8:399–401.

140   *PJMC*, 8:401–02, nn. 1 and 2.

141   JM to Thomas Jefferson, January 22, 1786, *PJMC*, 8:472–81, at 474.

142   *PJMC*, 8:405, n. 4.

143   JM to James Monroe, August 7, 1785, *PJMC*, 8:333–36. No sooner had Madison arrived at this conclusion than Richard Henry Lee, one of the twin titans of the General Assembly, confided his own conception that giving Congress this power would leave the five southern states at the mercy of the other eight states, whose interest would be to exploit the South. Lee thought it preferable to rely on the thirteen states to adopt agreed trade policy one by one. Richard Henry Lee to JM, August 11, 1785, *PJMC*, 8:339–40.

Chapter Three   *The Philadelphia Convention, 1787*

1   Biographical material in this paragraph comes from "William Leigh Pierce," in M.
    E. Bradford, *Founding Fathers: Brief Lives of the Framers of the United States Con-
    stitution* 2nd ed. (Lawrence, KS: University Press of Kansas, 1994), 208–09.

2   William Pierce's Madison sketch is found among his "Character Sketches of Del-
    egates to the Federal Convention," which are reprinted in Max Farrand, ed., *The
    Records of the Federal Convention of 1787* (hereafter *RFC*) (New Haven, CT: Yale
    University Press, 1937), 3:87–97. The Madison sketch is at 94–95.

3   William Lee Miller, *The Business of May Next: James Madison and the Founding*
    (Charlottesville: University Press of Virginia, 1993).

4   James Madison, "Notes on Ancient & Modern Confederacies," April–June? 1786,
    PJMC, 9:4–22.

5   "Vices of the Political System of the United States," *PJMC*, 9:348–57.

6   For a contrasting evaluation of the states' compliance with federal measures during
    the Revolutionary War, see Keith L. Dougherty, *Collective Action Under the Articles
    of Confederation* (New York: Cambridge University Press, 2003).

7   This paragraph and the next depend in large part on Editors' Note, "The Annapolis
    Convention September 1786," *PJMC*, 9:115–19, at 116.

8   JM to Ambrose Madison, September 8, 1786, *PJMC*, 9:120–21.

9   JM to James Monroe, September 11, 1786, *PJMC*, 9:121–22.

10 Alexander Hamilton, "Annapolis Convention. Address of the Annapolis Conven-
    tion," *The Papers of Alexander Hamilton*, eds. Harold Syrett et al. (New York:
    Columbia University Press, 1962), 3:686–90. The note adduces two letters writ-
    ten by Madison many years later as the evidence that the address was written by
    Hamilton and an 1876 Hamilton biography as the source for the claim that it was
    modified to mollify Edmund Randolph.

11 Madison's correspondence and notes of congressional debates concerning the so-
    called Jay-Gardoquì negotiation run through *PJMC* 9.

12 Accounts of the Jay mission can be found in Walter Stahr, *John Jay: Founding
    Father* (New York: Hambledon & London, 2006); and at James Monroe to JM,
    May 31, 1786, *PJMC*, 9:68–71, n. 5.

13 Madison too believed that access to the Mississippi was a natural right. See JM to
    James Monroe, June 21, 1786, *PJMC* 9:82–83.

14 See James Monroe to JM, August 14, 1786, *PJMC*, 9:104; James Monroe to JM,
    August 30, 1786, *PJMC*, 9:109; James Monroe to JM, September 1, 1786, *PJMC*,
    9:111–12; James Monroe to JM, September 3, 1786, *PJMC*, 9:112–114; James
    Monroe to JM, September 12, 1786, *PJMC*, 9:122–23; James Monroe to JM, Sep-
    tember 29, 1786, *PJMC*, 9:134–35.

15 JM to James Monroe, October 5, 1786, *PJMC*, 9:140–42.

16 JM to James Monroe, October 30, 1786, *PJMC*, 9:146.

17 Stuart Leibiger, *Founding Friendship: George Washington, James Madison, and the Creation of the American Republic* (Charlottesville: University Press of Virginia, 1999).

18 JM to George Washington, November 1, 1786, *PJMC*, 9:155–56.

19 George Washington to JM, November 5, 1786, *PJMC*, 9:161–62.

20 The parliamentary information in this paragraph and the next is at "Bill for Providing Delegates to the Convention of 1787," *PJMC*, 9:163–64, n. 1.

21 JM to George Washington, November 6, 1786, *PJMC*, 9:166–67.

22 George Washington to JM, November 18, 1786, *PJMC*, 9:170–71.

23 "Resolutions Reaffirming American Rights to Navigate the Mississippi," *PJMC*, 9:182–83, n. 1.

24 Madison and his colleagues may have been unaware that although the Treaty of Paris concluded with Britain at the end of the American Revolution resolved the Mississippi issue in the Americans' favor insofar as Britain was concerned, the treaty between Britain and Spain at the war's end omitted the issue entirely. In other words, Spain had no reason to think itself bound by treaty obligation to respect an American right of access.

25 JM to Edmund Pendleton, November 30, 1786, *PJMC*, 9:185–87.

26 JM to James Monroe, *PJMC*, 9:185.

27 "Resolutions Reaffirming American Rights to Navigate the Mississippi," *PJMC*, 9:182–83, n. 1. For the Senate vote, see JM to James Madison, Sr., December 12, 1786, *PJMC*, 9:205–06.

28 *PJMC*, 9:187.

29 Edmund Randolph to JM, *PJMC*, 9:198 and n. 2.

30 Edmund Pendleton to JM, December 9, 1786, *PJMC*, 9:201–04; Thomas Jefferson to JM, December 16, 1786, *PJMC*, 9:210–13.

31 George Washington to JM, December 16, 1786, *PJMC*, 9:215–17.

32 *Ibid.*, n. 1.

33 JM to George Washington, December 24, 1786, *PJMC*, 9:224–25.

34 Ibid., n. 2.

35 Thomas Jefferson to JM, *PJMC*, 9:247–52.

36 Ibid., n. 1.

37 The following account of Madison's service in Congress relies upon Editors' Note, "Madison in Congress February–May 1787," *PJMC*, 9:261–66.

38 JM to Edmund Randolph, *PJMC*, 9:271–73.

39 Virginia Delegates to Edmund Randolph, February 12, 1787, *PJMC*, 9:266.

40 Virginia Delegates to Edmund Randolph, February 19, 1787, *PJMC*, 9:274–75.

41 "Notes on Debates," February 19, 1787, *PJMC*, 9:276–79.

42 "Notes on Debates," February 21, 1787, *PJMC*, 9:290–92.

43 JM to Edmund Pendleton, February 24, 1787, *PJMC*, 9:294–95, n. 3.

44 This paragraph is based on JM to Edmund Pendleton, February 24, 1787, *PJMC*, 9:294–95. Madison said virtually the same thing in JM to Edmund Randolph, February 25, 1787, *PJMC*, 9:299, and then closed with an expression of hope that Randolph was planning to head off both monarchy and disunion through his participation in the upcoming Philadelphia Convention.

45 Edmund Randolph to JM, March 7, 1787, *PJMC*, 9:303–04, n. 2.

46 PJM to George Washington, March 18, 1787, *PJMC*, 9:314–16. Madison offered a similar evaluation of Henry's decision not to participate in the Philadelphia Convention in JM to Edmund Randolph, March 25, 1787, *PJMC*, 9:331–32. Henry, for his part, said that he could not afford to go. Ibid., n. 1.

47 For a good summary of Rhode Island developments in 1786–1787, see JM to James Madison, Sr., April 1, 1787, *PJMC*, 9:358–59, n. 2.

48 JM to Edmund Randolph, April 2, 1787, *PJMC*, 9:361–62. Elsewhere, Madison joined in referring to Rhode Island's "madness." Virginia Delegates to Edmund Randolph, April 2, 1787, *PJMC*, 9:362–63.

49 JM to Edmund Randolph, April 8, 1787, *PJMC*, 9:368–71. Madison wrote to Washington along the same lines, and in fact largely in the same language, in JM to George Washington, April 16, 1787, *PJMC*, 9:382–87. Interestingly, however, Madison said in this epistle that the federal government ought to have "a negative *in all cases whatsoever* on the legislative acts of the States," not just a veto on unconstitutional acts or acts contrary to federal policy. Among the positive effects of such a power, he hoped, would be to keep state majorities from oppressing minorities.

50 "Notes on Debates," Thursday, April 26, 1787, *PJMC*, 9:407.

51 JM to Thomas Jefferson, May 15, 1787, *PJMC*, 9:415.

52 Manasseh Cutler: Journal, July 13, 1787, Farrand, *RFC*, 3:58.

53 James Monroe to JM, May 23, 1787, *PJMC*, 9:416–17.

54 Farrand, *RFC*, n. at 1:10–11.

55 George Mason to George Mason, Jr., May 20, 1787, Farrand, *RFC*, 3:22–24, at 23.

56 The account of the Philadelphia Convention that follows is taken chiefly from the primary materials collected in Farrand's four-volume *The Records of the Federal Convention of 1787*, supplemented occasionally by the additional materials found in *PJMC* 9. I will not provide a citation to each statement that is made in reliance on Farrand's materials when the citation would be to Madison's notes. When referring to what another note taker said, I will note which it was. In every case, I will

provide the date of the address, so that the interested reader can easily locate the relevant passage in Farrand's collection.

57 Farrand, *RFC,* 1:xvi. Besides Madison's notes, other significant inside sources of information about the Convention's proceedings include the Journal, the notes kept up to mid-July by New York delegate Chief Justice Robert Yates, the disconnected memoranda of Massachusetts delegate Rufus King, some notes kept by delegate James McHenry of Maryland, the aforementioned notes of Georgia delegate William Pierce, notes kept by New Jersey delegate William Paterson, a few "brief memoranda" written by delegate Alexander Hamilton of New York, the plan of government presented in the Convention by South Carolina's delegate Charles Pinckney, and "a few notes and memoranda" by Virginia delegate George Mason. *Ibid.*, 1:xiv–xv, xix–xxii.

58 *PJMC*, 10:9.

59 JM to TJ, June 6, 1787, *PJMC*, 10:28–30, at 29; JM to William Short, June 6, 1787, *PJMC*, 10:31–2, at 31. The one exception was Rhode Island, which never sent a delegation.

60 Edmund Pendleton had said virtually the same thing on being chosen president of the Virginia Convention in 1776 and would repeat the performance at the Richmond ratification convention in 1788. Gutzman, *Virginia's American Revolution*, chapters 1 and 3. Early presidential inaugurals, including Washington's first (which Madison drafted) and Madison's, would sound the same theme as well.

61 James H. Hutson, ed., *Supplement to Max Farrand's The Records of the Federal Convention of 1787* (New Haven, CT: Yale University Press, 1987), 327–38, provides detailed information of the Philadelphia weather each day of the Convention from three different sources.

62 Madison in his old age, long since retired from politics but concerned to show himself always the consistent Jeffersonian, denied that the word "national" had here meant what it actually had meant: centralized, unitary, ultimate. JM to Robert S. Garnett, February 11, 1824, Gaillard Hunt, ed., *The Writings of James Madison* (New York: G. P. Putnam's Sons, 1910) (hereafter, *WJM*), 9:176–77; JM to John Tyler (Jr.), 1833, *WJM*, 9:502–510.

63 Bradford, "George Read," in *Founding Fathers*, 105–07.

64 This matter came up on June 5.

65 Speech of James Madison, June 6, Farrand, *RFC*, 1:134–36.

66 This statement is found in Rufus King's notes.

67 JT to TJ, June 6, 1787, *PJMC*, 10:28–30

68 Despite JM's concern, Adams's book seems to have received a hostile press in Virginia. See James McClurg to JM, August 22, 1787, *PJMC*, 10:154–55, at 55. Benjamin Rush, on the other hand, believed that Adams's book would reinforce

Americans' commitment to bicameralism. Benjamin Rush to Richard Price, June 2, 1787, Farrand, *RFC*, 3:33.

69 JM to William Short, June 6, 1787, *PJMC*, 10:31–32, at 32.

70 King quotation at Farrand, *RFC*, 1:158.

71 Madison's fn. at Farrand, *RFC*, 1:242.

72 Farrand, *RFC*, 1:268.

73 For Hamilton's political science, far the best treatment is Karl-Friedrich Walling, *Republican Empire: Alexander Hamilton on War and Free Government* (Lawrence: University Press of Kansas, 1999).

74 That is what Madison has him saying. According to Hamilton's fellow New Yorker—but political opponent—Yates's notes of the same address, Hamilton denied that the New York delegates' commissions bound them merely to propose amendments to the Articles. In Yates's account, Hamilton's explanation of this point was very lawyerly.

75 Farrand, *RFC*, 1:298.

76 Farrand, *RFC*, 1:323.

77 Farrand, *RFC*, 1:299.

78 The quotation is from Yates (Farrand, *RFC* I:301), but the rest of this paragraph is from Madison.

79 Farrand, *RFC*, 1:293, n. 9.

80 King's notes on Madison's June 19 speech, which are the source for this paragraph are at Farrand I:329–30. Hamilton's notes, though less complete, corroborate King's insofar as this paragraph is concerned; see Farrand, *RFC*, 1:333.

81 William Blount to John Gray Blount, July 19, 1787, Hutson, *Supplement to Max Farrand's RFC*, 175.

82 Both Madison and Lansing provided extensive accounts of this speech. My version draws on both.

83 Farrand, *RFC*, 1:363.

84 Farrand, *RFC*, 1:364.

85 This account of Ellsworth's June 25 speech is from Yates's notes, Farrand, *RFC*, 1:414–15.

86 Farrand, *RFC*, 1:421–23.

87 Farrand, *RFC*, 1:437–38

88 Paterson found a contrary example in Poland, which in the eighteenth century was partitioned into extinction by its neighbors Russia, Austria, and Prussia; see Farrand, *RFC*, 1:459. One cannot tell whether Paterson is ascribing this observation to Martin or making it himself.

89 Farrand, *RFC*, 1:464.

90 Yates's notes of Speech of James Madison, June 29, 1787, Farrand, *RFC*, 1:471–72.

91   Madison's proposal foreshadowed the South Carolina Constitution of 1808, which gave the Low Country (heavily enslaved) counties control of one house of the legislature and the Up Country counties control of the other.

92   Yates's notes, Speech of James Madison, June 30, 1787, Farrand, *RFC,* 1:499–500.

93   Farrand, *RFC,* 1:536.

94   Farrand, *RFC,* 2:2–11.

95   Farrand, *RFC,* 2:36, Madison's note at *.

96   JM to TJ, July 18, 1787, *PJMC,* 10:105–6, at 105.

97   James McClurg to JM, September 5, 1787, *PJMC,* 10:162.

98   JM to TJ, July 18, 1787, *PJMC,* 10:105–6.

99   [New Jersey delegate] David Brearly to Jonathan Dayton, July 27, 1787, Hutson, *Supplement to Max Farrand's RFC,* 195–96.

100   Elbridge Gerry to Ann Gerry, August 14, 1787, Hutson, *Supplement to Max Farrand's RFC,* 222–24, at 223.

101   Appendix: The Weather during the Convention, Ibid., 325–26.

102   Madison's notes say that Pinckney recommended these amendments, but Farrand suggests that Gerry, Rutledge, and Mason likely drafted some of them; see Farrand, *RFC,* 2, notes at 324, 325.

103   Here Mason echoed the essay on "Manners" in Thomas Jefferson, *Notes on the State of Virginia,* ed. William Peden (Chapel Hill: University of North Carolina Press, 1996).

104   Edward Coles: History of the Ordinance of 1787, Hutson, *Supplement to Max Farrand's RFC,* 321.

105   McHenry, Notes for September 5, Farrand, *RFC,* 2:516.

106   JM to TJ, September 6, 1787, *PJMC,* 10:163–64.

107   Madison's objection here betrayed his lack of legal expertise. The phrase "high misdemeanor" in English impeachment precedents did not mean "relatively unimportant crime," but rather referred to abuses of office less significant than treason and bribery. See Raoul Berger, *Impeachment: The Constitutional Problems* (Cambridge, MA: Harvard University Press, 1974).

108   In private correspondence, Gerry predicted that "the proceedings of the Convention . . . [would] if not altered materially lay the foundation of a civil war. This entre nous." Alas for his reputation as prognosticator, he did not explain how. Elbridge Gerry to Ann Gerry, August 26, 1787, Hutson, *Supplement to Max Farrand's RFC,* 241–42, at 241.

109   McHenry's notes, September 17, 1787, Farrand, *RFC,* 2:649–50, at 650; George Washington's Diary, September 17, 1787, Huston, *Supplement to Max Farrand's RFC,* 276.

Chapter Four   Ratifying the Constitution, Part One:
The Federalist, *1787–88*

1   JM to Edmund Pendleton, September 20, 1787, *PJMC*, 10:171.
2   Edward Carrington to JM, September 23, 1787, *PJMC*, 10:172.
3   *PJMC*, 10:172, n. 2.
4   JM to George Washington, September 30, 1787, *PJMC*, 10:179–80. On the question of the public's understanding of the Congress's unanimity in referring the proposal to the states, see also Ibid., n. 5.
5   JM to Edmund Randolph, c. September 28, 1787, *PJMC*, 10:178.
6   *PJMC*, 10:179, n. 1.
7   Edmund Randolph to JM, September 30, 1787, *PJMC*, 10:181–82.
8   George Washington to JM, October 10, 1787, *PJMC*, 10:189–90.
9   JM to Ambrose Madison, October 11, 1787, *PJMC*, 10:191–92.
10 JM to Edmund Randolph, October 21, 1787, *PJMC*, 10:199–200.
11 George Washington to JM, October 22, 1787, *PJMC*, 10:203–04.
12 Editorial Note, JM to Thomas Jefferson, October 24, 1787, *PJMC*, 10:205–06, at 205.
13 Here is the inspiration of the title of the most famous account of the convention, Catherine Drinker Bowen, *Miracle at Philadelphia: The Story of the Constitutional Convention, May to September 1787* (Boston: Little, Brown, 1966).
14 Madison repeated that last point in JM to William Short, October 24, 1787, *PJMC*, 10:220–22 and JM to Tench Coxe, October 26, 1787, *PJMC*, 10:222–23.
15 JM to Edmund Pendleton. October 28, 1787, *PJMC*, 10:223–24. Madison repeated this last point in virtually the same words in JM to George Washington, October 28, 1787, *PJMC*, 10:225–26.
16 For an explanation of the imprecise dating of this letter, see Edmund Randolph to JM, c. October 29, 1787, *PJMC*, 229–31, nn. 1 and 2. Note 1 is also the source for the rest of this paragraph.
17 JM to Archibald Stuart, October 30, 1787, *PJMC*, 10:232–33.
18 Virginia Delegates to Edmund Randolph, November 3, 1787, *PJMC*, 10:236–41.
19 Ibid., n. 9.
20 JM to Ambrose Madison, November 8, 1787, *PJMC*, 10:243–45.
21 The following account of *The Federalist*'s conception and organization relies heavily upon Editors' Note, "Madison's Authorship of *The Federalist*, 22 November 1787–1 March 1788," *PJMC*, 10:259–63; and Albert Furtwangler, *The Authority of Publius: A Reading of the Federalist Papers* (Ithaca, NY: Cornell University Press, 1984).

22   For Hamilton the practical statesman, see *American Machiavelli: Alexander Hamilton and the Origins of U.S. Foreign Policy* (Cambridge, UK: Cambridge University Press, 2004).

23   Easily the best Clinton biography is John Kaminski, *George Clinton: Yeoman Politician of the New Republic* (Madison, WI: Madison House Publishers, 1993).

24   The best book on the subject, Albert Furtwangler, *The Authority of Publius: A Reading of the Federalist Papers*, adduces ample evidence that Madison and Hamilton worked together on the series nearly from its conception.

25   Federalist No. 9, Alexander Hamilton, James Madison, and John Jay, *The Federalist*, ed. Jacob E. Cooke (Middletown, CT: Wesleyan University Press, 1961), 50–56. All references to *The Federalist* are to this edition, which is generally adjudged authoritative.

26   *The Federalist*, 56–65.

27   Editors' Note, "Additional Memorandums on Ancient and Modern Confederacies," *PJMC*, 10:273–74.

28   *The Federalist*, 83–89.

29   *The Federalist*, 110–17.

30   For a brilliant, iconoclastic account, see Leonard L. Richards, *Shays's Rebellion: The American Revolution's Final Battle* (Philadelphia: University of Pennsylvania Press, 2003).

31   *The Federalist*, 117–23.

32   Madison here has in mind the Treaty of Westphalia (1648). That treaty concluded the Thirty Years War, a struggle fought chiefly within Germany by armies led chiefly by the emperor on one side and by the king of Sweden on the other over the question whether a German state might adopt Protestantism as its state religion. In the end, the emperor had to concede Sweden's point that, yes, it might.

33   JM to Thomas Jefferson, December 9, 1787, *PJMC*, 10:310–14.

34   Virginia Delegates to Edmund Randolph, December 11, 1787, *PJMC*, 10:319–20.

35   *The Federalist*, 124–29.

36   Jonathan Israel, *The Dutch Republic: Its Rise, Greatness, and Fall 1477–1806* (New York: Oxford University Press, 1998).

37   Dull, *A Diplomatic History of the American Revolution*.

38   Throughout this book, I employ the numbering used by publishers of the essays in book form rather than the numbering that originally appeared in the newspapers. I also accept Cooke's allocation of essays among Hamilton, Madison, and Jay. For a full explanation of these matters, see Editors' Note, "Madison's Authorship of *The Federalist*, 22 November 1787–1 March 1788," *PJMC*, 10:259–63.

39 JM to Archibald Stuart, December 14, 1787, *PJMC*, 10:325–26; also see Thomas Jefferson to JM, December 20, 1787, *PJMC*, 10:333–34.

40 JM to Thomas Jefferson, December 20, 1787, *PJMC*, 10:331–33.

41 Thomas Jefferson to JM, December 20, 1787, *PJMC*, 10:335–39.

42 Edmund Randolph to JM, December 27, 1787, *PJMC*, 10:346–47.

43 Edmund Randolph to JM, January 7, 1788, *PJMC*, 10:350.

44 JM to Edmund Randolph, January 10, 1788, *PJMC*, 10:354–56.

45 *The Federalist*, 7.

46 I borrow this organization from Furtwangler, *The Authority of Publius*, 57.

47 Essays 37–40 appear at *The Federalist* 231–239, 239–249, 250–257, and 258–267.

48 Archibald Stuart to James Madison, January 14, 1788, *PJMC*, 10:373–74. Stuart named several significant figures who had changed their minds and come around to support for ratification.

49 For details regarding the state constitutions of the revolutionary era, see Marc W. Kruman, *Between Authority and Liberty: State Constitution-Making in Revolutionary America* (Chapel Hill: University of North Carolina Press, 1999); and Willi Paul Adams, *The First American Constitutions: Republican Ideology and the Making of the State Constitutions* (expanded edition; Lanham, MD: Rowman & Littlefield Publishers, 2001). For the case of Madison's own Virginia, see Gutzman, *Virginia's American Revolution*, especially chapters 1 and 6.

50 For a useful corrective to Federalist claims about the states' exertions on behalf of the revolutionary cause, see Keith L. Dougherty, *Collective Action Under the Articles of Confederation* (New York: Cambridge University Press, 2001).

51 *The Federalist*, 268–78.

52 *The Federalist*, 279–87, 288–98.

53 *The Federalist*, 299–308.

54 *The Federalist*, 308–14, 314–23

55 For numbers 47–51, see *The Federalist*, 323–31, 332–38, 338–43, 343–47, and 347–53.

56 *The Federalist*, 353–59, 359–66, 366–72, 372–78, 378–83, 384–90, 391–97.

57 *The Federalist*, 415–22, 422–31.

Chapter Five Ratifying the Constitution, Part Two:
The Richmond Convention, 1788

1 John P. Kaminski, ed., *The Documentary History of the Ratification of the Constitution* (hereafter, *DHRC*) (Madison: State Historical Society of Wisconsin, 1988), 8:11.

2 Edward Carrington to James Madison, September 23, 1787, *DHRC* 8:14.

3   Editors' Note, "The Confederation Congress and the Constitution, New York, 26–28 September, *DHRC*, 8:20–21. For full details (including the interesting excision of a reference to the Constitution as having created "a *national* Government"), see JM to GW, September 30, 1787, *DHRC*, 8:26–7.

4   The following description of Lee's argument is based primarily on Richard Henry Lee to Samuel Adams, October 5, 1787, *DHRC*, 8:36–8.

5   George Mason to GW, October 7, 1787, *DHRC*, 8:43–6.

6   GW to JM, *DHRC*, 8:49–50.

7   *DHRC*, 8:58, 112–19.

8   James Monroe to JM, February 7, 1788, *DHRC*, 8:354–55.

9   *Virginia Independent Chronicle*, September 26, 1787, *DHRC*, 8:19, fn. 1.

10 JM to GW, October 18, 1787, *DHRC*, 8:76–7.

11 Patrick Henry to Thomas Madison, October 21, 1787, *DHRC*, 8:88.

12 Edmund Randolph to JM, c. October 29, 1787, *DHRC*, 8:132–34, at 133.

13 GW to JM, November 5, 1787, quoting Archibald Stuart (one of two delegates, with Mason, from Fairfax) to GW, *DHRC*, 8:145–46.

14 JM to GW, November 18, 1787, *DHRC*, 8:167.

15 This paragraph on the distribution of *The Federalist* in Virginia is taken from two very helpful editorial notes in the *DHRC*: "Editors' Note: The Republication of The Federalist in Virginia, 28 November 1787–9 January 1788," 8:180–83, and "The Circulation of the Book Version of The Federalist in Virginia: Norfolk and Portsmouth Journal, 2 April," *DHRC*, 10:652–54.

16 This paragraph is taken from JM to TJ, December 9, 1787, *DHRC*, 8:226–28, at 226–27.

17 Henry Lee to James Madison, c. December 20, 1787, *DHRC*, 8:248–49.

18 Edmund Randolph to Speaker of the House of Delegates, October 10, 1787, *DHRC*, 8:262–74.

19 St. Jean de Crevecoeur to William Short, February 20, 1788, *DHRC*, 8:385, n. 2.

20 GW to JM, January 1, 1788, *DHRC*, 8:281–82.

21 Edmund Randolph to JM, January 3, 1788, *DHRC*, 8:284.

22 Nicholas Gilman to John Langdon, March 6, 1788, *DHRC*, 8:454, n. 4.

23 This sentiment was expressed in many surviving documents, and most clearly in Edward Carrington to Henry Knox, March 13, 1788, *DHRC*, 8:491–92.

24 This paragraph relies on the Introduction to the section on the elections at *DHRC*, 9:561–62.

25 James Monroe to Thomas Jefferson, April 10, 1788, *DHRC*, 9:733–34.

26 The account in this and the following paragraph comes from JM to Eliza Trist, March 25, 1788, *DHRC*, 9:603.

27   Hugh Blair Grigsby, *The History of the Virginia Federal Convention of 1788,* 2 vols.
      (Richmond: Virginia Historical Society, 1890–91); 1:79 (deformity), 1:79, n. 96
      (caricature), 2:295 (height).

28   George Nicholas to James Madison, April 5, 1788, *DHRC,* 9:702–05.

29   JM to George Nicholas, April 8, 1788, *DHRC,* 9:707–10.

30   Madison soon did this, orally to some and in writing to others. JM to John Brown,
      April 9, 1788, *DHRC,* 9:711–12; JM to George Washington, April 10, 1788, *DHRC,*
      9:732–33.

31   JM to Edmund Randolph, April 10, 1788, *DHRC,* 9:730–31.

32   Edmund Randolph to JM, April 17, 1788, *DHRC,* 9:741–42.

33   Nicholas Gilman to John Sullivan, April 19, 1788, *DHRC,* 9:742–43; George Wash-
      ington to Thomas Johnson, April 20, 1788, *DHRC,* 9:743–44; JM to Thomas
      Jefferson, April 22, 1788, *DHRC,* 9:744–46, at 744.

34   George Washington to John Armstrong, Sr., April 25, 1788, *DHRC,* 9:758–61.

35   Governor George Clinton to Governor Edmund Randolph, May 8, 1788, *DHRC,*
      9:790–91. For a full account of this imbroglio, see the Editors' Note, "The First
      Attempt at Cooperation Between Virginia and New York Antifederalists, 8 May–
      15 October," *DHRC,* 9:788–90.

36   George Washington to John Jay, May 15, 1788, *DHRC,* 9:803–04.

37   George Nicholas to JM, May 9, 1788, *DHRC,* 9:793.

38   JM to George Nicholas, May 17, 1788, *DHRC,* 9:804–10.

39   Hugh Blair Grigsby, *The History of the Virginia Federal Convention of 1788,* 119,
      n. 123.

40   The following information about the convention's schedule and the sources upon
      which historians may draw comes from the "Introduction" to Section IV of *DHRC,*
      9, which is found at 9:897–900.

41   I here use the words "Federalist" and "Anti-Federalist" to denote respectively pro-
      ponents of ratifying the Constitution immediately and opponents of ratifying the
      Constitution without first amending it. This usage should not obscure the validity
      of George Mason's objection to these names. George Mason to John Francis Mer-
      cer, May 1, 1788, *DHRC,* 9:779–80. As far as Mason was concerned, the Federal-
      ists were actually nationalists who "improperly style[d] themselves" Federalists. As
      we have seen, this was certainly true of Madison.

42   The following two paragraphs are drawn from Editors' Note, "Sources for the
      Virginia Convention," *DHRC,* 9:901–06. The Madison and editors' quotations
      are from p. 906.

43   Edmund Pendleton: Address to the General Convention, June 2, 1788, *DHRC,*
      9:910–11.

44 *DHRC*, 9:911, n. 3.

45 Jay Fliegelman, *Declaring Independence: Jefferson, Natural Language, and the Culture of Performance* (Palo Alto, CA: Stanford University Press, 1993), 94–107.

46 *DHRC*, 9:918.

47 For more on Henry and the Virginia Revolution, see Gutzman, *Virginia's American Revolution*, chs. 1–4.

48 James Breckinridge to John Breckinridge, June 13, 1788, *DHRC*, 10:1620–21. A similar appraisal of Madison's abilities came from Samuel A. Otis of Massachusetts. Otis to Theodore Sedgwick, June 15, 1788, *DHRC*, 10:1629.

49 Gouverneur Morris, lately a vocal participant in the Philadelphia Convention and another partisan Federalist, offered a Shakespearean appraisal of Henry's speech as calculated "to stir Men's Blood." Gouverneur Morris to Alexander Hamilton, June 13, 1788, *DHRC*, 10:1622, and n. 3 at 1623. Another delegate echoed the appraisal that Henry's chief effect would be upon "the desperate & ignorant." Charles Yates to James Maury, June 13, 1788, *DHRC*, 10:1623.

50 Speech of Edmund Randolph, June 4, 1788, *DHRC*, 9:931–36.

51 JM to Rufus King, June 4, 1788, *DHRC*, 10:1573–74; JM to George Washington, June 4, 1788, *DHRC*, 10:1574.

52 Speech of Edmund Pendleton, June 5, 1788, *DHRC*, 9:944–49; Speech of Henry Lee, June 5, 1788, *DHRC*, 9:949–51; Speech of Patrick Henry, June 5, 1788, *DHRC*, 9:951–68.

53 Speech of Edmund Randolph, June 6, 1788, *DHRC*, 9:971–89.

54 Speech of JM, June 6, 1788, *DHRC*, 9:989–98.

55 Speech of Edmund Randolph, June 7, 2010, *DHRC*, 9:1016–28.

56 Speech of JM, June 7, 1788, *DHRC*, 9:1028–35.

57 Speech of Patrick Henry, June 7, 1788, *DHRC*, 9:1035–47.

58 Editors' Note, "The Second Attempt at Cooperation between Virginia and New York Antifederalists, 18 May–27 June," *DHRC*, 9:811–13.

59 William Grayson to John Lamb, June 9, 1788, *DHRC*, 9:816–17; George Mason to John Lamb, June 9, 1788, *DHRC*, 9:818–19.

60 Patrick Henry to John Lamb, June 9, 1788, *DHRC*, 9:817.

61 Speech of Patrick Henry, June 9, 1788, *DHRC*, 9:1050–72.

62 Speech of Henry Lee, June 9, 1788, *DHRC*, 9:1072–81.

63 Speech of Edmund Randolph, June 9, 1788, *DHRC*, 9:1081–87.

64 *New York Journal*, June 20, 1788, *DHRC*, 10:1658–60, at 1659.

65 JM to Alexander Hamilton, June 9, 1788, *DHRC*, 10:1589.

66 JM to Rufus King, June 9, 1788, *DHRC*, 10:1590.

67 For his inability to attend "for several days," see JM to Tench Coxe, June 11, 1788, *DHRC*, 10:1595.

68 Speech of Edmund Randolph, June 10, 1788, *DHRC*, 9:1092–1103; Speech of James Monroe, June 10, 1788, *DHRC*, 9:1103–15; Speech of John Marshall, June 10, 1788, *DHRC*, 9:1115–27.

69 Speech of George Nicholas, June 10, 1788, *DHRC*, 9:1127–37.

70 Speech of JM, June 11, 1788, *DHRC*, 9:1142–54.

71 The speeches by Madison, Henry, and Madison again are at *DHRC*, 9:1154, while Mason's is at *DHRC*, 9:1154–63.

72 Speech of JM, June 11, 1788, *DHRC*, 9:1172.

73 JM to Tench Coxe, June 11, 1788, *DHRC*, 10:1595.

74 Speech of William Grayson, June 12, 1788, *DHRC*, 10:1184–92.

75 Speech of JM, June 12, 1788, *DHRC*, 10:1202–09.

76 Speech of JM, June 12, 1788, *DHRC*, 10:1222–26.

77 The speeches of Nicholas, Henry, Madison, and Lee mentioned in this paragraph are found at *DHRC*, 10:1228–29.

78 Speech of James Monroe, June 13, 1788, *DHRC*, 10:1229–35.

79 Speech of William Grayson, June 13, 1788, *DHRC*, 10:1235–39.

80 Speech of JM, June 13, 1788, *DHRC*, 10:1239–42.

81 Speech of William Grayson, June 13, 1788, *DHRC*, 10:1242–44.

82 Speech of Patrick Henry, June 13, 1788, *DHRC*, 10:1245–49; Speech of George Nicholas, June 13, 1788, *DHRC*, 10:1249–52.

83 As, for example, at Ibid., 10:1265. The debates for June 14 are found at *DHRC*, 10:1258–97.

84 Gouverneur Morris, Extempore at the Convention in Virginia, c. June 14, 1788, *DHRC*, 10:1628–29.

85 Speech of JM, June 14, 1788, *DHRC*, 10:1287.

86 Speech of JM, June 16, 1788, *DHRC*, 10:1301–03.

87 *DHRC*, 10:1320.

88 Speech of George Mason, June 16, 1788, *DHRC*, 10:1328; Speech of Patrick Henry, June 16, 1788, *DHRC*, 10:1328–32; Speech of William Grayson, June 16, 1788, *DHRC*, 10:1332.

89 JM to Alexander Hamilton, June 16, 1788, *DHRC*, 10:1630.

90 Speech of George Mason, June 17, 1788, *DHRC*, 10:1338.

91 Speech of JM, June 17, 1788, *DHRC*, 10:1338–39.

92 Contrast Paul Finkelman, "Making a Covenant with Death: Slavery and the Constitutional Convention," in *Slavery and the Founders: Race and Liberty in the Age of Jefferson* (2nd ed., Armonk, New York: M. E. Sharpe, Inc., 2001), 3–36.

93 Speech of JM, June 17, 1788, *DHRC*, 10:1343–44.

94   For example, on June 16, 1788, *DHRC*, 10:1323.

95   Speech of Edmund Randolph, June 17, 1788, *DHRC*, 10:1347–54.

96   For a full exploration of Randolph's role in developing the Virginia tradition of federalism, see Kevin R. C. Gutzman, "Edmund Randolph and Virginia Constitutionalism," *Review of Politics* 66 (2004): 469–97.

97   Speech of Edmund Randolph, June 17, 1788, *DHRC*, 10:1366–67.

98   William Grayson to Nathan Dane, June 18, 1788, *DHRC*, 10:1636; JM to Rufus King, June 18, 1788, *DHRC*, 10:1637; JM to George Washington, June 18, 1788, *DHRC*, 10:1637–38.

99   Speech of JM, June 19, 1788, *DHRC*, 10:1395–97.

100   Speech of George Mason, June 19, 1788, *DHRC*, 10:1401–02.

101   Speech of George Mason, June 19, 1788, *DHRC*, 10:1403–09.

102   Speech of JM, June 19, 1788, *DHRC*, 10:1409.

103   Speech of JM, June 20, 1788, *DHRC*, 10:1412–19.

104   Speech of John Marshall, June 20, 1788, *DHRC*, 10:1430–39.

105   JM to Alexander Hamilton, June 20, 1788, *DHRC*, 10:1656–57; JM to James Madison Sr., June 20, 1788, *DHRC*, 10:1657.

106   Speech of JM, June 24, 1788, *DHRC*, 10:1498–1504.

107   Speech of George Wythe, June 24, 1788, *DHRC*, 10:1473–74.

108   This account is taken from Speech of Patrick Henry, June 24, 1788, *DHRC*, 10:1504–6, and "Reminiscences of Patrick Henry's Thunderstorm Speech, 24 June," *DHRC*, 10:1511.

109   Speech of Ronald, June 24, 1788, *DHRC*, 10:1507.

110   Speech of JM, June 24, 1788, *DHRC*, 10:1507.

111   Speech of John Tyler, June 25, 1788, *DHRC*, 10:1524–29.

112   Speech of Patrick Henry, June 25, 1788, *DHRC*, 10:1534–37.

113   Speech of Edmund Randolph, June 25, 1788, *DHRC*, 10:1538. Federalists', chiefly Randolph's, argument against the possibility of prior amendments seems to have swayed at least one Anti-Federalist to vote "aye" on ratification. *DHRC*, 10:1651, n. 2.

114   The roll-call votes are at *DHRC*, 10:1538–41.

115   *DHRC*, 10:1542.

116   JM to Alexander Hamilton, June 22, 1788, *DHRC*, 10:1665.

117   From JM, June 25, 1788, *DHRC*, 10:1675 and n. 1; JM to Rufus King, June 25, 1788, *DHRC*, 10:1676; JM to George Washington, June 25, 1788, *DHRC*, 10:1676.

118   Convention Debates, June 27, 1788, *DHRC*, 10:1550–58.

119   An introductory editors' note and several newspaper accounts are at *DHRC*, 10:1560–62.

Chapter Six Inaugurating the Constitution, 1788–1800

1   For this and the following paragraph, see Stuart Leibiger, *Founding Friendship: George Washington, James Madison, and the Creation of the American Republic* (Charlottesville: University Press of Virginia, 1999), 97–98.

2   JM to Edmund Randolph, November 2, 1788, *PJMC*, 11:328–30.

3   JM to George Lee Turberville, November 2, 1788, *PJMC*, 11:330–32.

4   Leibiger, *Founding Friendship*, 99.

5   George Lee Turberville to JM, November 10, 1788, *PJMC*, 11:339–41.

6   George Lee Turberville to JM, November 16, 1788, *PJMC*, 11:346–47.

7   Leibiger, *Founding Friendship*, 99.

8   Thomas Jefferson to JM, November 18, 1788, *PJMC*, 11:353–55, at 353.

9   JM to Thomas Jefferson, December 8, 1788, *PJMC*, 11:381–84, at 382.

10 Ibid., at 384.

11 *PJMC*, 11:438, n. 1.

12 JM to George Eve, January 2, 1789, *PJMC*, 11:404–05.

13 Leibiger, *Founding Friendship*, 100.

14 JM to Edmund Randolph, March 1, 1789, *PJMC*, 11:453.

15 Leibiger, *Founding Friendship*, chapter 4.

16 "Address of the President to Congress," April 30, 1789, *PJMC*, 12:121–24.

17 *Ibid.*, 104.

18 Leibiger, *Founding Friendship*, 105, 109; *PJMC*, vols. 6–11.

19 For a brief account and the primary documents, see Editorial Note, "Address of the President to Congress," *PJMC*, 12:120–21.

20 Leibiger, *Founding Friendship*, 110.

21 For the contours of Madison's and other soon-to-be-Republicans' ideological opposition to Hamiltonianism in the 1790s, the leading account is Lance Banning, *The Jeffersonian Persuasion: Evolution of a Party Ideology* (Ithaca, NY: Cornell University Press, 1980).

22 Isaac Kramnick, *Bolingbroke and His Circle: The Politics of Nostalgia in the Age of Walpole* (Cambridge, MA: Harvard University Press, 1968).

23 Forrest McDonald, *The Presidency of George Washington* (Lawrence: University Press of Kansas, 1974), 69.

24 Ibid., 70.

25 The most insightful account of Hamiltonian finance is Herbert E. Sloan, "Hamilton's Second Thoughts: Federalist Finance Revisited," in Doron Ben-Atar and Barbara B. Oberg, eds., *Federalists Reconsidered* (Charlottesville: University Press of Virginia, 1999), 61–76.

26 The following account of the famous "Compromise of 1790" comes from Ralph Ketcham, *James Madison: A Biography* (Charlottesville: University Press of Virginia, 1990), 309.

27 The following discussion of Henry's Resolution and the General Assembly address draws upon Gutzman, *Virginia's American Revolution*, 116–17.

28 The most famous contemporary expression of the idea that Madison's change of heart regarding amendments arose out of political necessity is Representative Fisher Ames's. Ames said, "[He] is afraid of [Virginia's] state politics and of his popularity there more than I think he should be." Fisher Ames to George Richards Minot, May 3, 1789, W. B. Allen, ed., *Works of Fisher Ames, as Published by Seth Ames* (Indianapolis, IN: Liberty Fund, 1983), 1:567–69, at 569.

29 *PJMC*, 12:125, headnote.

30 "Address of the President to Congress," April 30, 1789, *PJMC*, 12:121–24, at 123.

31 George Washington to JM, c. May 31, 1789, *PJMC*, 12:191 and n.

32 Richard Labunski, *James Madison and the Struggle for the Bill of Rights* (New York: Oxford University Press, 2006), 189.

33 The following discussion of the chronology, Madison's speech, and his proposals comes from "Amendments to the Constitution," June 8, 1789, *PJMC*, 12:196–210.

34 Richard Labunski, *James Madison and the Struggle for the Bill of Rights* (New York: Oxford University Press, 2006), 201.

35 Ibid., 207.

36 William R. Davie to JM, June 10, 1789, *PJMC*, 12:210–11.

37 Edward Carrington to JM, May 12, 1789, *PJMC*, 12:156–57; John Dawson to JM, June 28, 1789, Ibid., 263–64. Dawson allowed that he would have preferred that the amendments go further.

38 "Amendments to the Constitution," August 13, 1789, *PJMC*, 12:332–33.

39 Labunski, *James Madison and the Struggle for the Bill of Rights*, 217.

40 "Amendments to the Constitution," August 15, 1789, *PJMC*, 12:339.

41 "Amendments to the Constitution," August 15, 1789, *PJMC*, 12:341–42.

42 JM to Richard Peters, August 19, 1789, *PJMC*, 12:346–48.

43 "Amendments to the Constitution," August 17, 1789, *PJMC*, 12:344.

44 Labunski, *James Madison and the Struggle for the Bill of Rights*, 230.

45 Both the Morris and the Butler information are at Labunski, *James Madison and the Struggle for the Bill of Rights*, 235.

46 Fisher Ames to George Richards Minot, May 3, 1789, *Works of Fisher Ames*, 1:567–69, at 569.

47 Fisher Ames to George Richards Minot, May 18, 1789, *Works of Fisher Ames*, 1:627–28, at 628.

48 Labunski, *James Madison and the Struggle for the Bill of Rights,* 239.

49 This paragraph and the next two are based on Henry Mayer, *A Son of Thunder: Patrick Henry and the American Republic* (New York: Franklin Watts, 1986), 458–60; and Labunski, *James Madison and the Struggle for the Bill of Rights,* 250–255.

50 James Roger Sharp, *American Politics in the Early Republic: The New Nation in Crisis* (New Haven, CT: Yale University Press, 1993), 38.

51 This account of Madison's role in the dispute relies on McDonald, *The Presidency of George Washington,* 76; Sharp, *American Politics in the Early Republic,* 38–41; Thomas Jefferson, "Opinion on the Constitutionality of a National Bank," February 15, 1791, in *The Portable Thomas Jefferson,* ed. Merrill D. Peterson (New York: Penguin Books, 1975), 261–67; and Alexander Hamilton, "Opinion on the Constitutionality of a National Bank," *Alexander Hamilton: Writings* (New York: Library of America, 2001), 613–46.

52 The following discussion is based on "The Bank Bill," February 2, 1791, *PJMC,* 13:373–81, as well as on the headnote at 12:372.

53 Memorandum to JM from Roger Sherman, c. February 4, 1791, *PJMC,* 13:382, and n. 2.

54 Speech on the Bank Bill, February 8, 1791, *PJMC,* 13:383–387.

55 *PJMC,* 13:388, n. 6.

56 Ralph Ketcham, *Presidents Above Party: The First American Presidency, 1789–1829* (Chapel Hill: University of North Carolina Press, 1987).

57 "Opinion on the Constitutionality of a National Bank," February 15, 1791, Peterson, *The Portable Thomas Jefferson,* 261–67.

58 This sentence and the following one rely on Sharp, *American Politics in the Early Republic,* 43.

59 The following account is based upon "Madison's *National Gazette* Essays, 19 November 1791–20 December 1792," *PJMC,* 14:110–12.

60 "For *Dunlop's American Daily Advertiser,*" October 21, 1792, *PJMC,* 14:387–92.

61 Of several treatments of the popular movement, the best is Simon P. Newman's *Parades and the Politics of the Street: Festive Culture in the Early American Republic* (Philadelphia: University of Pennsylvania Press, 1997).

62 McDonald, *The Presidency of George Washington,* 118.

63 For Randolph, see John Reardon, *Edmund Randolph: A Biography* (New York: Macmillan Publishing, 1974), 225.

64 JM to Thomas Jefferson, June 19, 1793, *PJMC,* 14:33–34.

65 The following account is indebted to Editorial Note, "Madison's 'Helvidius' Essays, 14 August–18 September 1793," *PJMC,* 15:64–66.

66 Thomas Jefferson to JM, July 7, 1792, *PJMC,* 15:43.

67 JM, "Helvidius" Number 1, *PJMC,* 15:66–73, at 72.

68   Kaminski, *George Clinton*, 229–36.

69   George Washington to JM, May 29, 1792, *PJMC*, 14:310–12.

70   Enclosure, JM to George Washington, June 20, 1792, *PJMC*, 14:321–24.

71   This account of the Madison courtship is based on Ketcham, *James Madison: A Biography*, 379–82.

72   The following account is based chiefly on William Jay, *The Life of John Jay: With Selections from His Correspondence and Miscellaneous Papers* (New York: J. & J. Harper, 1833).

73   For Burr and the Republican leadership in 1796, see Nancy Isenberg, *Fallen Founder: The Life of Aaron Burr* (New York: Viking, 2007), 148–54.

74   David N. Mayer, *The Constitutional Thought of Thomas Jefferson* (Charlottesville: University Press of Virginia, 1994), 199–201. Interestingly, Merrill Peterson did not consider this petition to merit inclusion in the 1,599-page collection, *Thomas Jefferson: Writings*. For Peterson, federalism ranked only as a secondary issue. For Jefferson, it was primary. See Kevin R. C. Gutzman, "Thomas Jefferson's Federalism, 1774–1825," *Modern Age* 53 (2011, forthcoming).

75   The following account is based primarily on Gutzman, *Virginia's American Revolution*, chapter 4.

76   For the Chase matter, see Raoul Berger, *Impeachment: The Constitutional Problems* (enlarged edition, Cambridge, MA: Harvard University Press, 1999), chapter 8.

77   For the novelty of Republicans' First Amendment argument, see Leonard Levy, *Legacy of Suppression: Freedom of Speech and Press in Early American History* (Cambridge, MA: Harvard University Press, 1960).

78   Thomas Jefferson, "Kentucky Resolutions" (draft), *Works of Thomas Jefferson*, ed. Paul Leicester Ford (New York: G. P. Putnam's Sons, 1892–1904), 8:458–77; James Madison, "Virginia Resolutions," December 21, 1798, *PJMC*, 17:188–90.

79   Thomas Jefferson to John Taylor, June [4], 1798, Peterson, *The Portable Thomas Jefferson*, 474–77, at 475.

Chapter Seven   Secretary of State, Then President, 1800–17

1   Alexander Hamilton to John Jay, May 7, 1800, Joanne B. Freeman, ed., *Alexander Hamilton: Writings* (New York: Library of America, 2001), 923–25.

2   Garry Wills, *"Negro President": Jefferson and the Slave Power* (Boston: Houghton Mifflin, 2003).

3   James E. Lewis, Jr., " 'What Is to Become of Our Government?' The Revolutionary Potential of the Election of 1800," in *The Revolution of 1800: Democracy, Race, and the New Republic*, eds. James Horn, Jan Ellen Lewis, and Peter S. Onuf (Charlottesville: University of Virginia Press, 2002), 3–29, at 10–12.

4   Ibid., 10.

5   Ibid., 11.

6   The following paragraph comes from Ibid., 14–15.

7   Ibid., 16.

8   Ibid., 17.

9   Thomas Jefferson, "First Inaugural Address," March 4, 1801, Peterson, *The Portable Thomas Jefferson*, 290–95.

10 Merrill D. Peterson, *Thomas Jefferson and the New Nation* (New York: Oxford University Press, 1970), 656.

11 Richard Samuelson, "The Midnight Appointments of John Adams," *White House History* 7 (Spring 2000): 14–25.

12 5 U.S. 137 (1803).

13 The best Marshall biography is R. Kent Newmyer, *John Marshall and the Heroic Age of the Supreme Court* (Baton Rouge: Louisiana State University Press, 2007).

14 For lower courts' claims to the power of judicial review, see Scott Douglas Gerber, ed., *Seriatim: The Supreme Court Before John Marshall* (New York: NYU Press, 1998).

15 The primary materials of the congressional proceedings form the best sources for the following paragraphs on the Republicans' impeachment efforts. The best secondary account of American impeachment is Raoul Berger, *Impeachment: The Constitutional Problems* (Cambridge, MA: Harvard University Press, 1974), which has been expanded and updated since. Also see Kevin R. [C.] Gutzman, Problems in Federal Judicial Impeachment (Master of Public Affairs Professional Report, University of Texas LBJ School of Public Affairs, 1990).

16 Nancy Isenberg, *Fallen Founder: The Life of Aaron Burr* (New York: Viking, 2007), chapter 8, includes a colorful account. For legal issues, consult Berger, *Impeachment: The Constitutional Problems*.

17 JM to Charles Pinckney, November 27, 1802, Robert J. Brugger et al., eds., *Papers of James Madison: Secretary of State Series* (hereafter *PJMSS*) (Charlottesville: University Press of Virginia, 1986–), 4:146–48.

18 William E. Hulings to JM, October 18, 1802, *PJMSS*, 4:30.

19 Peterson, *Jefferson and the New Nation*, 749–50.

20 Bonaparte quotation at Irving Brant, *James Madison: Secretary of State, 1800–1809* (Indianapolis, Indiana: Bobbs-Merrill, 1953), 125.

21 JM to Robert R. Livingston and James Monroe, April 18, 1803, *PJMSS*, 4: 527–32.

22 Madison conveyed the date he had received the treaty, along with his response, in JM to Robert R. Livingston and James Monroe, July 29, 1803, *PJMSS*, 5:238–40.

23 The best book on Jeffersonian Republican political economy is Drew R. McCoy,

The Elusive Republic: Political Economy in Jeffersonian America (New York: W. W. Norton, 1980).

24 Peterson, *Thomas Jefferson and the New Nation*, 770–71; Brant, *James Madison: Secretary of State, 1800–1809*, 141–42.

25 Robert R. Livingston to JM, July 30, 1803, *PJMSS*, 5:250–53, at 251.

26 Brant, *James Madison: Secretary of State, 1800–1809*.

27 The following account relies heavily on Ibid., 234–40.

28 JM to Thomas Jefferson, April 26, 1802, *PJMSS*, 3:160, and n. 1 at 160–161. Besides the details of the agreement, the note also includes the following point about Gallatin's authorship and Madison's receiving the "credit."

29 10 U.S. 87.

30 New York's George Clinton, New Yorker Aaron Burr's successor, had been that state's Anti-Federalist colossus in 1787–1788, and then had joined Jefferson and Madison in founding the Republican Party. See Kaminski, *George Clinton*.

31 Ketcham, *James Madison: A Biography*, 446–47.

32 Peter Onuf and Nicholas Onuf, *Federal Union, Modern World: The Law of Nations in an Age of Revolutions, 1776–1814* (Madison, WI: Madison House Publishers, 1993), 199. The following discussion of the international response to this new enunciation of the Rule of 1756 is heavily reliant on Ibid., 199–201.

33 James Madison, "An Examination of the British Doctrine, Which Subjects to Capture a Neutral Trade, Not Open in Time of Peace," 1806, *WJM*, 7:204–375.

34 Brant, *James Madison: Secretary of State, 1800–1809*, 312–16.

35 Thomas Jefferson to John Holmes, April 22, 1820, Peterson, *The Portable Thomas Jefferson*, 567–69.

36 The balance of this paragraph draws upon McDonald, *The Presidency of Thomas Jefferson* (Lawrence: University Press of Kansas, 1976), 119.

37 Ibid., 132.

38 For Jefferson's withholding the treaty from the Senate, see JM to John Armstrong, May 22, 1807, *WJM*, 7:446–49.

39 Madison explained the reasons for the treaty's rejection in JM to James Monroe and William Pinkney, May 20, 1807, *WJM*, 7:407–45 (quotations at 444).

40 McDonald, *The Presidency of Thomas Jefferson*, 135–37; JM to James Monroe, July 6, 1807, *WJM*, 7:454–60.

41 JM to John Armstrong and James Bowdoin, July 15, 1807, *WJM*, 7:460–62, at 462.

42 Brant, *James Madison: Secretary of State, 1800–1809*, 375.

43 McDonald, *The Presidency of Thomas Jefferson*, 143–44.

44 Henry Adams, *History of the United States of America During the Administrations of Thomas Jefferson and James Madison*, 9 vols., 1889–1891; reprinted 2 vols. (New York: Library of America, 1986), title of vol. 1, chapter 10.

45   Ibid., 1:1099.

46   Ibid., 1099–1101.

47   Ibid., 1107.

48   Ibid., 1108.

49   Ibid., 1109.

50   Ibid., 1143.

51   Ibid., 1171.

52   Ibid., 1172–73.

53   This and the following paragraph are based on McDonald, *The Presidency of Thomas Jefferson*, 158.

54   JM, First Inaugural Address, March 4, 1809, Robert Rutland et al., eds., *The Papers of James Madison, Presidential Series* (hereafter, *PJMP*) (Charlottesville: University Press of Virginia, 1984–), 1:15–18.

55   Catherine Allgor, *Parlor Politics: In Which the Ladies of Washington Help Build a City and a Government* (Charlottesville: University Press of Virginia, 2000), 90.

56   Robert Rutland, *The Presidency of James Madison* (Lawrence: University Press of Kansas, 1990), 15–17.

57   Adams, *History of the United States of America*, 2:11.

58   Catherine Allgor, *Parlor Politics: In Which the Ladies of Washington Help Build a City and a Government*, 48–101 provides the leading account of Dolley Madison's novel role in the Madison Administration.

59   Ibid., 84.

60   Quotation at Allgor, *Parlor Politics*, 71.

61   Ibid., 72.

62   Ibid., 75.

63   The best account of the Erskine affair is Rutland, *The Presidency of James Madison*, 39–43. Also see Garry Wills, *James Madison* (New York: Henry Holt, 2002), chapter 6, for Madison's twin foreign policy gaffes in 1809–1810. The following account is based primarily on these sources.

64   Presidential Proclamation, April 19, 1809, *PJMP*, 1:125–26.

65   The following account of George III's supposedly taking offense is from Rutland, *The Presidency of James Madison*, 42.

66   Wills, *James Madison*, 85.

67   John C. Calhoun, "Resolutions on the Chesapeake-Leopard Affair," August 3, 1807, *The Papers of John C. Calhoun*, 1:34–35. Also see K[evin] R. Constantine Gutzman, "Paul to Jeremiah: Calhoun's Abandonment of Nationalism," *Journal of Libertarian Studies* 16, no. 2 (Spring 2002): 3–33.

68   JM to Thomas Jefferson, June 22, 1810, *PJMP*, 2:388.

69   *PJMP*, 2;219, n. 2.

70 *PJMP*, 2:296, n. 1.

71 Rutland, *The Presidency of James Madison*, 69–70.

72 The following account comes from "Tammany" to JM, April 18, 1810, *PJMP*, 2:304–05.

73 The following account is based on JM to the House of Representatives, February 21, 1811, *PJMP*, 3:176, and n. 1 at 177. See also Rutland, *The Presidency of James Madison*, 77–78.

74 JM to Alexander I, February 25, 1811, *PJMP*, 3:184.

75 JM to the House of Representatives, February 28, 1811, *PJMP*, 3:193.

76 Rutland, *The Presidency of James Madison*, 77–78.

77 R. Kent Newmyer, *Supreme Court Justice Joseph Story: Statesman of the Old Republic* (Chapel Hill: University of North Carolina Press, 1985).

78 Rutland, *The Presidency of James Madison*, 57.

79 The case is *Martin v. Hunter's Lessee*, 14 U.S. 304 (1816). An excellent though markedly Federalist account is F. Thornton Miller, *Judges and Juries versus the Law: Virginia's Provincial Legal Perspective, 1783–1828* (Charlottesville: University Press of Virginia, 1994).

80 JM, Annual Message to Congress, November 5, 1811, *PJMP*, 4:1–5.

81 JM to Thomas Jefferson, May 25, 1812, *PJMP*, 4:415–16.

82 JM to Congress, April 1, 1812, *PJMP*, 4:279; the following information regarding the Foster-Madison conversation is at 280, n. 1.

83 Editors' Preface, *PJMP*, 4:xxix.

84 JM to Thomas Jefferson, April 24, 1812, *PJMP*, 4:345–46.

85 JM to Congress, December 18, 1811, *PJMP*, 4:73–74.

86 K[evin] R. Constantine Gutzman, "William Henry Harrison," *American National Biography*, ed. John A. Garraty and Mark C. Carnes (New York: Oxford University Press, 1999), 10:223–26.

87 For an account of the Shawnee Prophet and Tecumseh's anti-American campaign, see Gregory Evans Dowd, *A Spirited Resistance: The North American Indian Struggle for Unity, 1745–1815* (Baltimore, MD: Johns Hopkins University Press, 1993).

88 Jack N. Rakove, *James Madison and the Creation of the American Republic* (New York: Longman, 2007), 187.

89 This paragraph is drawn from JM to John Nicholas, *WJM*, 8:242–44, at 242.

90 "Draft of a Message to Congress," c. May 31, 1812, *PJMP*, 4:431

91 Rutland, *The Presidency of James Madison*, 102.

92 This paragraph is based on Adams, *History of the United States of America*, 2:490–91.

93 Presidential Proclamation, July 9, 1812, *PJMP*, 4:581–82.

94   *PJMP*, 4:582, n. 2.

95   David Chandler, *The Campaigns of Napoleon* (New York: Scribner, 1973) is the
     standard account not only of Napoleon's campaigns, but also of his strategic ap-
     proach. Also see Carl von Clausewitz, *On War* (Princeton, NJ: Princeton Univer-
     sity Press, 1989); and Baron Antoine Henri de Jomini, *On the Art of War: Restored
     Edition* (Kingston, Canada: Legacy Books Press, 2008).

96   Wills, *James Madison*, 99.

97   Walter R. Borneman, *1812: The War That Forged a Nation* (New York: Harper-
     Collins, 2004), 53, 57.

98   Wills, *James Madison*, 103.

99   Ibid., 103–05.

100 Ibid., 106.

101 Ibid., 116, is the primary source for this paragraph. The reference to Dolley
     Madison is from Allgor, *Parlor Politics*, 81.

102 Borneman, *1812: The War That Forged a Nation*, 100.

103 Ibid., 132.

104 Ibid., 105.

105 Rakove, *James Madison and the Creation of the American Republic*, 197.

106 For this subject generally, see Alan Taylor, *The Civil War of 1812: American Citi-
     zens, British Subjects, Irish Rebels, and Indian Allies* (New York: Knopf, 2010).

107 K[evin] R. Constantine Gutzman, "Jefferson's Draft Declaration of Independence,
     Richard Bland, and the Revolutionary Legacy: Giving Credit Where Credit Is
     Due."

108 Rutland, *The Presidency of James Madison*, 144.

109 Ibid., 146–47.

110 Adams, *History of the United States of American*, 2:890–91.

111 Rutland, *The Presidency of James Madison*, 147.

112 Ibid., 149; Russell Kirk, *John Randolph of Roanoke*, 2nd ed. (Indianapolis, IN:
     Liberty Fund, 1997); Henry Adams, *John Randolph* (Armonk, NY: M. E.
     Sharpe, 1995); Norman Risjord, *The Old Republicans: Southern Conservatism
     in the Age of Jefferson* (New York: Columbia University Press, 1965).

113 Ketcham, *James Madison: A Biography*, 550.

114 Adams, *History of the United States of America*, 993.

115 Ibid., 993, 995.

116 Rutland, *The Presidency of James Madison*, 157.

117 Ibid., 158–59.

118 Adams, *History of the United States of American*, 1001–03.

119 Rutland, *The Presidency of James Madison*, 160–62, is one source for the following
     account.

120 Ibid., 163.

121 For Dolley Madison, see Allgor, *Parlor Politics*, 95.

122 Borneman, *1812: The War That Forged a Nation*, 291.

123 The acerbic account of Adams is *History of the United States of America*, vol. 2, chapter 11.

124 Rutland, *The Presidency of James Madison*, 184.

125 Adams, *History of the United States of America*, 1114.

126 John Taylor of Caroline, "A Pamphlet Containing a Series of Letters, Written by Colonel John Taylor, of Caroline, to Thomas Ritchie, Editor of the 'Enquirer'" (Richmond, 1809).

127 The amendments are enumerated at Rutland, *The Presidency of James Madison*, 186. Ironically, it had been Virginian George Mason who repeatedly urged the Philadelphia Convention to require a two-thirds vote in each house for commercial legislation and a New England–Deep South axis that defeated his efforts.

128 Rutland, *The Presidency of James Madison*, 187.

129 Ibid., 187.

130 Ibid., 189.

131 James Madison, "Seventh Annual Message," December 5, 1815, *WJM*, 8:335–44.

132 Rutland, *The Presidency of James Madison*, 195.

133 Ibid., 197.

134 Ibid., 198.

135 JM, Eighth Annual Message, *WJM*, 8:375–85.

136 This last clause is a slight reworking of the Authorized Version's Luke 2:14. In Madison's day, all educated Anglophones would have recognized it as such.

137 Rutland, *The Presidency of James Madison*, 198.

138 JM, Veto Message, March 3, 1817, *WJM*, 8:386–88.

139 Margaret L. Coit, *John C. Calhoun: American Portrait* (Boston: Houghton Mifflin, 1950), 116–17.

Chapter Eight   An Active Retirement, 1817–36

1 Editor's Note, "Address to the Agricultural Society of Albemarle," *Papers of James Madison: Retirement Series* (hereafter *PJMR*), ed. David B. Mattern, et al. (Charlottesville: University of Virginia Press, 2009), 1:257–59; M. E. Bradford, "A Virginia Cato: John Taylor of Caroline and the Agrarian Republic," in John Taylor of Caroline, *Arator*, ed. M. E. Bradford (Indianapolis: Liberty Fund, 1977), 11–46.

2 JM, "Address to the Agricultural Society of Albemarle," May 12, 1818, *PJMR*, 1:260–83.

3   Samples of the criticism are found in Francis Walker Gilmer to Peter Minor, May
    20, 1818, Gilmer Letterbooks, University of Virginia; Francis Walker Gilmer to
    Peter Minor, June 29, 1818, Gilmer Letterbooks, University of Virginia. A hint of
    the public's evaluation of the address may be found in Richard Peters's account of
    a local farmer's refusal to take some of Madison's advice (that related to oxen and
    horses—the same score on which Madison's address was still being mocked
    twenty years later). Richard Peters to JM, July 30, 1818, *PJMR*, 1:320–21. For Jef-
    ferson's predictable encomium, see Editor's Note, "Address to the Agricultural
    Society of Albemarle," *PJMR*, 1:257–59. For criticism of Madison's address at the
    Virginia Constitutional Convention of 1829–30, see Hugh Blair Grigsby, *The Vir-
    ginia Convention of 1829–1830* (1854; reprint New York: DaCapo Press, 1969),
    70–71.

4   JM to Frederick Beasley, December 22, 1824, *WJM*, 9:210–13.

5   JM to Thomas Jefferson, September 10, 1824, *WJM*, 9:202–05.

6   The most recent account is Robert Pierce Forbes, *The Missouri Compromise and
    Its Aftermath* (Chapel Hill: University of North Carolina Press, 2007).

7   For Virginians among the early Missourians, see Robert J. Brugger, *Beverley
    Tucker: Heart Over Head in the Old South* (Baltimore, MD: Johns Hopkins Uni-
    versity Press, 1978).

8   JM to Robert Walsh, November 27, 1819, *PJMR*, 1:553–58.

9   JM to James Monroe, February 10, 1820, *WJM*, 9:21–23.

10 JM to James Monroe, February 23, 1820, *WJM*, 9:23–26.

11 JM to James Monroe, November 19, 1820, *WJM*, 9:30–35.

12 JM to marquis de LaFayette, November 25, 1820, *WJM*, 9:35–38.

13 For Virginians' response to these developments, see Gutzman, *Virginia's Ameri-
    can Revolution*, chapter 6.

14 JM to Spencer Roane, September 2, 1819, *PJMR*, 1:500–03, quotation at 501.

15 JM to Spencer Roane, June 29, 1821, *WJM*, 9:65–68.

16 Victor Dennis Golladay, "The Nicholas Family of Virginia, 1722–1820," PhD dis-
    sertation, University of Virginia, 1973; Elinor Janet Weeder, "Wilson Cary Nich-
    olas, Jefferson's Lieutenant," MA thesis, University of Virginia, 1946; David
    Nicholas Mayer, "Of Principles and Men: The Correspondence of John Taylor of
    Caroline with Wilson Cary Nicholas, 1804–1809," MA thesis, University of Vir-
    ginia, 1982.

17 JM to Thomas Jefferson, February 24, 1826, *WJM*, 9:243–46.

18 JM to Nicholas Biddle, April 16, 1825, *WJM*, 9:221–22, and n. 1.

19 K[evin] R. Constantine Gutzman, *Old Dominion, New Republic: Making Virginia
    Republican, 1776–1840,* PhD dissertation, University of Virginia, 1999, 364,
    421–22.

20 For Jefferson's gloom in the 1820s, see Peter S. Onuf, *Jefferson's Empire: The Language of American Nationhood* (Charlottesville: University Press of Virginia, 2000); and Alan Pell Crawford, *Twilight at Monticello: The Final Years of Thomas Jefferson* (New York: Random House, 2008).

21 John Taylor, *An Inquiry into the Principles and Policy of the Government of the United States* (1814; reprint New Haven, CT: Yale University Press, 1950); John Taylor, *Construction Construed, and Constitutions Vindicated* (Richmond, VA: Shepherd and Pollard, 1820); John Taylor, *New Views of the Constitution of the United States* (1823; reprint New York: Da Capo Press, 1971); and, particularly, John Taylor, *Tyranny Unmasked* (1821; reprint Indianapolis, IN: Liberty Fund, 1992).

22 The best account of the constitutional aspect of the nullification crisis is Richard E. Ellis, *The Union at Risk: Jacksonian Democracy, States' Rights, and the Nullification Crisis* (New York: Oxford University Press, 1989). For Calhoun's "Fort Hill Address" and "South Carolina Exposition," see John C. Calhoun, *Union and Liberty*, ed. Ross M. Lence (Indianapolis, IN: Liberty Fund, 1992).

23 For Virginia and the tariff in the 1820s, see Kevin R. [C.] Gutzman, "Preserving the Patrimony: William Branch Giles and Virginia versus the Federal Tariff," *Virginia Magazine of History and Biography* 104 (1996), 341–372.

24 K[evin] R. Constantine Gutzman, "Paul to Jeremiah: Calhoun's Abandonment of Nationalism."

25 JM to Thomas Cooper, March 23, 1824, *WJM*, 9:177–81.

26 It was to that speech that former senator William Branch Giles responded with an anti-protection campaign that soon won him elevation to the Virginia governorship. See Gutzman, "Preserving the Patrimony."

27 Madison expanded upon his reasoning, while retaining the same list, in JM to Joseph C. Cabell, October 30, 1828, *WJM*, 9:317 ff., n. 1.

28 TJ to Joseph C. Cabell, March 22, 1827, *WJM*, 9:284–87.

29 JM to Thomas Lehre, August 2, 1828, *WJM*, 9:314–16.

30 For Madison's discomfiture, see Kevin R. [C.] Gutzman, "A Troublesome Legacy: James Madison and 'The Principles of '98,'" *Journal of the Early Republic* 15 (1995): 569–589.

31 JM to Joseph C. Cabell, August 16, 1829, *WJM*, 9:341–44.

32 JM to Joseph C. Cabell, September 7, 1829, *WJM*, 9:346–51.

33 "Notes on Nullification," 1835, 1836, *WJM*, 9:573–607.

34 "Outline," *WJM*, 9:351–357, at 353–55.

35 For this last quotation, JM to Henry Clay, March 22, 1832, *WJM*, 9:477–78.

36 JM to Robert Y. Hayne, April 3 or 4 (?), 1830, *WJM*, 9:383 ff., n. 2.

37 JM to Nicholas P. Trist, December 1831, *WJM*, 9:471–77.

38 John Taylor of Caroline, *New Views of the Constitution of the United States* (1823; reprint Washington, D.C.: Regnery Publishing, 2000).

39 JM to C. E. Haynes, August 27, 1832, *WJM*, 9:482–84.

40 JM to Alexander Rives, January 1833, *WJM*, 9:495–98. The explanation of Madison's views regarding secession and the Constitution may be found in this letter as well. Also see JM to William Cabell Rives, March 12, 1833, *WJM*, 9:511–14.

41 JM to Edward Coles, August 29, 1834, *WJM*, 9:536–42.

42 "Notes on Nullification," 1835–36, *WJM*, 9:573–607, at 589.

43 JM to John Quincy Adams, February 24, 1829, *WJM*, 9:340–41.

44 JM to William Cogswell, March 10, 1834, *WJM*, 9:533–34.

45 In fact, he already had for years—as in JM to Thomas Ritchie, August 13, 1822, *WJM*, 9:110–11, where he insisted Jefferson receive full credit for his draft of the Declaration of Independence.

46 Gutzman, *Virginia's American Revolution*, 183–97; Dickson D. Bruce, *The Rhetoric of Conservatism: The Virginia Convention of 1829–30 and the Conservative Tradition in the South* (San Marino, CA: Huntington Library Press, 1982); Robert P. Sutton, *Revolution to Secession: Constitution Making in the Old Dominion* (Charlottesville: University Press of Virginia, 1989), 21–102.

47 Sutton, *Revolution to Secession: Constitution Making in the Old Dominion*, 60.

48 Gutzman, *Virginia's American Revolution*, 186–87.

49 Ibid., 187.

50 JM, "Speech in the Virginia Constitutional Convention," December 2, 1829, *WJM*, 9:358–64, and "Notes During the Convention for Amending the Constitution of Virginia," *WJM*, 9:358 ff., n. 1.

51 Kevin R. C. Gutzman, "Lincoln as Jeffersonian: The Colonization Chimera," in *Lincoln Emancipated: The President and the Politics of Race*, ed. Brian Dirck (DeKalb: Northern Illinois University Press, 2007), 46–72.

52 For Jefferson and slavery generally, see Paul Finkelman, "Jefferson and Slavery: 'Treason Against the Hopes of the World,'" in Peter S. Onuf, ed., *Jeffersonian Legacies* (Charlottesville: University Press of Virginia, 1993), 181–224.

53 JM to R. R. Gurley, December 28, 1831, *WJM*, 9:468–70.

54 JM to Thomas R. Dew, February 23, 1833, *WJM*, 9:498–502.

55 "Madison's Will," *WJM*, 9:548–52.

56 This account of the fate of Madison's slaves upon his death is based upon Drew McCoy, *The Last of the Fathers: James Madison & The Republican Legacy* (New York: Oxford University Press, 1989), 308–22.

57 For Dolley Madison as the legatee of the James Madison papers, see David W. Houpt, "Securing a Legacy: The Publication of James Madison's Notes from the Constitutional Convention," *Virginia Magazine of History and Biography*

118 (2010): 5–39; and Holly C. Shulman, "'A Constant Attention': Dolley Madison and the Publication of the Papers of James Madison, 1836–1837," *Virginia Magazine of History and Biography* 118 (2010): 41–70.

58 David W. Houpt and Holly C. Shulman, in the works cited in the preceding note, assert that Calhoun was disingenuous and inconsistent here. They might more graciously have conceded that his argument was right on the money (so to speak).

59 JM, "Advice to My Country" (in Dolley Madison's hand), *WJM*, 9 (photograph opposite page 610).

60 Details in this paragraph and the second sentence of the next are from Ketcham, *James Madison: A Biography*, 669–70.

Index